Customizing AutoCAD

Customizing AutoCAD

Sham Tickoo

Associate Professor
Department of Manufacturing Engineering Technologies
and Supervision
Purdue University Calumet
Hammond, Indiana

DELMAR PUBLISHERS INC.

NOTICE TO THE READER

Cover design by Mike Speke
Cover concepts by Santosh Tickoo, Sumit Tickoo and Sandeep Tickoo

Delmar Staff
Associate Editor: Kevin Johnson
Editing Supervisor: Marlene McHugh Pratt
Production Supervisor: Larry Main
Design Supervisor: Susan C. Mathews

For information, address
Delmar Publishers Inc.
2 Computer Drive West, Box 15-015
Albany, New York 12212

COPYRIGHT © 1992
BY DELMAR PUBLISHERS INC.

Printed in the United States of America
Published simultaneously in Canada
by Nelson Canada,
a division of The Thomson Corporation

10 9 8 7 6 5 4 3 2 1

Library of Congress Cataloging-in-Publication Data

Tickoo, Sham.
  Customizing AutoCAD/Sham Tickoo
  p. cm
  Includes index
  ISBN 0-8273-5041-4
  1. AutoCAD (Computer program) I. Title
  T385.T525 1992
  620'.0042'02855369--dc20

92-10478
CIP

Table of Contents

Appendices

Preface

AutoCAD, developed by Autodesk is the most popular PC-CAD system available in the market. Half a million people in 80 countries around the world are using AutoCAD to generate various kinds of drawings. In 1991 the market share of AutoCAD grew to 70 percent, making it the world wide standard for generating drawings. Also, AutoCAD's open architecture has allowed third party developers to write application software that have significantly added to its popularity. For example, the author of this book has developed a software package "SMLayout" for sheet metal products that generates flat layout of various geometrical shapes like: transitions, intersections, cones, elbows, and tank heads. Several companies in Canada and the USA are using this software package with AutoCAD to design and manufacture various products. AutoCAD has also provided facilities that allow users to customize AutoCAD to make it more efficient and therefore increase productivity.

The purpose of this book is to unravel the customizing power of AutoCAD and explain it in a way that is easy to understand. Every customizing technique has been thoroughly explained with examples and illustrations that should make it easy to comprehend the customizing concepts of AutoCAD. When you are done reading this book, you will be able to generate prototype drawing, write script files, edit existing menus, write your own menus, write shape and text files, create new linetypes and hatch patterns, define new commands, write programs in the AutoLISP programming language, and edit the existing drawing database. In the process, you will discover some new applications of AutoCAD that are unique and might have a significant effect on your drawings. You will also get a better idea of why AutoCAD has become such a popular software package and an international standard in PC-CAD.

To use this book, you do not need to be an AutoCAD expert or a programmer. If you know the basic AutoCAD commands, you will have no problem in understanding the material presented in this book. The book contains a detailed description of various customizing techniques that you can use to customize your system. Every chapter has several examples that illustrate some possible applications of these customizing techniques. At the end of each chapter are some exercises that provide a challenge to the user to solve the problems on his/her own. In a class situation, these exercises can be assigned to students to test their understanding of the material explained in the chapter. The chapters on AutoLISP programming assume that the user has no programming background and therefore all commands have been thoroughly explained in a way that makes programming easy to understand and interesting to learn. **All chapters, except Slide Shows and Editing Drawing Database, are independent and can be read in any order and used without reading the rest of the book.** The user needs only to read the chapters on Script Files before the chapter on Slide Shows and the chapter on AutoLISP before the chapter on Editing Drawing Database.   However, in order to get a good understanding of customizing techniques, it is recommended to start from chapter 1 and then progress through the chapters.   The following is a summary of different chapters in the book.

Chapter 1: Prototype Drawings

This chapter explains how to create prototype drawing and how to standardize the information that is common to all drawings.   This chapter also describes how to create a prototype drawing with paper space and pre-defined viewports.

Chapter 2: Script Files

This chapter introduces the user to script files and how to utilize them to group AutoCAD commands in a pre-determined sequence to perform a given operation.

Chapter 3: Slide Shows

This chapter explains how to use script files to create a slide show that can be used for product presentation.

Chapter 4: Creating and Modifying Linetypes

This chapter explains how to create a new linetype and how to edit the linetype file, ACAD.LIN.   This chapter also explains the effect of LTSCALE on a line.

Chapter 5: Creating Hatch Patterns

This chapter describes the techniques of creating a new hatch pattern, and the effect of hatch scale and hatch angle on hatch.

Chapter 6: Screen Menu

This chapter describes the procedure to write a screen menu with multiple submenus and how to load icon or pull-down menus from the screen menu.

Chapter 7: Tablet Menu

This chapter explains how to write a tablet menu, and how to load other menus from the tablet menu.   Advantages of the tablet menu, design of the tablet menu, and how AutoCAD assigns commands to different blocks of the tablet menu are also discussed in this chapter.

Chapter 8: Pull-down Menus

This chapter explains how to write a pull-down menu, and how to load screen and icon menus from the pull-down menus.

Chapter 9: Icon Menus

This chapter explains the icon menus and how to write an icon menu.   The chapter also discusses submenus and how to make slides for the icon menu.

Chapter 10: Buttons and Aux1 Menus

This chapter deals with buttons and auxiliary menus and how to assign AutoCAD commands to different buttons of a multi button pointing device.

Chapter 11: Customizing Standard AutoCAD Menu
This chapter describes how to edit and change various menu sections of the standard AutoCAD menu, ACAD.MNU. The chapter also contains information about submenus and how to load different submenus.

Chapter 12: Shapes and Text Fonts
This chapter explains what shapes are and how to create shape and text fonts. The chapter also contains a detailed description of special codes and their application to creating shapes and text fonts.

Chapter 13: AutoLISP
This chapter explains different AutoLISP functions and how to use these functions to write a program. It also introduces the user to basic programing techniques and use of relational and conditional statements in a program.

Chapter 14: AutoLISP - Editing Drawing Database
This chapter describes those AutoLISP function that allow a user to edit the drawing database.

In the end, it is the author's sincere hope that the material provided in this book will prove valuable in mastering the customizing techniques of AutoCAD.

DEDICATION

*To teachers, who make it possible to disseminate knowledge
to enlighten the young and curious minds
of our future generations.*

*To students, who are dedicated to learning new technologies
and make the world a better place to live.*

Thanks

*To the faculty and students of the METS department of
Purdue University Calumet for their cooperation.*

Chapter 1

Prototype Drawings

The Standard Prototype Drawing

The AutoCAD software package comes with a standard prototype drawing called ACAD.DWG. When you start a new drawing the standard prototype drawing, ACAD.DWG, is automatically loaded. (provided AutoCAD's initial drawing setup configuration has not been changed). The following is a list of the settings and variable values that are assigned to the AutoCAD's standard prototype drawing, ACAD.DWG.

AXIS	Off, spacing(0.0,0.0)
BASE	Insertion base point (0.0,0.0,0.0)
BLIPMODE	On
CHAMFER	Distance 0.0
COLOR	Bylayer
DIMCEN	0.0900
DIMCLRD	BYBLOCK
DIMCLRE	BYBLOCK
DIMCLRT	BYBLOCK
DIMDLE	0.0000
DIMDLI	0.3800
DIMEXE	0.1800
DIMEXO	0.0625
DIMGAP	0.0900
DIMLFAC	1.0000
DIMLIM	Off
DIMRND	0.0000
DIMSAH	Off
DIMSCALE	1.0000
DIMSE1	Off
DIMSE2	Off
DIMSHO	On
DIMSOXD	Off
DIMTAD	Off
DIMTFAC	1.0000
DIMTIH	On

DIMTIX	Off
DIMTM	0.0000
DIMTOFL	Off
DIMTOH	On
DIMTOL	Off
DIMTP	0.0000
DIMTSZ	0.0000
DIMTVP	0.0000
DIMTXT	0.1800
DIMZIN	0
DRAGMODE	Auto
ELEVATION	Elevation 0.0, thickness 0.0
FILL	On
FILLET	Radius 0.0
GRID	Off, spacing (0.0, 0,0)
HANDLES	Off
Highlighting	Enabled
ISOPLANE	Left
LAYER	Layer 0 with color white and linetype continuous.
LIMITS	Off, limits (0.0,0.0) - (12.0,9.0)
LINETYPE	Loaded linetype CONTINUOUS
LTSCALE	1.0
MENU	Acad
MIRROR	Text mirrored like other entities
OBJECT SELECTION	Pick box, size 3 pixels
ORTHO	Off
OSNAP	None
PLINE	Line-width 0.0
POINT	Display mode 0, size 0.00
QTEXT	Off
REGENAUTO	On
SKETCH	Record increment 0.10
SHADE	Rendering type 3 percent ambient 70
SNAP	Off, spacing (1.0,1.0)
Space	Model
Spline curves	Frame off, segment 8, spline type = cubic
STYLE	Text style STANDARD
Surfaces	6 tabulations in M and N directions
TABLET	Off
TEXT	Style standard, height 0.20 rotation 0.0 degrees
TILEMODE	On
TIME	User elapsed timer ON
TRACE	Trace width 0.05
UCS	Current UCS same as WORLD
UNITS(linear)	Decimal, 4 decimal places
UNITS (angular)	Decimal degrees, 0 decimal places 0 angle along positive X-Axis, angle positive if measured counterclockwise

Viewing modes	One active viewport, plan view perspective off, target point (0,0,0), front and back clipping off, lens length 50mm, twist angle 0.0, fast zoom on, circle zoom percent 100, World View 0
ZOOM	To drawing limits

Customizing Prototype Drawings

One of the ways to customize AutoCAD is to generate prototype drawings that contain initial drawing setup information so that when the user starts a new drawing, the settings that are associated with the prototype drawing are automatically loaded. If you start a new drawing, AutoCAD loads the drawing ACAD.DWG, with its default setup values. For example, the default limits are (0.0, 0.0), (12.0, 9.0) and the default layer is 0 with white color and continuous line type. Generally, these default parameters need to be reset before generating a drawing on the computer using AutoCAD. A considerable amount of time is required to setup the layers, colors, linetypes, limits, snap, units, text height, dimensioning variables and various other parameters. Sometimes, the border lines and a title block may also be needed.

In production drawings, most of the drawing setup values remain the same. For example, the company title block, border, layers, linetypes, dimension variables, text height, ltscale and various other drawing setup values do not change. It will save considerable time if these values could be saved and reloaded when starting a new drawing. This can be accomplished by making prototype drawings. These prototype drawings can contain the initial drawing setup information, set according to company specifications. They can also contain a border, title block, tolerance table and may be some notes and instructions that are common to all drawings.

Example 1

Create a prototype drawing with the following specifications. (Name of the prototype drawing PROTO1)

Limits	18.0, 12.0
Snap	0.25
Grid	0.50
Text height	0.125
Units	decimal
	2 decimal places
	decimal degrees
	0 decimal places
	0 angle along positive X-axis
	angle positive if measured counterclockwise

Start AutoCAD and from the main menu select option 1 to start a new drawing. Type the name of the new drawing, PROTO1 and press the ENTER key.

Main Menu

0. Exit AutoCAD
1. Begin a NEW drawing
2. Edit an EXISTING drawing
3. Plot a drawing
4. Printer Plot a drawing

5. Configure AutoCAD
6. File Utilities
7. Compile shape/font description file
8. Convert Old drawing file
9. Recover damaged drawing

Enter selection:<u>1</u> *(Begin a New drawing)*
Enter Name of Drawing:<u>PROTO1</u>

Once you are in the drawing editor, use the following AutoCAD commands to set up the values as given in Example 1.

Command: LIMITS
ON/OFF/<Lower left corner> <0.00,0.00>:0,0
Upper right corner <12.0,9.0>: 18.0,12.0

Command: SNAP
Snap spacing or ON/OFF/Aspect/Rotate/Style <1.0>: 0.25

Command: GRID
Grid spacing(X) or ON/OFF/Snap/Aspect <0.00>: 0.50

Command: SETVAR
Variable name or ?: TEXTSIZE
New value for textsize <0.02>: 0.125

Command: Units

Report formats:	**(Examples)**
1. Scientific	1.55E+01
2. Decimal	15.50
3. Engineering	1'-3.50"
4. Architectural	1'-3 1/2"
5. Fractional	15 1/2

With the exception of Engineering and Architectural formats, these formats can be used with any basic units of measurements. For example, Decimal mode is perfect for metric units as well as decimal English units.

Enter choice, 1 to 5 <2>: 2
Number of digits to right of decimal point (0 to 8) <4>: 2

Systems of angle measure: **(Examples)**

1.	Decimal degrees	45.0000
2.	Degrees/minutes/seconds	45d0'0"
3.	Grads	50.0000g
4.	Radians	0.7854r
5	Surveyor's units	N 45d0'0"

Enter choice, 1 to 5 <1>: 1
Number of fractional places for display of angles (0 to 8) <0>: 2

Direction for angle 0.00:

East	3 o'clock	= 0.00
North	12 o'clock	= 90.00
West	9 o'clock	= 180.00
South	6 o'clock	= 270.00

Enter direction for angle 0.00 <0.00>: 0
Do you want angles measured clockwise? <N>: N

Now, save the drawing as PROTO1 using AutoCAD's SAVE or END command. This drawing is now saved as PROTO1 on the default drive. You can also save this drawing on the floppy diskette in one of the drives, A or B.

Command: SAVE
File name <PROTO1>: A:PROTO1

Loading a Prototype Drawing

You can use the prototype drawing anytime you want to start a new drawing. To utilize the preset value of the prototype drawings, start AutoCAD and the main menu will be displayed on the screen.

Main Menu

0. Exit AutoCAD
1. Begin a NEW drawing
2. Edit an EXISTING drawing
3. Plot a drawing
4. Printer Plot a drawing

5. Configure AutoCAD
6. File Utilities
7. Compile shape/font description file
8. Convert Old drawing file
9. Recover damaged drawing

Enter selection:1   *(Begin a New drawing)*

Select option 1 (Begin a NEW drawing) and AutoCAD will display the following prompt.

Enter NAME of drawing:

AutoCAD has provided the following three options to respond to this prompt. (The name of the new drawing is assumed to be GEAR1).

>   **1. New Drawing Name**
>   (Example   GEAR1)
>
>   **2. New Drawing Name=**
>   (Example   GEAR1=)
>
>   **3. New Drawing Name=Prototype Drawing Name**
>   (Example   GEAR1=PROTO1)

1. New Drawing Name

Let us assume that the name of the new drawing that you want to start is GEAR1. If you enter the name of the new drawing as GEAR1, AutoCAD will load the standard prototype drawing ACAD.DWG. The new drawing GEAR1 will assume the same setup values as that of ACAD.DWG drawing. The format of entering the new drawing name is:

Enter NAME of drawing: (New drawing name)

Example
Enter NAME of drawing: GEAR1

2. New Drawing Name=

If the name of the new drawing that you want to start is GEAR1 and you put equal to sign (=) after the name of the drawing (GEAR1=), AutoCAD will start a new drawing GEAR1 and this drawing will assume AutoCAD's default values. For example, the default drawing limits are (0.00, 0.00), (12.00, 9.00) and the default layer is 0 with continuous line type and the color associated with this layer is white.

Therefore, if you want to make sure that your drawing has AutoCAD's default setup, it is recommended that you type equal sign (=) after the name of the new drawing. For example, Gear1=. If you save this drawing with the file name ACAD, the drawing will be saved as ACAD.DWG. That is how the AutoCAD drawing ACAD.DWG was created. The format of entering the new drawing name is:

Enter NAME of drawing: (New drawing name=)

Example
Enter NAME of drawing: GEAR=

Note

If the standard prototype drawing ACAD.DWG, and the initial drawing setup has not been changed, the two options discussed above (GEAR1 and GEAR1=) will produce the same results.

3. New Drawing Name=Prototype Drawing Name

This option can be used if you want to start a new drawing that has the same setup as that of any previously created prototype drawing. For example, if you enter the name of the new drawing as GEAR1=PROTO1, where GEAR1 is the name of the new drawing and PROTO1 is the name of the prototype drawing. AutoCAD will start a new drawing GEAR1, but it will have the same setup as that of prototype drawing, PROTO1.

You can have several prototype drawings, each drawing having a different setup. For example, PROTO1 for 12" by 18" drawing, PROTO2 for 24" by 36" drawing and PROTO3 for 36" by 48" drawing. Each prototype drawing can be created according to the user defined specifications. You can then load any of these prototype drawings by entering the name of new drawing, followed by equal to "=" sign and the name of the prototype drawing. The format for entering the new drawing name is:

Enter NAME of drawing: (New drawing name=prototype drawing)

Example
Enter NAME of drawing: GEAR=PROTO1

Note

If the prototype drawings are not in the current subdirectory, then you need to define the path with the name of the prototype drawing. For example, if the prototype drawing PROTO1 is in the PROTODWG subdirectory of the C drive, then the prototype drawing name and the path will be defines as:

Enter NAME of drawing: GEAR=C:\PROTODWG\PROTO1

Initial Drawing Setup

AutoCAD has provided a facility to change the default drawing that AutoCAD initially loads when you start a new drawing. For example, if you start a new drawing GEAR1, AutoCAD loads the default drawing ACAD.DWG, because AutoCAD has been configured to load ACAD.DWG drawing. You can reconfigure AutoCAD to load PROTO1.DWG or any other drawing by changing AutoCAD's initial drawing setup. Use the following procedure to configure the initial drawing setup.

Start AutoCAD and the main menu will be displayed on the screen.

Main Menu

0. Exit AutoCAD
1. Begin a NEW drawing
2. Edit an EXISTING drawing
3. Plot a drawing
4. Printer Plot a drawing

5. Configure AutoCAD
6. File Utilities
7. Compile shape/font description file
8. Convert Old drawing file
9. Recover damaged drawing

Enter selection: 5   *(Configure AutoCAD)*

This will display the existing configuration. If you press the ENTER key one more time, the configuration menu will be displayed on the screen.

Configuration Menu

0. Exit to Main Menu
1. Show current configuration
2. Allow detailed configuration

3. Configure video display
4. Configure digitizer
5. Configure plotter
6. Configure printer plotter
7. Configure system console
8. Configure operating parameters

Enter Selection <0>: 8   (Configure operating parameters)

In the configuration menu select option number 8, **"Configure operating parameters"** and press the ENTER key. The operating parameter menu will be displayed on the screen.

Operating parameter menu

0. Exit to configuration menu
1. Alarm on error
2. Initial drawing setup
3. Default plot file name
4. Plot spooler directory
5. Placement of temporary files
6. Network node name
7. AutoLISP feature
8. Full-time CRC validation
9. Automatic Audit after IGESIN, DXFIN, or DXBIN
10. Login name
11. Server authorization and file locking

Enter selection <0>: 2   *(Initial drawing setup)*

Enter name of default prototype file for new drawings or . for none <acad>:

The default prototype file for the new drawing is ACAD (ACAD.DWG). If you want to change the default drawing, type the name of the drawing in response to the above prompt. For example, if you want the PROTO1.DWG drawing to be the default drawing, type PROTO1 and press the ENTER key. Press the ENTER key again till you are back in the main menu. Now, if you start a new drawing GEAR1, AutoCAD will load the default drawing PROTO1. Again, if you want to start a new drawing that has the AutoCAD's default values, then the name of the new drawing should be followed by "=" sign ("Gear1=").

Customizing Drawings with Layers

Most production drawings need multiple layers for different groups of entities. In addition to layers, it is a good practice to assign different colors to different layers for controlling the line width at the time of plotting. You can generate a prototype drawing that contains the desired number of layers with linetypes and colors according to your company specifications. You can then use this prototype drawing for making a new drawing. The next example illustrates the procedure used for customizing a drawing with layers, linetypes and colors.

Example 2

A user wants to create a prototype drawing that has a border and the company's title block as shown in Figure 1. In addition to this, the user also wants the following initial drawing setup. (Name of the prototype drawing PROTO2)

Limits	48.0, 36.0
Snap	1.0
Grid	4.00
Text height	0.25
PLINE width	0.02
Ltscale	4.0
Dimscale	4.0

Layers

Layer Names	Line Type	Color
0	Continuous	White
OBJ	Continuous	Red
CEN	Center	Yellow
HID	Hidden	Blue
DIM	Continuous	Green
BOR	Continuous	Magenta

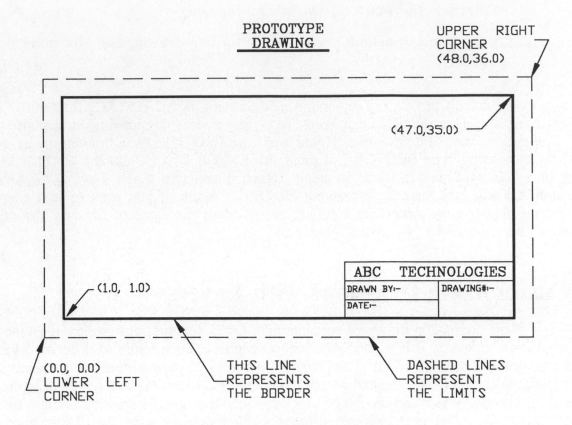

Figure 1 Prototype drawing

Start a new drawing with default parameters. You can do this by typing equal sign (=) after the name of the drawing. **(Enter NAME of drawing:** New drawing name=). Once you are in the drawing editor, use the AutoCAD commands to set up the values as given in Example 2. Also, draw a border and a title block as shown in Figure 1. In this figure the hidden lines indicate the drawing limits. The border lines are 0.5 units inside the drawing limits. For the border lines use a polyline of width 0.02 units. Use the following command sequence to produce the prototype drawing for Example 2.

Command: LIMITS
ON/OFF/<Lower left corner> <0.00,0.00>:0,0
Upper right corner <12.0,9.0>: 48.0,36.0

Command: SNAP
Snap spacing or ON/OFF/Aspect/Rotate/Style <1.0>: 1.0

Command: GRID
Grid spacing(X) or ON/OFF/Snap/Aspect <1.0>: 4.0

Command: SETVAR
Variable name or ?: TEXTSIZE
New value for textsize <0.180>: 0.25

Command: PLINE
From point: 1.0,1.0
Current line-width is 0.00
Arc/Close/Halfwidth/Length/Undo/Width/ < Endpoint > :W
Starting width < 0.00 > : 0.02
Ending width < 0.02 > : 0.02
Arc/Close/Halfwidth/Length/Undo/Width/ < Endpoint > :47,1
Arc/Close/Halfwidth/Length/Undo/Width/ < Endpoint > :47,35
Arc/Close/Halfwidth/Length/Undo/Width/ < Endpoint > :1,35
Arc/Close/Halfwidth/Length/Undo/Width/ < Endpoint > :C

Command: LTSCALE
New scale factor < 1.0 > : 4

Command: DIM
Dim: DIMSCALE
Current value < 1.00 > New value: 4.0
Dim: EXIT

Command: Layer
?/Make/Set/New/ON/OFF/Color/Ltype/Freeze/Thaw: N
New layer name(s): OBJ,CEN,HID,DIM,BOR

?/Make/Set/New/ON/OFF/Color/Ltype/Freeze/Thaw: L
Linetype (or ?) < CONTINUOUS > : HIDDEN
Layer name(s) for linetype HIDDEN < 0 > : IIID

?/Make/Set/New/ON/OFF/Color/Ltype/Freeze/Thaw: L
Linetype (or ?) < CONTINUOUS > : CENTER
Layer name(s) for linetype CENTER < 0 > : CEN

?/Make/Set/New/ON/OFF/Color/Ltype/Freeze/Thaw: C
Color: RED
Layer name(s) for color 1 (red) < 0 > : OBJ

?/Make/Set/New/ON/OFF/Color/Ltype/Freeze/Thaw: C
Color: YELLOW
Layer name(s) for color 2 (yellow) < 0 > : CEN

?/Make/Set/New/ON/OFF/Color/Ltype/Freeze/Thaw: C
Color: BLUE
Layer name(s) for color 5 (blue) < 0 > : HID

?/Make/Set/New/ON/OFF/Color/Ltype/Freeze/Thaw: C
Color: GREEN
Layer name(s) for color 3 (green) < 0 > : DIM

?/Make/Set/New/ON/OFF/Color/Ltype/Freeze/Thaw: C
Color: MAGENTA

Layer name(s) for color 6 (magenta) <0>: BOR
?/Make/Set/New/ON/OFF/Color/Ltype/Freeze/Thaw: (RETURN)

Note

1. *Add the title block and the text as shown in Figure 1*
2. *You can also use the pull-down menu to create the layers, and to set the color and linetype.*
3. *After completing the drawing save it as PROTO2. Now, you have created a prototype drawing (PROTO2) that contains all information given in Example 2.*

Customizing Drawings according to Plot Size and Drawing Scale

You can generate a prototype drawing according to plot size and scale. For example, if the scale is 1/16" = 1' and the drawing is to be plotted on a 36" x 24" area, you can calculate the drawing parameters like: limits, dimscale, ltscale, etc and save them in a prototype drawing. This will save considerable time in the initial drawing setup and provide uniformity in the drawings. The next example explains the procedure involved in customizing a drawing according to a certain plot size and scale.

Example 3

Generate a prototype drawing with the following specifications. (Name of the prototype drawing PROTO3)

Plotted sheet size	36" x 24" (Figure 2)
Scale	1/8" = 1.0'
Snap	3'
Grid	6'
Text height	1/4" on plotted drawing
Ltscale	Calculate
Dimscale	Calculate
Units	Architectural
	16 - denominator of smallest fraction
	Angle in degrees/minutes/seconds
	4 - number of fractional places for display of angles
	0 angle along positive X-axis
	Angle positive if measured counterclockwise

Border   1" inside the edges of the
                                        plotted drawing sheet,
                                        using PLINE 1/32" wide
                                        when plotted (Figure 2)

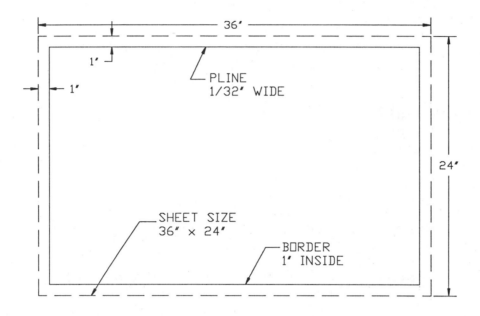

Figure 2 Border of prototype drawing

In this exercise there are some values that you need to calculate before setting various parameters. For example, the limits of the drawing depend on the plotted size of the drawing and the scale of the drawing. Similarly, the LTSCALE and DIMSCALE depend on the limits of the drawing. The following calculations explain the procedure for finding the values of limits, ltscale, dimscale, and text height.

Limits

```
Given:
Sheet Size    36" x 24"
Scale        1/8" = 1'
         or 1" = 8'

Calculate:
X-Limit
Y-Limit

Since sheet size is 36" x 24" and scale is 1/8"=1'
Therefore, X-Limit = 36 x 8' = 288'
           Y-Limit = 24 x 8' = 192'
```

Text height

```
Given:
Text height when plotted = 1/4"
```

```
        Sheet size                    36" x 24"
        Scale                         1/8" = 1'


        Calculate:
        Text height
        Since scale is 1/8" = 1'
                   or 1/8" = 12"
                   or   1" = 96"
        Therefore, scale factor = 96
                   Text height  = 1/4" x 96
                                = 24" = 2'
```

Ltscale and Dimscale

```
        Known:
        Limits    288' x 192'


        Calculate:
        ltscale and Dimscale

        Since X-Limit is 288'
                  = 288 x 12"
        Therefore
        Ltscale = X-Limits of the drawing / 12
                = 288 x 12 / 12
                = 288
        Dimscale = 96 (because scale is 1/8"=1' or 1=96")
        (All dimension variables like DIMTXT, DIMASZ  will
        be multiplied by 96).
```

Pline Width

```
        Given:
        Scale is  1/8" = 1'


        Calculate:
        PLINE width

        Since Scale is 1/8" = 1'
                  or    1" = 8'
                  or    1" = 96


        Therefore
        PLINE width = 1/32 x 96
                    = 3"
```

After calculating the unknown parameters, use the following AutoCAD commands to set up the drawing. Then save the drawing as PROTO3.

Command: Units
Report formats: (Examples)
    1. Scientific   1.55E+01
    2. Decimal   15.50
    3. Engineering   1'-3.50"
    4. Architectural   1'-3 1/2"
    5. Fractional   15 1/2

With the exception of Engineering and Architectural formats, these formats can be used with any basic units of measurements. For example, Decimal mode is perfect for metric units as well as decimal English units.

Enter choice, 1 to 5 <2>: 4
**Denominator of smallest fraction to display
(1, 2, 4, 8, 16, 32, or 64 <16>:** 16

Systems of angle measure: (Examples)
   1. Decimal degrees   45.0000
   2. Degrees/minutes/seconds   45d0'0"
   3. Grads   50.0000g
   4. Radians   0.7854r
   5   Surveyor's units   N 45d0'0"

Enter choice, 1 to 5 <1>: 2
Number of fractional places for display of angles (0 to 8) <0>: 2

Direction for angle 0.00:
   East   3 o'clock   = 0d0'0'
   North   12 o'clock   = 90d0'0"
   West   9 o'clock   = 180d0'0"
   South   6 o'clock   = 270d0'0"

Enter direction for angle 0d0'0" <0d0'0">: RETURN
Do you want angles measured clockwise? <N>: N

Command: LIMITS
ON/OFF/<Lower left corner> <0'-0",0'-0">:0,0
Upper right corner <1'-0",0'-9">: 288',192'

Command: SNAP
Snap spacing or ON/OFF/Aspect/Rotate/Style <0'-1">: 3'

Command: GRID
Grid spacing(X) or ON/OFF/Snap/Aspect <0'-0">: 6'

Command: SETVAR
Variable name or ?: TEXTSIZE
New value for textsize <0'-0 3/16">: 2'

Command: LTSCALE
New scale factor <1.0>: 288

Command: DIM
Dim: Dimscale
Current value <1.00> New value: 96
Dim: EXIT

Command: PLINE
From point: 8',8'
Current line-width is 0.00
Arc/Close/Halfwidth/Length/Undo/Width/<Endpoint>:W

Starting width <0.00>: 3
Ending width <0'-3">: RETURN
Arc/Close/Halfwidth/Length/Undo/Width/<Endpoint of line>:280',8'
Arc/Close/Halfwidth/Length/Undo/Width/<Endpoint of line>:280',184'
Arc/Close/Halfwidth/Length/Undo/Width/<Endpoint of line>:8',184'
Arc/Close/Halfwidth/Length/Undo/Width/<Endpoint of line>:C

Customizing Drawings with Dimensioning Specifications

In productions drawings it is very important to maintain a uniformity in dimensioning and follow certain dimensioning specifications. This can be accomplished by generating a prototype drawing that has the dimension variables set according to company specifications. It is extremely useful in an environment where there are several operators working on the same project or the company has some special dimensioning requirements. The next example illustrates the procedure for customizing a drawing with dimensioning specifications.

Example 4

Generate a prototype drawing with the following specifications. (Name of the prototype drawing PROTO4)

Plotted sheet size	24" x 18" (Figure 3)
Scale	1 = 25
Border	1" inside the edges of the plotted drawing sheet, using PLINE 0.05" wide when plotted (Figure 4)
DIMTAD	ON
DIMTIX	ON
DIMTOH	OFF
DIMTIH	OFF
DIMSCALE	25

Limits

Given:
Sheet Size   24" x 18"
Scale   1 = 25

Calculate:
X-Limit
Y-Limit

Since sheet size is 24" x 18" and scale is 1 = 25
Therefore X-Limit = 24 x 25 = 600

Y-Limit = 18 x 25 = 450

Pline Width

Given:
Scale 1 = 25

Calculate:
PLINE width

Since Scale is 1 = 25
Therefore
PLINE width = 0.05 x 25
            = 1.25

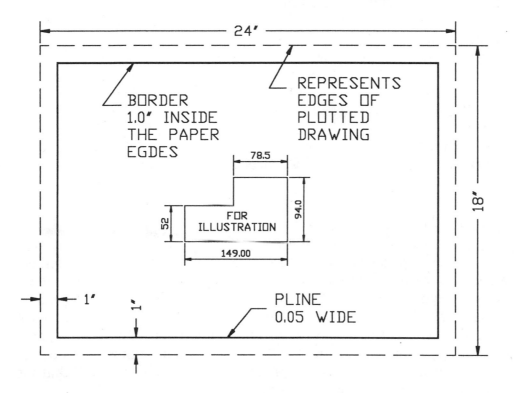

Figure 3   Prototype drawing

After calculating the unknown parameters, use the following AutoCAD commands to set up the drawing. Then save the drawing as PROTO4.

Command: LIMITS
ON/OFF/<Lower left corner> <0.00,0.00>:0,0
Upper right corner <12.0,9.0>: 600,450

Command: PLINE
From point: 25,25
Current line-width is 0.00
Arc/Close/Halfwidth/Length/Undo/Width/<Endpoint>:W

Starting width <0.00>: 1.25
Ending width <1.2500>: RETURN
Arc/Close/Halfwidth/Length/Undo/Width/<Endpoint of line>:575.25
Arc/Close/Halfwidth/Length/Undo/Width/<Endpoint of line>:575,425
Arc/Close/Halfwidth/Length/Undo/Width/<Endpoint of line>:25,425
Arc/Close/Halfwidth/Length/Undo/Width/<Endpoint of line>:C

Command: DIM
Dim: Dimtix
Current value <Off> New value: ON

Dim: Dimtad
Current value <Off> New value: ON

Dim: Dimtoh
Current value <On> New value: OFF

Dim: Dimtih
Current value <On> New value: OFF

Dim: Dimscale
Current value <1.0000> New value: 25

Customizing Drawings with Viewports

In certain applications you might need a standard viewport configuration to display different views of an object. It involves setting up the desired viewports and then changing the vpoint for different viewports.   You can generate a prototype drawing that contains a required number of viewports and the vpoint information. Now, if you insert a 3D object in one of the viewports of the prototype drawing, you will automatically get different views of the object without setting viewports or vpoints. The following example illustrates the procedure to create a prototype drawing with a standard number (4) of viewports and vpoints.

Example 5

Generate a prototype drawing with 4 viewports as shown in Figure 4.   The viewports should have the following vpoints.

VIEWPORTS	VPOINT	VIEW
Top right	1,-1,1	3D view
Top left	0,0,1	Top view
Lower right	1,0,0	Right side view
Lower left	0,-1,0	Front view

From the main menu select option number 1 to start a new drawing, PROTO5. Use the following commands to set the viewports and vpoints.

Command:VPORTS
Save/Restore/Delete/Join/SIngle/?/2/3/4: 4
Regenerating drawing

Make the top right viewport current and use the following command to set up the vpoint.

```
┌─────────────────────────┬─────────────────────────┐
│                         │                         │
│                         │                         │
│                         │                         │
│        VPⷯINT           │        VPⷯINT           │
│        0,0,1            │        1,-1,1           │
│                         │                         │
│                         │    (CURRENT VIEWPⷯRT)    │
│                         │                         │
├─────────────────────────┼─────────────────────────┤
│                         │                         │
│                         │                         │
│                         │                         │
│        VPⷯINT           │        VPⷯINT           │
│        0,-1,0           │        1,0,0            │
│                         │                         │
│                         │                         │
│                         │                         │
└─────────────────────────┴─────────────────────────┘
```

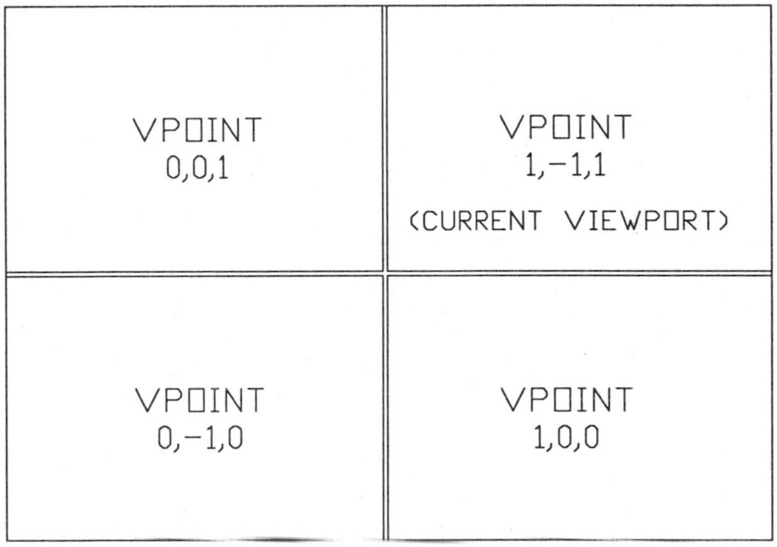

Figure 4   Viewports with different viewpoints

Command: <u>VPOINT</u>
Rotate/ <View point>: <0.00,0.00,1.00>: <u>1,-1,1</u>
Regenerating drawing

Make the top left viewport current and use the following command to set up the vpoint.

Command: <u>VPOINT</u>
Rotate/ <View point>: <0.00,0.00,1.00>: <u>0,0,1</u>
Regenerating drawing

Make the lower right viewport current and use the following command to set up the vpoint.

Command: <u>VPOINT</u>
Rotate/ <View point>: <0.00,0.00,1.00>: <u>1,0,0</u>
Regenerating drawing

Make the lower left viewport current and use the following command to set up the vpoint.

Command: VPOINT
Rotate/ < View point > : < 0.00,0.00,1.00 > : <u>0,-1,0</u>
Regenerating drawing

Command: END

From the main menu select option number 1 to start a new drawing, TBLOCK. Draw the following 3D tapered block as shown in Figure 5, and save it as TBLOCK. (Assume proportionate dimensions for the tapered block).

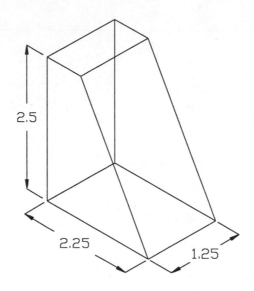

Figure 5   3D Tapered block

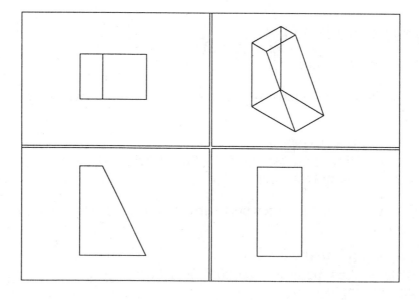

Figure 6   Different views of 3D tapered block

From the main menu again select option number 1 to start a new drawing, TEST=PROTO5. Make the top right viewport current and insert the drawing TBLOCK. Four different views will be automatically displayed on the screen as shown in Figure 6.

Customizing a Drawing with Paper Space

The paper space provides a convenient way to plot multiple views of a 3D drawing or multiple views of a regular 2D drawing. It takes quite some time to set up the viewports in the model space with different vpoints and scale factors. You can create prototype drawings that contains predefined viewports settings, with vpoint and other desired information. Now, if you create a new drawing, or insert a drawing, the views are automatically generated. The following example illustrates the procedure to generate a prototype drawing with paper space and model space viewports.

Example 6

Generate a prototype drawing Figure 7 with four views in paper space that display front, top, side and 3D views of the object. The plot size is 9 x 6 inches. The plot scale of the model space is 0.5 or 1/2" = 1". The model space viewports should have the following vpoint setting.

Model Space VIEWPORTS	VPOINT	VIEW
Top right	1,-1,1	3D view
Top left	0,0,1	Top view
Lower right	1,0,0	Right side view
Lower left	0,-1,0	Front view

Start AutoCAD and from the main menu select option number 1 to start a new drawing, PROTO6. Use the following commands to set up various parameters.

The first step is to change the TILEMODE to 0 and set up the limits for the paper space. At the time of plotting, if you want to use a plot scale factor of 1=1, set up the paper space limits equal to plot size. In this example, the plot size is 9 x 6, therefore the limits are 0,0 and 9,6. After setting the limits, use the AutoCAD's ZOOM-ALL command to display the new limits.

Command: TILEMODE
New value for TILEMODE <1>: 0
Regenerating drawing.

Command: LIMITS
Reset Paper space limits:
ON/OFF/<Lower left corner> <0.00,0.00>: (Press ENTER)
Upper right corner <12.00,9.00>: 9.0,6.0

Command: ZOOM
All/Center/Dynamic/Extents/Left/Previous/Vmax/Window/
<Scale (X/XP)>: ALL
Regenerating drawing.

The second step is to set up a layer (VIEW) for viewports and assign it a color (GREEN).

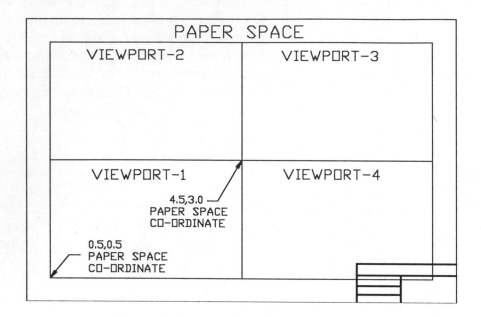

Figure 7   Paper space with 4 viewports

Command: Layer
?/Make/Set/New/ON/OFF/Color/Ltype/Freezw/Thaw: M
New current layer<0>:VIEW
?/Make/Set/New/ON/OFF/Color/Ltype/Freezw/Thaw: C
Color: GREEN
Layer name(s) for color 3 (green)<VIEW>: (Press ENTER)
?/Make/Set/New/ON/OFF/Color/Ltype/Freezw/Thaw: (ENTER)

Now, use AutoCAD's MVIEW command to set up a viewport and then switch to modelspace to zoom the display to half the size..

Command: MVIEW
ON/OFF/Hideplot/Fit/2/3/4/Restore/<First Point>:0.5,0.5
Other corner: 4.5,3.0

Command: MSPACE
Command: ZOOM
All/Center/Dynamic/Extents/Left/Previous/Vmax/Window/
<Scale (X/XP)>: 0.5XP

Use AutoCAD's PSPACE command to change to paper space and make four copies of the viewport as shown in Figure 7.

Use AutoCAD's MSPACE command to change to model space and then change the vpoints of different model space viewports by using the VPOINT command. The vpoint values for different viewports is shown in Example 6.

Use PSPACE command to change to paper space and set a new layer PBORDER with color yellow. Make the PBORDER layer current and draw a border and if needed, a title block using PLINE command.

Command: PSPACE
Command: PLINE
From point: 0,0
Current line-width is 0.00
Arc/Close/Halfwidth/Length/Undo/Width/<Endpoint of line>: 9.0,0
Arc/Close/Halfwidth/Length/Undo/Width/<Endpoint of line>: 9.0,6.0
Arc/Close/Halfwidth/Length/Undo/Width/<Endpoint of line>: 0,6.0
Arc/Close/Halfwidth/Length/Undo/Width/<Endpoint of line>: C

The last step is to change the **TILEMODE to 1** and save the prototype drawing. To test the paper space that you just created, insert the TBLOCK drawing that was created in Example 5. If you change TILEMODE to 0, you will find four different views of TBLOCK (Figure 8). You can freeze the layer VIEW so that the viewports do not appear on the drawing. Now, you can plot this drawing with a plot scale factor of 1=1 and the size of the plot will be exactly 9 x 6 inches.

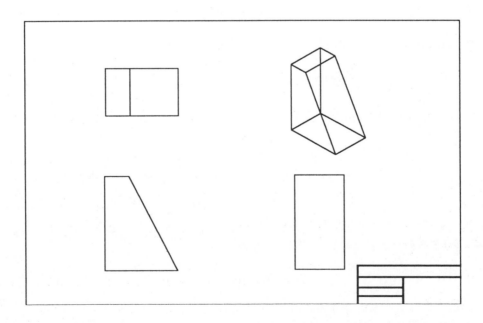

Figure 8   Four views of TBLOCK in paper space

Review

Fill in the blanks

1. The name of the standard prototype drawing that comes with AutoCAD software is ....

2. The default prototype drawing is automatically ...., provided the .... has not been changed.

3. If the name of the new drawing is HOUSE, AutoCAD will load the default prototype drawing as specified in the AutoCAD's .... menu.

4. If the name of the new drawing is HOUSE=, AutoCAD will load a drawing that has AutoCAD's .... settings.

5. If the name of the new drawing is HOUSE=PROTOH, AutoCAD will load the .... prototype drawing.

6. The ACAD.DWG standard prototype drawing was created by entering the name of the new drawing as ....

7. The default prototype drawing can be changed by selecting item number .... from the main menu, item number .... from Configuration menu and then item number 2 from ....

8. The default value of DIMSCALE is ....

9. The default value of DIMTXT is ....

10. The default value for SNAP is ....

11. The architectural units can be selected by using AutoCAD's .... command.

12. If plot size is 36" x 24", and the scale is 1/2" = 1', the X-Limit = ... and Y-Limit = ...

13. If the plot size is 24" x 18", and the scale is 1 = 20, the X-Limit = ... and Y-Limit = ...

14. If the limits are (0.00, 0.00) and (600.00, 450.00), the LTSCALE factor = ...

15. .... provides a convenient way to plot multiple views of a 3D drawing or multiple views of a regular 2D drawing

16. You can use AutoCAD's .... command to set up a viewport in model space.

17. You can use AutoCAD's .... command to change to paper space

18. You can use AutoCAD's .... command to change to model space

19. The values that can be assigned to TILEMODE are .... and ....

20. In the model space if you want to reduce the display size by half, the scale factor that you will enter in ZOOM-Scale command is ....

Exercises

Exercise 1

Generate a prototype drawing with the following specifications. (Name of the prototype drawing PROTOE1)

Limits	36.0, 24.0
Snap	0.5
Grid	1.0
Text height	0.25
Units	decimal
	2 decimal places
	decimal degrees
	0 decimal places
	0 angle along positive X-axis
	angle positive if measured
	counterclockwise

Exercise 2

Generate a prototype drawing with the following specifications. (Name of the drawing PROTOE2)

Limits	48.0, 36.0
Snap	0.5
Grid	2.0
Text height	0.25
PLINE width	0.03
Ltscale	Calculate
Dimscale	Calculate

Layers

Layer Names	Line Type	Color
0	Continuous	White
OBJECT	Continuous	Green
CENTER	Center	Magenta
HIDDEN	Hidden	Blue
DIM	Continuous	Red
BORDER	Continuous	Cyan

Exercise 3

Generate a prototype drawing with following specifications.   (Name of the drawing PROTOE3)

Plotted sheet size	36" x 24" (Figure 9)
Scale	1/2" = 1.0'
Text height	1/4" on plotted drawing
Ltscale	Calculate
Dimscale	Calculate
Units	Architectural
	32 - denominator of smallest fraction
	Angle in degrees/minutes/seconds
	4 - number of fractional places for display of angles
	0 angle along positive X-axis
	Angle positive if measured counterclockwise
Border	1-1/2" inside the edges of the plotted drawing sheet, using PLINE 1/32" wide when plotted (Figure 9)

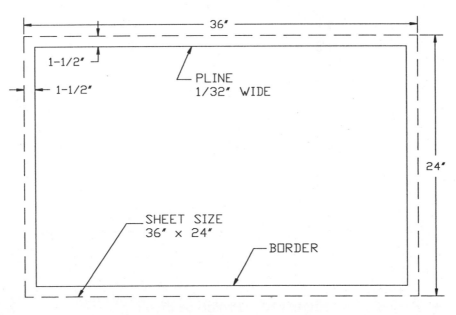

Figure 9   Prototype drawing

Exercise 4

Generate a prototype drawing with following specifications. (Name of the drawing PROTOE4)

Plotted sheet size	24" x 18" (Figure 10)
Scale	1 = 50
Border	1" inside the edges of the plotted drawing sheet, using PLINE 0.05" wide when plotted (Figure 10)
DIMTAD	ON
DIMTIX	ON
DIMTOH	OFF
DIMTIH	OFF
DIMSCALE	Calculate
DIMALT	ON
DIMASO	OFF
DIMTOFL	ON

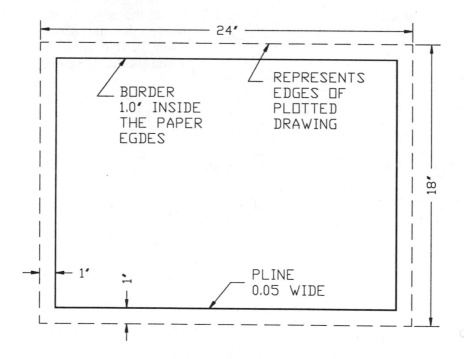

Figure 10   Prototype drawing

Exercise 5

A user wants to set up a prototype drawing with the following specifications. (Name of the drawing PROTOE5)

Limits	36.0, 24,0
Border	35.0, 23.0
Grid	1.0
Snap	0.5
Text Height	0.15
Dimscale	2.0
Units	Decimal (Up to 2 Places)
Ltscale	3
Current Layer	Object

Layers

Layer Name	Line Type	Color
0	Continuous	White
Object	Continuous	Red
Hidden	Hidden	Yellow
Center	Center	Green
Dim	Continuous	Blue
Border	Continuous	Magenta
Notes	Continuous	White

This prototype drawing should also have a border line and a title block as shown in Figure 11.

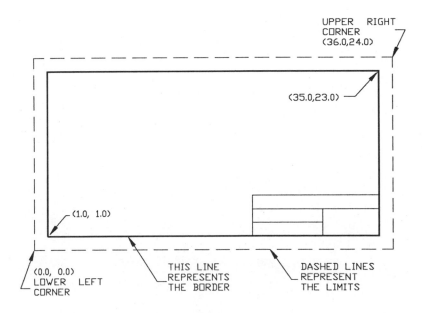

Figure 11 Prototype drawing

Chapter 2

Script Files

What are Script Files

AutoCAD has provided a facility called script files that allow the user to combine different AutoCAD commands and execute them in a predetermined sequence. The commands can be written as a text file by using the "EDLIN" function of DOS, AutoCAD's EDIT command (provided ACAD.PGP file is present and EDIT is defined in the file), or any other text editor. These files, generally known a script files, have an extension .SCR (Example PLOT.SCR). A script file can be executed with AutoCAD's SCRIPT command.

Script files can be used to generate a slide show, do the initial drawing setup, or plot a drawing to a predefined specification. They can also be used to automate some command sequences that are used frequently in generating, editing, or viewing a drawing.

Example 1

Write a script file that will perform the following initial set up for a drawing. (File name SCRIPT1.SCR)

Ortho	On
Grid	2.0
Grid	Off
Snap	0.5
Limits	0,0
	48.0,36.0
Zoom	All
Axis	On
Text height	0.25
Ltscale	4.0
Dimscale	4.0

Before writing a script file it is very important to know the AutoCAD commands and the entries required in response to the command prompts. To find out the sequence of the prompt entries, you can type the command from the keyboard and then respond to different prompts. The following commands is a list of AutoCAD commands and prompt entries for Example 1.

Command: ORTHO
ON/OFF <Off>: ON

Command: GRID
Grid spacing(X) or ON/OFF/Snap/Aspect <1.0>: 2.0

Command: GRID
Grid spacing(X) or ON/OFF/Snap/Aspect <1.0>: Off

Command: SNAP
Snap spacing or ON/OFF/Aspect/Rotate/Style <1.0>: 0.5

Command: LIMITS
ON/OFF/<Lower left corner> <0.00,0.00>:0,0
Upper right corner <12.0,9.0>: 48.0,36.0

Command:ZOOM
All/Center/Dynamic/Extents/Left/Previous/Vmax/Window/<Scale(X/XP)>:A

Command: SETVAR
Variable name or ?: TEXTSIZE
New value for textsize <0.02>: 0.125

Command: LTSCALE
New scale factor <1.0000>: 4.0

Command: SETVAR
Variable name or ?: DIMSCALE
New value for dimscale <1.0000>: 4.0

Once you know the AutoCAD commands and the required prompt entries, you can write the script file using AutoCAD's EDIT command or any text editor. The following file is a listing of the script file for Example 1.

```
ORTHO
ON
GRID
2.0
GRID
Off
SNAP
0.5
LIMITS
0,0
48.0,36.0
ZOOM
```

```
ALL
AXIS
ON
SETVAR
TEXTSIZE
0.25
LTSCALE
4
SETVAR
DIMSCALE
4.0
```

You will notice that the commands and the prompt entries in this file are in the same sequence as mentioned before. You can also combine several statements in one line as shown in the following listing.

```
ORTHO ON
GRID 2.0 GRID Off
SNAP 0.5 SNAP ON
LIMITS 0,0 48.0,36.0 ZOOM ALL
AXIS ON
SETVAR TEXTSIZE 0.25
LTSCALE 4
SETVAR DIMSCALE 4.0
```

Note

1. *In the script files the spaces are used to terminate a command, or a prompt entry. Therefore the spaces are very important in the script files. Make sure there are no extra spaces, unless they are required to enter RETURN more than once.*

2. *After you change the limits, it is a good practice to use ZOOM command with ALL option to display the new limits on the screen.*

SCRIPT Command

AutoCAD's SCRIPT command allows the user to run a script file while you are in the drawing editor. To execute the script file, type the SCRIPT command and press ENTER key on the keyboard. AutoCAD will prompt you to enter the name of the script file. You can accept the default file name, or enter a new file name. The default script file name is the same as the drawing name. If you want to enter a new file name, type the name of the script file, without the file extension (.SCR). The file extension is assumed and need not to be included with the file name.

To run the script file of Example 1, type the SCRIPT command and press ENTER. In response to file name, enter SCRIPT1 and then press the ENTER key again. You will see the changes taking place on the screen as the script file commands are executed. The format of the SCRIPT command is:

Command: SCRIPT
Script file <default>: Script file name

Example
Command: SCRIPT
```
Script file <CUSTOM>: SCRIPT1
```
```
                              └─ Name of the script file
              └─ Default drawing file name
```

Example 2

Write a script file that will set up the following layers with the given colors and linetypes. (File name SCRIPT2.SCR)

Object	Red	Continuous
Center	Yellow	Center
Hidden	Blue	Hidden
Dimension	Green	Continuous
Border	Magenta	Continuous
Hatch	Cyan	Continuous

As mentioned earlier, before writing a script file you need to know the AutoCAD commands and the required prompt entries. For Example 2, the following commands are needed to create the layers with the given colors and linetypes.

Command: Layer
?/Make/Set/New/ON/OFF/Color/Ltype/Freeze/Thaw: N
New layer name(s):OBJECT,CENTER,HIDDEN,DIM,BORDER,HATCH

?/Make/Set/New/ON/OFF/Color/Ltype/Freeze/Thaw: L
Linetype (or ?) <CONTINUOUS>: HIDDEN
Layer name(s) for linetype HIDDEN <0>: HIDDEN

?/Make/Set/New/ON/OFF/Color/Ltype/Freeze/Thaw: L
Linetype (or ?) <CONTINUOUS>: CENTER
Layer name(s) for linetype CENTER <0>: CENTER

?/Make/Set/New/ON/OFF/Color/Ltype/Freeze/Thaw: C
Color: RED
Layer name(s) for color 1 (red) <0>: OBJECT

?/Make/Set/New/ON/OFF/Color/Ltype/Freeze/Thaw: C
Color: YELLOW
Layer name(s) for color 2 (yellow) <0>: CENTER
?/Make/Set/New/ON/OFF/Color/Ltype/Freeze/Thaw: C
Color: BLUE
Layer name(s) for color 5 (blue) <0>: HIDDEN

?/Make/Set/New/ON/OFF/Color/Ltype/Freeze/Thaw: C
Color: GREEN
Layer name(s) for color 3 (green) <0>: DIM

?/Make/Set/New/ON/OFF/Color/Ltype/Freeze/Thaw: C
Color: MAGENTA
Layer name(s) for color 6 (magenta) <0>: BORDER

?/Make/Set/New/ON/OFF/Color/Ltype/Freeze/Thaw: C
Color: CYAN
Layer name(s) for color 4 (cyan) <0>: HATCH

?/Make/Set/New/ON/OFF/Color/Ltype/Freeze/Thaw: (RETURN)

The following file is a listing of the script file that creates different layers and assigns the given colors and linetypes to these layers.

```
LAYER
NEW
OBJECT,CENTER,HIDDEN,DIM,BORDER,HATCH
L
CENTER
CENTER
L
HIDDEN
HIDDEN
C
RED
OBJECT
C
YELLOW
CENTER
C
BLUE
HIDDEN
C
GREEN
DIM
C
MAGENTA
BORDER
C
CYAN
HATCH
```
——————— (This is a blank line to terminate
the LAYER command)

Example 3

Write a script file that will rotate the circle and the line, as shown in Figure 1, around the lower end point of the line through 45 degree increments. The script file should be able to produce a continuous rotation of the given objects with a delay of 2 seconds after every 45 degrees rotation. (File name SCRIPT3.SCR)

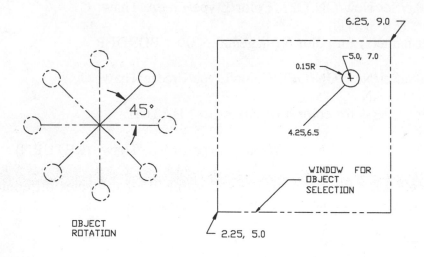

Figure 1   Line and circle rotated through 45 degree increments

Before writing the script file, enter the required command and the prompt entries from the key board. Write down the exact sequence of the entries in which they have been entered to perform the given operations. The following is a listing of the AutoCAD command sequence needed to rotate the circle and the line around the lower end point of the line.

> **Command**: Rotate ——————— (Enter Rotate Command)
> **Select objects**:W ——————— (Window Option to select objects)
> **First corner**: 2.25,5.0
> **Other corner**: 6.25,9.0
> **Select objects**: < RETURN >
> **Base point**: 4.25,6.5
> **< Rotation angle >/Reference**: 45

Once the AutoCAD commands, command options and their sequence is known, you can write a script file. As mentioned earlier, you can use EDLIN function of DOS, or any other text editor to write a script file. If you are in the drawing editor and you want to use the Edlin function to write a text file, type SHELL or SH and press the "Enter" key to access DOS commands

> **Command: SHELL**
> **OS Command: EDLIN ROTATE.SCR**

The following file is a listing of the script file that will create the required rotation of the circle and the line of Example 1.

```
ROTATE
W
2.25,5.0
6.25,9.0
                        ——————————— Blank line for RETURN

4.25,6.5
45
```

Line 1
ROTATE   In this line ROTATE is an AutoCAD command that rotates the objects.

Line 2
W   In this line W is the window option for selecting the objects that need to be edited.

Line 3
2.25,5.0   In this line 2.25 defines the X coordinate and 5.0 defines the Y coordinate of the lower left corner of the object selection window.

Line 4
6.25,9.0   In this line 6.25 defines the X coordinate and 9.0 defines the Y coordinate of the upper right corner of the object selection window.

Line 5
Line 5 is a blank line that terminates the object selection process.

Line 6
4.25,6.5   In this line 4.25 defines the X coordinate and 6.5 defines the Y coordinate of the base point for rotation.

Line 7
45   In this line 45 is the incremental angle for rotation.

Note

One of the limitations of the script files is that all the information has to be contained within the file. These files do not let the user enter information. For example, in Example 3, if you want to use the window option for selecting the objects then the window option (W) and the two points that define this window must be contained within the script file. Same is true for the base point and all other information that goes in a script file. There is no way that a script file can prompt the user to enter a particular piece of information and then resume the script file.

RSCRIPT Command

AutoCAD's RSCRIPT command allows the user to execute the script file indefinitely until cancelled. It is very desirable feature when the user wants to run the same file continuously. For example, in the case of a slide show for a product demonstration, the RSCRIPT command can be used to run the script file again and again until it is terminated by pressing CTRL-C from the key board. Similarly, in Example 3, the rotation command needs to be repeated indefinitely to create a continuous rotation of the objects. This can be accomplished by adding RSCRIPT command at the end of the file as shown in the following file.

```
ROTATE
W
2.25,5.0
6.25,9.0
                          ──────────── Blank line for RETURN
6. 4.25,6.5
45
RSCRIPT
```

The RSCRIPT command on line 8 will repeat the commands from line 1 to line 7, and thus set the script file in an indefinite loop. The script file can be stopped by pressing CTRL C or the BACKSPACE key on the key board.

Note

You can not provide a conditional statements in a script file to terminate the file when a particular condition is satisfied.

DELAY Command

In the script files some of the operation happen very quickly that might make it difficult for the user to see the operations that are taking place on the screen. Sometimes, it might be even necessary to intentionally introduce a pause between certain operations in a script file. For example, in a slide show for a product demonstration, it is very important to have a time delay between different slides so that the audience has enough time to see the slides. This is accomplished by using AutoCAD's DELAY command that introduces a delay before the next command is executed. The general format of DELAY command is:

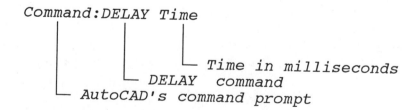

```
Command:DELAY Time
                     └── Time in milliseconds
             └── DELAY  command
   └── AutoCAD's command prompt
```

The DELAY command is to be followed by the delay time in milliseconds. For example, a delay of 2000 milliseconds means that AutoCAD will pause for approximately 2 seconds before executing the next command. The reason it is approximately 2 seconds is because the computers vary in their processing speeds. The maximum time delay you can enter is 32767 milliseconds (about 33 seconds).   In Example 3, a 2 second delay can be introduced by inserting a DELAY command line between line 7 and line 8 as shown in the following file listing.

```
ROTATE
W
2.25,5.0
6.25,9.0
                              ———————— Blank line for RETURN

4.25,6.5
45
DELAY 2000
RSCRIPT
```

The first seven lines of this file rotate the objects through 45 degree angle. Before the RSCRIPT command on line 8 is executed, there is a delay of 2000 milliseconds (about 2 seconds). The RSCRIPT command will repeat the script file that rotates the objects through another 45 degree angle. Thus, a slide show is created with a time delay of 2 seconds after every 45 degrees increment.

RESUME Command

If the script file was cancelled and you want to continue the script file, you can do so by using AutoCAD's RESUME command.

Command: <u>RESUME</u>

The RESUME command can also be used if the script file has encountered an error causing the script file to be suspended. The RESUME command will skip the command that caused the error and continue with rest of the script file. If the error has occurred when the command was in progress, use a leading apostrophe with the RESUME command ('RESUME) to invoke the RESUME command in transparent mode.

Command: <u>'RESUME</u>

Invoking a Script File
when Loading AutoCAD

The script files can also be run when loading AutoCAD, without getting into the drawing editor. The format of the command for running a script file when loading AutoCAD is:

Drive > ACAD (Default drawing) (Script file name)

Example

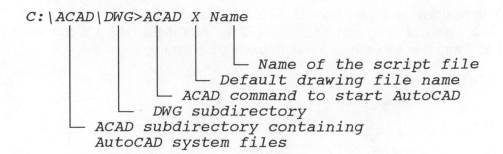

```
C:\ACAD\DWG>ACAD X Name
```

Here, it is assumed that the AutoCAD system files are loaded in ACAD subdirectory and the user is in the DWG subdirectory. If the path has not been set before, you can use the following command format to invoke a script file.

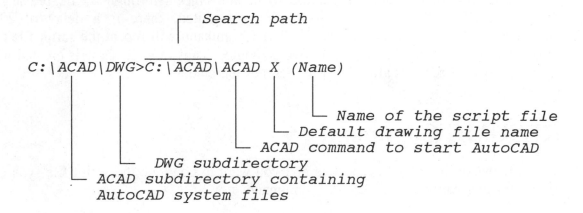

```
C:\ACAD\DWG>C:\ACAD\ACAD X (Name)
```

Note

1.   *When a script file is invoked at the time of loading AutoCAD, the AutoCAD message (ACAD.MSG) is skipped.*

2.   *It is recommended to avoid the use of abbreviations to prevent any confusion.*

Example 4

Write a script file that can be invoked when loading AutoCAD and creates a new drawing EX4 with the following set up. (File name SCRIPT4.SCR)

Grid	3.0
Snap	0.5
Limits	0,0
	36.0,24.0
Zoom	All
Text Height	0.25
Ltscale	3.0
Dimscale	3.0
Layers	

Name	Color	Linetype
Obj	Red	Continuous
Cen	Yellow	Center
Hid	Blue	Hidden
Dim	Green	Continuous

The following file is a listing of the script file that creates a new drawing EX4 and does the initial setup for the drawing.

```
1                     ───────────── Selects option 1 from main menu
                      ───────────── Blank line for RETURN
GRID 2.0
SNAP 0.5
LIMITS 0,0 36.0,24.0 ZOOM ALL
SETVAR TEXTSIZE 0.25
LTSCALE 3
SETVAR DIMSCALE 3.0
LAYER NEW
OBJ,CEN,HID,DIM
L CENTER CEN
L HIDDEN HID
C RED OBJ
C YELLOW CEN
C BLUE HID
C GREEN DIM
                      ───────────── Blank line for RETURN
```

To run the script file SCRIPT4, when loading AutoCAD use the following command.

```
C:\ACAD\DWG>ACAD EX4 SCRIPT4
        │       │      │
        │       │      └─ Name of the script file
        │       └─ Default drawing file name
        └─ ACAD to load AutoCAD
```

The second ACAD starts AutoCAD and displays the main menu on the screen. After this, script file SCRIPT4 is automatically executed. The first line in the script file is 1 that picks option number 1, "Begin a NEW drawing", from the main menu.

Main Menu

0. Exit AutoCAD
1. Begin a NEW drawing
2. Edit an EXISTING drawing
3. Plot a drawing
4. Printer Plot a drawing

5. Configure AutoCAD
6. File Utilities
7. Compile shape/font description file
8. Convert Old drawing file
9. Recover damaged drawing

Enter selection: 1

Enter name of drawing < EX4 > : RETURN

The new drawing automatically assumes the default file name EX4. Since the second line of the script file is a blank line, it causes a RETURN. This does not change the file name. However, if the second line of the script file contained a file name, for example DWG4, then AutoCAD will ignore the default file name EX4 and assign the name DWG4 to the new drawing. The following script file will create a new drawing DWG4 and then completes the initial setup for the drawing.

```
1                      ─────────────── Select option 1 from main menu
DWG4                   ─────────────── New drawing name
GRID 2.0
SNAP 0.5
LIMITS 0,0 36.0,24.0 ZOOM ALL
SETVAR TEXTSIZE 0.25
LTSCALE 3
SETVAR DIMSCALE 3.0
LAYER NEW
OBJ,CEN,HID,DIM
L CENTER CEN
L HIDDEN HID
C RED OBJ
C YELLOW CEN
C BLUE HID
C GREEN DIM
                       ─────────────── Blank line for RETURN
```

Example 5

Write a script file that will plot a 36 x 24 drawing on a 9 x 6 Inch size paper. Use the window option to select the drawing to be plotted. (File name SCRIPT5.SCR)

Before writing a script file for plotting a drawing, it is important to set up the plotter specification to obtain the desired output. To determine the prompt entries and their sequence to set up the plotter specifications, enter the AutoCAD's PLOT command from the keyboard. Write down the entries you make and also the sequence of these entries. The following file is a listing of the plotter specification with the new entries.

```
PLOT
What to plot -- Display, Extents, Limits, View, or Window <D>: W
```

First corner: 0,0
Other corner: 36,24
Plot will be written to a selected file
Sizes are in Inches
Plot origin is at (0.00,0.00)
Plotting area is 10.22 wide by 7.53 high (MAX size)
Plot is NOT rotated
Pen width is 0.010
Area fill will NOT be adjusted for pen width
Hidden lines will NOT be removed
Plot will be scaled to fit available area

Do you want to change anything? <N>: Y

Entity Color	Pen No.	Line Type	Pen Speed	Entity Color	Pen No.	Line Type	Pen Speed
1 (red)	1	0	36	9	1	0	36
2 (yellow)	1	0	36	10	1	0	36
3 (green)	1	0	36	11	1	0	36
4 (cyan)	1	0	36	12	1	0	36
5 (blue)	1	0	36	13	1	0	36
6 (magenta)	1	0	36	14	1	0	36
7 (white)	1	0	36	15	1	0	36
8	1	0	36				

Line type   0 = continuous line
                   1 = ...
                   2 = ----   ----   ----   ----
                   3 = -----   -----   -----
                   4 = ------. ------. ------. ------.
                   5 = ---- - ------ - ------
                   6 = --- - - --- - - ---
Do you want to change any of the above parameters? <N>: N
Write the plot to a file? <Y>: N
Size units (Inches or Millimeters) <I>: I
Plot origin in Inches <0.00,0.00>: 0,0

Standard values for plotting size

Size	Width	Height
MAX	10.22	7.53

Enter the Size or Width, Height (in Inches) <MAX>: 9,6
Rotate plot 0/90/180/270 <0>:0
Pen width <0.010>:0.010
Adjust area fill boundaries for pen width? <N>: N
Remove hidden lines? <N>: N

Specify scale by entering:
Plotted Inches=Drawing Units or Fit or ? <F>: 1=4
Effective plotting area: 6.00 wide by 4.50 high
Position paper in plotter.
Press RETURN to continue or S to Stop for hardware setup
Plot completed.

Press RETURN to continue:

The following file is a listing of the script file that will plot a 36 x 24 drawing on a 9 x 6 Inch paper after making the necessary changes in the plot specifications.

```
PLOT
W                    ————— Window option
0,0 36,24            ————— First corner, other corner
Y                    ————— Do you want to change anything
N
N
I
0,0
9,6
0                    ————— Rotation angle
0.010                ————— Pen width
N
N
1=4

                     ————— Blank line for RETURN
                     ————— Blank line for RETURN
```

Example 6

Write a script file that will plot a 144' x 96' drawing on a 36 x 24 inch sheet of paper. The drawing scale is 1/8" = 1'. The following table lists the assignment of pens for different colors and speeds. (File name SCRIPT6.SCR)

Entity Color	Pen No.	Line Type	Pen Speed
1 (red)	1	0	25
2 (yellow)	2	0	30
3 (green)	3	0	36
4 (cyan)	4	0	36
5 (blue)	5	0	36
6 (mag.)	6	6	36

The following file is a listing of the script file for plotting a 144' x 96' drawing on a 36 x 24 inch size paper after making the necessary changes in the plot specifications.

```
PLOT
L
Y        ————— Do you want to change anything
Y        ————— Do you want to change any of the above parameters? <N>
1 0 25   ————— Pen NO., Linetype, Pen Speed
2 0 30
3 0 36
4 0 36
5 0 36
```

```
6 6 36
X                  ————————— X for Exit
N
I
0,0
9,6
0
0.010
N
N
1=96               ————————— Plotted Inches = Drawing units
                   ————————— Blank line for RETURN
                   ————————— Blank line for RETURN
```

Review

Fill in the blanks

1. AutoCAD has provided a facility of .... that allows the user to combine different AutoCAD commands and execute them in a predetermined sequence.

2. The .... files can be used to generate a slide show, do the initial drawing setup, or plot a drawings to a predefined specification

3. Before writing a script file it is very important to know the AutoCAD .... and the .... required in response to the command prompts.

4. In a script file you can .... several statements in one line.

5. In the script file the .... are used to terminate a command, or a prompt entry.

6. AutoCAD's .... command is used to run a script file.

7. When you run a script file the default script file name is the same as the .... name.

8. When you run a script file, type the name of the script file without the file ....

9. One of the limitations of the script files is that all the information has to be contained .... the file.

10. AutoCAD's .... command allows the user to execute the script file indefinitely until cancelled.

11. You can not provide a .... statements in a script file to terminate the file when a particular condition is satisfied.

12. AutoCAD's .... command introduces a delay before the next command is executed.

13. The DELAY command is to be followed by .... in milliseconds

14. If the script file was cancelled and you want to continue the script file, you can do so by using AutoCAD's .... command.

Exercises

Exercise 1

Write a script file that will do the following initial set up for a drawing. (File name SCRIPTE1.SCR)

Grid	2.0
Snap	0.5
Limits	0,0
	18.0,12.0
Zoom	All
Text Height	0.25
Ltscale	2.0
Dimscale	2.0
Dimtix	On
Dimtoh	Off
Dimtih	Off
Dimtad	On
Dimcen	0.75

Exercise 2

Write a script file that will set up the following layers with the given colors and linetypes. (File name SCRIPTE2.SCR)

Contour	Red	Continuous
SPipes	Yellow	Center
WPipes	Blue	Hidden
Power	Green	Continuous
Manholes	Magenta	Continuous
Trees	Cyan	Continuous

Exercise 3

Write a Script file that will do the following initial setup for a new drawing. (File name SCRIPT3E.SCR)

Limits	0,0 24,18
Grid	1.0
Snap	0.25
Ortho	On
Snap	On
Zoom	All
Pline Width	0.02

PLine	0,0 24,0 24,18 0,18 0,0
Units:	Decimal Units
	Number of decimal digits (2)
	Decimal degrees
	Number of decimal digits (2)
	Direction of 0 angle (3 O'CLOCK)
	Angle measured counter-clockwise
Ltscale	1.5

Layers

Name	Color	Linetype
Obj	Red	Continuous
Cen	Yellow	Center
Hid	Blue	Hidden
Dim	Green	Continuous

Exercise 4

Write a Script file that will PRPLOT a given drawing according to the following specifications. (File name SCRIPT4E.SCR)

Prplot, using the window option.
Window size (0,0 24,18)
Do not write the plot to file.
Size in Inch-Units.
Plot origin (0.0, 0,0)
Maximum plot size (8.0, 10.5)
90 Deg. plot rotation.
No removal of hidden lines.
Plotting scale (Fit)

Chapter 3

Slide Shows

What is a Slide Show

AutoCAD provides a facility using script files to combine the slides in a text file and display them on the screen in a predetermined sequence. In this way, a user can generate a slide show for a slide presentation. A time delay can also be introduced in the display so that the viewer gets enough time to view a slide.

A drawing or the parts of a drawing can also be displayed by using AutoCAD's display commands. For example, you can use ZOOM, PAN, or other commands to display the details that you want to show to your client. If the drawing is very complicated, it takes quite sometime to display the desired information and it may not be possible to get the desired views in the right sequence. However, with slide shows you can arrange the slides in any order and present them to your client in a definite sequence. In addition to saving the time, it will also help in minimizing the distraction that might be caused by constantly changing the drawing display. Also, there are some drawings that are confidential in nature and the user may not want to display some portions or views of the drawing. By making slides you can restrict the information that is presented through the slides. You can send a slide show to your client without loosing control of the drawings and the information that is contained in the drawing.

What are Slides

Slides are the snap-shots of a screen display. It is like taking a picture of a display with a camera. The slides do not contain any vector information, which means that the entities do not have any information associated with them. For example, the slides do not retain any information about the layers, colors, linetypes, start point and end point of a line, or viewpoint. Therefore, the slides can not be edited like a drawing. If you want to make any changes in the slide, you need to edit the drawing and then make a new slide from the edited drawing.

MSLIDE Command

The slides are created by using the AutoCAD's MSLIDE command. The command will prompt the user to enter the slide file name.

    Command: MSLIDE
    Slide file <Default>: (Name)

    Example
    Command: MSLIDE
    Slide File: <NEWDWG> SLIDE1
                         | |
                         | |
                         | └─Slide file name
                         └─Default slide file name

The slide file name can be a maximum of 8 characters long, but without an extension (SLIDE1). In the above mentioned example, AutoCAD will save the slide file under the name SLIDE1.SLD.

Note

1.   *In the model space, you can use the MSLIDE command to make a slide of the existing display in the current viewport.*

2.   *If you are in the paper space, you can make a slide of the display in the paper space that includes any viewports.*

3.   *In case the viewports are not active, the MSLIDE command will make the slide of the current screen display.*

VSLIDE Command

To view a slide, use the command VSLIDE. AutoCAD will then prompt you to enter the slide file name. Enter the name of the slide you want to view and press the ENTER key. Do not enter the extension after the slide file name. AutoCAD automatically assumes the extension .SLD.

    Command: VSLIDE
    Slide file <Default>: (Name)

    Example
    Command: VSLIDE
    Slide file <NEWDWG>: SLIDE1
                     | |
                     | └─ Name of slide file
                     └─ Default slide file name

If the slide is in the slide library, and you want to view that slide, the slide library name has to be specified with the slide file name. The slide library is discussed later in this chapter. The format of the library and slide file name is:

```
Command: VSLIDE
```
Slide file <default>:<u>Library file name</u>(Slide file name)

Example
```
Command: VSLIDE
Slide file <NEWDWG>: SLDLIB(SLIDE1)
```
```
                              └─ Name of slide file
                        └─ Name of slide library
              └─ Default slide file name
```

Note

1. *After viewing a slide, you can use AutoCAD's REDRAW command to remove the slide display and return to existing drawing on the screen.*

2. *Any command that is automatically followed by a redraw will also display the existing drawing. For example, AutoCAD's GRID, ZOOM ALL, or REGEN commands will automatically return to the existing drawing on the screen.*

3. *You can view the slides on high or low resolution monitors. Depending on the resolution of the monitor, AutoCAD automatically adjusts the image. However, if you are using a high resolution monitor, it is better to make the slides on the same monitor to take full advantage of the high resolution monitor.*

Example 1

Write a script file that will generate a slide show of the following slide files with a time delay of 15 seconds after every slide.

SLIDE1, SLIDE2, SLIDE3, SLIDE4

The first step in a slide show is to create the slides. Fig 1 shows the drawings that have been saved as slide files SLIDE1, SLIDE2, SLIDE3, SLIDE4. The second step is to find out the sequence in which you want these slides to be displayed on the screen with the necessary time delay, if any, between the slides. Then you can use any text editor or AutoCAD's EDIT command (provided ACAD.PGP file is present and EDIT is defined in the file) to write the script file with the extension .SCR.

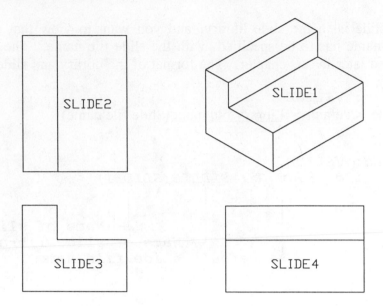

Figure 1   Slides for slide show

The following file is a listing of the script file that will create a slide show of the given slide. The name of the script file is SLDSHOW1.

```
VSLIDE SLIDE1
DELAY 15000
VSLIDE SLIDE2
DELAY 15000
VSLIDE SLIDE3
DELAY 15000
VSLIDE SLIDE4
DELAY 15000
```

To run this slide show, type SCRIPT in response to AutoCAD's Command prompt. Now, type the name of the script file (SLDSHOW1) and press the ENTER key. The slides will be displayed on the screen with an approximate time delay of 15 seconds between the slides.

Preloading Slides

In the script file of Example 1, VSLIDE SLIDE1 in line 1, loads the slide file SLIDE1 and displays it on the screen. After 15000 milliseconds pause, it starts loading the second slide file SLIDE2. Depending on the computer and the disk access time, you will notice that it takes some time to load the second slide file, and the same is true for the other slides. To avoid the delay in loading the slide files, AutoCAD has provided a facility to preload a slide while viewing the previous slide. This is accomplished by placing a "*" (asterisk) mark in front of the slide file name.

VSLIDE SLIDE1   ———— (View slide, SLIDE1)

VSLIDE *SLIDE2	——— (Preload slide, SLIDE2)
DELAY 15000	——— (Delay of 15 seconds)
VSLIDE	——— (Display slide, SLIDE2)
VSLIDE *SLIDE3	——— (Preload slide, SLIDE3)
DELAY 15000	——— (Delay of 15 seconds)
VSLIDE	——— (Display slide, SLIDE3)
VSLIDE *SLIDE4	
DELAY 15000	
VSLIDE	
DELAY 15000	
RSCRIPT	——— (Re-start the script file)

Example 2

Write a script file to generate a continuous slide show of the following slide files with a time delay of 2 seconds between the slides.

SLD1, SLD2, SLD3

The slide files are located in different sub-directories as shown in Figure 2. The subdirectory SUBDIR1 is the current subdirectory.

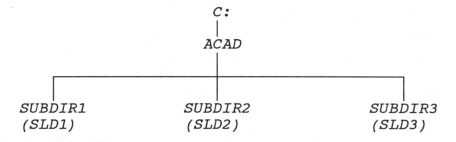

Figure 2   Subdirectories of C drive

Where:
C:	(root directory)
ACAD	(subdirectory where the AutoCAD files are loaded)
SUBDIR1	(drawing subdirectory)
SUBDIR2	(drawing subdirectory)
SUBDIR3	(drawing subdirectory)
SLD1	(slide file in SUBDIR1 subdirectory)
SLD2	(slide file in SUBDIR2 subdirectory)
SLD3	(slide file in DUBDIR3 subdirectory)

The following file is the listing of the script file that will generate a slide show for the slides of Example 2.

```
VSLIDE SLD1
DELAY 2000
VSLIDE C:\ACAD\SUBDIR2\SLD2
```

```
DELAY 2000
VSLIDE C:\ACAD\SUBDIR3\SLD3
DELAY 2000
RSCRIPT
```

Line 1
VSLIDE SLD1
In this line the AutoCAD command VSLIDE loads the slide file SLD1. Since, in this example it is assumed that the user is in the subdirectory SUBDIR1 and the first slide file SLD1 is located in the same subdirectory, therefore it does not require any path definition.

Line 2
DELAY 2000
This line uses AutoCAD's DELAY command to create a pause of approximately 2 seconds before the next slide is loaded.

Line 3
VSLIDE C:\ACAD\SUBDIR2\SLD2
In this line the AutoCAD command VSLIDE loads the slide file SLD2 that is located in the subdirectory SUBDIR2. If the slide file is located in a different subdirectory, then you need to define the path with the slide file.

Line 5
VSLIDE C:\ACAD\SUBDIR3\SLD3
In this line the VSLIDE command loads the slide file SLD3 that is located in the subdirectory SLD3.

Line 7
RSCRIPT
In this line the RSCRIPT command executes the script file again and displays the slides on the screen. This process continues indefinitely until the script file is cancelled by pressing CTRL-C or the BACKSPACE key from the key board.

Slide Libraries

AutoCAD provides a utility SLIDELIB that constructs a library of the slide files. The format of the SLIDELIB utility command is:

C:\ > SLIDELIB (Library file name) < (Slide list file name)

Example
```
C:\>SLIDELIB SLDLIB <SLDLIST
         │         │      │
         │         │      └─ List of slide file names
         │         └─ Slide library file name
         └─ AutoCAD's SLIDELIB utility
```

The SLIDELIB utility is supplied with the AutoCAD software package. You can find this utility on the support diskette that comes with the software. The slide file list is a list of the slide file names that you want in a slide show. It is a text file that can be written by using any text editor or AutoCAD's EDIT command (provided ACAD.PGP file is present and EDIT is defined in the file). The slide files in the slide file list should not contain any file extension (.SLD). However, if you want to give a file extension it should be .SLD.

When you use the SLIDELIB utility, it reads the slide files names from the file that is specified in the slide list and the file is then written to the file specified by library. In the following example, the SLIDELIB utility reads the slide file names from the file SLDLIST and writes them to the library file SLDLIB.

C:\ > SLIDELIB SLDLIB < SLDLIST

Note

1. *You can not edit a slide library file. If you want to change anything, you have to create a new list of the slide files and then use the SLIDELIB utility to create a new slide library.*

2. *If you edit a slide while the slide is being displayed on the screen, the slide is not edited. Instead, the current drawing that is behind the slide will get edited. Therefore, it is recommended not to use any editing commands while a slide is being viewed. Use VSLIDE and DELAY commands only when viewing a slide.*

3. *The path name is not saved in the slide library. Therefore, if you have more than one slide with the same name, although in different subdirectories, only one slide will be saved in the slide library.*

4. *If you are using DOS, it is recommended to use a smaller library files. If the library file contains a large number of files, it might exceed the computer's memory. In that case, the SLIDELIB utility will display a warning message.*

Example 3

Use AutoCAD's SLIDELIB utility to generate a continuous slide show of the following slide files with a time delay of 2.5 seconds between the slides. (The file names are: SLDLIST for slide list file, SLDSHOW1 for slide library, SHOW1 for script file)

FRONT, TOP, RSIDE, STAIRS, 3DVIEW, LROOM, FROOM, BROOM

The slide files are located in different sub-directories as shown in Figure 3.

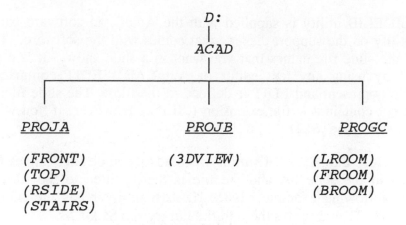

Figure 3   Subdirectories of D drive

Where
D   (D drive)
ACAD   (subdirectory where the AutoCAD files are loaded)
PROJA   (drawing subdirectory)
PROJB   (drawing subdirectory)
PROJC   (drawing subdirectory)

Step 1

The first step is to create a list of the slide file names with the drive and the directory information. Assume that you are in the ACAD subdirectory. You can use a text editor or AutoCAD's EDIT function to create the list of the slide files that you want to include in the slide show. These files do not need a file extension. However, if you choose to give a file extension, it should be .SLD. The following file is a listing of the file SLDLIST for Example 3.

```
D:\ACAD\PROJA\FRONT
D:\ACAD\PROJA\TOP
D:\ACAD\PROJA\RSIDE
D:\ACAD\PROJA\STAIRS
D:\ACAD\PROJB\3DVIEW
D:\ACAD\PROJC\LROOM
D:\ACAD\PROJC\FROOM
D:\ACAD\PROJC\BROOM
```

Step 2

The second step is to use AutoCAD's SLIDELIB utility program to create the slide library. The name of the slide library is assumed to be SLDSHOW1 for this example.

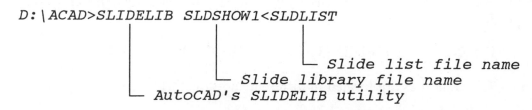

Step 3

Now, you can write a script file for the slide show that will use the slides in the slide library. The name of the script file for this example is assumed to be SHOW1

```
VSLIDE SLDSHOW1(FRONT)
DELAY 2500
VSLIDE SLDSHOW1(TOP)
DELAY 2500
VSLIDE SLDSHOW1(RSIDE)
DELAY 2500
VSLIDE SLDSHOW1(STAIRS)
DELAY 2500
VSLIDE SLDSHOW1(3DVIEW)
DELAY 2500
VSLIDE SLDSHOW1(LROOM)
DELAY 2500
VSLIDE SLDSHOW1(RROOM)
DELAY 2500
VSLIDE SLDSHOW1(BROOM)
DELAY 2500
RSCRIPT
```

Step 4

Start AutoCAD and get into the drawing editor. With the AutoCAD's SCRIPT command run the script file, SHOW1, and you will see the slides being displayed on the screen.

Command: SCRIPT
Slide file < default > :SHOW1

Review

Fill in the blanks

1.   AutoCAD provides a facility through .... files to combine the slides in a text file and display them on the screen in a predetermined sequence.

2.   A .... can also be introduced in the script file so that the viewer gets enough time to view a slide.

3.   Slides are the .... of a screen display.

4.   The slides do not contain any .... information, which means that the entities do not have any information associated with them.

5.   The slides .... be edited like a drawing.

6.   The slides can be created by using the AutoCAD's .... command.

7.   The slide file name can be up to .... characters long.

8.   In the model space, you can use the MSLIDE command to make a slide of the .... display in the .... viewport.

9.   If you are in the paper space, you can make a slide of the display in the paper space that .... any viewports.

10.   To view a slide, use AutoCAD's .... command.

11.   If the slide is in the slide library, and you want to view that slide, the slide library name has to be .... with the slide file name.

12.   AutoCAD provides a utility that constructs a library of the slide files. This is done with the AutoCAD's utility program called ....

13.   You can not .... a slide library file. If you want to change anything, you have to create a new list of the slide files and then use the .... utility to create a new slide library.

14.   The path name .... saved in the slide library. Therefore, if you have more than one slide with the same name, although different subdirectories, only one slide will be saved in the slide library.

15.   If you want to make any changes in the slide, you need to .... the drawing and then make a new slide from the edited drawing.

Exercises

Exercise 1

Make the slides as shown in Figure 4, and write a script file for a continuous slide show. Provide a time delay of 10 seconds after every slide.

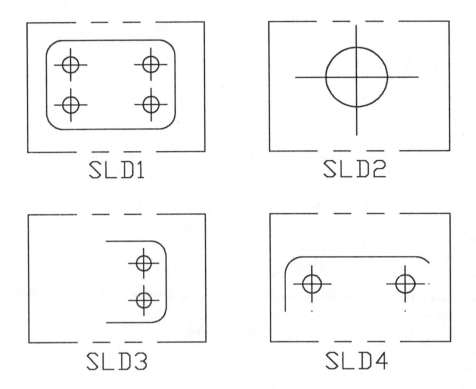

Figure 4   Slides for slide show

Exercise 2

In Exercise 1 above, list the slides in a file SLDLIST2 and create a slide library file SLDLIB2. Then write a script file SHOW2 using the slide library with a time delay of 5 seconds after every slide.

Exercise 3

Write a script file to generate a continuous slide show of the following slide files with a time delay of 3 seconds between the slides.

SLDX1, SLDX2, SLDX3
SLDY1, SLDY2, SLDY3
SLDZ1, SLDZ2, SLDZ3

It is assumed that the slide files are located in different sub-directories as shown in Figure 5 and ACAD is the current subdirectory.

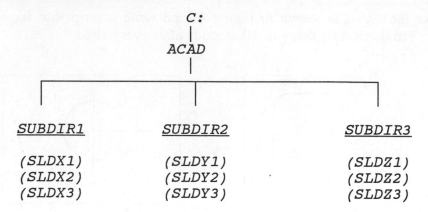

Figure 5   Subdirectories of C drive

Where
C: (C drive)
ACAD   (subdirectory where the AutoCAD
                   files are loaded)
SUBDIR1   (drawing subdirectory)
SUBDIR2   (drawing subdirectory)
SUBDIR3   (drawing subdirectory)

Chapter 4

Creating and Modifying Linetypes

Standard Linetypes

The AutoCAD software package comes with a library of standard linetypes that has 8 different groups of linetypes, with each group having 3 linetypes as shown in Figure 1. These linetypes are saved in the file ACAD.LIN. You can modify the existing linetypes or create a new linetype of your choice.

Linetype Definition

All linetype definitions consist of the following two parts.

1. Header Line
2. Pattern Line

1. Header Line

The header line consists of an asterisk sign followed by the name of the linetype and the linetype description. The name and the line description should be separated by a comma. If there is no description then the comma that separates the linetype name and the description is not required.

The format of the header line is:

* Linetype Name, Description

```
DASHED       _  __  __  __  __  __  __  __
DASHED2      _ __ __ __ __ __ __ __ __ __ __ __
DASHEDX2     ____    ____    ____    ____

HIDDEN       _ __ __ __ __ __ __ __ __ __ __
HIDDEN2      -------------------------------------
HIDDENX2     _  __  __  __  __  __  __  __

CENTER       ____   ____   ____  _  ____
CENTER2      ____ _ ____ _ ____ _ ____ _
CENTERX2     _____    ____   __    _____

PHANTOM      ____  _  _  ____  _  _  ____
PHANTOM2     __ _ _ __ _ _ __ _ _ __ _ _
PHANTOMX2    _____   ____   ____   _____

DOT          . . . . . . . . . . . . . . . . . . .
DOT2         ....................................
DOTX2        .     .     .     .     .     .     .

DASHDOT      ___  .  ___  .  ___  .  ___  .
DASHDOT2     _ . _ . _ . _ . _ . _ . _ . _ .
DASHDOTX2    _____   .   _____   .   _____

BORDER       __ __ . __ __ . __ __ . __ __ .
BORDER2      _ _ . _ _ . _ _ . _ _ . _ _ .
BORDERX2     _____   __   __ . _____

DIVIDE       __ _ . __ _ . __ _ . __ _ .
DIVIDE2      __ _ . __ _ . __ _ . __ _ . __ _ .
DIVIDEX2     _____   .   _____   .   _____
```

Figure 1   Standard Linetypes

Example
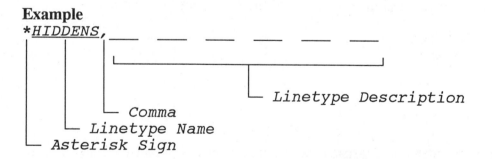

All linetype definitions require a linetype name. When you want to load a linetype, or assign a linetype to an entity, AutoCAD recognizes the linetype by the name that you have assigned to the linetype definition. The names of the linetype definition should be selected in way that will help the user to recognize the linetype by its name. For example, a linetype name LINEFCX does not give the user any idea about the type of the line. However, a linetype name like DASHDOT gives a better idea about the type of line that a user can expect.

The linetype description is a graphical representation of the line. This graphics can be generated by using dashes, dots and spaces from the keyboard. The graphics is utilized by AutoCAD when you want to display the linetypes on the screen by using AutoCAD's LINETYPE command with ? option, or the dialogue box. The linetype description can not be more than 47 characters long.

Pattern Line

The pattern line contains the definition of the line pattern. The definition of line pattern consists of the alignment field specification and the linetype specification. The alignment field specification and the linetype specification are separated by a comma.

The format of the pattern line is:

Alignment Field Specification, Linetype Specification

Example

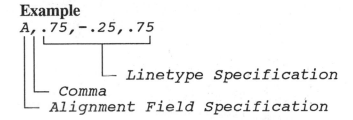

The letter used for alignment field specification is A. This is the only alignment field supported by AutoCAD. Therefore the pattern line will always start with the letter A. The linetype specification defines the configuration of the dash dot pattern to generate a line. The maximum number of dash length specification in the linetype is 12, provided the linetype pattern definition fits on one 80 character line.

Elements of Linetype Specification

All linetypes are created by a combining the basic elements in a desired configuration. There are three basic elements that can be utilized to define a linetype specification.

DASH	(Pen down)
DOT	(Pen down, 0 length)
SPACE	(Pen up)

Example

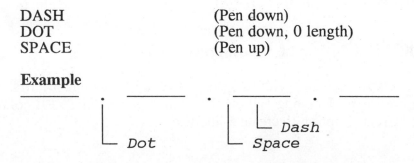

The dashes are generated by defining a positive number. For example, .5 will generate a dash that is 0.5 units long. Similarly, spaces are generated by defining a negative number. For example, -.2 will generate a space that is 0.2 units long. The dot is generated by defining a 0 length.

Example
```
A,.5,-.2,0,-.2,.5
```

Length of dash (pen down)
Length of space (pen up)
Dot (Zero length)

Creating Linetypes

Before creating a linetype it is important to decide the type of line that you want to generate. Draw the line on a piece of paper and measure the length of each element that constitutes the line. You need to define only one segment of the line, because the pattern is then repeated when you draw a line. The linetypes can be created or modified by one of the following methods

1. Using AutoCAD's Linetype command
2. Using a Text Editor (such as EDLIN)

Consider the following example that creates a new linetype using AutoCAD's linetype command, and text editor.

Example 1

Using the AutoCAD's LINETYPE command, create a linetype DASH3DOT (Figure 2A) with the following specifications:

Length of the first dash 0.5
Blank Space 0.125
Dot
Blank Space 0.125
Dot
Blank Space 0.125
Dot
Blank Space 0.125

Using AutoCAD's Linetype Command

To create a linetype by using AutoCAD's LINETYPE command, first make sure that you are in the Drawing Editor. Then enter the LINETYPE command and select the "Create" option to create a linetype.

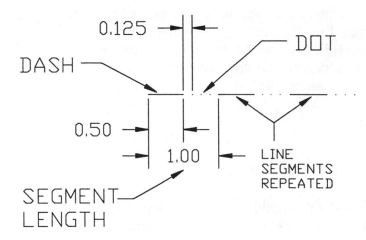

Figure 2A Linetype specifications of DASH3DOT

Command: <u>Linetype</u>
?/Create/Load/Set: <u>C</u>

Enter the name of the linetype and the name of the library file in which you want to store the definition of the new linetype.

Name of linetype to create: <u>DASH3DOT</u>
File for storage of linetype < default > : <u>Acad</u>

If the linetype already exists, following message will be displayed on the screen.

(Name) already exists in this file.
Current definition is:
__*Linetype name [,description]__
alignment, dash-1, dash-2,...
Overwrite? <N>

If you want to redefine the existing line style then enter Y otherwise type N or just hit the RETURN key to pick the default value of N. You can then repeat the process with a different name of the linetype.

After entering the name of the linetype and the library file name, AutoCAD will prompt you to enter the Descriptive text and the pattern of the line.

Descriptive text: *DASH3DOT,____ . . . ____ . . . ____
Enter pattern (on next line):
A,.5,-.125,0,-.125,0,-.125,0,-.125

Descriptive Text

*DASH3DOT,____ . . . ____ . . . ____

For the descriptive text you have to type asterisk (*) followed by the name of the linetype. For Example 1, the name of the linetype is DASH3DOT. The name *DASH3DOT can be followed by the description of the linetype, the length of this description can not exceed 47 characters. In this example, the description is dashes and dots ____ . . . ____ . It could be any text or alphanumeric string. The description is displayed on the screen when you list the linetypes.

Pattern
A,.5,-.125,0,-.125,0,-.125,0,-.125

The line pattern should start with the alignment definition. At present, AutoCAD supports only one type of alignment and that is A. Therefore it is automatically displayed on the screen when you select the LINETYPE command with CREATE option. After entering A for pattern alignment, you must define the pen position. A positive number (.5 or 0.5) indicates a "pen-down" position and a negative number (-.25 or -0.25) indicates a "pen-up" position. The length of the dash or the space is designated by the magnitude of the number. For example, 0.5 will draw a dash of 0.5 units long and -0.25 will leave a blank space of 0.25 units. A dash length of zero (0) will draw a dot (.). The following list is the pattern definition elements for Example 1.

.5	**pen down**	**0.5 units long dash**
-.125	**pen up**	**.125 units blank space**
0	**pen down**	**dot**
-.125	**pen up**	**.125 units blank space**
0	**pen down**	**dot**
-.125	**pen up**	**.125 units blank space**
0	**pen down**	**dot**
-.125	**pen up**	**.125 units blank space**

After entering pattern definition, the linetype (DASH3DOT) is automatically saved in the file ACAD.LIN. The linetype (DASH3DOT) can be loaded by using AutoCAD's **LINETYPE** command and selecting **LOAD** option.

Note

The name and the description should be separated by a comma (,). The description is optional and in case you decide not to give the description, the comma after the linetype name DASH3DOT should be omitted.

Using a Text Editor

You can also use the EDLIN Command of DOS or any other text editor to create a new linetype. If you are in the AutoCAD drawing editor, type SH or SHELL to access the DOS commands. To load the ACAD.LIN file, use the following EDLIN function of DOS.

Command: SHELL
OS Command: Edlin ACAD.LIN

If you are in a different subdirectory, you can load the ACAD.LIN file by defining the path with the file name as shown in the following command line.

OS Command: Edlin C:\ACAD11\ACAD.LIN

List the file and insert the lines that define the new linetype. The following file is a partial listing of ACAD.LIN file after adding a new linetype to the file

```
*BORDER,___ __ . ___ . __ __ . __ __ . __ __ . __ __ .
A,.5,-.25,.5,-.25,0,-.25
*BORDER2,__ . _ . _ . _ . __ _ . _ . _ . _ . _ . _ .
A,.25,-.125,.25,-.125,0,-.125
*BORDERX2,____ ____ . ___ ___ . ___ ___ .
A,1.0,-.5,1.0,-.5,0,-.5

*CENTER,____ _ ___ _ ___ _ ___ _ ___ _ ____
A,1.25,-.25,.25,-.25
*CENTER2,___ _ __ _ __ _ __ _ __ _ __ _ __
A,.75,-.125,.125,-.125
*CENTERX2,_____ __ _____ __ _____ __ ____
A,2.5,-.5,.5,-.5

*DASHDOT,__ . _ . _ . _ . _ . _ . _ . _ . __ .
A,.5,-.25,0, .25
```

```
*DOT,. . . . . . . . . . . . . . . . . . . . . . . .
A,0,-.25
*DOT2,. . . . . . . . . . . . . . . . . . . . . . . . . . . . . . .
A,0,-.125
*DOTX2,. . . . . . . . . . . . .
A,0,-.5
*HIDDEN,__ _ _ _ _ _ _ _ _ _ _ _ _ _ _ _ _ __
A,.25,-.125
*HIDDEN2,__ _ _ _ _ _ _ _ _ _ _ _ _ _ _ _
A,.125,-.0625
*HIDDENX2,___ __ __ __ __ __ __ __ __ __
A,.5,-.25
*PHANTOM,_____ __ __ ____ __ __
A,1.25,-.25,.25,-.25,.25,-.25
*PHANTOM2,_____ _ _ _ _ __ _ _
A,.625,-.125,.125,-.125,.125,-.125
*PHANTOMX2,_____ __ __ _____
A,2.5,-.5,.5,-.5,.5,-.5
*DASH3DOT,____ . . . ____ . . . ___
A,.5,-.125,0,-.125,0,-.125,0,-.125
```

The last two lines of this file define the new linetype DASH3DOT. The first line contains the name DASH3DOT and the description of the line (___ . . .___). The second line contains the alignment and the pattern definition. Save the file and then load the linetype by using AutoCAD's LINETYPE command with LOAD option. The lines and polylines that this linetype will generate are shown in Figure 2B

Figure 2B   Lines created by linetype DASH3DOT

Creating Linetype Files

You can start a new linetype file and then add the line definitions to this file. The following example uses the EDLIN function of DOS to create a new file NEWLT.LIN.   Two lines have been inserted in this file to define the linetype DASH3DOT.

Command: SHELL
OS Commands: <u>EDLIN NEWLT.LIN</u>

*DASH3DOT,___ . . .___ . . . ___
A,.5,-.125,0,-.125,0,-.125,0,-.125

You can load the linetype DASH3DOT from this file by using AutoCAD's LINETYPE command, and then selecting the LOAD option.

Command: <u>LINETYPE</u>
?/Create/Load/Set: <u>L</u>
Linetype(s) load: <u>DASH3DOT</u>
File to search <default>: <u>NEWLT</u>

Alignment Specification

The alignment specifies the pattern alignment at the start and the end of the line, circle or arc. In other words, the line would always start and end with the dash (___). The alignment definition "A" requires that the first element be a dash or dot (pen-down), followed by a negative (pen-up) segment. The minimum number of dash segments for this alignment A is two. If there is not enough space for the line then AutoCAD will draw a continuous line.

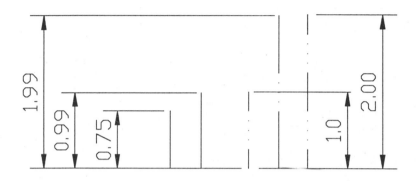

Figure 3   Alignment of linetype DASH3DOT

For example, in the linetype DASH3DOT of Example 1, the length of each line segment is (.5 + .125 + .125 + .125 + .125 = 1.0) 1.0. If the length of the line drawn is less than 1.00, the line will be drawn as a continuous line (Figure 3). If the length of the line is 1.00 or greater, the line will be drawn according to linetype DASH3DOT. AutoCAD automatically adjusts the length of the dashes and the line will always start and end with a dash. The length of the starting and the ending dashes will be at least half the length of the dash as specified in the file. If the length of the dash as specified in the file is 0.5, the length of the starting and the ending dashes will be at least 0.25. To fit a line that starts and ends with a dash, the length of these dashes can also increase as shown in Figure 3.

LTSCALE Command

As mentioned in the previous section the length of each line segment in the linetype DASH3DOT is 1.0 (.5 + .125 + .125 + .125 + .125 = 1.0). If you draw a line that is less than 1.0 units long, AutoCAD will draw a single dash that looks like a continuous line (Figure 4). This problem can be rectified by changing the linetype scale factor variable LTSCALE to a smaller value. This can be accomplished by using AutoCAD's LTSCALE command.

Command: LTSCALE
New scale factor <default>: (new value)

The default value of LTSCALE variable is 1.0. If the LTSCALE is changed to 0.75, the length of each segment is reduces by 0.75 (1.0 x 0.75 = 0.75). Then, if you draw a line 0.75 units or longer, it will be drawn according to the definition of DASH3DOT (___ . . . ___) (Figure 5 and Figure 6).

LTSCALE = 1

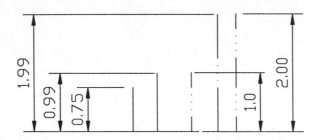

Figure 4 Alignment when Ltscale=1

LTSCALE = 0.99

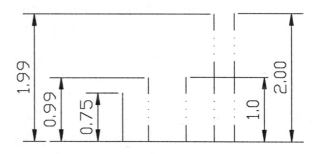

Figure 5 Alignment when Ltscale=0.99

LTSCALE = 0.75

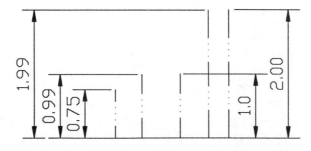

Figure 6 Alignment when Ltscale=0.75

The appearance of the lines is also effected by the limits of the drawing. Most of the AutoCAD linetypes work fine for a drawing that has the limits 12, 9. Figure 7 shows a line of linetype DASH3DOT that is 4 units long and the limits of the drawing are 12,9. If you increase the limits to 48, 36 the lines will appear like a continuous lines. If you want the line to appear the same as before, the LTSCALE should be changed. Since the limits of the drawing have increased 4 times, therefore the LTSCALE should also increase by the same amount. If you change the scale factor to 4, the line segments will also increase by a factor of 4. As shown in Figure 7, the length of the starting and the ending dash has increased to 1 unit.

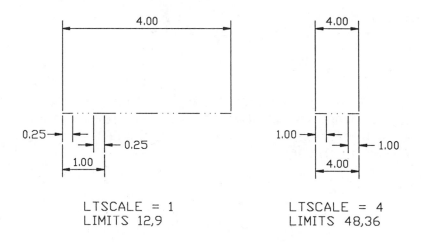

Figure 7 Linetype DASH3DOT before and after changing Ltscale

In general the approximate LTSCALE factor can be obtained by dividing the X-Limit of the drawing by the default X-Limit (12.00).

Ltscale Factor = X-Limits of the drawing/12.00

Example
Drawing Limits are 48,36
Ltscale Factor = 48/12 = 4

Drawing Limits are 9,6
Ltscale Factor = 9/12 = 0.75

Drawing Sheet Size is 12,9 and scale is 1/4" = 1'
Ltscale Factor = 12 x 4 (12 / 12) = 48

Drawing Sheet Size is 36,24 and scale is 1/4" = 1'
Ltscale Factor = 12 x 4 x (36 / 12) = 144

Note

If you change the LTSCALE factor, all lines in the drawing are affected by the same ratio.

Alternate Linetypes

One of the problems with the LTSCALE factor is that it affects all the lines in the drawing. As shown in Figure 8(A), the length of each segment in all DASH3DOT type lines is approximately equal, no matter how long the lines are. Sometime a user would like to have small segment length if the lines are small and a longer segment length if the lines are long. You can accomplish this by defining an alternate linetype with a different segment length. For example, you can define a linetype DASH3DOT and DASH3DOTX with different line pattern specification.

```
*DASH3DOT,___ . . . ___ . . .___ . . . ___
A,0.5,-.125,0,-.125,0,-.125,0,-.125
*DASH3DOTX,_____ . . . _____
A,1.0,-.25,0,-.25,0,-.25,0,-.25
```

In DASH3DOT linetype the segment length is 1 unit, whereas in DASH3DOTX linetype the segment length is 2 units. You can have several alternate linetypes to produce the lines with different segment lengths. Figure 8(B) shows the lines generates by DASH3DOT and DASH3DOTX.

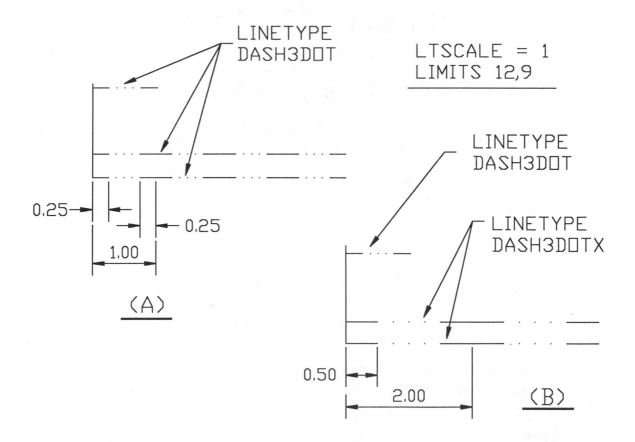

Figure 8 Linetypes generated by DASH3DOT and DASH3DOTX

Note

Although you might have used different linetypes with different segment lengths, the lines will be affected equally when you change the LTSCALE factor. For example, if the LTSCALE factor is 0.5, the segment length of DASH3DOT line will be 0.5 and the segment length of DASH3DOTX will be 1.0 units.

Modifying Linetypes

You can also modify the linetypes that are defined in the ACAD.LIN file. To modify the linetype you need a text editor. You can also use the EDLIN function of DOS, or AutoCAD's EDIT command (provided ACAD.PGP file is present and EDIT is defined in the file). For example, if you want to change the dash length of border linetype from 0.5 to 0.75, load the file and then edit the pattern line of border linetype. The following file is a partial listing of ACAD.LIN file after changing the border and centerx2 linetypes.

```
;;
*BORDER,
A,.75,-.25,.75,-.25,0,-.25
*BORDER2,
A,.25,-.125,.25,-.125,0,-.125
*BORDERX2,
A,1.0,-.5,1.0,-.5,0,-.5
*CENTER,
A,1.25,-.25,.25,-.25
*CENTER2,
A,.75,-.125,.125,-.125
*CENTERX2,
A,3.5,-.5,.5,-.5
*DASHDOT,
A,.5,-.25,0,-.25



A,0,-.5
*HIDDEN,
A,.25,-.125
*HIDDEN2,
A,.125,-.0625
*HIDDENX2,
A,.5,-.25
*PHANTOM,
A,1.25,-.25,.25,-.25,.25,-.25
*PHANTOM2,
A,.625,-.125,.125,-.125,.125,-.125
*PHANTOMX2,
A,2.5,-.5,.5,-.5,.5,-.5
```

Example 2

Create a new file NEWLINET.LIN and define a linetype VARDASH with the following specifications.

Length of first dash 1.0
Blank Space 0.25
Length of second dash 0.75
Blank Space 0.25
Length of third dash 0.5
Blank Space 0.25
Dot
Blank Space 0.25
Length of next dash 0.5
Blank Space 0.25
Length of next dash 0.75

To use the EDIT command, type EDIT at AutoCAD prompt and then enter the name of the file.

Command: <u>EDIT</u>
File name: <u>NEWLINET.LIN</u>

Now, insert the following lines that define the new linetype VARDASH.

*VARDASH,-------- ---- -- . -- ---- --------
A,1,-.25,.75,-.25,.5,-.25,0,-.25,.5,-.25,.75,-.25

The type of lines that this linetype will generate is shown in Figure 9.

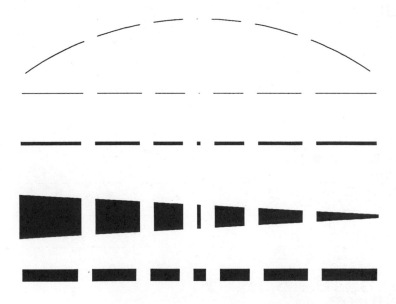

Figure 9   Lines generated by linetype VARDASH

Review

Fill in the blanks

1.   The AutoCAD command .... can be used to create a new linetype.

2.   The AutoCAD command .... can be used to load a linetype.

3.   The AutoCAD command .... can be used to change the ltscale factor.

4.   In AutoCAD the linetypes are saved in .... file.

5.   The linetype description should not be .... characters long.

6.   A positive number denotes a pen .... segment.

7.   The segment length .... generates a dot.

8.   AutoCAD supports only .... alignment.

9.   A line pattern definition always start with ....

10.   A header line definition always starts with ....

Exercises

Exercise 1

Using AutoCAD's LINETYPE command to create a new linetype "DASH3DASH" with the following specifications.

Length of the first dash 0.75
Blank Space 0.125
Dash Length 0.25
Blank Space 0.125
Dash Length 0.25
Blank Space 0.125
Dash Length 0.25
Blank Space 0.125

Exercise 2

Use a text editor to create a new file NEWLT2.LIN and a new linetype DASH2DASH with the following specifications.

Length of the first dash 0.5
Blank Space 0.1
Dash Length 0.2
Blank Space 0.1
Dash Length 0.2
Blank Space 0.1

Exercise 3

Using the AutoCAD's LINETYPE command, create a linetype DASH3DOT with the following specifications.

Length of the first dash 0.75
Blank Space 0.25
Dot
Blank Space 0.25
Dot
Blank Space 0.25
Dot
Blank Space 0.25

Exercise 4

Using AutoCAD's EDIT command, create a new file NEWLINET.LIN and define a linetype VARDASHX with the following specifications.

Length of first dash 1.5
Blank Space 0.25
Length of second dash 0.75
Blank Space 0.25
Dot
Blank Space 0.25
Length of third dash 0.75

Chapter 5

Creating Hatch Patterns

The AutoCAD software comes with a hatch pattern library file, **ACAD.PAT** that contains 53 different hatch patterns. These hatch patterns are sufficient for general drafting work. However, sometimes a user might need a hatch pattern that is different than those that are supplied with the software. AutoCAD lets you create your own hatch patterns. There is no limit to the number of hatch patterns you can define.

Hatch Pattern Definition

The hatch patterns that you define can be added to the hatch pattern library file ACAD.PAT. You can also create a new hatch pattern library file, provided the file contains only one hatch pattern definition and the name of the hatch is the same as the name of the file. The hatch pattern definition consists of the following two parts.

1. Header Line
2. Hatch Descriptors

1. Header Line

Header Line consists of an asterisk (*) followed by the name of the hatch pattern. The hatch name is the name that is used in the hatch command to hatch an area. After the name, you can give the hatch description that is separated from the hatch name by a comma (,). The general format of the header line is:

```
*HATCH Name [, Hatch Description]
 |      |                |
 |      |                └─ Description of hatch pattern
 |      └─ Name of hatch pattern
 └─ Asterisk
```

The description can be any text that describes the hatch pattern. It can also be omitted, in which case no comma should follow the hatch pattern name.

Example

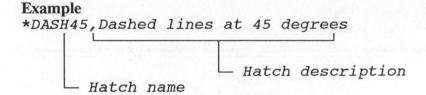

2. Hatch Descriptors

The hatch descriptors consists of one or more lines that contain the definition of the hatch lines. The general format of the hatch descriptor is:

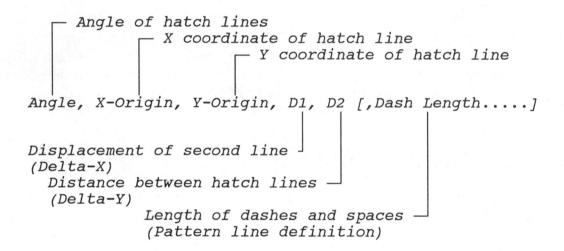

Example

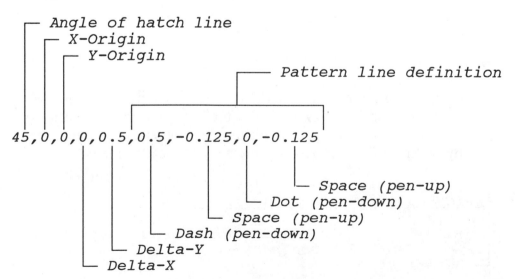

Hatch Angle

The hatch angle is the angle that the hatch lines make with the positive X axis. The angle is positive if measured counter clockwise (Figure 1), and it is negative if the angle is measured counterclockwise.

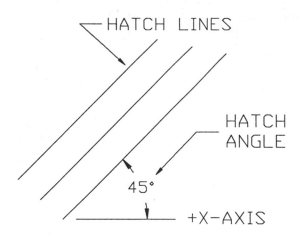

Figure 1   Hatch angle

X-Origin and Y-Origin

When you draw a hatch pattern, the first line of the hatch line starts from the point defined by X-Origin and Y-Origin. The remaining lines are generated by offsetting the first hatch line by a distance specified by Delta-X and Delta-Y. In Figure 2(A), the first hatch line starts from the point with coordinates of X=0 and Y=0, and in Figure 2(B) the first line of hatch starts from a point with coordinates X=0 and Y=0.25.

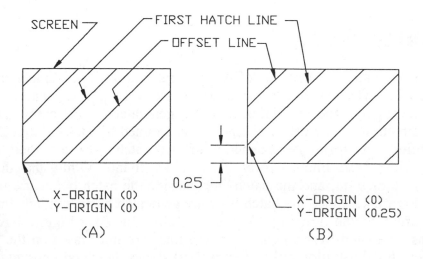

Figure 2   X-Origin and Y-Origin of hatch lines

Delta-X and Delta-Y

Delta-X is the displacement of the offset line in the direction in which the hatch lines are generated. For example, if the lines are drawn at 0 degree angle and Delta-X = 0.5, the offset line will be displaced by a distance Delta-X (0.5) along 0 angle direction. Similarly, if the hatch lines are drawn at 45 degree angle, the offset line will be displaced by a distance Delta-X (0.5) along 45 degree direction (Figure 3).

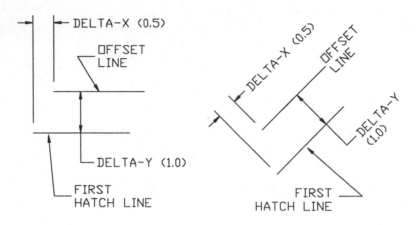

Figure 3 Delta-X and Delta-Y of hatch lines

Delta-Y is the displacement of the offset lines measured perpendicular to the hatch lines. For example, if Delta-Y = 1.0, the space between any two hatch lines will be 1.0 (Figure 3).

How Hatch Works

When you hatch an area, AutoCAD generates an infinite number of hatch lines of infinite length. The first hatch line always passes through the point specified by X-Origin and Y-Origin. The remaining lines are generated by offsetting the first hatch line in both directions. The offset distance is determined by Delta-X and Delta-Y. All selected entities that form the boundary of the hatch area are then checked for intersection with these lines. Any hatch lines found within the defined hatch boundaries are turned on, and the hatch lines outside the hatch boundary are turned off as shown in Figure 4. Since the hatch lines are generated by offsetting, the hatch lines in different areas of the drawing are automatically aligned. Figure 4(A) shows the hatch lines as computed by AutoCAD. These lines are not drawn on the screen, they are shown here for illustration only. Figure 4(B) shows the hatch lines generated in the circle that was defined as the hatch boundary.

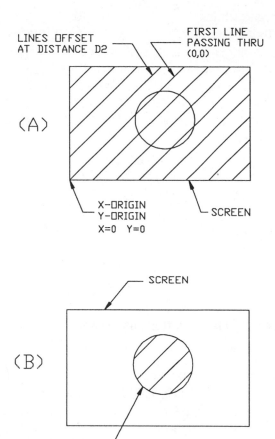

Figure 4 Hatch lines outside the hatch boundary are turned off

Simple Hatch Pattern

It is a good practice to develop the hatch pattern specification before writing a hatch pattern definition. For simple hatch patterns it may not be that important, but for more complicated hatch patterns it is very important to know the detailed specifications. The following example illustrates the procedure to develop a simple hatch pattern.

Example 1

Write a hatch pattern definition for the hatch pattern as shown in the Figure 5, with the following specifications.

Name of the hatch pattern	HATCH1
X-Origin =	0
Y-Origin =	0
Distance between hatch lines =	0.5

Displacement of hatch lines=   0
Hatch line pattern   Continuous

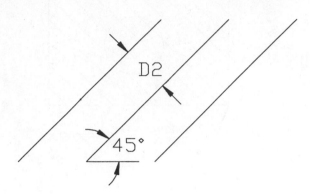

Figure 5   Hatch pattern angle and offset distance

This hatch pattern definition can be added to the existing hatch file ACAD.PAT. You can use AutoCAD's EDIT command (provided ACAD.PGP file is present and EDIT command is defined in the file), or the Edlin function of DOS to edit the file. If you are in the drawing editor type **"SH"** or **"SHELL"** to access DOS commands. **OS Commands**: prompt will appear on the screen. Type EDLIN followed by the name of the file, with path if necessary as shown in the following command line.

OS Commands:EDLIN C:\ACAD\ACAD.PAT

In this example, it is assumed that the AutoCAD files are in the ACAD subdirectory and the user is working in a different subdirectory. List the ACAD.PAT file and insert the following two lines at the end of the file.

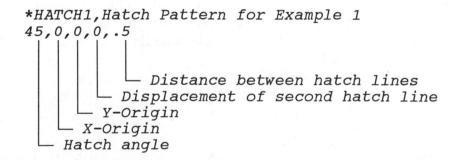

The first field of hatch descriptors contains the angle of the hatch lines. That angle is 45 degrees with respect to the positive X axis. The second and third field describe the X and Y coordinate of the first hatch line origin. The first line of the hatch pattern will pass through this point. If the values of X-Origin and Y-Origin were

0.5 and 1.0 respectively, then the first line would pass through the point with X coordinate of 0.5 and the Y coordinate of 1.0 with respect to the drawing origin 0,0. The remaining lines are generated by offsetting the first line by a distance 0.5 on both sides of the line as shown in Figure 5.

Effect of Angle and Scale Factor on Hatch

When you hatch an area, the angle and the displacement of hatch lines that you have specified in the hatch pattern definition can be altered to get a desired hatch spacing. This can be accomplished by entering an appropriate value for angle and scale factor in AutoCAD's HATCH command.

Command: Hatch
Pattern(? or name/U,style) < default > : Hatch1
Scale for pattern < default > : 1
Angle of pattern < default > : 0

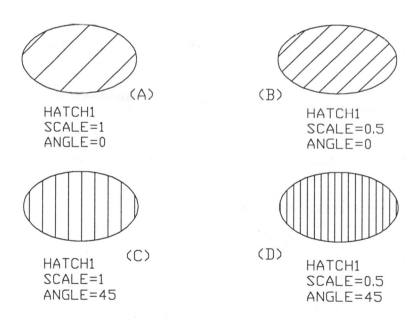

Figure 6   Effect of angle and scale factor on hatch

To understand how the angle and the displacement can be changed, hatch an area with the hatch pattern HATCH1 of Example 1. You will notice that the hatch lines have been generated according to the definition of hatch pattern HATCH1. Notice the effect of hatch angle, and scale factor on the hatch. Figure 6(A) shows a hatch that is generated by AutoCAD's HATCH command with 0 degree angle and a scale factor of 1.0. If the angle is 0, the hatch will be generated with the same angle as defined in the hatch pattern definition (45 degrees in Example 1). Similarly, if the scale factor is 1.0, the distance between the hatch lines will be same as defined in the hatch pattern definition (0.5 in Example 1). Figure 6(B) shows a hatch that is generated when the hatch scale factor is 0.5. If you measure the distance between the successive hatch lines, it will be 0.25 (0.5 X 0.5 = 0.25). Figure 6(C) and Figure 6(D) show the hatch when the angle is 45 degrees and the scale factors are 1.0 and 0.5 respectively. You can enter any value in response to HATCH command prompts to generate hatch lines at any angle and with any line spacing.

Hatch Pattern with Dashes and Dots

The lines you can use in a hatch pattern definition is not restricted to continuous lines. You can define any line pattern to generate a hatch pattern. The lines could be a combination of dashes, dots and spaces in any configuration. However, the maximum number of dashes you can specify in the line pattern definition of a hatch pattern is 6. The next example uses a dash-dot line to create a hatch pattern.

Example 2

Write a hatch pattern definition for a hatch pattern as shown in Figure 7, with the following specifications

Name of the hatch pattern	HATCH2
Hatch angle=	0
X-Origin=	0
Y-Origin=	0
Displacement of lines (D1)=	0.25
Distance between lines (D2)=	0.25
Length of each dash=	0.5
Space between dashes and dots=	0.125
Space between dots=	0.125

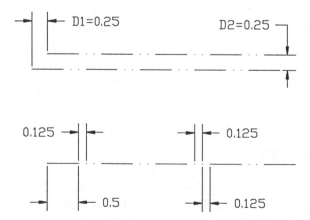

Figure 7   Hatch lines made of dashes and dots

You can use AutoCAD's EDIT command to edit the file ACAD.PAT. The general format of the header line and the hatch descriptors is:

*HATCH NAME, Hatch Description
Angle, X- Origin, Y-Origin, D1, D2 [,Dash Length.....]

Substitute the value from Example 2 in the corresponding fields of header line and field descriptor.

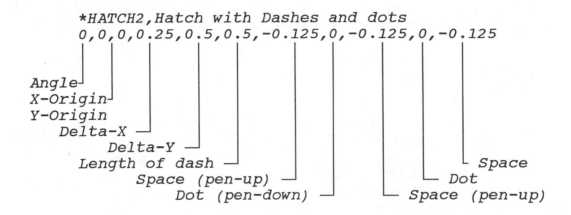

```
*HATCH2,Hatch with Dashes and dots
0,0,0,0.25,0.5,0.5,-0.125,0,-0.125,0,-0.125
```

Angle
X-Origin
Y-Origin
Delta-X
Delta-Y
Length of dash
Space (pen-up)
Dot (pen-down)
Space (pen-up)
Dot
Space

The hatch pattern that this hatch definition will generate is shown in Figure 8. The first figure, Fig 8(A) shows the hatch with 0 angle and a scale factor of 1.0. Figure 8(B) shows the hatch with 45 degree angle and a scale factor of 0.5.

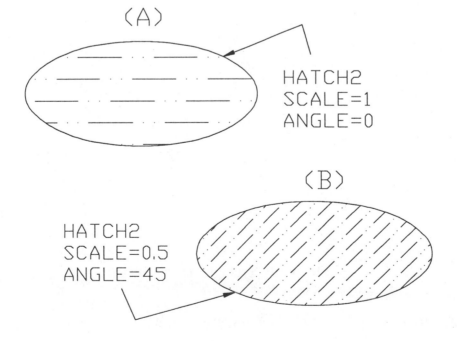

Figure 8   Hatch pattern at different angles

Hatch with Multiple Descriptions

Some hatch pattern require multiple lines to generate a shape. For example, if you want to create a hatch pattern of a brick wall, you need a hatch pattern that has four hatch descriptors to generate a rectangular shape. You can have any number of hatch descriptor lines in a hatch pattern definition. It is up to the user to combine them in any conceivable order. However, there are some shapes that you can not generate. A shape that has a nonlinear element, like an arc, can not be generated by hatch pattern definition. You can use only straight lines, to generate a hatch pattern. The next example uses three lines to define a triangular hatch pattern.

Example 3

Write a hatch pattern definition for a hatch pattern as shown in the Figure 9 with the following specifications:

Hatch pattern name: HATCH3
Vertical height of the triangle: 0.5
Horizontal length of the triangle: 0.5
Vertical distance between the triangles: 0.5
Horizontal distance between the triangles: 0.5

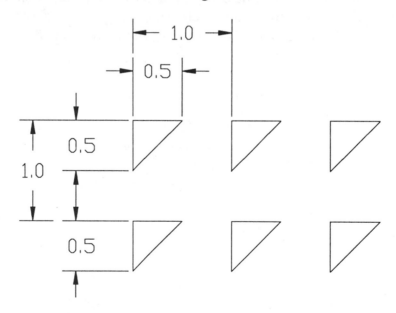

Figure 9   Triangle hatch pattern

Each triangle in this hatch pattern consists of the following three elements.

1. Vertical Line
2. Horizontal Line
3. Line inclined at 45 Degrees

1. Vertical Line

For the vertical line the specifications are:

Hatch angle=	90 Degrees
X-Origin=	0
Y-Origin=	0
Delta-X (D1)=	0
Delta-Y (D2)=	1.0
Dash Length	0.5
Space	0.5

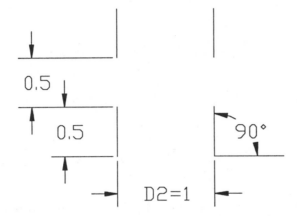

Figure 10   Vertical line

Substitute the values from the vertical line specification in various fields of hatch descriptor to get the following line.

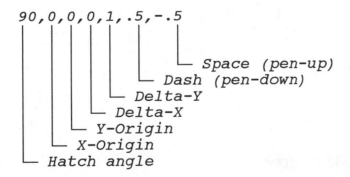

2. Horizontal Line

For the horizontal line the specifications are:

Hatch angle=	0 Degrees
X-Origin=	0

Y-Origin =   0.5
Delta-X (D1) =   0
Delta-Y (D2) =   1.0
Dash Length =   0.5
Space =   0.5

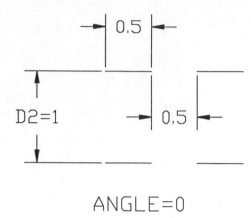

ANGLE=0

Figure 11   Horizontal line

The only difference between the vertical and the horizontal line is the angle. For the horizontal line the angle is 0 degree, whereas for the vertical line the angle is 90 degrees. Substitute the values from the vertical line specification to obtain the following line.

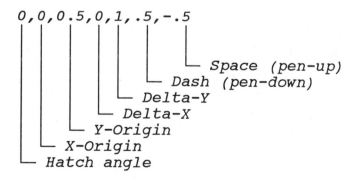

3. Line inclined at 45 Degrees

This line is at an angle, therefore you need to calculate the distances Delta-X (D1), Delta-Y (D2), length of the dash line, and the length of space. Figure 12 shows the calculations to find these values.

Hatch angle =   45 Degrees
X-Origin =   0
Y-Origin =   0

Delta-X (D1)=	0.7071
Delta-Y (D2)=	0.7071
Dash Length=	0.7071
Space=	0.7071

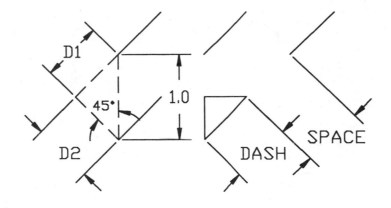

$$D1 = 1.0 \times COS\ 45 \qquad D2 = 1.0 \times SIN\ 45$$

$$D1 = 0.7071 \qquad D2 = 0.7071$$

$$DASH = SQRT(0.5**2 + 0.5**2)$$
$$= .7071$$
$$SPACE = DASH = .7071$$

Figure 12   Line inclined at 45 degrees

After substituting the values in the general format of the hatch descriptor, you will obtain the following line.

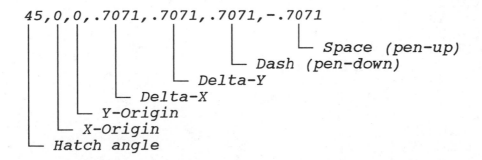

```
45,0,0,.7071,.7071,.7071,-.7071
                                    Space (pen-up)
                              Dash (pen-down)
                        Delta-Y
                  Delta-X
              Y-Origin
          X-Origin
      Hatch angle
```

Now, you can combine these three lines and insert them at the end of ACAD.PAT file. You can also use AutoCAD's EDIT command to edit the file and insert the lines.

Figure 13 shows the hatch pattern that will be generated by this hatch pattern (HATCH3). In Fig 13(A) the hatch pattern is at 0 degree angle and the scale factor is 0.5. In Fig 13(B) the hatch pattern is at -45 degree angle and the scale factor is 0.5

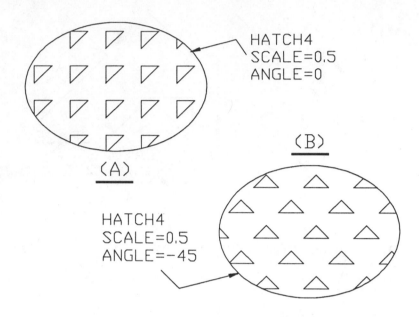

Figure 13   Hatch generated by HATCH3 pattern

The following file is a partial listing of ACAD.PAT file, after adding the hatch pattern definitions from Example 1, Example 2 and Example 3.

```
*angle,Angle steel
0, 0,0, 0,.275, .2,-.075
90, 0,0, 0,.275, .2,-.075
*ansi31,ANSI Iron, Brick, Stone masonry
45, 0,0, 0,.125
*ansi32,ANSI Steel
45, 0,0, 0,.375
45, .176776695,0, 0,.375
*ansi33,ANSI Bronze, Brass, Copper
45, 0,0, 0,.25
45, .176776695,0, 0,.25, .125,-.0625
*ansi34,ANSI Plastic, Rubber
45, 0,0, 0,.75
45, .176776695,0, 0,.75
45, .353553391,0, 0,.75
45, .530330086,0, 0,.75
*ansi35,ANSI Fire brick, Refractory material
45, 0,0, 0,.25
45, .176776695,0, 0,.25, .3125,-.0625,0,-.0625
*ansi36,ANSI Marble, Slate, Glass
45, 0,0, .21875,.125, .3125,-.0625,0,-.0625
*ansi37,ANSI Lead, Zinc, Magnesium, Sound/Heat/Elec Insulation
```

```
45, 0,0, 0,.125
135, 0,0, 0,.125
*ansi38,ANSI Aluminum
45, 0,0, 0,.125
135, 0,0, .25,.125, .3125,-.1875


*steel,Steel material
45, 0,0, 0,.125
45, 0,.0625, 0,.125
*swamp,Swampy area
0, 0,0, .5,.866025403, .125,-.875
90, .0625,0, .866025403,.5, .0625,-1.669550806
90, .078125,0, .866025403,.5, .05,-1.682050806
90, .046875,0, .866025403,.5, .05,-1.682050806
60, .09375,0, .5,.866025403, .04,-.96
120, .03125,0, .5,.866025403, .04,-.96
*trans,Heat transfer material
0, 0,0, 0,.25
0, 0,.125, 0,.25, .125,-.125
*triang,Equilateral triangles
60, 0,0, .1875,.324759526, .1875,-.1875
120, 0,0, .1875,.324759526, .1875,-.1875
0, -.09375,.162379763, .1875,.324759526, .1875,-.1875
*zigzag,Staircase effect
0, 0,0, .125,.125, .125,-.125
90, .125,0, .125,.125, .125,-.125
```

*HATCH1,Hatch at 45 Degree Angle
45,0,0,0,.5
*HATCH2,Hatch with Dashes & Dots:
0,0,0,.25,.25,0.5,-.125,0,-.125,0,-.125
*HATCH3,Triangle Hatch:
90,0,0,0,1,.5,-.5
0,0,0.5,0,1,.5,-.5
45,0,0,.7071,.7071,.7071,-.7071

Saving Hatch Patterns in a Separate File

When you load a certain hatch pattern, AutoCAD looks for that definition in the ACAD.PAT file. Therefore, the hatch pattern definitions must be in the ACAD.PAT file. However, you can add the new pattern definition to a different file and then copy that file to ACAD.PAT. Make sure that you make a copy of the original ACAD.PAT file so that you can copy that file back when needed. Let us assume the name of the file that contain your custom hatch pattern definitions is CUSTOMH.PAT. Use the following command to copy the original ACAD.PAT file to another file (ACADORG.PAT)

COPY C:\ACAD\ACAD.PAT C:\ACAD\ACADORG.PAT

Now you can copy the COSTOMH.PAT file to ACAD.PAT

COPY CUSTOMH.PAT C:\ACAD\ACAD.PAT

In this example it is assumed that the AutoCAD files are loaded in ACAD subdirectory and the user is in a different directory. If you want to use the original file, use the following command to copy ACADORG.PAT to ACAD.PAT.

COPY C:\ACAD\ACADORG.PAT C:\ACAD\ACAD.PAT

Custom Hatch Pattern File

As mentioned earlier, you can add the new hatch pattern definitions to the file ACAD.PAT. There is no limit to the number of hatch pattern definitions you can add to this file. However, if you have only one hatch pattern definition, you can define a separate file. It has the following three requirements.

1. The name of the file has to be same as the hatch pattern name.
2. The file can contain only one hatch pattern definition.
3. The hatch pattern name and therefore the hatch file name should be unique.

Example
File name HATCH3.PAT

```
*HATCH3,Triangle Hatch:
90,0,0,0,1,.5,-.5
0,0,0.5,0,1,.5,-.5
45,0,0,.7071,.7071,.7071,-.7071
```

Note

1. *The hatch lines can be edited after exploding the hatch with AutoCAD's EXPLODE command. After exploding, each hatch line becomes a separate entity.*

2. *It is a good practice not to explode a hatch, because it increases the size of the drawing database. For example, if a hatch consists of 100 lines, it is saved as a single entity. However, after exploding the hatch, every line becomes a separate entity and now you have 99 additional entities in the drawing.*

3. *Keep the hatch lines in a separate layer to facilitate editing of the hatch lines.*

4. *Assign a unique color to hatch lines so that the line width of the hatch lines can be controlled at the time of plotting.*

Review

Fill in the blanks

1. The ACAD.PAT file contains .... number of hatch pattern definitions.

2. The header line consists of the pattern name and ....

3. The first hatch line passes through a point whose coordinates are specified by .... and ....

4. The perpendicular distance between the hatch lines in a hatch pattern definition is specified by ....

5. The displacement of the second hatch line in a hatch pattern definition is specified by ....

6. The maximum number of dash lengths that can be specified in the line pattern definition of a hatch pattern is ....

7. The hatch lines in different areas of the drawing will automatically ....

8. The hatch angle as defined in the hatch pattern definition can be further changed when you use AutoCAD's .... command.

9. The hatch lines have a unknown .... definition.

10. The hatch lines can be edited after .... the hatch by using AutoCAD's .... command.

Exercises

Exercise 1

Determine the hatch specifications and write a hatch pattern definition for the hatch pattern as shown in Figure 14.

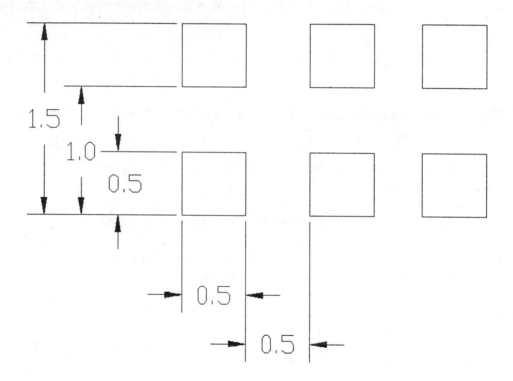

Figure 14   Square hatch pattern

Exercise 2

Determine the hatch pattern specifications and write a hatch pattern definition for the hatch pattern as shown in Figure 15.

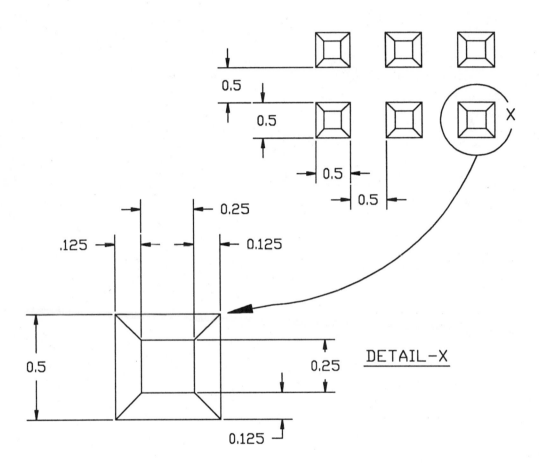

Figure 15 Hatch pattern

Chapter 6

Screen Menu

AutoCAD Menu

The AutoCAD menu provides an important and powerful tool to customize AutoCAD. The AutoCAD software package comes with a standard menu file. The name of this file is ACAD.MNU. When you start AutoCAD, ACAD menu file is automatically loaded, provided the AutoCAD configuration has not been changed. The ACAD menu file contains AutoCAD commands, separated under different headings for easy identification. For example, all draw commands are under DRAW, and all editing commands are under EDIT. The headings are named and arranged in a way that makes it easier for a user to locate and access the commands. However, there are some commands that a user may never use. Also, some users might like to regroup and rearrange the commands so that it is easier to get access to the most frequently used commands.

AutoCAD lets the user eliminate commands from the menu file that are rarely used and define new commands. This is made possible by editing the existing ACAD.MNU file, or writing a new menu file. There is no limit to the number of files you can write. You can have a separate menu file for each application. For example, you can have separate menu files for mechanical, electrical or architectural drawings. You can load these menu files any time by using AutoCAD's MENU command. The menu files are text files with the extension .MNU. These files can be written by using AutoCAD's EDIT command (provided ACAD.PGP file is present and EDIT command is defined in the file), EDLIN function of DOS, or a text editor.

The menu file can be divided into several sections, each section identified by a section label. AutoCAD uses the following labels to identify different sections of AutoCAD menu file.

***SCREEN
***TABLET(n)   ------- n is from 1 to 4
***TABLET(n)ALT   ------- n is from 1 to 4

```
***ICON
***POP(n)                  ------- n is from 1 to 10
***BUTTONS
***AUX1
***COMMENT
```

The tablet menu and the alternate tablet menu can have up to 4 different sections. The POP menu (pull-down menu) can have up to 10 sections.

<u>**Tablet Menus**</u>

```
***TABLET1
***TABLET2
***TABLET3
***TABLET4
```

<u>**Alt. Tablet Menus**</u>

```
***TABLET1ALT
***TABLET2ALT
***TABLET3ALT
***TABLET4ALT
```

<u>**Pull-Down Menus**</u>

```
***POP1
***POP2
***POP3
***POP4
***POP5
***POP6
***POP7
***POP8
***POP9
***POP10
```

Screen Menu

When you are in the AutoCAD drawing editor the screen menu is displayed on the right hand side of the computer screen. The AutoCAD screen menu displays AutoCAD at the top followed by asterisk signs(* * * *) and a list of commands (Figure 1).

The screen menu is a powerful tool when customizing AutoCAD. If it is developed properly it can save lot of time, and make the system more efficient. Depending on the scope of the menu, the size of the menu file can vary from a few lines to several hundred lines. A menu file consists of section labels, submenus, and menu items. A menu item consists of an item label and a command definition. The menu item label is enclosed in brackets and the command definition is outside the brackets.

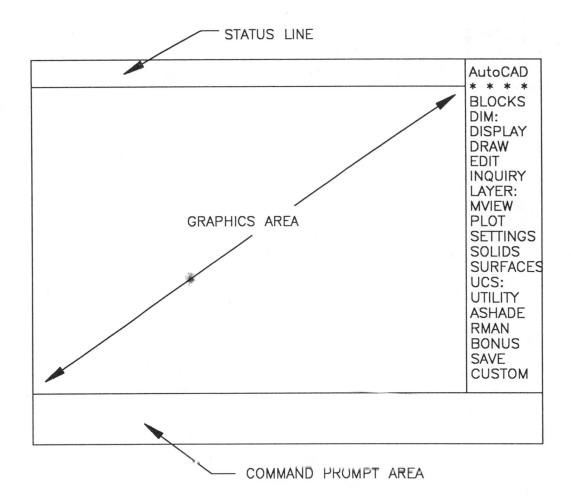

Figure 1   Screen display

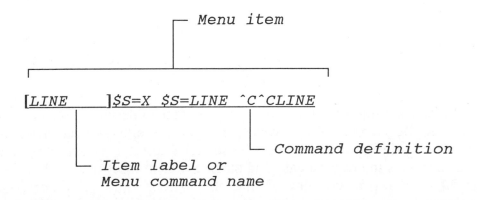

The menu item label that is enclosed in the brackets is displayed in the screen menu area of the monitor and it is not a part of the command definition. The command definition, the part of the menu item outside the bracket, is the executable part of the menu item. To understand the process of developing and writing a screen menu, consider the following example.

Example 1

Write a screen menu for the following AutoCAD commands. (File name SM1.MNU)

Line
Circle C,R
Circle C,D
Circle 2P
Erase
Move

The layout of these commands is shown in Figure 2. This menu is named MENU-1 and it should be displayed at the top of the screen menu. It lets the user know the menu that he is using.

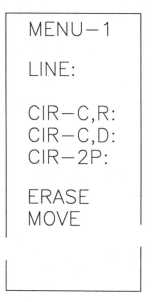

Figure 2   Layout of screen menu

Before writing a menu, it is very important to design a menu , know the exact sequence of the AutoCAD commands, and the prompts associated with a particular command. To design a menu, the user should select and arrange the commands in a way that provides the user an easy and quick access to most frequently used commands. A careful design will save lot of time in the long run. Therefore, it is strongly recommended to consider several possible designs with different command combinations, and then select the one that is best suited for the job. Suggestions from other CAD operators in the company can prove very valuable. The screen menu in Example 1 shows one of the possible designs.

The second very important thing in developing a screen menu is to know the exact sequence of the commands and the prompts associated with the command. To better determine the prompt entries that are required in a command, you should enter all the commands and the prompt entries from the keyboard. The following is a description of the commands and the prompt entries required for Example 1.

LINE Command

Command: LINE

Notice the command and prompt entry sequence

>   LINE
>   <RETURN>

CIRCLE (C,R) Command

Command: CIRCLE
3P/2P/TTR/<Center point>:
Diameter/<Radius>:

Notice the command and prompt entries sequence

CIRCLE
<RETURN>
Center Point
<RETURN>
Radius
<RETURN>

CIRCLE (C,D) Command

Command: CIRCLE
3P/2P/TTR/<Center point>:
Diameter/<Radius>: D
Diameter:

Notice the command and prompt entries sequence

CIRCLE
<RETURN>
Center Point
<RETURN>
D
<RETURN>
Diameter
<RETURN>

CIRCLE (2P) Command

Command: CIRCLE
3P/2P/TTR/ < Center Point > : 2P
First point on diameter:
Second point on diameter:

Notice the command and prompt entries sequence

CIRCLE
< RETURN >
2P
< RETURN >
Select first point on diameter
< RETURN >
Select second point on diameter
< RETURN >

ERASE Command

Command: ERASE

Notice the command and prompt entry sequence

ERASE
< RETURN >

MOVE Command

Command: MOVE

Notice the command and prompt entry sequence

MOVE
< RETURN >

The difference between the Center-Radius and Center-Diameter option of the CIRCLE command is that in the first one the RADIUS is the default, whereas in the second one you need to enter D to use the diameter option. This difference, although minor, is very important when writing a menu file. Similarly, the 2P (2 point) option of the CIRCLE command is different from the other two. Therefore, it is important to know the correct sequence of the AutoCAD commands, and the entries made in response to the prompts associated with those commands.

You can use AutoCAD's edit command or the Edlin function of DOS to write the menu file. If you use the EDIT command, AutoCAD will prompt you to enter the file name that you want to edit. The file name can be up to eight characters long and the file extension should be .MNU. If the file name exists it will be automatically loaded, otherwise a new file will be created. For Example 1 the file name is SM1.MNU. SM1 is the name of the screen menu file, and .MNU is the extension of this file. All menu files have an extension of .MNU.

If you want to use the EDLIN function of DOS, you can access the DOS command from the drawing editor by typing SHELL or SH, and then use the Edlin function. If these commands do not work, check the ACAD.PGP file and make sure that this file is present. **The line numbers are not a part of the file. They are shown here for reference only.**

```
***SCREEN                            1
[ MENU-1    ]                        2
[           ]                        3
[           ]                        4
[LINE       ]^C^CLINE                5
[           ]                        6
[CIR-C,R    ]^C^CCIRCLE              7
[CIR-C,D    ]^C^CCIRCLE;\D           8
[CIR- 2P    ]^C^CCIRCLE;2P           9
[           ]                       10
[ERASE      ]^C^CERASE              11
[MOVE       ]^C^CMOVE               12
```

Line 1
***SCREEN
***SCREEN is the section label for the screen menu. The lines that follow the screen menu are treated as a part of this menu. The screen menu definition will be terminated by another section label like ***TABLET1 or ***POP1.

Line 2
[MENU-1]
This menu item displays MENU-1 on the screen. Anything that is inside the brackets is for display only and does not have any effect on the command. The maximum number of characters or spaces that you can put inside these brackets is 8, because the width of the screen menu column on the screen is 8 characters. If the number of characters is more than 8, the remaining characters in excess of 8 are not displayed on the screen. The part of the menu item that is outside the brackets is executed even if the number of characters inside the bracket is more than 8.

Line 3
[   ]
This menu item prints a blank line on the screen menu. There are 8 blank spaces inside the bracket. When 8 blank spaces are printed on the screen menu, it displays a blank line. This line does not contain anything outside the bracket, and therefore no command is executed. To provide the space in the menu you can also leave a blank space in the menu file, or have two brackets ([ ]). The next line, line 4, also prints a blank line.

Line 5
[LINE   ]^C^CLINE. [LINE   ]
This menu item displays LINE on the screen. The first ^C (Caret C) cancels the existing command, and the **second ^C** cancels the command again. The two

CANCEL (^C^C) commands are required to make sure that the existing commands are cancelled before executing a new command. Most AutoCAD commands can be cancelled by just one CANCEL command. However, there are some commands like dimensioning command that need to be cancelled twice to get out of the command. The **LINE** is an AutoCAD command that will prompt the user to enter the points to draw a line. Since there is nothing after the LINE, it automatically enters a RETURN.

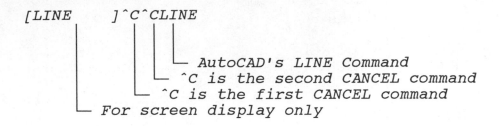

```
[LINE     ]^C^CLINE
                       └─ AutoCAD's LINE Command
                    └─ ^C is the second CANCEL command
                 └─ ^C is the first CANCEL command
          └─ For screen display only
```

Line 7
[CIR-C,R]^C^CCIRCLE
The part of the menu item that is enclosed within the brackets is for screen display only. The part of the menu item that is outside the brackets is executed when this line is selected. ^C^C (Caret C) cancels the existing command twice. CIRCLE is an AutoCAD command that generates a circle. **The space after CIRCLE automatically causes a RETURN.**

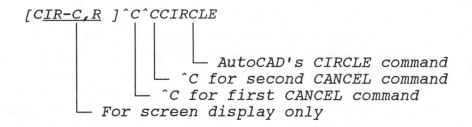

```
[CIR-C,R ]^C^CCIRCLE
                       └─ AutoCAD's CIRCLE command
                    └─ ^C for second CANCEL command
                 └─ ^C for first CANCEL command
          └─ For screen display only
```

Line 8
[CIR-C,D]^C^CCIRCLE;\D
The part of the menu item that is enclosed in the brackets is for screen display only, and the part that is outside the brackets is the executable part. ^C^C will cancel the existing command twice.

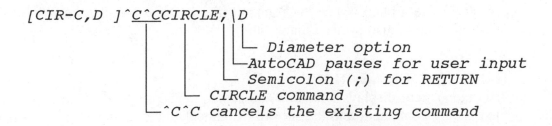

```
[CIR-C,D ]^C^CCIRCLE;\D
                           └─ Diameter option
                          └─ AutoCAD pauses for user input
                       └─ Semicolon (;) for RETURN
                 └─ CIRCLE command
          └─ ^C^C cancels the existing command
```

The CIRCLE command is followed by a semicolon, back slash (\), and D for diameter option. **The semicolon (;) after the CIRCLE command causes RETURN which has the same effect as entering RETURN from the keyboard. The back slash (\) pauses for the user input.** In this case it is the center point of the circle. D is for the diameter option and it is automatically followed by RETURN. The semicolon, in above example, can also be replaced by a blank space as shown in the following line:

```
[CIR-C,R ]^C^CCIRCLE \D
                      |
                      |
                      |__ Blank space for RETURN
```

Line 9
[CIR- 2P]^C^CCIRCLE;2P
In this menu item ^C^C cancels the existing command twice and the semicolon after CIRCLE enters a RETURN. 2P is for the two point option followed by the blank space that cause RETURN. You will notice that the sequence of commands is same as discussed earlier in this section. Therefore it is essential to know the exact sequence of the commands, otherwise the screen menu is not going to work.

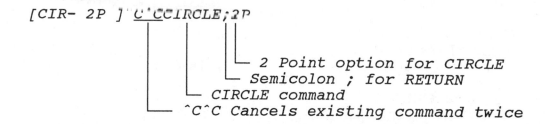

```
[CIR- 2P ] C^CCIRCLE;2P
          |  |      | |
          |  |      | |__ 2 Point option for CIRCLE
          |  |      |__ Semicolon ; for RETURN
          |  |__ CIRCLE command
          |__ ^C^C Cancels existing command twice
```

The semicolon after the CIRCLE command can be replaced by a blank space as shown in the following line. The blank space causes a RETURN like a semicolon (;).

```
[CIR- 2P ]^C^CCIRCLE 2P
                     |
                     |
                     |__ Blank space for RETURN
```

Line 11
[ERASE]^C^CERASE
In this menu item ^C^C cancels the existing command twice and ERASE is an AutoCAD command that erases the selected entities.

```
[ERASE     ]^C^CERASE
            └── AutoCAD's ERASE command
```

Line 12
[MOVE   ]^C^CMOVE
In this menu item ^C^C cancels the existing command twice, and the MOVE command will move the selected entities.

```
[MOVE     ]^C^CMOVE
               └── AutoCAD's MOVE command
```

From this example it is clear that every statement in the screen menu is based on the AutoCAD commands and the information that is needed to complete that command. This forms the basis for creating a menu file and should be given an important consideration. Following is a summary of the AutoCAD commands used in Example 1, and their equivalent in the menu file.

Command: LINE

[LINE   ]^C^CLINE

Command: CIRCLE
3P/2P/TTR/ < Center point > :
Diameter/ < Radius > :

[CIR-C,R]^C^CCIRCLE

Command: CIRCLE
3P/2P/TTR/ < Center point > :
Diameter/ < Radius > : D
Diameter:

[CIR-C,D]^C^CCIRCLE;\D

Command: CIRCLE
3P/2P/TTR/ < Center Point > : 2P
First point on diameter:
Second point on diameter:

[CIR- 2P]^C^CCIRCLE;2P

Command: ERASE

[ERASE   ]^C^CERASE

Command: MOVE

[MOVE   ]^C^CMOVE

Loading Menus

AutoCAD automatically loads the ACAD.MNX (ACAD.MNX file is the compiled form of ACAD.MNU file) file when you get into AutoCAD's drawing editor, provided AutoCAD configuration has not been changed. However, you can also load a different menu file by using AutoCAD's MENU command.

Command: Menu
Menu file name <ACAD>: SM1

                                 └─ *Name of menu file*
                    └─ *Default menu file*

After entering the MENU command, AutoCAD will prompt for the file name. Enter the name of the menu file without the file extension (.MNU), since AutoCAD assumes the extension to be .MNU.   AutoCAD will compile the menu file and then load the new compiled menu file.   The extension of a compiled menu file is .MNX.   It is the compiled file that is displayed on the screen.   If you make any changes in the menu file, you must use the menu command again to recompile the file.   After you load the menu file SM1, the following menu will be displayed on the screen:

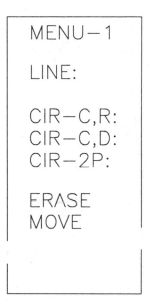

Figure 3   Screen menu display

Now, you can test the menu by selecting different commands from this menu.

Note

1.   After you load the new menu, you can not use the pull-down menu, button menu, or the digitizer, because the original menu ACAD.MNU is not present and the new menu does not contain these menu areas.

2.   To activate the original menu again, load the menu file by using MENU command.

Command: Menu
Menu file name or . for none < SM1 >: ACAD

3.   *If you need to use input from a keyboard or a pointing device use back slash "\".   The system will pause for the user to enter data.*

4.   *There should be no space after the back slash "\".*

5.   *The menu items, menu labels, and the command definition can be in upper case, lower case or mixed.*

6.   *You can introduce spaces between the menu items to improve the readability of the menu file.*

7.   *If there are more items in the menu than the number of spaces available, the excess items are not displayed on the screen.   For example, in the screen menu if the menu device limits the number of items to 21, the items in excess of 21 will not be displayed on the screen, and are therefore inaccessible.*

8.   *If you configure AutoCAD and turn the screen prompt area off, you can increase the number of lines that can be displayed on the screen menu.   On some devices it is 24 lines.*

9.   *If you want to protect your menu files from accidental editing, compile the new menu file by loading the menu and then delete the menu file.   Do not delete the file with extension .MNX (Compiled file).*

Exercise 1

Design and write a screen menu for the following AutoCAD commands.   (File name SME1.MNU)

PLINE
ELLIPSE (Center)
ELLIPSE (Axis Endpoint)
ROTATE
OFFSET
SCALE

Submenus

The number of items in the screen menu file can be very large that can not be accommodated on one screen. For example, the maximum number of items that can be displayed on some of the menu devices is 21. If the screen menu has more than 21 items, the menu items in excess of 21 are not displayed on the screen and can not therefore be accessed. The user can overcome this problem by using submenus that let the user define smaller groups of items within a menu section. When a submenu is selected, it loads the submenu items and displays them on the screen. However, depending on the resolution of the monitor and the graphics card, the number of items that you can display on the screen can be higher and you may not need submenus.

Submenu Definition

A submenu definition consists of two asterisk signs (**) followed by the name of the submenu. A menu can have any number of submenus, and every submenu should have a unique name. The items that follow a submenu, up to the next section label, or submenu label, belong to that submenu. The format of a submenu definition is:

```
**Name
  |   |
  |   └─ Name of the submenu
  └─ Two asterisk signs (**) designate a submenu
```

Example
```
**DRAW1
  |   |
  |   └─ Name of the submenu
  └─ ** Designates that DRAW1 is a submenu
```

Note

1. The submenu name can be up to 31 characters long.

2. The submenu name can consist of letters, digits, and the special characters like: $ (dollar), - (hyphen), and _ (underscore).

3. The submenu name should not have any embedded blanks (spaces).

4. The submenu names should be unique in a menu file.

Submenu Reference

The submenu reference is used to reference or load a submenu. It consists of a "$" sign followed by a letter that specifies the menu section. The letter that specifies a screen menu section is S. The section is followed by "=" sign, and the name of the submenu that the user wants to activate. The submenu name should be without "**". The following is the format of a submenu reference:

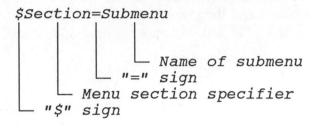

```
$Section=Submenu
```
            Name of submenu
        "=" sign
    Menu section specifier
"$" sign

Example
```
$S=EDIT
```
        Name of submenu
    S-Specifies screen menu section

Note

S	*specifies the SCREEN menu*
P1 - P10	*specifies the POP menus, POP1 to POP10*
I	*specifies the ICON menu*
B	*specifies the BUTTONS menu*
T1 - T4	*specifies the TABLET menus, T1 to T4*
A1	*specifies the AUX1 menu*

Nested Submenus

When a submenu is activated, the current menu is copied to a stack. If you select another submenu, the submenu that was current will be copied or pushed to the top of the stack. The maximum number of menus that can be stacked is 8. If the stack size increases to more than 8, the menu that is at the bottom of the stack is removed and forgotten. You can call the previous submenu by using the nested submenu call. The format of the call is:

```
$S=
```
        "=" sign
    Screen menu specifier
"$" sign

The maximum number of nested submenu calls is 8. Each time you call a submenu, this pops the last item from the stack and reactivates it.

Example 2

Design a menu layout and write a screen menu for the following commands.

LINE	ERASE
PLINE	MOVE
ELLIPSE-C	ROTATE
ELLIPSE-E	OFFSET
CIR-C,R	COPY
CIR-C,D	SCALE
CIR- 2P	

As mentioned earlier, the first and the most important part of writing a menu is the design of the menu and knowing the commands and the prompts associated with these commands. You should know the way you want the menu to look, and the way you want to arrange the commands for maximum efficiency. Write the menu on a piece of paper and check it thoroughly to make sure that you have arranged the commands the way you want them. Use submenus to group the commands together based on their use, function, and relationship with other submenus. Make provision to access other frequently used commands without going through the root menu.

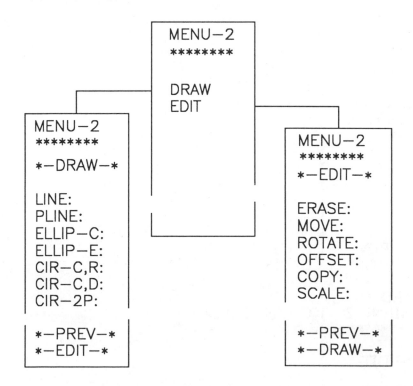

Figure 4 Screen menu design

Figure 4 shows one of the possible arrangements of the commands and the design of the screen menu. It has one main menu and 2 submenus. One of the submenus is for draw commands and the other submenu is for edit commands. The colon (:) at the end of the commands is not required. They are used here to distinguish the commands from those items that are not used as commands. For example, DRAW in the root menu is not a command, therefore it has no colon at the end. On the other hand, if you select ERASE from the EDIT menu it executes ERASE command, therefore it has a colon (:) at the end of the command.

The following file is a listing of the menu file of Example 1. **The line numbers are not a part of the file, they are given here for reference only.**

```
***SCREEN                                      1
[ MENU-2     ]                                 2
[********    ]                                  3
[            ]                                  4
[            ]                                  5
[            ]                                  6
[            ]                                  7
[DRAW        ]^C^C$S=DRAW                       8
[EDIT        ]^C^C$S=EDIT                       9
                                               10
**DRAW                                         11
[ MENU-2     ]^C^C$S=SCREEN                     12
[********    ]                                  13
[            ]                                  14
[*-DRAW-*    ]                                  15
[            ]                                  16
[LINE:       ]^C^CLINE                          17
[PLINE:      ]^C^CPLINE;\W;0.1;0.1              18
[ELLIP-C:    ]^C^CELLIPSE;C                     19
[ELLIP-E:    ]^C^CELLIPSE                       20
[CIR-C,R:    ]^C^CCIRCLE                        21
[CIR-C,D:    ]^C^CCIRCLE;\D                     22
[CIR-2P:     ]^C^CCIRCLE;2P                     23
[            ]                                  24
[            ]                                  25
[            ]                                  26
[            ]                                  27
[            ]                                  28
[            ]                                  29
[*-PREV-*    ]^C^C$S=                           30
[*-EDIT-*    ]^C^C$S=EDIT                       31
                                               32
**EDIT                                         33
[ MENU-2     ]^C^C$S=SCREEN                     34
[********    ]                                  35
[            ]                                  36
[*-EDIT-*    ]                                  37
[            ]                                  38
[ERASE:      ]^C^CERASE                         39
[MOVE:       ]^C^CMOVE                          40
[ROTATE:     ]^C^CROTATE                        41
```

```
[OFFSET:    ]^C^COFFSET                        42
[COPY:      ]^C^CCOPY                          43
[SCALE:     ]^C^CSCALE                         44
[          ]                                    45
[          ]                                    46
[          ]                                    47
[          ]                                    48
[          ]                                    49
[          ]                                    50
[          ]                                    51
[*-PREV-*  ]^C^C$S=                            52
[*-DRAW-*  ]^C^C$S=DRAW                        53
```

Line 1
***SCREEN
***SCREEN is the section label for the screen menu.

Line 2
[MENU-2]
This menu item displays MENU-2 at the top of the screen menu.

Line 3
[********]
This menu item prints eight asterisk signs (********) on the screen menu.

Line 4-7
[   ]
This menu item prints four blank lines on the screen menu. The brackets are not required. They could be just four blank lines without brackets.

Line-8
[DRAW   ]^C^C$S=DRAW
[DRAW   ] displays DRAW on the screen letting the user know that by selecting this function he can access the draw commands. ^C^C cancels the existing command twice, and $S=DRAW loads the DRAW submenu on the screen.

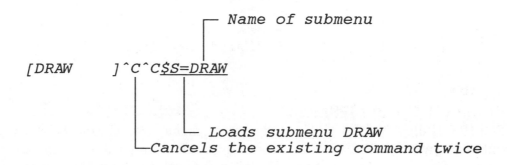

Line 9
[EDIT   ]^C^C$S=EDIT

[EDIT   ] displays EDIT on the screen. ^C^C cancels the existing command, and $S=EDIT loads the submenu **EDIT**.

Line 10
The blank lines between the submenus or menu items is not required. It just makes it easy to read the file.

Line 11
**DRAW
**DRAW is the name of the submenu, and the lines 12 through 31 are defined under this submenu.

Line 15
[*-DRAW-*]
It prints *-DRAW-* on the screen menu as a heading that lets the user know that the commands listed on the screen menu are draw commands.

Line 18
[PLINE:]^C^CPLINE;\W;0.1;0.1
[PLINE:] displays PLINE: on the screen. ^C^C cancels the command twice, and PLINE is AutoCAD's polyline command.   The semicolons are for RETURN. The semicolons can be replaced by a blank space. The back slash (\) is for user input. In this case it is the start point of the polyline. W is to select the width option of the polyline. The first 0.1 is the starting width and the second 0.1 is the ending width of the polyline. This command will draw a polyline of 0.1 width.

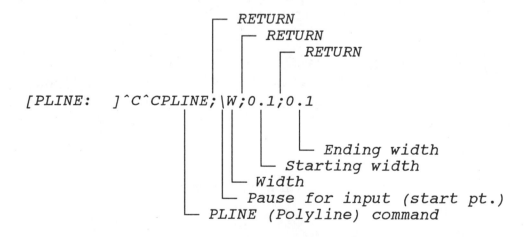

Line 19
[ELLIP-C:]^C^CELLIPSE;C
[ELLIP-C:] displays ELLIP-C: on the screen menu. ^C^C cancels the existing command twice, and ELLIPSE is an AutoCAD command for generating an ellipse. The semicolon is for RETURN, and C selects the center option of the ELLIPSE command.

```
[ELLIP-C:]^C^CELLIPSE;C
             |          |  |
             |          |  └─ Center option for ellipse
             |          └─ RETURN
             └─ ELLIPSE command
```

Line 20
[ELLIP-A:]^C^CELLIPSE
[ELLIP-A:] displays ELLIP-A: on the screen menu.   ^C^C cancels the existing
command twice, and ELLIPSE is an AutoCAD command.   Here the ELLIPSE
command uses the default options, axis end point, instead of center.

Line 30
[*-PREV-*]^C^C$S=
[*-PREV-*] displays *-PREV-* on the screen menu, and ^C^C cancels the
existing command twice. $S= restores the previous menu that was displayed
on the screen before loading the current menu.

```
[*-PREV-*]^C^C$S=
                 |
                 └─ Restores the previous screen menu
```

Line 31
[*-EDIT-*]^C^C$S=EDIT
[*-EDIT-*] displays *-EDIT-* on the screen menu, and ^C^C cancels the
existing command twice. $S=EDIT loads the submenu EDIT on the screen.
This lets the user access the EDIT commands without going back to root menu
and then selecting EDIT from there.

```
                        ┌─ Name of the submenu
                        |
[*-EDIT-*]^C^C$S=EDIT
                 |
                 └─ Loads the submenu EDIT
```

Line 33
**EDIT
**EDIT is the name of the submenu, and the lines 34 to 53 are defined under
this submenu.

Line 34
[MENU-2]^C^C$S=SCREEN

[MENU-2] displays MENU-2 on the screen menu, and ^C^C cancels the existing command twice. $S=SCREEN loads the root menu SCREEN on the screen menu.

Line 39
[ERASE:]^C^CERASE
[ERASE:] displays ERASE: on the screen menu, and ^C^C cancels the existing command twice. ERASE is an AutoCAD command for erasing the selected entities.

Line 53
[*-DRAW-*]^C^C$S=DRAW
$S=DRAW loads the DRAW submenu on the screen. It lets the user load the DRAW menu without going through the root menu.

When you select DRAW from the root menu, the submenu DRAW is loaded on the screen. The menu items in the draw submenu completely replace the menu items of the root menu. Now, if you select MENU-2 from the screen menu, the root menu will be loaded on the screen, but some of the items are not cleared from the screen menu (Figure 5). This is because the root menu does not have enough menu items to completely replace the menu items of the DRAW submenu.

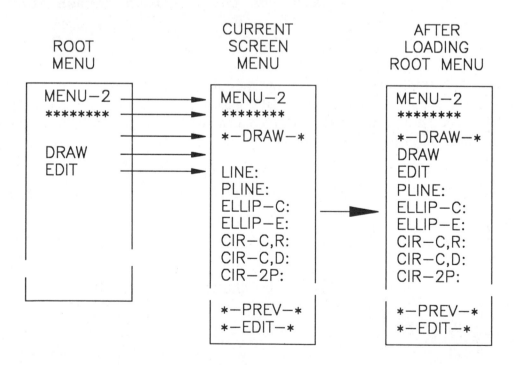

Figure 5   Screen menu display after loading the root menu

One of the ways to clear the screen is to define a submenu that has 21 blank lines. When this submenu is loaded it will clear the screen. Now, if you load another submenu there will be no overlap, because the screen menu has been already cleared and there are no menu items left on the screen (Figure 6). Example 3 illustrates the use of such a submenu.

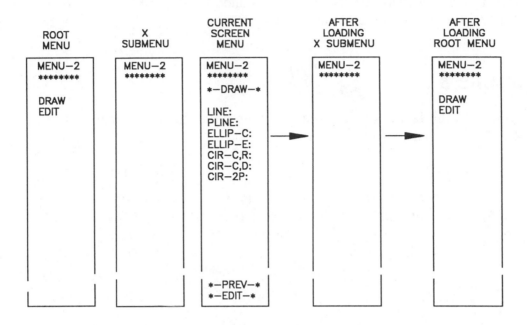

Figure 6   Screen menu display after loading the root menu

Another way to avoid overlapping of the menu items is to define every submenu in a way so that all of them have the same number of menu items. The disadvantage with this approach is that the menu file will get long, because every submenu will have 20 or 21 lines. (The number of lines will depend on the menu device)

Exercise 2

Write a Screen Menu file for the following AutoCAD commands. (File name SM2.MNU)

ARC	MIRROR
-3P	BREAK-F
-SCE	BREAK-@
-SCA	EXTEND
-SCL	STRETCH
-SEA	FILLET-0
POLYGON-C	FILLET
POLYGON-E	CHAMFER

Multiple Submenus

A menu file can have any number of submenus. All the submenu names have two asterisk signs (**) in front of them, even if there is a submenu within a submenu. Also, several submenus can be loaded in a single statement. If there is more than one submenu in a menu item they should be separated by a space. The following example, Example 3, illustrates the use of multiple submenus.

Example 3

Design the layout of the menu and then write the screen menu for the following AutoCAD commands.

Draw	**Edit**	**Display**
LINE	EXTEND	ZOOM
Continue	STRETCH	REGEN
Close	FILLET	SCALE
Undo		PAN
.X		
.Y		
.Z		
.XY		
.XZ		
.YZ		
ARC		
3Point		
SCE		
SCA		
CSE		
CSA		
CSL		

There are several different ways of arranging the commands depending on the requirements of the user. However, the following layout is one of the possible designs of the screen menu for the given AutoCAD commands.

The name of the following menu file is SM3.MNU. You can use the Edlin function of DOS or a text editor to write the file. The following file is the listing of the menu file SM3.MNU. The line numbers are not a part of the file. They are shown here for reference only.

```
***SCREEN                           1
**S                                 2
[ MENU-3    ]^C^C$S=X $S=S          3
[********   ]$S=OSNAP               4
[          ]                        5
[          ]                        6
```

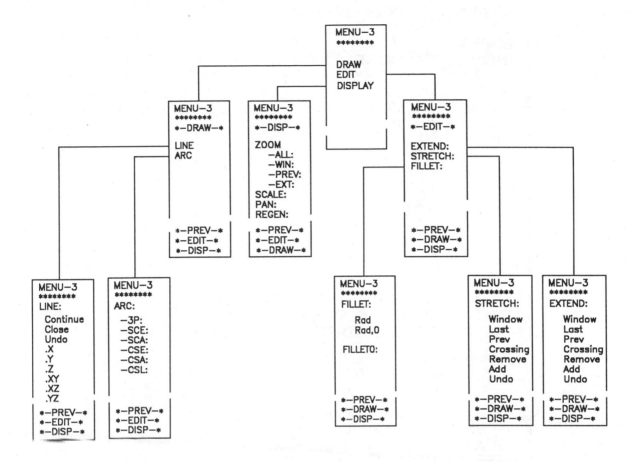

Figure 7 Screen menu design with submenus

```
[DRAW        ]^C^C$S=X $S=DRAW                        7
[EDIT        ]^C^C$S=X $S=EDIT                        8
[DISPLAY     ]^C^C$S=X $S=DISP                        9
                                                     10
**DRAW 3                                             11
[*-DRAW-* ]                                           12
[         ]                                           13
[         ]                                           14
[LINE:       ]$S=X $S=LINE ^C^CLINE                   15
[ARC:        ]$S=X $S=ARC                             16
[         ]                                           17
[         ]                                           18
[         ]                                           19
[         ]                                           20
[         ]                                           21
[         ]                                           22
[         ]                                           23
[         ]                                           24
[         ]                                           25
[         ]                                           26
[*-PREV-*    ]$S= $S=                                 27
[*-EDIT-*    ]^C^C$S=X $S=EDIT                        28
```

```
[*-DISP-*      ]$S=X $S=DISP                              29
                                                         30
**LINE 3                                                 31
[LINE:         ]^C^CLINE                                 32
[              ]                                         33
[              ]                                         34
[Continue      ]^C^CLINE;;                               35
[Close         ]CLOSE                                    36
[Undo          ]U                                        37
[.X            ].X                                       38
[.Y            ].Y                                       39
[.Z            ].Z                                       40
[.XY           ].XY                                      41
[.XZ           ].XZ                                      42
[.YZ           ].YZ                                      43
[              ]                                         44
[              ]                                         45
[              ]                                         46
[*-PREV-*      ]$S= $S=                                  47
[*-EDIT-*      ]^C^C$S=X $S=EDIT                         48
[*-DISP-*      ]$S=X $S=DISP                             49
                                                         50
**ARC 3                                                  51
[ARC           ]                                         52
[              ]                                         53
[  -3P:        ]^C^CARC \\DRAG                           54
[  -SCE:       ]^C^CARC \C \DRAG                         55
[  -SCA:       ]^C^CARC \C \A DRAG                       56
[  -CSE:       ]^C^CARC C \\DRAG                         57
[  -CSA:       ]^C^CARC C \\A DRAG                       58
[  -CSL:       ]^C^CARC C \\L DRAG                       59
[              ]                                         60
[              ]                                         61
[              ]                                         62
[              ]                                         63
[              ]                                         64
[              ]                                         65
[              ]                                         66
[*-PREV-*      ]$S= $S=                                  67
[*-EDIT-*      ]^C^C$S=X $S=EDIT                         68
[*-DISP-*      ]$S=X $S=DISP                             69
                                                         70
**EDIT 3                                                 71
[*-EDIT-*      ]                                         72
[              ]                                         73
[              ]                                         74
[EXTEND:       ]$S=X $S=EXTEND ^C^CEXTEND                75
[STRETCH:      ]$S=X $S=STRETCH ^C^CSTRETCH C            76
[FILLET:       ]$S=X $S=FILLET ^C^CFILLET                77
[              ]                                         78
[              ]                                         79
[              ]                                         80
[              ]                                         81
[              ]                                         82
```

```
[                ]                                    83
[                ]                                    84
[                ]                                    85
[                ]                                    86
[*-PREV-*    ]$S= $S=                                 87
[*-DRAW-*    ]^C^C$S=X $S=DRAW                        88
[*-DISP-*    ]$S=X $S=DISP                            89
                                                     90
**EXTEND  3                                           91
[EXTEND:     ]^C^CEXTEND                              92
[                ]                                    93
Window                                               94
Last                                                 95
Prev                                                 96
Crossing                                             97
Remove                                               98
Add                                                  99
Undo                                                100
[                ]                                   101
[                ]                                   102
[                ]                                   103
[                ]                                   104
[                ]                                   105
[                ]                                   106
[*-PREV-*    ]$S= $S=                                107
[*-DRAW-*    ]^C^C$S=X $S=DRAW                       108
[*-DISP-*    ]$S=DISP                                109
                                                    110
**STRETCH  3                                         111
[STRETCH:  ]^C^CSTRETCH C                            112
[                ]                                   113
Window                                              114
Last                                                115
Prev                                                116
Crossing                                            117
Remove                                              118
Add                                                 119
Undo                                                120
[                ]                                   121
[                ]                                   122
[                ]                                   123
[                ]                                   124
[                ]                                   125
[                ]                                   126
[*-PREV-*    ]$S= $S=                                127
[*-DRAW-*    ]^C^C$S=X $S=DRAW                       128
[*-DISP-*    ]$S=X $S=DISP                           129
                                                    130
**FILLET  3                                          131
[FILLET:     ]^C^CFILLET                             132
[   Rad       ]R \FILLET                             133
[   Rad 0    ]R 0 FILLET                             134
[                ]                                   135
[FILLET0:   ]^C^CFILLET R 0;;                        136
```

```
[                ]                                    137
[                ]                                    138
[                ]                                    139
[                ]                                    140
[                ]                                    141
[                ]                                    142
[                ]                                    143
[                ]                                    144
[                ]                                    145
[                ]                                    146
[*-PREV-*       ]$S= $S=                              147
[*-DRAW-*       ]^C^C$S=X $S=DRAW                     148
[*-DISP-*       ]$S=X $S=DISP                         149
                                                     150
**DISP 3                                             151
[*-DISP-*       ]                                     152
[                ]                                    153
[                ]                                    154
[ZOOM:          ]'ZOOM                                155
[  -ALL         ]A                                    156
[  -WIN         ]W                                    157
[  -PREV        ]P                                    158
[  -EXT         ]E                                    159
[                ]                                    160
[SCALE:         ]'ZOOM                                161
[PAN:           ]'PAN                                 162
[REGEN:         ]^C^CREGEN                            163
[                ]                                    164
[                ]                                    165
[                ]                                    166
[*-PREV-*       ]$S= $S=                              167
[*-EDIT-*       ]^C^C$S=X $S=EDIT                     168
[*-DRAW-*       ]$S=X $S=DRAW                         169
                                                     170
**X 3                                                171
[                ]                                    172
[                ]                                    173
[                ]                                    174
[                ]                                    175
[                ]                                    176
[                ]                                    177
[                ]                                    178
[                ]                                    179
[                ]                                    180
[                ]                                    181
[                ]                                    182
[                ]                                    183
[                ]                                    184
[                ]                                    185
[                ]                                    186
[                ]                                    187
[                ]                                    188
[                ]                                    189
                                                     190
```

```
**OSNAP 2                                                  191
[-OSNAPS-   ]                                              192
[           ]                                              193
[Center     ]CEN $S=                                       194
[Endpoint   ]END $S=                                       195
[Insert     ]INS $S=                                       196
[Intersec   ]INT $S=                                       197
[Midpoint   ]MID $S=                                       198
[Nearest    ]NEA $S=                                       199
[Node       ]NOD $S=                                       200
[Perpend    ]PER $S=                                       201
[Quadrant   ]QUA $S=                                       202
[Tangent    ]TAN $S=                                       203
[None       ]NONE $S=                                      204
[           ]                                              205
[           ]                                              206
[           ]                                              207
[           ]                                              208
[           ]                                              209
[*-PREV-*   ]$S=                                           210
```

Line 3
[MENU-3]^C^C$S=X $S=S
In this menu item [MENU-3] displays MENU-3 at the top of the screen menu. ^C^C cancels the command twice, and $S=X loads the submenu X. Similarly, $S=S loads the submenu S. The submenu X, defined on line number 171, consists of 18 blank lines. Therefore, when this submenu is loaded it prints blank lines on the screen and clears the screen menu area. After loading the submenu X, the system loads the submenu S, and the items that are defined in this submenu are displayed on the screen menu.

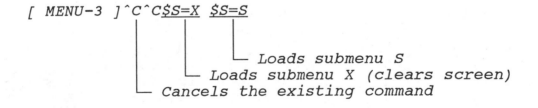

Line 4
[*******]$S=OSNAP
This menu item prints eight asterisk signs on the screen menu, and $S=OSNAP loads the submenu OSNAP. The OSNAP submenu is defined on line 191 and it consists of different OSNAP modes.

Line 7
[DRAW   ]^C^C$S=X $S=DRAW
This menu item displays DRAW on the screen menu area, cancels the existing command twice, and then loads the submenus X and then the submenu DRAW.

The submenu X clears the screen menu area, and the submenu DRAW, as defined on line 11, loads the items defined under the DRAW submenu.

Line 11
**DRAW 3
This line is the submenu label for DRAW, and 3 indicates that the first line of the DRAW submenu will be printed on line 3. Nothing will be printed on line 1 or line 2. The first line of the DRAW submenu will be on line 3, followed by rest of the menu. All the submenus except the submenus S and OSNAP have a 3 at the end of the line. Therefore the first two lines (MENU-3) and (********) will never be cleared and will be displayed on the screen all the time. If you select MENU-3 in any menu, it will load the submenu S. If you select ********, it will load the submenu OSNAP.

```
**DRAW 3
      |
      |         |
      |          - Leaves 2 blank lines and prints from 3rd.
       - Submenu name
```

Line 15
[LINE:]$S=X $S=LINE ^C^CLINE
In this menu item $S=X, loads the submenu X, and $S=LINE loads the submenu LINE. The submenu name LINE has nothing to do with the AutoCAD's LINE command. It could also have been any other name. However, it is recommended to select the names that reflect the contents of the menu. ^C^C cancels the existing command twice, and LINE is the AutoCAD's LINE command.

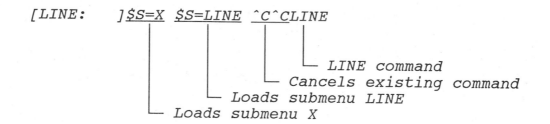

```
[LINE:     ]$S=X  $S=LINE  ^C^CLINE
                |       |        |      |
                |       |        |       - LINE command
                |       |         - Cancels existing command
                |        - Loads submenu LINE
                 - Loads submenu X
```

Line 16-26
[   ]
These menu items print blank lines on the screen, because there are eight spaces inside the brackets. You can also get the blank lines on the screen by blank lines in the screen menu file, or using open and close bracket ([ ]). The brackets make it easier to see the blank lines in the menu file.

Line 27
[*-PREV-*]$S= $S=

This menu item recalls the previous menu twice. AutoCAD keeps a track of the submenus that were loaded on the screen. The first **$S=** will load the previously loaded menu, and the second **$S=** will load the submenu that was loaded before that. For example, in line 16 ([ARC:]$S=X $S=ARC) two submenus have been loaded: first X and then ARC. The submenu X is stacked before loading the submenu ARC that is current and is not stacked yet. The first **$S=** will recall the previous menu, in this case submenu X. The second **$S=** will load the menu that was on the screen before selecting the item in line 16.

```
[*-PREV-*]$S=  $S=
                │      │
                │      │
                │      └── Loads last to last menu
                └── Loads last menu
```

Line 29
[*-DISP-*]$S=X $S=DISP
In this menu item $S=X loads the submenu X, and $S=DISP loads the submenu DISP. You will notice that there is no CANCEL (^C^C) command in the line. There are some menus that the user might like to load without cancelling the existing command. For example, if you are drawing a line you might want to zoom without cancelling the existing command. You can select [*-DISP-*], select the appropriate zoom option and then continue with the line command. However, if the line had a CANCEL command ([*-DISP-*]^C^C$S=X $S=DISP), then you can not continue with the LINE command, because the existing command will be cancelled when you select *-DISP-* from the screen.

In line 28 ([*-EDIT-*]^C^C$S=X $S=EDIT), cancel command has been used to cancel the existing command, because the user can not use any editing command unless the existing command is cancelled.

Line 35
[Continue]^C^CLINE;;
In this menu item the LINE command is followed by two semicolons that continue the LINE command. To understand it, take a look at the LINE command and how a continue option is used in this command.

Command: LINE
From point:RETURN   (Continue)
To point:

Following is the command and prompt entry sequence for the LINE command, if the user wants to start a line from the last point.

LINE
RETURN

RETURN
SELECT A POINT

Therefore, in the screen menu file the LINE command has to be followed by two RETURNS to continue from the previous point.

Line 38
[.X   ].X
In this menu item .X extracts the X co-ordinate from a point. The bracket, .X and spaces inside the brackets ([.X   ]) are not needed. The line could consist of .X only. Same is true for the lines 39 thru 43.

For example
[.X   ].X   can also be written as   .X
[.Y   ].Y   .Y
[.Z   ].Z   .Z

Line 76
[STRETCH:]$S=X $S=STRETCH ^C^CSTRETCH C
In this menu item $S=X loads the submenu X, and $S=STRETCH loads the STRETCH submenu.   ^C^C cancels the existing command twice, and STRETCH is an AutoCAD command. The C is for the crossing option that prompts the user to enter two points to select the objects.

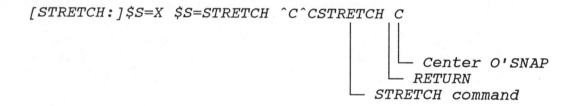

```
[STRETCH:]$S=X  $S=STRETCH  ^C^CSTRETCH  C
                                   │    │
                                   │    │
                                   │    └─ Center O'SNAP
                                   └─ RETURN
                              └─ STRETCH command
```

Line 133
[RAD]R \FILLET
This menu item selects the radius option of the FILLET command and then waits for the user to enter the radius. After entering the radius the FILLET command is executed again to generate the desired fillet between the two selected entities.

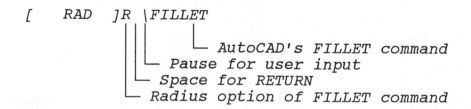

```
[    RAD    ]R  \FILLET
            │ │  │  │
            │ │  │  └─ AutoCAD's FILLET command
            │ │  └─ Pause for user input
            │ └─ Space for RETURN
            └─ Radius option of FILLET command
```

Line 134
[RAD 0]R 0 FILLET

This menu item selects the radius option of the FILLET command and assigns it a 0 value.   Then it executes the FILLET command to generate 0 fillet between the two selected entities.

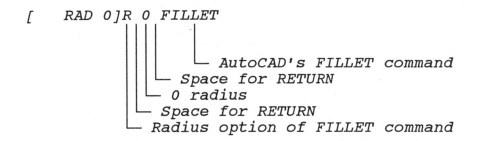

Line 136
[FILLET0:]^C^CFILLET R 0;;
This menu item defines a FILLET command with 0 radius and then generates 0 fillet between the two selected entities.

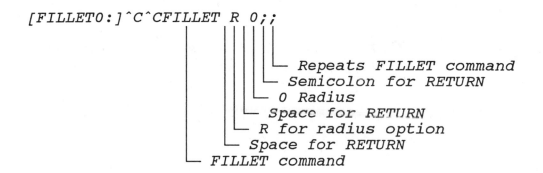

Line 155
[ZOOM:]'ZOOM
This menu item defines a transparent ZOOM command.

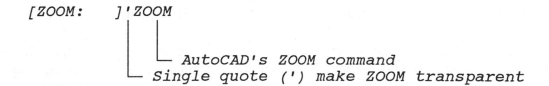

Note

The transparent zoom does not work with ZOOM All and ZOOM Extents, because these two commands regenerate the drawing.

Line 194
[Center]CEN $X=

In this menu item CEN is for center object snap, and $X= automatically recalls the previous screen menu after selecting the entity.

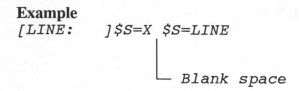

```
[Center  ]CEN $X=
                │    │
                │    └─ Loads previous menu
                └─ Center object snap
```

Note

If any menu item in a screen menu has more than one load command, they must be separated by a space.

Example

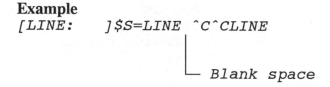

```
[LINE:   ]$S=X $S=LINE
              │
              └─ Blank space
```

2. *Similarly, if a menu item has load command and an AutoCAD command, they should also be separated by a space*

Example

```
[LINE:   ]$S=LINE ^C^CLINE
                 │
                 └─ Blank space
```

Changing Default Menu

When you start AutoCAD, the default menu file ACAD.MNU is automatically loaded, because AutoCAD is configured to load this menu. There are two ways to load the new menu automatically when you get into AutoCAD drawing editor.

One way to load the new menu automatically is to save the new menu file under the name ACAD.MNU. To try this, save the original ACAD.MNU file under a different name, let us say ACAD1.MNU. Now, copy the new menu file to ACAD.MNU. To copy the files, use the SHELL command and then the COPY command.

Command: SHELL
OS Commands: COPY ACAD.MNU ACAD1.MNU

Command: SHELL
OS Commands: COPY SM3.MNU ACAD.MNU

Exit AutoCAD, and then get back into the drawing editor by creating a new drawing or editing the existing drawing. You will notice that this time the new menu SM3.MNU has been loaded. You can also load the new menu automatically by configuring AutoCAD to load the new menu SM3 as discussed in chapter 1.

Note

1.   *Make sure the original ACAD.MNU file has been properly saved under a different name. If the ACAD menu file gets damaged you can always restore the original AutoCAD menu file.*

2.   *You may not have ACAD.MNU file loaded on the system. In that case copy ACAD.MNX to ACAD1.MNX and then load the modified ACAD.MNU file.*

Exercise 3

Write a screen menu for the following AutoCAD commands.   (File name SME3.MNU)

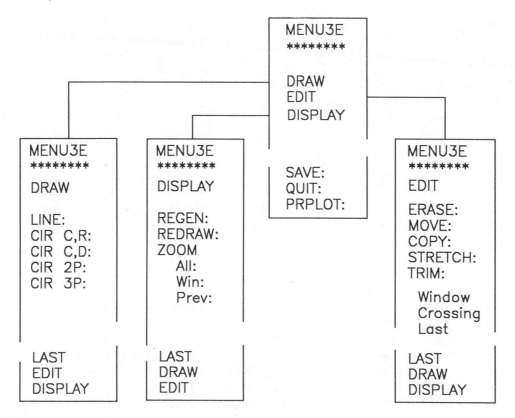

Figure 8   Screen menu design with submenus

Long Menu Definitions

You can put any number of commands in one screen menu line. There is no limit to the number of commands and the order in which they appear in the line, as long as they satisfy all the requirements of the command and the sequence of prompt entries. Again, it is very important to know the AutoCAD commands, the options in the command, the command prompts, and the entries for various prompts. If the statement can not fit on one line, you can put a plus (+) sign at the end of the first line and then continue with the second line. The command definition that involves several commands put together in one line is also called a macro. The following example illustrates a long menu item or a macro.

Example 4

Write a screen menu command definition that performs the following functions. (File name SM4.MNU)

Draw a border using polyline

Width =	0.01
Point-1	0,0
Point-2	12,0
Point-3	12,9
Point-4	0,9
Point-5	0,0

Initial drawing setup

Snap	0.25
Grid	0.5
Limits	12,9
Zoom	All

Before writing a menu the you should know the commands, options, prompts, and the prompt entries required for the commands. Therefore, first study the commands involved in the above mentioned drawing setup.

POLYLINE
Command: PLINE
From point: 0,0
Arc/Close/Halfwidth/Length/Undo/Width/<Endpoint of line>: W
Starting width <0.0000>:0.01
Ending width <0.01>: RETURN
Arc/Close/Halfwidth/Length/Undo/Width/<Endpoint of line>: 12,0
Arc/Close/Halfwidth/Length/Undo/Width/<Endpoint of line>: 12,9
Arc/Close/Halfwidth/Length/Undo/Width/<Endpoint of line>: 0,9
Arc/Close/Halfwidth/Length/Undo/Width/<Endpoint of line>: C

Screen menu command definition for PLINE
PLINE;0,0;W;0.01;;12,0;12,9;0,9;C

SNAP
Command: SNAP
Snap spacing or ON/OFF/Aspect/Rotate/Style <1.0000>: 0.25

Screen menu command definition for SNAP
SNAP;0.25

GRID
Command: GRID
Grid spacing(X) or ON/OFF/Snap/Aspect <0.0000>: 0.5

Screen menu command definition
GRID;0.5

LIMITS
Command: LIMITS
ON/OFF/<Lower left corner>: 0,0
Upper right corner <12.00,9,00>: 12,9

Screen menu command definition
LIMITS;0,0;12,9

ZOOM
Command: ZOOM
All/Center/Dynamic/Extents/Left/Previous/Window/<Scale(X)>: A

Screen menu command definition
ZOOM;A

Now, you can combine these individual command definitions to form a single screen menu command definition that will perform all the functions when you select NSETUP from the new screen menu.

Combined screen menu line

[-NSETUP-]PLINE;0,0;W;0.01;;12,0;12,9;0,9;C;+
SNAP;0.25;GRID;0.5;LIMITS;+
0,0;12,9;ZOOM;A

Exercise 4

Write a screen menu item that will set up the following parameters for the UNITS command. (File name SME4.MNU)
System of units: Scientific
Number of digits to right of decimal point: 2
System of angle measure: Decimal
Number of fractional places for display of angles: 2
Direction for angle: 0
Angles measured counter-clockwise

Use of Control Characters in Menu Items

You can use ASCII control characters in the command definition by using the caret sign (^) followed by the control character. For example, if you want to write a menu item that will toggle the SNAP off or on, you can use a caret sign followed by the control character B as shown in the following example.

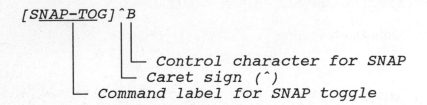

^B is equivalent to entering CTRL B from the keyboard that toggles the SNAP mode. SNAP-TOG is the menu item label that will be displayed on the screen menu. You can use any ASCII control character in the command definition. Following are some of the ASCII control characters:

^H	(Backspace)
^@	(ASCII code 0)
^[	(ASCII code 27)
^\	(ASCII code 28)
^]	(ASCII code 29)
^^	(ASCII code 30)
^-	(ASCII code 31)

Example 5

Write a screen menu for the following toggle functions.   (File name SM5.MNU)

ORTHO	SNAP
GRID	CO-ORDINATE DIAL
TABLET	ISOPLANE
PRINTER	CANCEL

Before writing a screen menu for these toggle functions, it is important to know the control characters that AutoCAD uses to turn these functions on or off.   The following is a list of the control characters for the functions in this example.

ORTHO	CTRL O
SNAP	CTRL B
GRID	CTRL G
COORDINATE DIAL	CTRL D
TABLET	CTRL T
ISOPLANE	CTRL E

```
PRINTER                CTRL Q
CANCEL                 CTRL C
```

The following file is a listing of the screen menu that toggle the given functions. You can use AutoCAD's EDIT command to write this file.

```
[-TOGGLE- ]
[         ]
[         ]
[         ]
[ORTHO    ]^O      ————————  turns ORTHO on/off
[SNAP     ]^B      ————————  turns SNAP on/off
[GRID     ]^G      ————————  turns GRID on/off
[CO-ORDS  ]^D      ————————  turns CO-ORD dial on/off
[TABLET   ]^T      ————————  turns TABLET on/off
[         ]
[ISOPLANE ]^E      ————————  turns ISOPLANE on/off
[PRINTER  ]^Q      ————————  turns PRINTER echo on/off
[         ]
[CANCEL   ]^C      ————————  AutoCAD command CANCEL
```

Command Definition without RETURN or SPACE

All command definitions that have been discussed so far use a semicolon (;) or a space for RETURN. However, sometimes a user might want to define a menu item that is not followed by a RETURN or a space. This is accomplished by using the backspace ASCII control character (^H). It is especially useful when you want to write a screen menu for a numeric keypad. ^H control character can be used with any character or a group of characters. The following is the format of menu item definition without a RETURN or space:

```
[9]9X^H
    │││└── ^H for backspace
    ││└─ X is erased because of ^H (backspace)
    ││    (X could be substituted by any character)
    │└─ character returned by selecting this item
    └─ Menu item label
```

^H is the ASCII control character for backspace. When you select this item, ^H erases the previous character X, and therefore returns 9 only. It is not necessary to have X preceding ^H. It could be any character. You can continue selecting more characters and when you are done, and you want to enter RETURN, use the keyboard or the digitizer.

Example 6

Write a screen menu for the following characters. (File name SM6.MNU)

```
0          5          .
1          6
2          7          X
3          8          Y
4          9          Z
```

The following file is a listing of the screen menu of Example 6 that will enable the user to pick the characters without a RETURN.

```
[-KEYPAD- ]
[          ]
[          ]
[          ]
[0]0Y^H                    ——————— returns 0
[1]1Y^H                    ——————— returns 1
[2]2Y^H                    ——————— returns 2
[3]3Y^H
[4]4Y^H
[5]5Y^H
[6]6Y^H
[7]7Y^H
[8]8Y^H
[9]9Y^H
[.].Y^H                    ——————— returns period (.)
[,],Y^H                    ——————— returns comma (,)
[]                         ——————— for space in the screen menu
[X]XX^H                    ——————— returns X
[Y]YX^H                    ——————— returns Y
[Z]ZZ^H                    ——————— returns Z
```

Note

You can also use a back slash, after the character, to continue selecting more characters. For example, [2]2\ will return 2 and then pause for the user input, which could be another character. The following file uses back slash (\) to let the user enter another character.

```
[-KEYPAD-
[          ]
[          ]
[          ]
[0]0\
[1]1\
[2]2\
[3]3\
[4]4\
[5]5\
```

```
[6]6\
[7]7\
[8]8\
[9]9\
[.].\
[,],\
[]
[X]X\
[Y]Y\
[Z]Z\
```

Menu Command Repetition

AutoCAD has made provision for repeating a menu item until cancelled by the user by entering CTRL C from the keyboard or selecting another menu item. It is particularly useful when editing a drawing and the same command is used several times. A command can be repeated if the menu command definition starts with an asterisk sign (*).

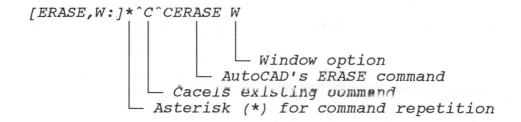

If you select this menu item, AutoCAD will prompt you to enter two points for selecting the objects, because window option for ERASE command requires two points. When you enter RETURN the objects you selected will be erased and the command will be repeated.

Example 7

Write a screen menu for the following AutoCAD commands. Make provision for automatically repeating the commands. (File name SM7.MNU)

LINE	LIST
ERASE	INSERT
TRIM	DIST

The following file is a listing of the screen menu of Example 7 that will repeat the selected command until cancelled by CTRL C.

```
[-REPEAT-  ]
[          ]
```

```
[                 ]
[LINE:            ]*^C^CLINE
[ERASE:           ]*^C^CERASE
[TRIM:            ]*^C^CTRIM
[LIST:            ]*^C^CLIST
[INSERT:          ]*^C^CINSERT
[DIST:            ]*^C^CDIST
```

Note

1. *If the command definition is incorrect and you happen to select that item, the screen prompt display will be repeated indefinitely. To get out of this infinite loop you must reboot the system. Entering CTRL C or selecting another command does not stop the display of the prompt.*

2. *One of the major drawbacks with the menu command repetition is that it does not let the user select a different command option. In the following menu item, the ERASE command uses C (Crossing) option to select the objects. When the command is repeated, it does not allow the user to use a different option for entity selection.*

    [ERASE,C:]*^C^CERASE C

Menu Items with "SIngle" and "AUto" Options

The "SIngle" and "AUto" options for object selection, combined with the menu item repetition can provide a powerful editing tool.

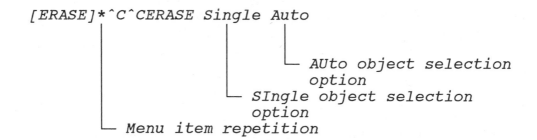

In this menu item the asterisk that follows the menu item label repeats the command. ^C^C cancels the existing command and ERASE is an AutoCAD command that erases the selected objects. The **Single** option enables the user to select the objects and then automatically terminate the object selection process. The editing command then edits the selected objects.

The **Auto** option enables the user to select one object using a pick box. If the point you pick is in a blank area (if there is no object), AutoCAD automatically defaults to BOX option of object selection, and the point you picked is taken as the first point of the BOX.

Menu Item Labels and HELP Command

As mentioned earlier, the menu item labels that are enclosed in the brackets is for screen display only and do not have any effect on the command definition. However, AutoCAD provides special handling for the HELP command and the menu item labels.

Normally, If you need help with any AutoCAD command, you type HELP followed by RETURN and the name of the command.

> **Command: HELP**
> **Command name (RETURN for list):**

To enter the command name you can also utilize AutoCAD's special help feature. When AutoCAD prompts for the Command name, you can select the menu item label from the screen menu. You can also obtain help while you are in the middle of a command by using **'HELP**. The following example illustrates the use of the HELP command and the menu item labels.

Example 8

Write a screen menu file for the following AutoCAD commands. Use the "SIngle" and "AUto" options for editing commands.

> LINE
> ERASE
> MOVE
> LIST
> HELP

The following file is a listing of the screen menu for Example 8.

```
[SI-A-HLP   ]
[           ]
[           ]
[LINE       ]*^C^CLINE
[ERASE      ]*^C^CERASE SI AU
[MOVE       ]*^C^CMOVE SI AU
[LIST       ]^C^CLIST SI AU
[           ]
[HELP       ]^C^CHELP
```

If you select the menu item HELP from the screen menu or if you type the HELP command, AutoCAD will prompt you to enter the command name. Instead of typing the command name, you can select the command (Menu item label) from the screen menu. In above example, if you select the menu label ERASE, AutoCAD will display the information about the ERASE command.

Use of AutoLISP in Menus

You can combine AutoLISP variables and expressions with the menu items as a command definition. When you select that item from the menu, it will evaluate all the expressions and generate the necessary output. The following examples illustrates the use of AutoLISP variables and expressions. (for more information on AutoLISP, see the chapters on AutoLISP)

Example 9

Write an AutoLISP program that draws a square and then write a screen menu that utilizes the AutoLISP variables and expressions to draw a square.

The following file is a listing of the AutoLISP program that generates a square. The program prompts the user to enter the starting point and the length of the side.

```
(DEFUN C:SQR()
(SETVAR "CMDECHO" 0)
(SETQ P1 (GETPOINT "\n ENTER STARTING POINT: "))
(SETQ S (GETDIST "\n ENTER LENGTH OF SIDE: "))
(SETQ P2 (LIST (+ (CAR P1) S) (CADR P1)))
(SETQ P3 (POLAR P2 (/ PI 2) S))
(SETQ P4 (POLAR P1 (/ PI 2) S))
(COMMAND "PLINE" P1 P2 P3 P4 "C")
(SETVAR "CMDECHO" 1)
(PRINC)
)
```

Following is the listing of the screen menu that utilizes the AutoLISP variables and expressions to draw a square.

```
[-SQUARE-  ]
[          ]
[          ]
[SQUARE:   ](SETQ P1(GETPOINT "ENTER STARTING POINT:+
 "));\+
(SETQ S (GETDIST "ENTER LENGTH OF SIDE: "));\+
(SETQ P2 (LIST (+ (CAR P1) S) (CADR P1)))+
(SETQ P3 (POLAR P2 (/ PI 2) S))+
(SETQ P4 (POLAR P1 (/ PI 2) S));+
PLINE !P1 !P2 !P3 !P4 C
```

If you compare the AutoLISP program with the screen menu, you will notice that the statements that prompt the user to enter the information, and the statements that do actual calculations are identical. Therefore the user can utilize AutoLISP variables and expressions in the menu file to customize AutoCAD.

Review

Fill in the blanks

1.   The name of the menu file that comes with AutoCAD software package is
      ....

2.   You can use .... command of DOS to write a menu file.

3.   The AutoCAD menu file can have up to .... sections.

4.   Tablet menu can have .... sections.

5.   The section label is designated by ....

6.   A submenu is designated by ....

7.   The part of the menu item that is inside the brackets is for .... only.

8.   Only the first .... characters can be displayed on the screen menu.

9.   If the number of characters inside the bracket exceeds 8 the screen menu
      .... work.

10.   In a menu file you can use .... to cancel the existing command.

11.   AutoCAD's .... command is used to load a new menu file.

12.   .... is used to input the information in a screen menu definition.

13.   The menu item .... be a combination of upper and lower case
      characters.

14.   Submenu names can be .... characters long.

15.   The maximum number of accessible menu items in a screen menu depends on the
      ....

Exercises

Exercise 5

Design and write a screen menu for the following AutoCAD commands. (File name SME5.MNU)

    POLYGON (Center)
    POLYGON (Edge)
    ELLIPSE (Center)
    ELLIPSE (Axis Endpoint)
    CHAMFER
    EXPLODE
    COPY

Exercise 6

Write a Screen Menu file for the following AutoCAD commands. Use submenus if required. (File name SME6.MNU)

ARC	ROTATE
-3P	ARRAY
-SCE	DIVIDE
-CSE	MEASURE
BLOCK	
INSERT	LAYER
WBLOCK	SET
MINSERT	LIST

Exercise 7

Write a screen menu item that will set up the following layers, linetypes and, colors. (File name SME7.MNU)

Layer Name	Color	Linetype
0	WHITE	CONTINUOUS
OBJECT	RED	CONTINUOUS
HIDDEN	YELLOW	HIDDEN
CENTER	BLUE	CENTER
DIM	GREEN	CONTINUOUS

Exercise 8

Write a screen menu for the following commands.   Use the menu item ******** to load O'Snaps, and the menu item   MENU-7   to load the root menu. (File name SME8.MNU)

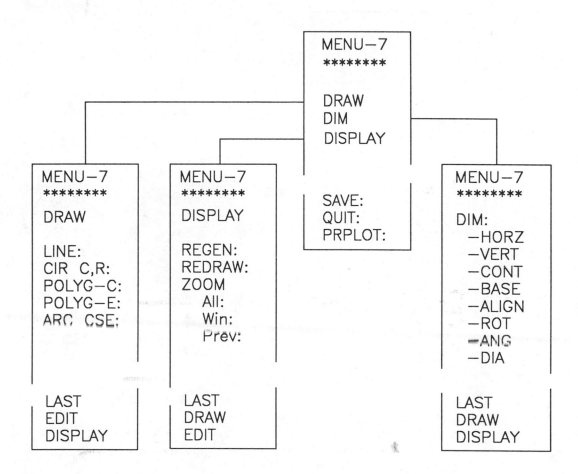

Figure 9   Screen menu displays

Chapter 7

Tablet Menu

Standard Tablet Menu

The tablet menu provides a powerful alternative for entering commands. In the tablet menu, the commands are picked from the template that is secured on the surface of a digitizing tablet. To use the tablet menu you need a digitizing tablet and a pointing device. You also need a tablet template (Fig 1) that contains AutoCAD commands arranged in various groups for easy identification.

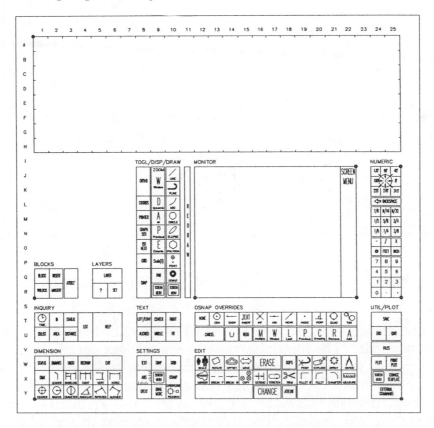

Figure 1   Sample Tablet Template

145

The AutoCAD menu file has 4 tablet menu sections TABLET1, TABLET2, TABLET3, and TABLET4. In addition to this the menu file also has 4 alternate tablet menu sections TABLET1ALT, TABLET2ALT, TABLET3ALT, and TABLET4ALT. When you start AutoCAD and get into the drawing editor, the tablet menu sections TABLET1, TABLET2, TABLET3, and TABLET4 are automatically loaded. The commands defined in these four sections are then assigned to various blocks of the template. To use the alternate tablet menu, you need to load the required tablet menu before you can select the commands from the alternate tablet menu. You can load the alternate tablet menus by selecting the appropriate block from the template swap menu. The template swap menu is located just below the screen pointing area on the right.

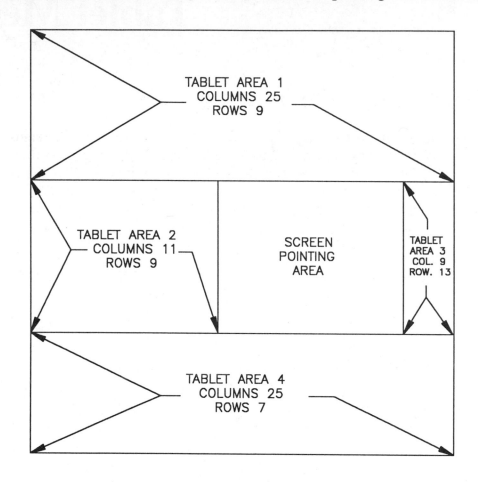

Figure 2A   Four tablet areas of AutoCAD tablet template

The first tablet menu section (TABLET1) has 225 lines that can be used to assign new commands. The remaining tablet menu sections contain various AutoCAD commands, arranged in different groups that make it easier for the user to identify and access these commands. The commands that are contained in the TABLET2 section include ucs, xref, display, draw, blocks and layer. The TABLET3 section contains numbers, fractions, and angles. The commands contained in the TABLET4 section include inquiry, text, osnap overrides, dimension, settings, edit, utility and plot commands.

The AutoCAD tablet template has four tablet areas (Fig 2A) that correspond to four tablet menu sections TABLET1, TABLET2, TABLET3, and TABLET4. If you are using the alternate tablet menus these tablet areas correspond to alternate tablet menu sections TABLET1ALT, TABLET2ALT, TABLET3ALT, and TABLET4ALT (Figure 2B).

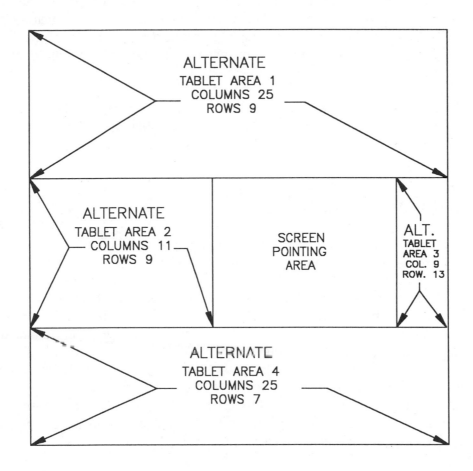

Figure 2B   Alternate tablet menu areas

Advantages of Tablet Menu

The tablet menu has the following advantages over the screen menu, pull-down menu, icon menu, or the keyboard.

1. In the tablet menu the commands can be arranged in way so that the most frequently used commands can be accessed directly. This can save considerable time in entering AutoCAD commands. Whereas in the screen menu some of the commands can not be accessed directly. For example, to generate a horizontal dimension the user has to go through several steps. First you select DIM from the root menu, then linear, and then horizontal dimensioning option. Whereas in the tablet menu you can select the horizontal dimensioning command directly from the digitizer. This saves

time, and eliminates the distraction that takes place as you page through different screens.

2. You can have the graphical symbols of the AutoCAD commands drawn on the tablet template. This makes it lot easier for the user to recognize and select the commands. For example, if the user is not an expert in AutoCAD dimensioning, the baseline and continue dimensioning can be confusing. But, if the command is supported by the graphical symbol of what a command does, the chances of selecting a wrong command are minimized.

3. You can assign any number of commands to the tablet overlay. The number of commands you can assign to a tablet is limited only by the size of the digitizer, and the size of the rectangular blocks.

Customizing Tablet Menu

Like screen menu, you can write a tablet menu to customize the AutoCAD tablet menu. It is a powerful tool to customize AutoCAD and makes it more efficient.

The tablet menu can have a maximum of 4 sections TABLET1, TABLET2, TABLET3, and TABLET4 or TABLET1ALT, TABLET2ALT, TABLET3ALT, TABLET4ALT. Each section represents a certain rectangular area on the digitizing tablet. These rectangular areas can be further divided into any number of rectangular blocks. The size of the blocks depends on the number of commands that are assigned to the tablet area. Also, the rectangular tablet areas can be located anywhere on the digitizer, and arranged in any order. AutoCAD's TABLET command can be used to configure the tablet. The MENU command then loads and assigns the commands to the rectangular blocks on the tablet template.

Before writing a tablet menu file, it is very important to design the layout of the tablet template. A well thought out design can save lot of revision time in the long run. The following points should be considered when designing a tablet template.

1. Get a good understanding of the AutoCAD commands that you use in your profession.

2. Group the commands based on their function, use, or their relationship with other commands.

3. Draw a rectangle representing a template, and locate the screen pointing area. The screen pointing area should be located so that it is convenient for the user to move around the pointing device. The size of this area should be appropriate to your application. It should not be too large or too small. Also, the size of the template depends on the active area of the digitizer.

4. Divide the remaining area into four different tablet areas for TABLET1, TABLET2, TABLET3, and TABLET4. It is not necessary to have 4 areas. You can have any number of tablet areas, but the maximum is four.

5. Determine the number of commands that you need to assign to a particular tablet area, and then determine the number of rows and columns you need to generate in each area. The size of the blocks do not need to be same in different tablet areas.

6. Use the text command to print the commands on the tablet overlay, and draw the symbols of the command, if possible.

7. Plot the tablet overlay on a good quality paper or a sheet of mylar. If you want the plotted side of the template to face the digitizer board, you can create a mirror image of the tablet overlay and then plot the mirror image.

Writing Tablet Menu

When writing a table menu it is very important to understand the AutoCAD commands and the prompt entries required for each command. Also, equally important is the design of the tablet template and the placement of various commands on the template. The user should give a considerable thought to the design and layout of the template, and if possible invite suggestions from AutoCAD users in your trade. To understand the process that is involved in developing and writing a tablet menu, consider the following example.

Example 1

Write a tablet menu for the following AutoCAD commands. The commands are to be arranged as shown in the Figure 3. Use the template at the end of this chapter for configuration and command selection. (File name TM1.MNU)

Line
Pline
Circle
Circle C,D
Circle 2P
Erase

Figure 3 represents one of the possible template designs where the AutoCAD commands are in one row at the top of the template, and the screen menu area is in the center. In this template there is only one area, therefore you can place all these commands under the section label TABLET1. To write a menu file you can use AutoCAD's EDIT command, Edlin function of DOS, or any text editor.

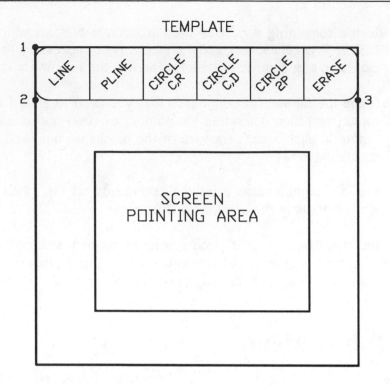

Figure 3   Design of tablet template

The name of the file is TM1, and the extension of the file is .MNU.   The line numbers are not a part of the file.   They are shown here for reference only.

***TABLET1	1
^C^CLINE	2
^C^CPLINE	3
^C^CCIRCLE	4
^C^CCIRCLE \D	5
^C^CCIRCLE 2P	6
^C^CERASE	7

Line 1
***TABLET1
TABLET1 is the section label of the first tablet area.   All the section labels are preceded by three asterisks (***).

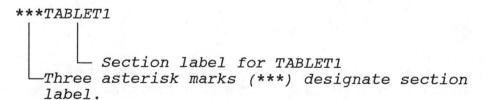

Line 2
^C^CLINE

^C^C cancels the existing command twice and LINE is an AutoCAD command. There is no space between the second ^C and LINE.

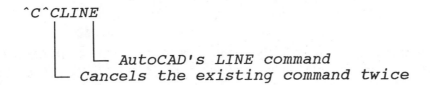

```
^C^CLINE


          └── AutoCAD's LINE command
     └── Cancels the existing command twice
```

Line 3
^C^CPLINE
^C^C cancels the existing command twice and the PLINE is an AutoCAD command.

Line 4
^C^CCIRCLE
^C^C cancels the existing command twice, and CIRCLE is an AutoCAD command. The default input for the CIRCLE command is the center and the radius of the circle. Therefore no additional input is required for this line.

Line 5
^C^CCIRCLE \D
^C^C cancels the existing command twice and the CIRCLE is an AutoCAD command like the previous line. However, in this command definition it requires the diameter option of the circle command. This is accomplished by using \D in the command definition. There should be no space between the back slash (\) and D, but there should always be a space before the back slash (\). The back slash (\) lets the user enter a point, and in this case it is the center point of the circle. After entering the center point, the diameter option is selected by the letter D that follows the back slash (\).

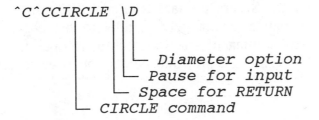

```
^C^CCIRCLE \D


               └── Diameter option
            └── Pause for input
         └── Space for RETURN
     └── CIRCLE command
```

Line 6
^C^CCIRCLE 2P
^C^C cancels the existing command twice and the CIRCLE is an AutoCAD command. The 2P selects the two point option of the CIRCLE command.

Line 7
^C^CERASE

^C^C cancels the existing command twice, and ERASE is an AutoCAD command that erases the selected entities.

Note

1. In the tablet menu, the part of the menu item that is enclosed in the brackets is ignored. For example, in the following menu item, T1-6 will be ignored and it will have no effect on the command definition.

```
        ┌ For reference only and has no effect
     ┌──┤  on the command definition
 ────┘  │
[T1-6]^C^CCIRCLE 2P
 │      │
 │      └─ Item number 6
 └─ Tablet area 1
```

2. The reference information can be used to designate the tablet area and the line number.

3. Before you can use the commands from the new tablet menu, you need to configure the tablet and load the tablet menu.

Tablet Configuration

To use the new template for selecting the commands the tablet needs to be configured so that the AutoCAD knows the location of the tablet template and the position of the commands that are assigned to each block. This is accomplished by using AutoCAD's TABLET command. Secure the tablet template (Figure 3) on the digitizer with the edges of the overlay approximately parallel to the edges of the digitizer. Enter AutoCAD's TABLET command, select the configure option, and then respond to the following prompts. Figure 4 shows the points you need to select to configure the tablet.

Command: TABLET
Options (ON/OFF/CAL/CFG):CFG
Enter number of tablet menus desired (0-4): 1
Do you want to realign tablet menu areas? <N>: Y
Digitize upper left corner of menu area 1; P1
Digitize lower left corner of menu area 1; P2
Digitize lower right corner of menu area 1; P3
Enter the number of columns for menu area 1; 7
Enter the number of rows for menu area 1; 1
Do you want to re-specify the screen pointing area? <N>:Y
Digitize lower left corner of screen pointing area: P4

Digitize upper right corner of screen pointing area: P5

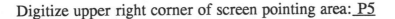

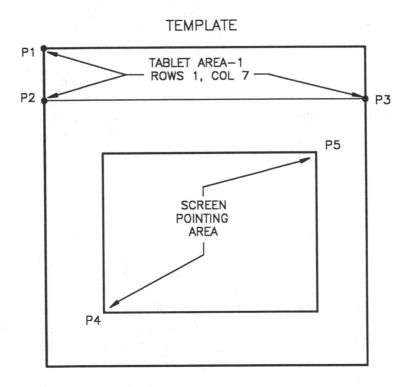

Figure 4 Points that need to be selected to configure the tablet

Note

1. *The three points p1, p2, p3 should form a 90 degree angle. If the selected points do not form a 90 degree angle the system will prompt you to enter the points again until they form a 90 degree angle.*

2. *The tablet areas should not overlap the screen pointing area.*

3. *The screen pointing area could be of any size and anywhere on the tablet as long as it is within the active area of the digitizer. The screen pointing area should not overlap other tablet areas. The screen pointing area you select will correspond to the monitor screen area. Therefore, the length to width ratio of the screen pointing area should be the same as that of the monitor, unless you are using the screen pointing area to digitize a drawing.*

Loading Menus

AutoCAD software comes with a compiled menu file ACAD.MNX that is automatically loaded when you get into drawing editor, provided the default settings have not been changed on your system. Otherwise, it will load the default menu file, or the menu that is referenced by the prototype drawing. To load a new menu you can use AutoCAD's MENU command.

Command: MENU
Menu file name or . for none <current>: (file name)

To load the new menu, enter the file name of the tablet menu (TM1) without the extension .MNU. AutoCAD will load the new tablet menu TM1, and then you can select the commands from the digitizer by picking a point in the block that contains the desired command.

Note

1. When you load the tablet menu, some of the commands will be displayed on the screen menu area. This happens because the screen menu area is empty. If the menu file contained a screen menu also, then the tablet menu commands will not be displayed in the screen menu.

2. When you load a new menu the original menu you had on the screen, prior to loading the new menu, is disabled. You can not select commands from the screen menu, pull-down menu, pointing device, or the digitizer, unless the new menu file contains these menus.

3. To load the original menu use the MENU command again, and enter the name of the menu file.

Exercise 1

Write a tablet menu for the following AutoCAD commands. Use the tablet menu template at the end of this chapter for configuration, and command selection. (File name is TME1.mnu)

Line	Text-Center
Circle C,R	Text-Left
Arc C.S.E	Text-Right
Ellipse	Text-Aligned
Donut	

Use the template in Figure 5 to arrange the commands. The draw and the text commands should be placed in two separate tablet areas.

TEMPLATE

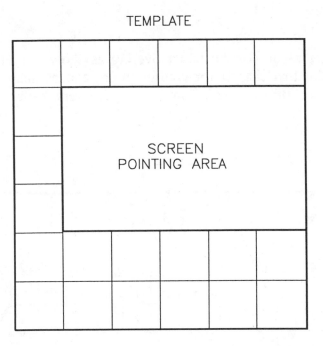

Figure 5   Template for Exercise 1

Tablet Menus with Different Block Sizes

As mentioned earlier, the size of each tablet area could be different. Also, the size of the blocks in these tablet areas could be different. But the size of every block in a particular tablet area must be same. This provides a lot of flexibility to the user in designing a template. For example, a user might prefer to have smaller blocks for numbers, fractions, or letters, and larger blocks for draw commands. You can also arrange these tablet areas to design a template layout with different shapes like: L shape, or a T shape.

Tablet Area-1   **Tablet Area-2**

The following example illustrates the use of multiple tablet areas with different block sizes.

Example 2

Write a tablet menu for the tablet overlay as shown in Figure 6A. Use the template at the end of this chapter for configuration, and command selection. Figure 6B shows the number of rows and columns in different tablet areas. (File name TM2.MNU)

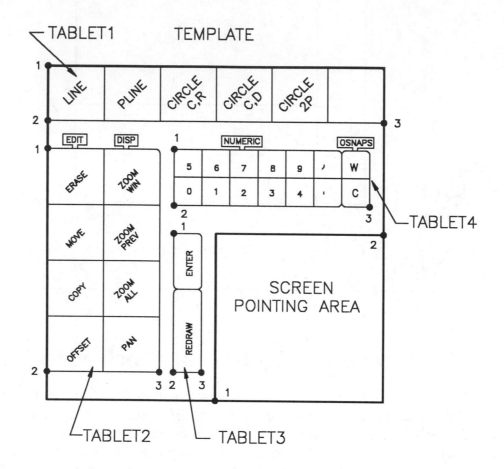

Figure 6A   Tablet overlay for Example 2

You will notice that this tablet template has four different sections in addition to the screen pointing area. Therefore, this menu will have four section labels TABLET1, TABLET2, TABLET3, and TABLET4. You can use AutoCAD's EDIT command to write the file.

The following file is a listing of the tablet menu of Example 2.

```
***TABLET1                                          1
 ^C^CLINE                                           2
 ^C^CPLINE                                          3
 ^C^CCIRCLE                                         4
 ^C^CCIRCLE \D                                      5
 ^C^CCIRCLE 2P                                      6
```

TEMPLATE

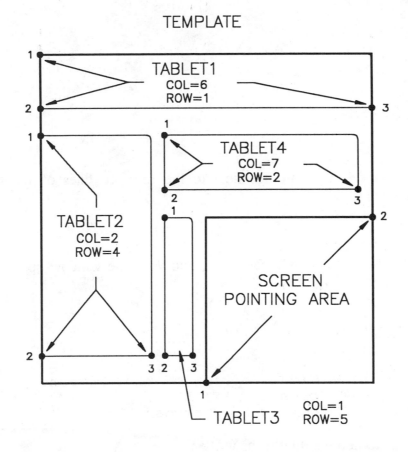

Figure 6B   Number of rows and columns in different tablet areas

***TABLET2	7
^C^CERASE	8
^C^CZOOM W	9
^C^CMOVE	10
^C^CZOOM P	11
^C^CCCOPY	12
^C^CZOOM A	13
^C^COFFSET	14
^C^CPAN	15
***TABLET3	16
;	17
;	18
REDRAW	19
REDRAW	20
REDRAW	21
***TABLET4	22
5\	23
6\	24
7\	25
8\	26
9\	27
,\	28

```
WINDOW                                              29
0\                                                  30
1\                                                  31
2\                                                  32
3\                                                  33
4\                                                  34
.\                                                  35
CROSSING                                            36
```

Line 1-6
The first six lines are identical to the first six lines of the tablet menu in Example 1.

Line 9
^C^CZOOM W
ZOOM is an AutoCAD command, and W is the window option of the ZOOM command.

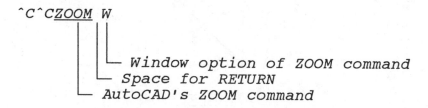

This menu item could also be written as

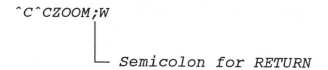

Line 17 & 18
The semicolon (;) is for RETURN. It has the same effect as entering RETURN form the keyboard.

Line 19-21
REDRAW
REDRAW is an AutoCAD command that redraws the screen. Notice that there are no ^C^C in front of the REDRAW command. If it had ^C^C then the existing command will be cancelled before redrawing the screen. This may not be a desired practice in most applications, because the user might like to redraw the screen without cancelling the existing command.

Line 23
5
The back slash (\) is used to introduce a pause for user input. Without the back slash you can not enter another number or a character, because after you select the digit 5 it will be automatically followed by RETURN. For example,

without the back slash (\) it will not be possible to enter a number like: 5.6. Therefore back slash is necessary to enable the user to enter decimal numbers or any characters. To terminate the input enter RETURN from the key board, or pick RETURN from the digitizer.

```
5 \
  |
  |
  └─  Back slash  (\)  for user input
```

Assigning Commands to Tablet

After loading the menu with the AutoCAD's MENU command, you must configure the tablet. It is at the time of configuration that AutoCAD actually generates and stores the information about the rectangular blocks on the tablet template. When you load the menu, the commands defined in the tablet menu are assigned to various blocks. For example, when you pick the three points for the tablet area 4 (Figure 6A), and enter the number of rows and columns, AutoCAD generates a grid of seven columns and two rows as shown in the following diagram.

After Configuration

When you load the new menu, AutoCAD takes the commands under the section label TABLET4 and starts filling the blocks from left to right. That means "5", "6", "7", "8", "9", "," and "Window" will be placed in the top row. The next seven commands will be assigned to the next row, starting from the left as shown in the following diagram.

After Loading Tablet Menu

5	6	7	8	9	,	Window
0	1	2	3	4	.	Cross

Similarly, the tablet area 3 has been divided into 5 rows and 1 column. At first, it appears that this tablet area has only two rows and one column (Figure 6A). When you configure this tablet area by picking the three points and entering the number of rows and columns, AutoCAD divides the area in one column and 5 rows as shown in the following diagrams

After Configuration   After Loading Menu

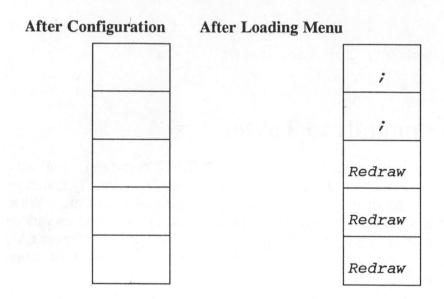

After loading the menu, AutoCAD takes the commands in the TABLET3 section of the tablet menu and assigns them to the blocks. The first command ";" is placed in the first block. Since there are no more blocks in the first row, therefore the next command ";" is placed in the second row. Similarly, the three REDRAW commands are placed in the next three rows. If you pick a point in the first two rows, you will select an ENTER command. Similarly, if you pick a point in the next three blocks, you will select the REDRAW command.

This process is carried out for all the tablet areas, and the information is stored in the AutoCAD configuration file ACAD.CFG. If for any reason the configuration is not right, the tablet menu may not perform the desired function.

Exercise 2

Write a tablet menu for the AutoCAD commands as shown in the Figure 7. Configure the tablet and then load the new menu. Use the tablet menu template at the end of this chapter for configuration, and command selection. (File name TME2.MNU)

TEMPLATE

SAVE	QUIT	END	PRPLOT	PLOT	⊕ / , 5 6 7 8 9 / X – • 0 1 2 3 4		
			ERASE	ZOOM WIN	REDRAW		
			MOVE	ZOOM PREV	SCREEN POINTING AREA		
			COPY	ZOOM ALL			
			OFFSET	PAN			
			TRIM	ZOOM EXTENTS	ENTER		
			CEN	ENDP	INT	LINE	PLINE	ELLIPSE
EDIT	CHANGE		MID	NEAR	PERP	CIRCLE	CIRCLE C,D	CIRCLE 2P

Figure 7   Tablet overlay for Exercise 2

Combined Screen and Tablet Menus

The screen menu and the tablet menu can be combined together in one file. The file can be written in a way so that if you select a command on the digitizer tablet, the corresponding screen menu will be loaded and displayed on the screen. For example, if you select the ARC command from the tablet menu, the corresponding ARC command with its options will be loaded on the screen menu, and you can select the ARC options from the screen menu. This is a very desired feature in a menu file, because it makes it convenient for the user to select the commands and their options.

You can load any menu that is defined in the screen menu section, from the tablet menu, by using the following load command.

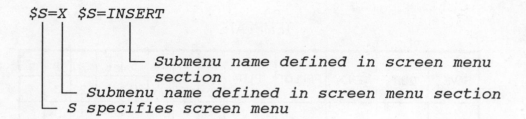

```
$S=X  $S=INSERT


                    Submenu name defined in screen menu
                    section
            Submenu name defined in screen menu section
      S specifies screen menu
```

The first load command ($S=X) loads the submenu X that has been defined in the screen menu section of the menu file. The X submenu can contain 21 blank lines, so that when it is loaded it clears the screen menu. The second load command ($S=INSERT) loads the submenu INSERT that has been defined in the screen menu section of the menu file. The following example illustrates the procedure to develop a combined menu.

Example 3

Write a combined screen and tablet menu for the commands shown in the tablet menu template Figure 8A, and the screen menu Figure 8B. When the user selects a command from the digitizer template, it should automatically load the corresponding screen menu on the screen. (File name TM3.MNU)

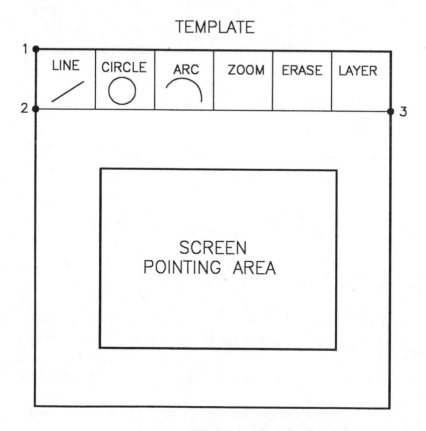

Figure 8A   Tablet menu template for Example 3

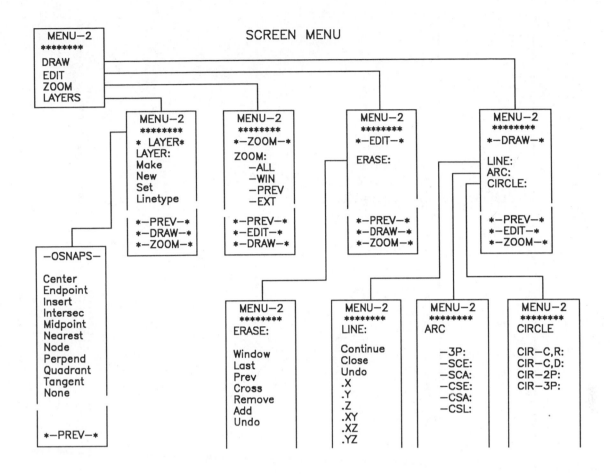

Figure 8B   Screen menu displays

The following file is a listing of the combined menu for Example 3.

```
***SCREEN                                              1
**S                                                    2
[ MENU-3    ]^C^C$S=X $S=S                             3
[********   ]$S=OSNAP                                  4
[           ]                                          5
[           ]                                          6
[DRAW       ]^C^C$S=X $S=DRAW                          7
[EDIT       ]^C^C$S=X $S=EDIT                          8
[ZOOM       ]^C^C$S=X $S=ZOOM                          9
[LAYER      ]^C^C$S=X $S=LAYER                        10
                                                      11
**DRAW 3                                              12
[*-DRAW-*   ]                                         13
[           ]                                         14
[           ]                                         15
[LINE:      ]$S=X $S=LINE ^C^CLINE                    16
[ARC:       ]$S=X $S=ARC                              17
[CIRCLE:    ]$S=X $S=CIRCLE ^C^CCIRCLE                18
```

```
[                  ]                                         19
[                  ]                                         20
[                  ]                                         21
[                  ]                                         22
[                  ]                                         23
[                  ]                                         24
[                  ]                                         25
[                  ]                                         26
[                  ]                                         27
[*-PREV-*   ]$S= $S=                                         28
[*-EDIT-*   ]^C^C$S=X $S=EDIT                                29
[*-ZOOM-*  ]$S=X $S=ZOOM                                     30
                                                             31
**LINE 3                                                     32
[LINE:      ]^C^CLINE                                        33
[                  ]                                         34
[                  ]                                         35
[Continue   ]^C^CLINE;;                                      36
[Close      ]CLOSE                                           37
[Undo       ]UNDO                                            38
[.X         ].X                                              39
[.Y         ].Y                                              40
[.Z         ].Z                                              41
[.XY        ].XY                                             42
[.XZ        ].XZ                                             43
[.YZ        ].YZ                                             44
[                  ]                                         45
[                  ]                                         46
[                  ]                                         47
[*-PREV-*   ]$S= $S=                                         48
[*-EDIT-*   ]^C^C$S=X $S=EDIT                                49
[*-ZOOM-*  ]$S=X $S=ZOOM                                     50
                                                             51
**ARC 3                                                      52
[ARC        ]                                                53
[                  ]                                         54
[   -3P:     ]^C^CARC \\DRAG                                 55
[   -SCE:    ]^C^CARC \C \DRAG                               56
[   -SCA:    ]^C^CARC \C \A DRAG                             57
[   -CSE:    ]^C^CARC C \\DRAG                               58
[   -CSA:    ]^C^CARC C \\A DRAG                             59
[   -CSL:    ]^C^CARC C \\L DRAG                             60
[                  ]                                         61
[                  ]                                         62
[                  ]                                         63
[                  ]                                         64
[                  ]                                         65
[                  ]                                         66
[                  ]                                         67
[*-PREV-*   ]$S= $S=                                         68
[*-EDIT-*   ]^C^C$S=X $S=EDIT                                69
[*-ZOOM-*  ]$S=X $S=ZOOM                                     70
                                                             71
**CIRCLE   3                                                 72
```

```
[CIRCLE:    ]                                          73
[           ]                                          74
[   -C,R:   ]^C^CCIRCLE                                75
[   -C,D:   ]^C^CCIRCLE \D                             76
[   -2P:    ]^C^CCIRCLE 2P                             77
[   -3P:    ]^C^CCIRCLE 3P                             78
[           ]                                          79
[           ]                                          80
[           ]                                          81
[           ]                                          82
[           ]                                          83
[           ]                                          84
[           ]                                          85
[           ]                                          86
[           ]                                          87
[*-PREV-*   ]$S= $S=                                   88
[*-EDIT-*   ]^C^C$S=X $S=EDIT                          89
[*-ZOOM-*   ]$S=X $S=ZOOM                              90
                                                       91
                                                       92
**EDIT 3                                               93
[*-EDIT-*   ]                                          94
[           ]                                          95
[           ]                                          96
[ERASE:     ]$S=X $S=ERASE ^C^CERASE                   97
[           ]                                          98
[           ]                                          99
[           ]                                          100
[           ]                                          101
[           ]                                          102
[           ]                                          103
[           ]                                          104
[           ]                                          105
[           ]                                          106
[           ]                                          107
[           ]                                          108
[*-PREV-*   ]$S= $S=                                   109
[*-DRAW-*   ]^C^C$S=X $S=DRAW                          110
[*-ZOOM-*   ]$S=X $S=ZOOM                              111
                                                       112
**ERASE 3                                              113
[ERASE:     ]^C^CERASE                                 114
[           ]                                          115
Window                                                 116
Last                                                   117
Prev                                                   118
Cross                                                  119
Remove                                                 120
Add                                                    121
Undo                                                   122
[           ]                                          123
[           ]                                          124
[           ]                                          125
[           ]                                          126
```

```
[                  ]                                    127
[                  ]                                    128
[*-PREV-*          ]$S= $S=                             129
[*-DRAW-*          ]^C^C$S=X $S=DRAW                    130
[*-ZOOM-*          ]$S=ZOOM                             131
                                                       132
**ZOOM 3                                               133
[*-ZOOM-*          ]                                    134
[                  ]                                    135
[                  ]                                    136
[ZOOM:             ]'ZOOM                               137
[  -ALL            ]A                                   138
[  -WIN            ]W                                   139
[  -PREV           ]P                                   140
[  -EXT            ]E                                   141
[                  ]                                    142
[                  ]                                    143
[                  ]                                    144
[                  ]                                    145
[                  ]                                    146
[                  ]                                    147
[                  ]                                    148
[*-PREV-*          ]$S= $S=                             149
[*-EDIT-*          ]^C^C$S=X $S=EDIT                    150
[*-DRAW-*          ]$S=X $S=DRAW                        151
                                                       152
***LAYER  3                                            153
[*-LAYER*          ]                                    154
[                  ]                                    155
[                  ]                                    156
[LAYER:            ]^C^CLAYER                           15
Make                                                   158
New                                                    159
Set                                                    160
Linetype                                               161
Color                                                  162
[List              ]?;;                                163
[                  ]                                    164
[                  ]                                    165
[                  ]                                    166
[                  ]                                    167
[                  ]                                    168
[*-PREV-*          ]$S= $S=                             169
[*-EDIT-*          ]^C^C$S=X $S=EDIT                    170
[*-DRAW-*          ]$S=X $S=DRAW                        171
                                                       172
**X 3                                                  173
[                  ]                                    174
[                  ]                                    175
[                  ]                                    176
[                  ]                                    177
[                  ]                                    178
[                  ]                                    179
[                  ]                                    180
```

```
[                    ]                                  181
[                    ]                                  182
[                    ]                                  183
[                    ]                                  184
[                    ]                                  185
[                    ]                                  186
[                    ]                                  187
[                    ]                                  188
[                    ]                                  189
[                    ]                                  190
[                    ]                                  191
                                                       192
**OSNAP 2                                              193
[-OSNAPS-  ]                                            194
[                    ]                                  195
[Center      ]CEN $S=                                  196
[Endpoint    ]END $S=                                  197
[Insert      ]INS $S=                                  198
[Intersec    ]INT $S=                                  199
[Midpoint    ]MID $S=                                  200
[Nearest     ]NEA $S=                                  201
[Node        ]NOD $S=                                  202
[Perpend     ]PER $S=                                  203
[Quadrant    ]QUA $S=                                  204
[Tangent     ]TAN $S=                                  205
[None        ]NONE $S=                                 206
[                    ]                                  207
[                    ]                                  208
[                    ]                                  209
[                    ]                                  210
[                    ]                                  211
[*-PREV-*    ]$S=                                       212
                                                       213
***TABLET1                                             214
$S=X $S=LINE ^C^CLINE                                   215
$S=X $S=CIRCLE ^C^CCIRCLE                               216
$S=X $S=ARC ^C^CARC                                     217
$S=X $S=ZOOM ^C^CZOOM                                   218
$S=X $S=ERASE ^C^CERASE                                 219
$S=X $S=LAYER ^C^CLAYER                                 220
```

Line 1
***SCREEN
This is the section label for the screen menu, and the line numbers 1 through 213 are defined in this section of the menu file.

Line 3
[MENU-3]^C^C$S=X $S=S
In this menu item $S=X loads the submenu X, and $S=S loads the submenu S.

Line 7
[DRAW   ]^C^C$S=X $S=DRAW

In this menu item $S=DRAW loads the submenu DRAW that is defined in the menu file.

Line 12
**DRAW 3
In this menu item DRAW is the name of the submenu, and the 3 forces the submenu to be displayed on line 3. Since nothing is printed on the first two lines, therefore [MENU-3] and [********] will be displayed on the screen all the time. If you select [MENU-3] from any menu, it will load the submenu S and display it on the screen, Similarly, if you pick [********] from any menu, it will load and display the OSNAP submenu.

Line 28
[*-PREV-*]$S= $S=
In this menu item $S= $S= loads the previous two submenus. One of them is the submenu X and the second submenu is the one that was displayed on the screen before the current menu.

Line 214
***TABLET1
TABLET1 is the section label for the tablet area 1. The line numbers 215 through 220 are defined in this section.

Line 215
$S=X $S=LINE ^C^CLINE
$S=X, defined in the screen menu section, loads the submenu X on the screen menu area. The purpose of loading the submenu X is to clear the screen so that there is no overlapping of the screen menu items. $S=LINE, defined in the screen menu section, loads the LINE submenu on the screen menu. ^C^CLINE cancels the existing command twice and then executes AutoCAD's LINE command.

When you select the LINE block from the digitizer, AutoCAD automatically clears the screen menu, loads the LINE submenu, and enters a LINE command. This makes it easier for the user to select the command options from the screen menu, since they are not on the digitizer template.

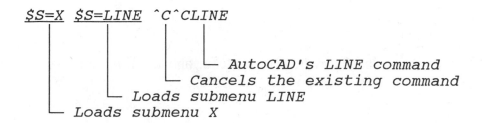

Exercise 3

Write a combined screen and tablet menu file for the commands shown in the tablet menu template in Figure 9. Design the screen menu as shown in Example 3. Use the tablet menu template at the end of this chapter for configuration, and command selection. (File name TME3.MNU)

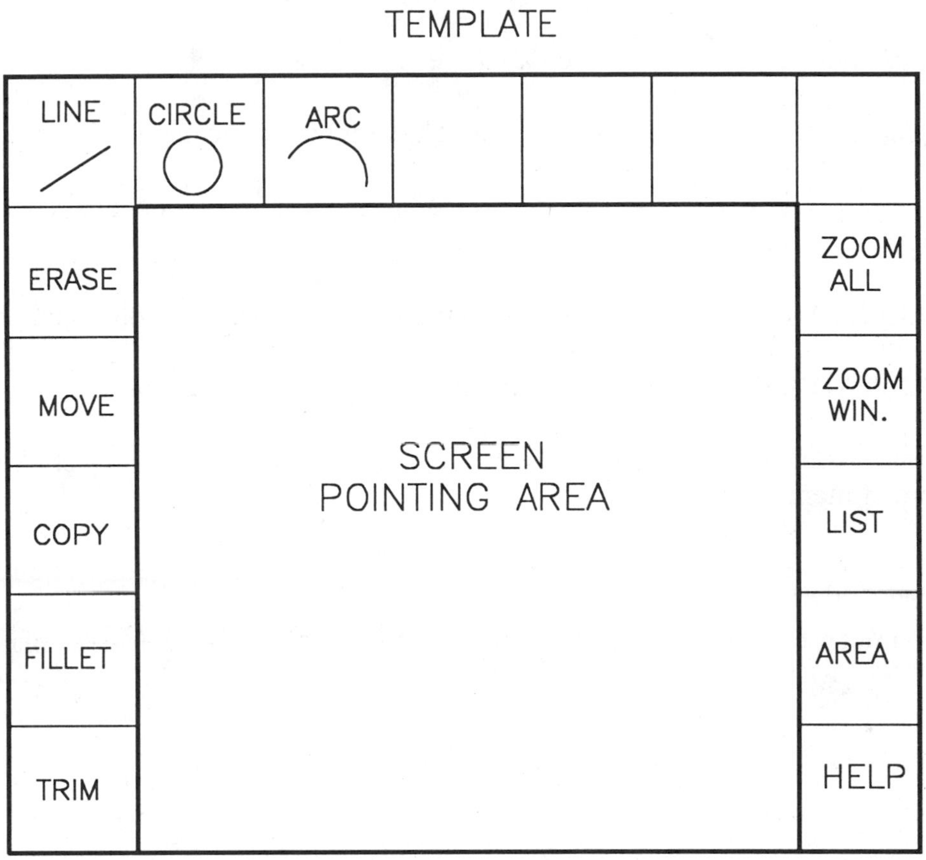

TEMPLATE

Figure 9   Tablet menu template for Exercise 3

Review

Fill in the blanks

1. The maximum number of tablet menu sections is ....

2. A tablet menu area is .... in shape

3. The blocks in any tablet menu area are .... in shape.

4. A tablet menu area can have .... number of rectangular blocks.

5. You .... assign same command to more than one block on the tablet menu template.

6. AutoCAD's .... command is used to configure the tablet menu template.

7. AutoCAD's .... command is used to load a new menu.

8. When using the tablet menu, you .... load a submenu defined under the screen menu section.

9. The screen menu and the tablet menu .... be combined in one file.

10. You need to enter .... points to configure any area in a template.

Exercises

Exercise 4

Design the template and write a tablet menu to insert the following user defined blocks.

BX1   BX5   BX9
BX2   BX6   BX10
BX3   BX7   BX11
BX4   BX8   BX12

Exercise 5

Design the template and the screen menu for the following AutoCAD commands.

LINE   ZOOM-Win   DIM-Horz
PLINE   ZOOM-Dyn   DIM-Vert
ARC   ZOOM-All   DIM-Alig
CIRCLE   ZOOM-Pre   DIM-Ang
ELLIPSE   ZOOM-Ext   DIM-Rad
POLYGON   ZOOM-Scl   DIM-Cen

Exercise 6

Write a combined tablet and screen menu file for the AutoCAD commands in Exercise 5.

Exercise 7

Write a tablet menu file for the AutoCAD commands shown in the template (Figure 10). Use the template at the end of the chapter for configuration, and command selection.

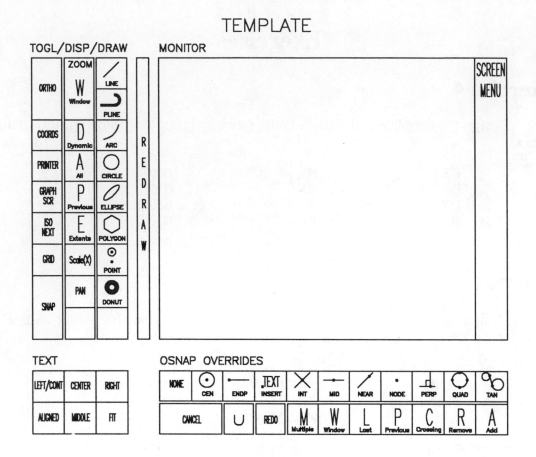

Figure 10   Tablet menu template for Exercise 7

Exercise 8

Write a combined tablet and screen menu file for the commands in Exercise 7. Design the screen menu as shown in Example 3.

Template for Example 1

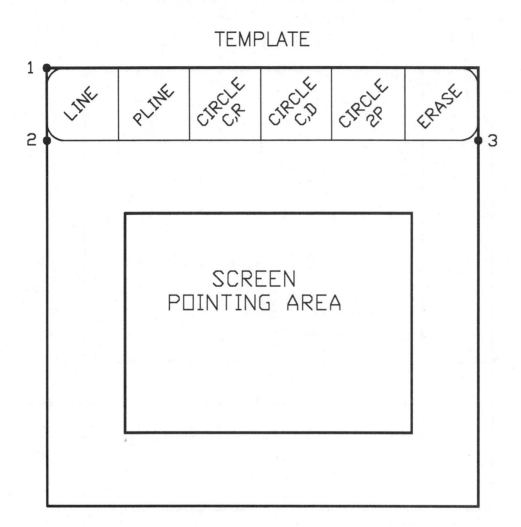

Note

This template is for tablet configuration. You can make a copy of this page and then secure it on the digitizer surface for configuration.

Template for Exercise 1

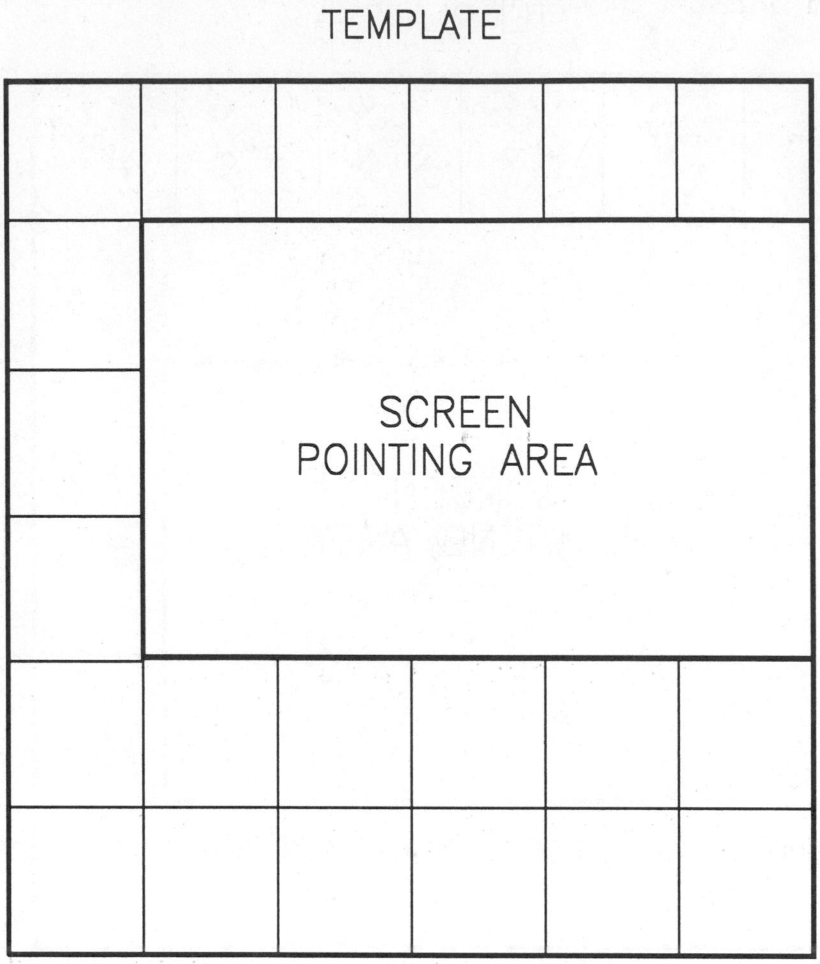

TEMPLATE

Note

This template is for tablet configuration. You can make a copy of this page and then secure it on the digitizer surface for configuration.

Template for Example 2

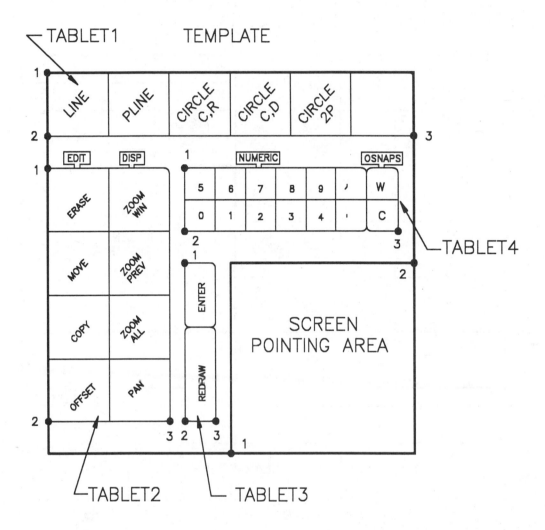

Note

This template is for tablet configuration. You can make a copy of this page and then secure it on the digitizer surface for configuration.

Template for Exercise 2

TEMPLATE

SAVE	QUIT	END	PRPLOT	PLOT	⊕ / ' 5 6 7 8 9
					X — · 0 1 2 3 4
			ERASE	ZOOM WIN	REDRAW
			MOVE	ZOOM PREV	SCREEN POINTING AREA
			COPY	ZOOM ALL	
			OFFSET	PAN	
			TRIM	ZOOM EXTENTS	ENTER
			CEN	ENDP	INT	LINE	PLINE	ELLIPSE
EDIT	CHANGE		MID	NEAR	PERP	CIRCLE	CIRCLE C,D	CIRCLE 2P

Note

This template is for tablet configuration. You can make a copy of this page and then secure it on the digitizer surface for configuration.

Template for Example 3

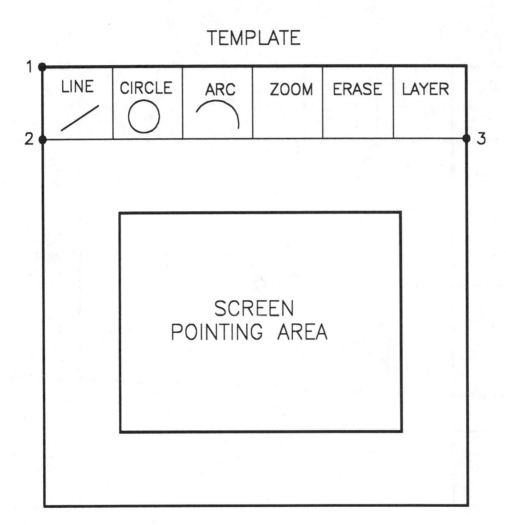

Note

This template is for tablet configuration. You can make a copy of this page and then secure it on the digitizer surface for configuration.

Template for Exercise 3

TEMPLATE

LINE /	CIRCLE ○	ARC				
ERASE						ZOOM ALL
MOVE		SCREEN POINTING AREA				ZOOM WIN.
COPY						LIST
FILLET						AREA
TRIM						HELP

Note

This template is for tablet configuration. You can make a copy of this page and then secure it on the digitizer surface for configuration.

Template for Exercise 7

TEMPLATE

TOGL/DISP/DRAW   MONITOR

ORTHO	ZOOM W Window	/ LINE
		⌐ PLINE
COORDS	D Dynamic	(ARC
PRINTER	A All	○ CIRCLE
GRAPH SCR	P Previous	⬭ ELLIPSE
ISO NEXT	E Extents	⬡ POLYGON
GRID	Scale(X)	⊙ · POINT
SNAP	PAN	● DONUT

R E D R A W

SCREEN MENU

TEXT

LEFT/CONT	CENTER	RIGHT
ALIGNED	MIDDLE	FIT

OSNAP OVERRIDES

NONE	⊙ CEN	•— ENDP	.TEXT INSERT	✕ INT	—•— MID	╱ NEAR	• NODE	⊥ PERP	◯ QUAD	○○ TAN
CANCEL		∪	REDO	M Multiple	W Window	L Last	P Previous	C Crossing	R Remove	A Add

Note

This template is for tablet configuration. You can make a copy of this page and then secure it on the digitizer surface for configuration.

Chapter 8

Pull-Down Menus

Standard Pull-Down Menus

The pull-down menu is a part of AutoCAD's standard menu file ACAD.MNU. The ACAD.MNU file is automatically loaded when you start AutoCAD, provided the standard configuration of AutoCAD has not been changed. The pull-down menu can be used if the display driver supports the advanced user interface (AUI).

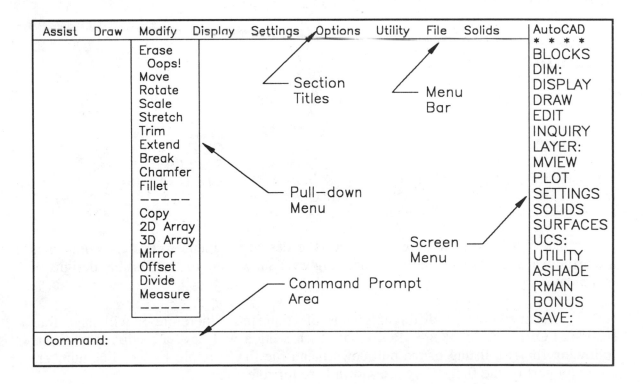

Figure 1 Pull-down menus

181

The different sections of pull-down menu can be selected by moving the cross hair to the top of the screen into the status line area. When the cross hair touches this area, the status line is replaced by the menu bar that displays the section titles (Figure 1). If you move the pointing device sideways, different section titles are highlighted and you can pick the desired item by pressing the pick button on your pointing device. Once the item is selected the corresponding pull-down menu is displayed directly under the title. The pull-down menu has 10 sections, defined as POP1, POP2, POP3 - - - - - - - - POP10.

Writing a Pull-Down Menu

The pull-down menus are similar to screen and tablet menus. The menu item consists of a menu item label and a command definition. The menu item is enclosed in the brackets, whereas the command definition is outside the brackets. As in other menus, before writing a pull-down menu you have to know the AutoCAD commands, command options and the prompts associates with each command. Equally important is the layout of various pull-down menus and submenus.

To write the pull-down menu file you can use AutoCAD's EDIT command (provided ACAD.PGP file is present and the EDIT command is defined in the file), Edlin function of DOS, or a text editor. To understand the process of developing a pull-down menu, consider the following example.

Example 1

Write a pull-down menu for the following AutoCAD commands.

LINE	ERASE	REDRAW	SAVE
PLINE	MOVE	REGEN	QUIT
CIRCLE C,R	COPY	ZOOM ALL	PRPLOT
CIRCLE C,D	STRETCH	ZOOM WIN	DIR Dwg Files
CIRCLE 2P	EXTEND	ZOOM PRE	
CIRCLE 3P	OFFSET		

The first step in writing any menu is to design the menu so that the commands are arranged in a desired configuration. Figure 2 shows one of the possible designs of this menu.

This menu has 4 different groups of commands, therefore it will have four sections POP1, POP2, POP3, POP4, and each section will have a section label. The following file is a listing of the pull-down menu file for Example 1. The line numbers are not a part of the file. They are shown here for reference only.

```
***POP1                                              1
[DRAW]                                               2
[LINE]*^C^CLINE                                      3
[PLINE]^C^CPLINE                                     4
```

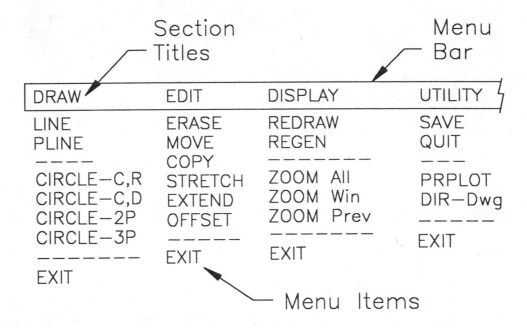

Figure 2 Design of pull-down menu

```
[~--]                               5
[CIR-C,R]^C^CCIRCLE                  6
[CIR-C,D]^C^CCIRCLE \D               7
[CIR-2P]^C^CCIRCLE 2P               8
[CIR-3P]^C^CCIRCLE 3P               9
[~--]                              10
[~Exit]^C                          11
***POP2                            12
[EDIT]                             13
[ERASE]*^C^CERASE                  14
[MOVE]^C^CMOVE                     15
[COPY]^C^CCOPY                     16
[STRETCH]^C^CSTRETCH;C             17
[OFFSET]^C^COFFSET                 18
[EXTEND]^C^CEXTEND                 19
[~--]                              20
[~Exit]^C                          21
***POP3                            22
[DISPLAY]                          23
[REDRAW]'REDRAW                    24
[REGEN]^C^CREGEN                   25
[~--]                              26
[ZOOM-All]^C^CZOOM A               27
[ZOOM-Window]'ZOOM W               28
[ZOOM-Prev]'ZOOM PREV              29
[~--]                              30
[Exit]^C                           31
***POP4                            32
```

```
[UTILITY]                              33
[SAVE]^C^CSAVE;                        34
[QUIT]^C^CQUIT                         35
[----]                                 36
[PRPLOT]^C^CPRPLOT                     37
[DIR-Dwg Files]^C^CDIR;*.DWG;          38
[~--]                                  39
[Exit]^C                               40
```

Line 1
***POP1
POP1 is the section label for the first pull-down menu. All section labels in the AutoCAD menu begin with three asterisk (***), followed by the section label name, like POP1

Line 2
[DRAW]
In this menu item DRAW is the section title that is displayed when the cursor is moved in the menu bar area. The title names should be chosen so that the user can identify the type of commands he can expect in that particular pull-down menu. In this example, all the draw commands are under the title DRAW, all edit commands are under EDIT, and same is true for other groups of items. Each title in the menu bar can be up to 14 characters long. However, most of the display devices provide a maximum of 80 characters. In order to have 10 sections in the menu bar, the length of each title should not exceed 8 characters.

If the first line in a pull-down menu section is a blank line, the title of that section is not displayed in the menu bar area. Since the section title is not displayed, therefore you **can not** access that pull-down menu. This allows the user to turn off the pull down menu section. For example, if you replace [DRAW] by a blank line, the DRAW section (POP1) of the pull-down menu will be disabled. The second section (POP2) will be displayed in its place.

Example
```
***POP1                    ——————— Section label
             .             ——————— Blank line (turns off POP1)
[LINE:]^CLINE              ——————— Menu item
[PLINE:]^CPLINE
[CIRCLE:]^CCIRCLE
```

The menu titles are left justified. If the first title is not displayed, the rest of the menu titles will be shifted to the left. In Example 1, if DRAW title is not displayed in the menu bar area, EDIT, DISPLAY and FILE sections of the pull-down menu will move to the left.

Line 3
*^C^CLINE
In this menu item the command definition starts with an asterisk sign (*). This feature allows the command to be repeated automatically until it is cancelled by

entering CTRL C or by selecting another menu command. ^C^C cancels the existing command twice, and LINE is an AutoCAD command that generates lines.

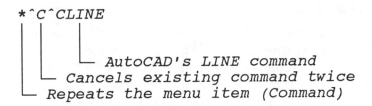

```
*^C^CLINE
```

└── AutoCAD's LINE command
└── Cancels existing command twice
└── Repeats the menu item (Command)

Line 5
[~--]
To separate the two groups of commands in any section, you can use a menu item that consists of two hyphens (--). This line automatically expands to fill the entire width of the pull-down menu or 39 characters, whichever is smaller. If you have one or more than two hyphens, the line does not expand. You can not use a blank line in a pull-down menu. If a pull-down menu has a blank line, the items beyond the blank line are not displayed on the screen.

If a menu items begins with a tilde sign (~), the item will be displayed little lighter than rest of the pull-down menu. You can use this feature to indicate that the item is not a valid selection or to activate a special command. If there is any instruction associated with the item, that instruction will be executed when you select the item. For example, [~OSNAPS]^C^C$S=OSNAPS will load the OSNAPS submenu on the screen, although the item begins with a tilde (~).

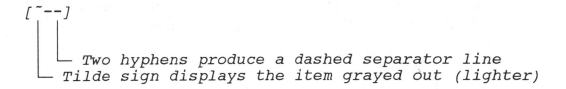

```
[~--]
```

└── Two hyphens produce a dashed separator line
└── Tilde sign displays the item grayed out (lighter)

Line 11
[~Exit]^C
In this menu item ^C command definition has been used to cancel the pull-down menu. The pull-down menu can also be cancelled by any of the following actions:

1. Select a point
2. Move cross hair to screen menu area
3. Select or type another command
4. Entering CTRL C from the key board

This item provides the user one more option for cancelling the pull-down menu. This is especially useful for new AutoCAD users who are not familiar with all AutoCAD features.

Line 28
[ZOOM-Window]'ZOOM W
In this menu item the single quote ('), preceding the ZOOM command, makes the ZOOM Window command transparent. When a command is transparent the existing command is not cancelled. After the ZOOM WINDOW command, AutoCAD will automatically resume the current operation. You can not use the transparent mode with those commands that regenerate the drawing. For example, ZOOM ALL regenerates the drawing, and therefore can not be used as a transparent command.

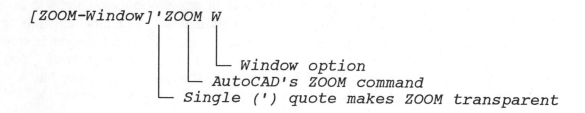

```
[ZOOM-Window]'ZOOM W
                │        │
                │        └─ Window option
                └─ AutoCAD's ZOOM command
              └─ Single (') quote makes ZOOM transparent
```

Line 31
[Exit]^C
This menu item is similar to the menu item in line 11, except the tilde sign (˜). Since this menu item does not have a tilde sign (˜), therefore the item will not be greyed out.

Line 34
[SAVE]^C^CSAVE;
In this menu item the semicolon (;) that follows the SAVE command enters RETURN. The semicolon is not required; the command will also work without a semicolon.

```
[SAVE]^C^CSAVE;
              │    │
              │    └─ Semicolon (;) enters RETURN
              └─ AutoCAD's SAVE command
```

Line 36
[----]
This menu item has four hyphens, therefore the line will not extend. It is only in the case of two hyphens (--) that the line extends to the entire width of the pull-down menu or 39 characters, whichever is smaller.

Line 38
[DIR-Dwg Files]^C^CDIR;*.DWG;

In this menu item DIR is an AutoCAD command for listing the files. The first semicolon (;) enters RETURN, and the second semicolon (;) lists the drawing files. The DIR command is defined in the ACAD.PGP file. This command will work if ACAD.PGP file is present and DIR command is defined in the file.

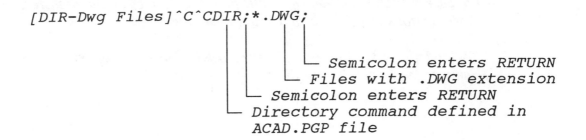

```
[DIR-Dwg Files]^C^CDIR;*.DWG;
```
                                    └─ Semicolon enters RETURN
                              └─ Files with .DWG extension
                       └─ Semicolon enters RETURN
              └─ Directory command defined in
                 ACAD.PGP file

Note

For all pull-down menus, the menu items are displayed directly beneath the menu title and are left justified. The rightmost pull-down menu (POP10) does not have enough space to display the entire menu item, therefore the characters that do not fit will be truncated. Most of the display devices display 80 characters. If you have 10 pull-down menus, the last pull-down menu POP10 will have only 8 character space for display. If the menu title or the menu items are longer than 8 characters, the characters beyond the 8th character will be truncated. However, the command associated with the menu items will still be executed.

Loading Menus

AutoCAD software comes with a menu file ACAD.MNU that is automatically loaded when you get into drawing editor, provided the default settings have not been changed on your system. Otherwise, it will load the menu file that AutoCAD is configured to load, or the menu that is referenced by the drawing. To load a new menu you can use AutoCAD's MENU command.

Command: MENU
Menu file name or . for none <current>: (file name)

To load the new menu, enter the file name of the menu file that you want to load without extension. AutoCAD will load the new menu, and then you can select the commands from the pull-down menu.

Note

1. *When you load the pull-down menu, some of the commands will be displayed on the screen menu area. This happens because the screen menu*

area is empty. If the menu file contained a screen menu also, the pull-down menu commands will not be displayed in the screen menu area.

2. *When you load a new menu, the original menu you had on the screen, prior to loading the new menu, is disabled. You can not select commands from the screen menu, pull-down menu, pointing device, or the digitizer, unless these sections are defined in the new menu file.*

3. *To load the original menu use the MENU command again, and enter the name of the original menu file.*

Restrictions

The pull-down menus are very easy to use and provide a quick access to some of the frequently used AutoCAD commands. However, the menu bar and the pull-down menus are disabled during the following commands.

DTEXT Command
After you assign the text height and the rotation angle to a DTEXT command, the pull down-menu is automatically disabled.

SKETCH Command
The pull-down menus are disabled after you set the record increment in the SKETCH command.

VPOINT Command
The pull-down menus are disabled while the axis tripod and compass are displayed on the screen.

ZOOM Command
The pull-down menus are disabled when the dynamic zoom is in progress.

VIEWPORTS AND VPORTS
The pull-down menus are disabled when viewports and vports are active.

Exercise 1

Write a pull-down menu for the following AutoCAD commands.

DRAW	EDIT	DISP/TEXT	UTILITY
LINE	FILLET0	DTEXT,C	SAVE
PLINE	FILLET	DTEXT,L	QUIT
ELLIPSE	CHAMFER	DTEXT,R	PRPLOT

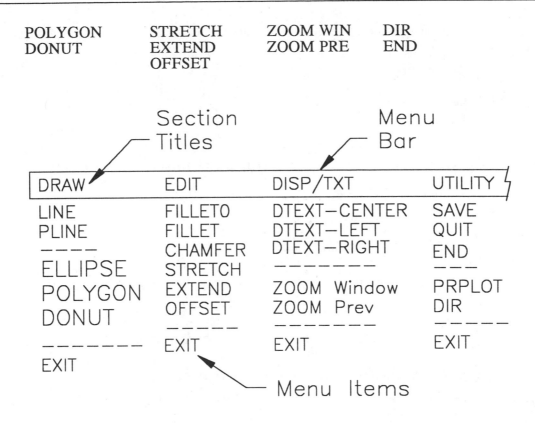

POLYGON   STRETCH   ZOOM WIN   DIR
DONUT   EXTEND   ZOOM PRE   END
            OFFSET

Figure 3   Pull-down menu display for Exercise 1

Submenus

The number of items in a pull-down menu file can be very large that may not be accommodated on one screen. For example, the maximum number of items that can be displayed on some of the menu devices is 21. If the pull-down menu has more than 21 items, the menu items in access of 21 are not displayed on the screen and can not therefore be accessed. The user can overcome this problem by using submenus that let the user define smaller groups of items within a menu section. When a submenu is selected, it loads the submenu items and displays them on the screen.

Submenu Definition

A submenu definition consists of two asterisk signs (**) followed by the name of the submenu. A menu can have any number of submenus, and every submenu should have a unique name. The items that follow a submenu, up to the next section label or submenu label, belong to that submenu. Following is the format of a submenu label:

```
**Name
  │     └─ Name of the submenu
  └─ Two asterisk signs (**) designate a submenu
```

Note

1. *The submenu name can be up to 31 characters long.*

2. *The submenu name can consist of letters, digits, and the special characters like: $ (dollar), - (hyphen), and _ (underscore).*

3. *The submenu name can not have any embedded blanks.*

4. *The submenu names should be unique in a menu file.*

Submenu Reference

The submenu reference is used to reference or load a submenu. It consists of a "$" sign followed by a letter that specifies the menu section. The letter that specifies a pull-down menu section is Pn, where n designates the number of the pull-down menu section. The menu section is followed by "=" sign, and the name of the submenu that the user wants to activate. The submenu name should be without "**". Following is the format of a submenu reference:

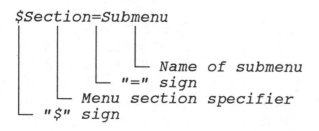

```
$Section=Submenu
 │   │      │   └─ Name of submenu
 │   │      └─ "=" sign
 │   └─ Menu section specifier
 └─ "$" sign
```

Example
```
$P1=P1A
 │    └─ Name of submenu
 └─ P1-Specifies pull-down menu section 1
```

Displaying Submenu

When you load a submenu in a pull-down menu, the submenu items are not automatically displayed on the screen. For example, when you load a submenu P1A that has DRAW-ARC as the first item, the current title of POP1 will be replaced by the DRAW-ARC. But the items that are defined under DRAW-ARC are not displayed on the screen. To force the display of the new items on the screen AutoCAD uses a special command $Pn=*

```
$Pn=*
   │ │ │
   │ │ └── Asterisk sign (*)
   │ └── Pull-down menu section number (1 to 10)
   └── P for pull-down menu
```

Loading Menus

From the pull-down menu, you can load any menu that is defined in the screen, or icon menu sections by using the appropriate load commands. It may not be needed in most of the applications, but if you want to, you can load the menus that are defined in other menu sections.

Loading Screen Menus

You can load any menu that is defined in the screen menu section, from the pull-down menu, by using the following load command.

```
$S=X $S=LINE
   │  │      │
   │  │      └── Submenu name defined in screen menu section
   │  └── Submenu name defined in screen menu section
   └── S specifies screen menu
```

The first load command ($S=X) loads the submenu X that has been defined in the screen menu section of the menu file. The X submenu can contain 21 blank lines, so that when it is loaded it clears the screen menu. The second load command ($S=LINE) loads the submenu LINE that has also been defined in the screen menu section of the menu file.

Loading an Icon Menu

You can also load an icon menu, from the pull-down menu, by using the following load command.

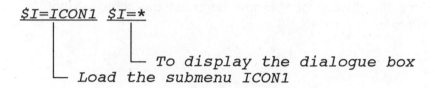

```
$I=ICON1 $I=*
        │       │
        │       └── To display the dialogue box
        └── Load the submenu ICON1
```

This menu item consists of two load commands. The first load command $I=ICON1 loads the icon submenu ICON1 that has been defined in the icon menu section of the file. The second load command $I=* displays the new dialogue box on the screen.

Example 2

Write a pull-down and screen menu for the following AutoCAD commands. Use submenus for ARC and CIRCLE commands. When the user selects an item from the pull-down menu the corresponding screen menu should be automatically loaded on the screen.

LINE	BLOCK	QUIT
PLINE	INSERT	SAVE
ARC	WBLOCK	----
ARC 3P		PLOT
ARC SCE		
ARC SCA		
ARC CSE		
ARC CSA		
ARC CSL		
CIRCLE		
CIRLCE C,R		
CIRCLE C,D		
CIRCLE 2P		

The layout shown in Figure 4A is one of the possible designs for this pull-down menu. The ARC and CIRCLE commands are in separate groups that will be defined as submenus in the menu file. The layout of the screen menu is shown in Figure 4B.

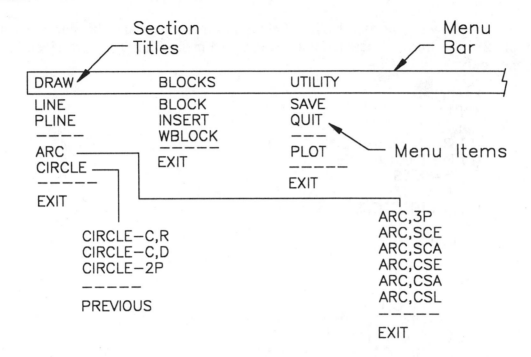

Figure 4A   Design of pull-down menu for Example 2

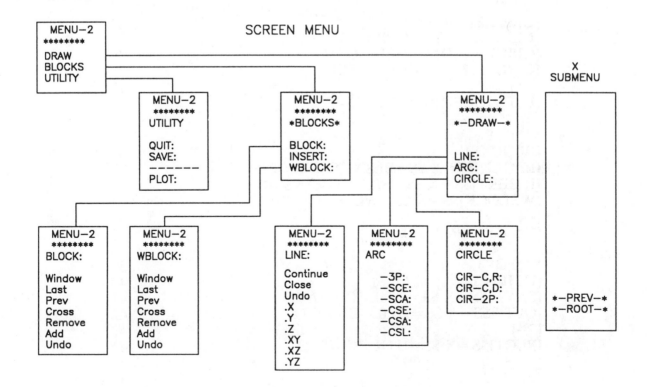

Figure 4B   Design of screen menu

The following file is a listing of the pull-down menu and the screen menu for Example 2. The line numbers are not a part of the menu file. They are given here for reference only.

```
***POP1                                                      1
**P1A                                                        2
[DRAW]                                                       3
[LINE]$S=X $S=LINE ^C^CLINE                                  4
[PLINE]^C^CPLINE                                             5
[--]$S=X $S=OSNAP                                            6
[ARC]^C^C$S=X $S=ARC $P1=P1B $P1=*                           7
[CIRCLE]^C^C$S=X $S=CIR $P1=P1C $P1=*                        8
[--]                                                         9
[Exit]^C                                                    10
                                                            11
**P1B                                                       12
[ARC]                                                       13
[ARC,3P]^C^CARC \\DRAG                                      14
[ARC,SCE]^C^CARC \C \DRAG                                   15
[ARC,SCA]^C^CARC \C \A DRAG                                 16
[ARC,CSE]^C^CARC C \\DRAG                                   17
[ARC,CSA]^C^CARC C \\A DRAG                                 18
[ARC,CSL]^C^CARC C \\L DRAG                                 19
[--]                                                        20
[Exit]^C                                                    21
                                                            22
**P1C                                                       23
[CIRCLE]                                                    24
[CIRCLE C,R]^C^CCIRCLE                                      25
[CIRCLE C,D]^C^CCIRCLE \D                                   26
[CIRCLE 2P]^C^CCIRCLE 2P                                    27
[--]                                                        28
[PREVIOUS]$P1=P1A $P1=*                                     29
                                                            30
***POP2                                                     31
[BLOCKS]                                                    32
[BLOCK]$S=X $S=BLKX ^C^CBLOCK                               33
[INSERT]$S=X $S=BLK *^C^CINSERT                             34
[WBLOCK]$S=X $S=WBLK ^C^CWBLOCK                             35
[--]                                                        36
[Exit]$P1=P1A $P1=*                                         37
                                                            38
***POP3                                                     39
[UTILITY]                                                   40
[SAVE]$S=X $S=UTIL ^C^CSAVE                                 41
[QUIT]$S=X $S=UTIL ^C^CQUIT                                 42
[~--]                                                       43
[PLOT]$S=X $S=UTIL ^C^CPLOT                                 44
[~--]                                                       45
[Exit]^C                                                    46
                                                            47
***SCREEN                                                   48
**S                                                         49
[ MENU-3   ]^C^C$S=X $S=S                                   50
```

```
[********     ]$S=OSNAP                          51
[            ]                                    52
[            ]                                    53
[DRAW        ]^C^C$S=X $S=DRAW                    54
[BLOCKS      ]^C^C$S=X $S=BLK                     55
[UTILITY     ]^C^C$S=X $S=UTIL                    56
                                                  57
**DRAW 3                                          58
[*-DRAW-*  ]                                      59
[            ]                                    60
[            ]                                    61
[LINE:       ]$S=X $S=LINE ^C^CLINE               62
[ARC:        ]$S=X $S=ARC                         63
[CIRCLE:     ]$S=X $S=CIR                         64
                                                  65
**LINE 3                                          66
[LINE:       ]^C^CLINE                            67
[            ]                                    68
[            ]                                    69
[Continue    ]^C^CLINE;;                          70
[Close       ]CLOSE                               71
[Undo        ]UNDO                                72
[.X          ].X                                  73
[.Y          ].Y                                  74
[.Z          ].Z                                  75
[.XY         ].XY                                 76
[.XZ         ].XZ                                 77
[.YZ         ].YZ                                 78
                                                  79
**ARC 3                                           80
[ARC        ]                                     81
[           ]                                     82
[  -3P:     ]^C^CARC \\DRAG                       83
[  -SCE:    ]^C^CARC \C \DRAG                     84
[  -SCA:    ]^C^CARC \C \A DRAG                   85
[  -CSE:    ]^C^CARC C \\DRAG                     86
[  -CSA:    ]^C^CARC C \\A DRAG                   87
[  -CSL:    ]^C^CARC C \\L DRAG                   88
                                                  89
**CIR 3                                           90
[CIRCLE     ]                                     91
[    ]                                            92
                                                  93
[]                                                94
[CIR-C,R:    ]^C^CCIRCLE                          95
[CIR-C,D:    ]^C^CCIRCLE \D                       96
[CIR-2P:     ]^C^CCIRCLE 2P                       97
                                                  98
                                                  99
**BLK 3                                           100
[*BLOCKS* ]                                       101
[            ]                                    102
[            ]                                    103
[BLOCK:      ]$S=X $S=BLKX ^C^CBLOCK              104
```

```
[INSERT:    ]^C^CINSERT                            105
[WBLOCK:    ]$S=X $S=WBLK ^C^CWBLOCK               106
                                                   107
**BLKX 3                                           108
[BLOCK:     ]^C^CBLOCK                             109
[           ]                                      110
Window                                             111
Last                                               112
Prev                                               113
Cross                                              114
Remove                                             115
Add                                                116
Undo                                               117
                                                   118
**WBLK 3                                           119
[WBLOCK:    ]^C^CWBLOCK                             120
[           ]                                      121
Window                                             122
Last                                               123
Prev                                               124
Cross                                              125
Remove                                             126
Add                                                127
Undo                                               128
                                                   129
**UTIL 3                                           130
[UTILITY    ]                                      131
[           ]                                      132
[           ]                                      133
[QUIT:      ]^C^CQUIT                              134
[SAVE:      ]^C^CSAVE                              135
[--------   ]                                      136
[PLOT:      ]^C^CPLOT                              137
                                                   138
**X 3                                              139
[           ]                                      140
[           ]                                      141
[           ]                                      142
[           ]                                      143
[           ]                                      144
[           ]                                      145
[           ]                                      146
[           ]                                      147
[           ]                                      148
[           ]                                      149
[           ]                                      150
[           ]                                      151
[           ]                                      152
[           ]                                      153
[           ]                                      154
[           ]                                      155
[           ]                                      156
[*-PREV-*   ]$S= $S=                               157
[*-ROOT-*   ]^C^C$S=X $S=S                         158
```

```
                                               159
    **OSNAP 2                                  160
    [-OSNAPS-   ]                              161
    [           ]                              162
    [Center     ]CEN $S=                       163
    [Endpoint   ]END $S=                       164
    [Insert     ]INS $S=                       165
    [Intersec   ]INT $S=                       166
    [Midpoint   ]MID $S=                       167
    [Nearest    ]NEA $S=                       168
    [Node       ]NOD $S=                       169
    [Perpend    ]PER $S=                       170
    [Quadrant   ]QUA $S=                       171
    [Tangent    ]TAN $S=                       172
    [None       ]NONE $S=                      173
    [           ]                              174
    [           ]                              175
    [           ]                              176
    [           ]                              177
    [           ]                              178
    [*-PREV-*   ]$S=                           179
```

Line 2
**P1A
**P1A defines the submenu P1A. All the submenus have two asterisk signs (**) followed by the name of the submenu. The submenu can have any valid name. In this example, P1A has been chosen because it is easy to identify the location of the submenu. P indicates that it is a pull-down menu, 1 indicates that it is in the first pull-down menu (POP1), and A indicates that it is the first submenu in that section.

Line 4
[LINE]$S=X $S=LINE ^C^CLINE
In this menu item, $S=X loads the submenu X that has been defined in the screen menu section of the menu file. Similarly, $S=LINE loads the submenu LINE that has also been defined in the screen menu section. The purpose of loading the submenu X is to clear the screen so that the menu items that are not needed are erased from the screen menu. When the submenu LINE is loaded, the menu items defined in this submenu are displayed on the screen menu without any overlap of the menu items.

Line 6
[--]$S=X $S=OSNAP
The two hyphens enclosed in the brackets will automatically expand to fill the entire width of the pull-down menu or 39 character space, whichever is smaller. This menu item can also be used to define a command. In this case $S=OSNAP loads the submenu OSNAP that has been defined in the screen menu section of the menu.

Line 7

[ARC]^C^C$S=X $S=ARC $P1=P1B $P1=*

In this menu item, $P1=P1B loads the submenu P1B and assigns it to the first menu section (POP1), but the new pull-down menu is not displayed on the screen. $P1=* forces the display of the new pull-down menu on the screen.

For example, if you select CIRCLE from the first pull-down menu (POP1), the menu bar title DRAW will be replaced by CIRCLE, but the new menu is not displayed on the screen. Now, if you select CIRCLE from the menu bar, the command defines under CIRCLE submenu will be displayed in the pull-down menu.

To force the display of the menu that is currently assigned to POP1, you can use AutoCAD's special command **$P1=***. If you select CIRCLE from the first pull-down menu (POP1), the CIRCLE submenu will be loaded and automatically displayed on the screen.

Line 21

[EXIT]^C

When you select this menu item the current pull-down menu will be cancelled. It will not return to the previous submenu (DRAW). If you check the menu bar, it will display ARC as section title, not DRAW. Therefore, it is not a good practice to cancel a submenu. It is better to return to the first menu before cancelling it, or define a command that will automatically loads the previous menu and then cancel the pull-down menu.

> **Example**
> [EXIT]$P1=P1A $P1=* ^C^C

Line 29

[PREVIOUS]$P1=P1A $P1=*

In this menu item $P1=P1A loads the submenu P1A, which happens to be the previous menu in this case. You can also use **$P1=** to load the previous menu. $P1=* forces the display of the submenu P1A.

Note

1. *It is a good practice to provide a escape mechanism in a pull down menu like: [EXIT] or [PREVIOUS] in Example 2. However, it not a must, because there are other ways of cancelling a pull-down menu as discussed earlier in this chapter..*

2. *In a pull down menu, do not cancel a menu when you are in a submenu. Always return to the first menu before cancelling it.*

Exercise 2

Write a pull-down and a screen menu for the following AutoCAD commands. Use a submenu for the LINE command options in the pull-down menu. When the user selects an item from the pull-down menu, the corresponding screen menu should be automatically loaded on the screen. (The layout of the screen menu, and the pull-down menu is shown in Figure 5A and Figure 5B)

LINE	ZOOM All	TIME
Continue	ZOOM Win	LIST
Close	ZOOM Pre	DISTANCE
Undo	PAN	AREA
.X		DBLIST
.Y		STATUS
.Z		
CIRCLE		
ELLIPSE		

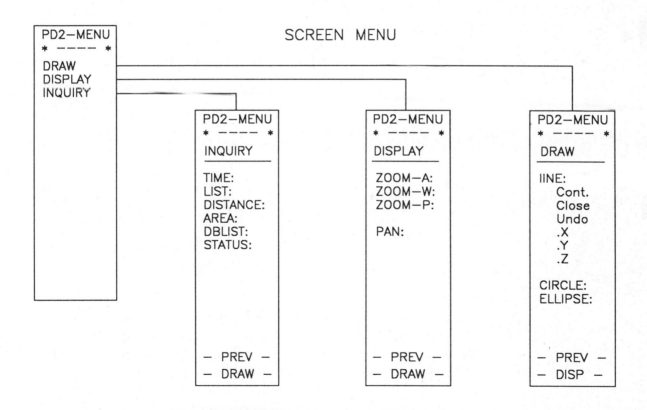

Figure 5A   Design of screen menu for Exercise 2

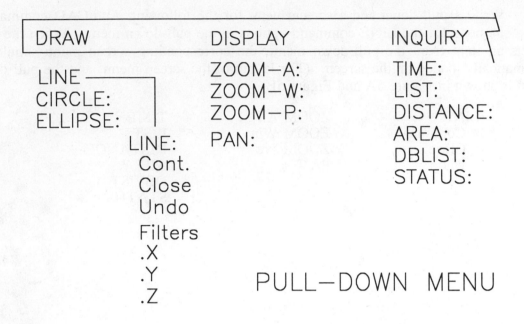

Figure 5B   Design of pull-down menu for Exercise 2

Review

Fill in the blanks

1. A pull-down menu can have .... sections.

2. The length of the section title should not exceed .... characters.

3. The section titles in a pull-down menu are .... justified.

4. In a pull-down menu a line consisting of two hyphens ([--]) ....
    automatically to fill the .... of the pull-down menu or ....
    characters, whichever is smaller.

5. If the menu item begins with the tilde (˜), the items will be displayed
    .... than rest of the menu.

6. The pull-down menus are .... when the dynamic zoom is in progress.

7. The pull-down menus can be used if the display driver supports ....
    interface.

8. Every submenu in menu file should have a .... name.

9. The submenu name can be .... characters long.

10. The submenu names should not have any .... blanks.

Exercises

Exercise 3

Write a pull-down menu for the following AutoCAD commands. (The layout of the pull-down menu is shown in Figure 6)

LINE	DIM HORZ	DTEXT LEFT
CIRCLE C,R	DIM VERT	DTEXT RIGHT
CIRCLE C,D	DIM RADIUS	DTEXT CENTER
ARC 3P	DIM DIAMETER	DTEXT ALIGNED
ARC SCE	DIM ANGULAR	DTEXT MIDDLE
ARC CSE	DIM LEADER	DTEXT FIT

PULL—DOWN MENU

DRAW	DIM	DTEXT
LINE	DIM—HORZ	DTEXT—LEFT
CIRCLE C,R	DIM—VERT	DTEXT—RIGHT
CIRCLE C,D	DIM—RADIUS	DTEXT—CENTER
ARC 3P	DIM—DIAMETER	DTEXT—ALIGNED
ARC SCE	DIM—ANGULAR	DTEXT—MIDDLE
ARC CSE	DIM—LEADER	DTEXT—FIT

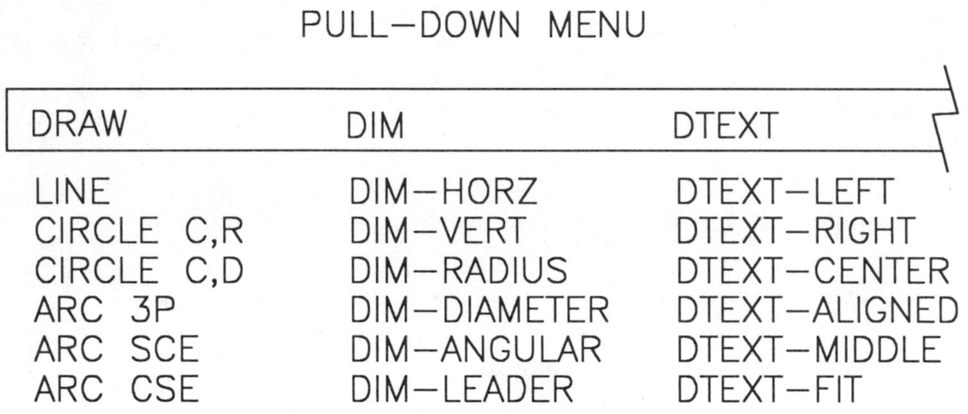

Figure 6   Layout of pull-down menu

Exercise 4

Write a pull-down and a screen menu for the following AutoCAD commands. When the user selects a command from the pull-down menu, it should automatically load the corresponding screen menu on the screen. (The layout of the screen menu and the pull-down menu is shown in Figure 7A and Figure 7B)

LAYER NEW	SNAP 0.25	UCS WORLD
LAYER MAKE	SNAP 0.5	UCS PREVIOUS
LAYER SET	GRID 1.0	VPORTS 2
LAYER LIST	DRID 10.0	VPORTS 4

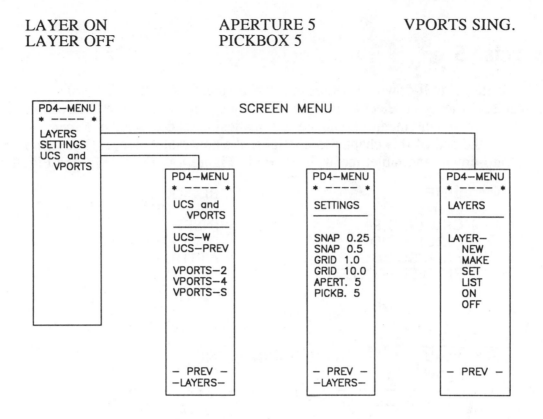

LAYER ON   APERTURE 5   VPORTS SING.
LAYER OFF   PICKBOX 5

Figure 7A   Design of screen menu for Exercise 4

PULL–DOWN MENU

DRAW	SETTINGS	UCS–PORT
LAYER–New	SNAP 0.25	UCS–World
LAYER–Make	SNAP 0.5	UCS–Pre
LAYER–Set	GRID 1.0	VPORTS–2
LAYER–List	GRID 10.0	VPORTS–4
LAYER–On	APERTURE 5	VPORTS–1
LAYER–Off	PICKBOX 5	

Figure 7B   Design of pull-down menu for Exercise 4

Exercise 5

Write a pull-down, screen and tablet menu for the following AutoCAD commands. When you select a command from the template or the pull-down menu, the corresponding screen menu should be automatically loaded on the screen. Use the template at the end of this chapter to configure the new tablet menu. (The layout of the screen, pull-down, and tablet menus is shown in Figure 8A, Figure 8B, and Figure 8C)

LINE	BLOCK
PLINE	WBLOCK
CIRCLE C,R	INSERT
CIRCLE C,D	BLOCK LIST
ELLIPSE EDGE	ATTDEF
ELLIPSE CENTER	ATTEDIT

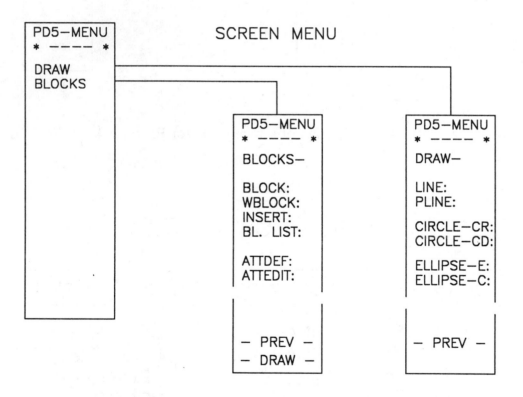

Figure 8A   Design of screen menu for Exercise 5

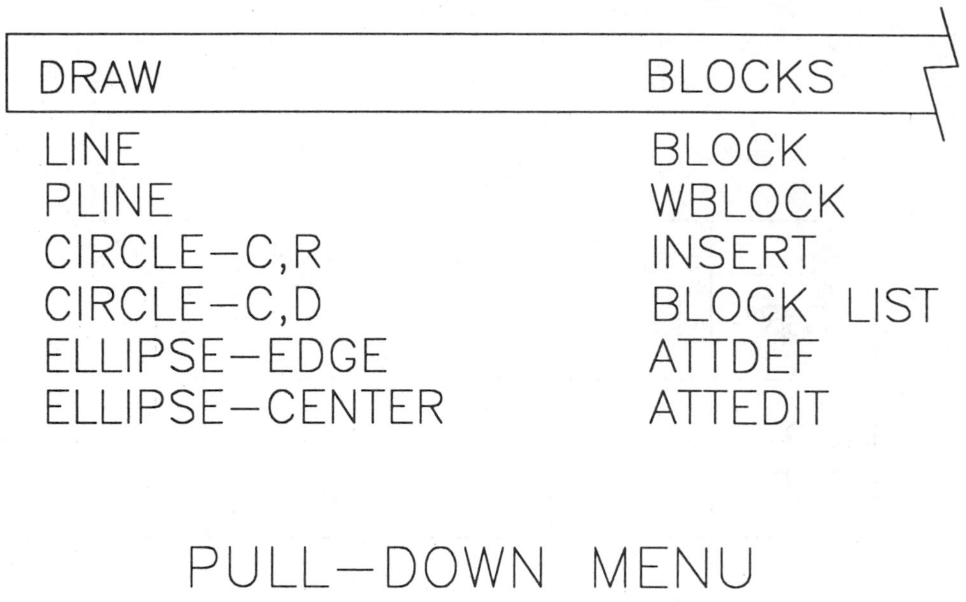

```
┌─────────────────────────────────────────────┐
│  DRAW                    BLOCKS               │
└─────────────────────────────────────────────┘
     LINE                  BLOCK
     PLINE                 WBLOCK
     CIRCLE−C,R            INSERT
     CIRCLE−C,D            BLOCK  LIST
     ELLIPSE−EDGE          ATTDEF
     ELLIPSE−CENTER        ATTEDIT
```

PULL−DOWN MENU

Figure 8B   Design of pull-down menu for Exercise 5

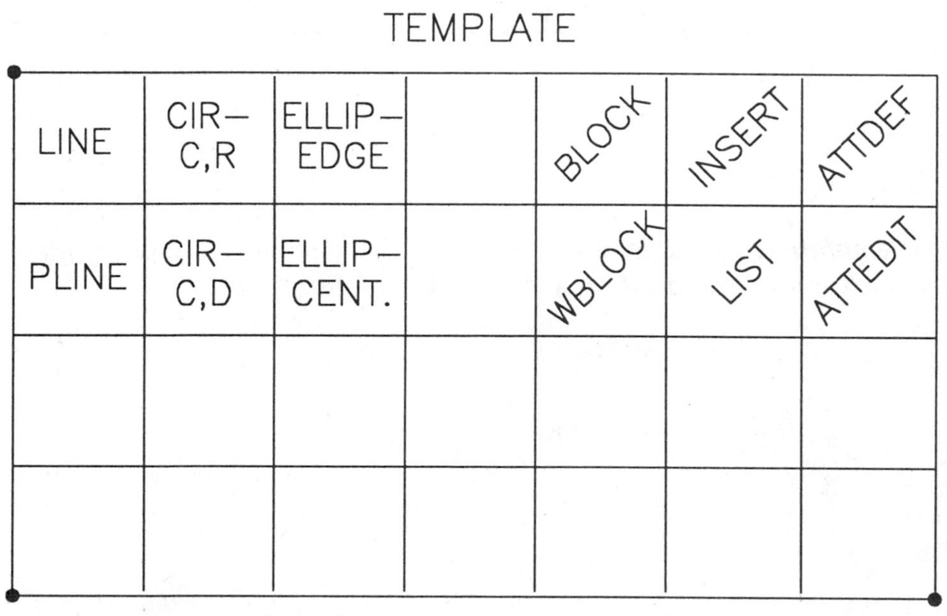

TEMPLATE

LINE	CIR−C,R	ELLIP−EDGE		BLOCK	INSERT	ATTDEF
PLINE	CIR−C,D	ELLIP−CENT.		WBLOCK	LIST	ATTEDIT

Figure 8C   Design of tablet template for Exercise 5

Template for Exercise 5

TEMPLATE

LINE	CIR— C,R	ELLIP— EDGE		BLOCK	INSERT	ATTDEF
PLINE	CIR— C,D	ELLIP— CENT.		WBLOCK	LIST	ATTEDIT

Note

This template is for tablet configuration. You can make a copy of this page and then secure it on the digitizer surface for configuration.

Chapter 9

ICON Menus

The icon menus are extremely useful when a user is inserting blocks, selecting a hatch pattern or a text font. You can also use the icon menus to load an AutoLISP routine, or a predefined macro. Therefore, the icon menu is a powerful tool for customizing AutoCAD.

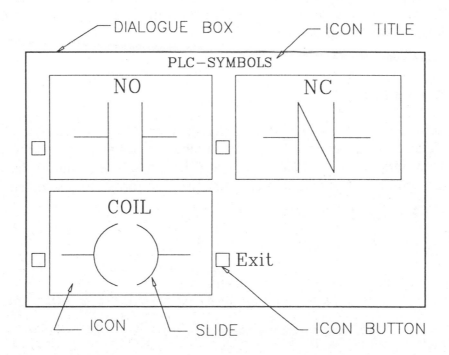

Figure 1   Sample icon menu display

The icon menus can be accessed from the pull-down, tablet, button, or screen menu. When the user selects an icon, a dialogue box is displayed on the screen that contains different icons. The title of the icon menu is displayed at the top of the dialogue box. (Figure 1). Also, an arrow appears on the screen that can be moved to select any icon. On the left hand side of each icon is a small rectangular box called a icon button or simply a button. You can select an icon by highlighting the button with the arrow and then pressing the pick button of the pointing device. You can cancel an icon menu by entering CTRL C, pressing ESCAPE key on the keyboard, or selecting the EXIT icon from the icon menu display.

The dialogue box can display 4,9, or 16 icons depending on the number of items in the icon menu section. For example, if there are 5 items in a submenu, AutoCAD will display 9 icons in the dialogue box. Out of these nine icons, the first five icons will display the slides as referenced in the corresponding menu item, and the remaining icons will be empty.

Submenus

The number of items in an icon menu file can be very large that may not accommodate on one screen. For example, the maximum number of items in an icon menu is 16. If the icon menu has more than 16 items, the menu items in access of 16 are not displayed on the screen, and therefore **can not** be accessed. The user can overcome this problem by using submenus that let the user define smaller groups of items within a icon menu section. When a submenu is selected, it loads the submenu items and displays them on the screen.

Submenu Definition

A submenu label consists of two asterisk signs (**) followed by the name of the submenu. The icon menu can have any number of submenus, and every submenu should have a unique name. The items that follow a submenu, up to the next section label, or submenu label, belong to that submenu. The format of a submenu label is:

```
**Name
 |  |
 |  |___ Name of the submenu
 |_____ Two asterisk signs (**) designate a submenu
```

Note

1. The submenu name can be upto 31 characters long.

2. The submenu name can consist of letters, digits, and the special characters like: $ (dollar), - (hyphen), and _ (underscore).

3. *The submenu name should not have any embedded blanks.*
4. *The submenu names should be unique in a menu file.*

Submenu Reference

The submenu reference is used to reference or load a submenu. It consists of a "$" sign followed by a letter that specifies the menu section. The letter that specifies a icon menu section is I. The menu section is followed by "=" sign, and the name of the submenu that the user wants to activate. The submenu name should be without "**". Following is the format of a submenu reference:

```
$Section=Submenu
 |     |      |    |
 |     |      |    └── Name of submenu
 |     |      └── "=" sign
 |     └── Menu section specifier
 └── "$" sign
```

Example

```
$I=ICON1
 |   |
 |   └── Name of submenu
 └── I  Specifies ICON menu section
```

Displaying a Submenu

When you load a submenu, the new dialogue box, and the icons are not automatically displayed on the screen. For example, if you load a submenu ICON1, the items contained in the this submenu will not be displayed. To force the display of the new icon menu on the screen, AutoCAD uses a special command $I=*

```
$I=*
 | |
 | └── Asterisk sign (*)
 └── I for icon menu
```

Loading Screen Menus

You can load any menu that is defined in the screen menu section, from the icon menu, by using the following load command.

```
$S=X  $S=SUBMENU
  │   │    │
  │   │    └─ Submenu name defined in screen menu section
  │   └─ Submenu name defined in screen menu section
  └─ S specifies screen menu
```

The first load command ($S=X) loads the submenu X that has been defined in the screen menu section of the menu file. The X submenu can contain 21 blank lines, so that when it is loaded it clears the screen menu. The second load command ($S=INSERT) loads the submenu INSERT that has been defined in the screen menu section of the menu file.

Writing an Icon Menu

An icon menu will work only if the device driver that you are using supports AutoCAD's Advanced User Interface (AUI). AutoCAD ignores the icon menu section (***ICON) if the display driver does not support AUI. Also, the system should be configured so that the status line is not disabled. Otherwise, the icon menus, or the pull down menus can not be used.

The icon menu consists of a section label ***ICON. There is only one icon menu in a file and all the icon menus are defined in this section.

```
***ICON
   │  │
   │  └─ Section Label for an icon
   └─ Three asterisks (***) designate a section label
```

You can define any number of submenus in the icon menu. All submenus have two asterisks followed by the name of the submenu (**PARTS or **ICON1).

```
**ICON1
  │   │
  │   └─ Name of submenu
  └─ Two asterisks (**) designate a submenu
```

The first item in the icon menu is the title of the icon menu that is displayed at the top of the dialogue box (Figure 1). The menu title has to be enclosed in brackets ([PLC-SYMBOLS]) and should not contain any command definition. If it does contain a command definition, AutoCAD ignores the definition. The remaining items in the icon menu file contain slide names in the brackets, and the command definition outside the brackets.

Example
***ICON —————— Icon menu section
**BOLTS —————— Submenu BOLTS
[HEX-HEAD BOLTS] —————— Icon title
[BOLT1]^C^CINSERT B1 —————— BOLT1 is slide name
                                INSERT is AutoCAD command
                                B1 is block name

Example 1

Write an icon menu that will enable a user to insert the following blocks in the drawing by selecting an icon from the dialogue box. Use the pull-down menu to load the icon menu. (The block shapes are shown in Figure 2)

PLC SYMBOLS   ELECTRIC SYMBOLS

NO (NORMALLY OPEN)   RESIS (RESISTANCE)
NC (NORMALLY CLOSED)   DIODE
COIL   GROUND

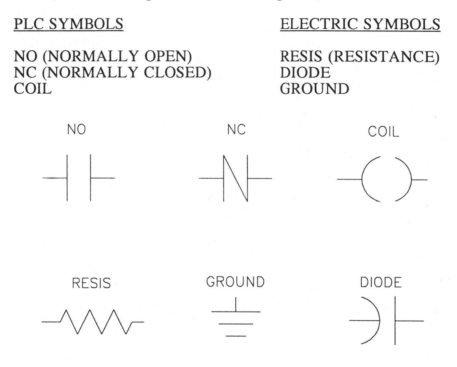

Figure 2   Block shapes for icon menu

As mentioned in the earlier chapters, the first step in writing a menu is to design the menu so that the commands are arranged in a desired configuration. Figure 3 shows one of the possible designs of the pull-down menu and the icon menu for Example 1.

To write the file you can use AutoCAD's EDIT command. The line numbers in the following file are for reference only and are not a part of the menu file.

```
***POP1                              1
[ELECTRIC]                           2
[PLC-SYMBOLS]$I=ICON1 $I=*           3
[ELEC-SYMBOLS]$I=ICON2 $I=*          4
```

```
***ICON                                                    5
**ICON1                                                    6
[PLC-SYMBOLS]                                              7
[NO]^C^CINSERT;NO;\1.0;1.0;0                               8
[NC]^C^CINSERT;NC;\1.0;1.0;0;                              9
[COIL]^C^CINSERT;COIL                                     10
[ EXIT]^C                                                 11
                                                          12
**ICON2                                                   13
[ELECTRICAL SYMBOLS]                                      14
[RESIS]^C^CINSERT;RESIS;\\\\                              15
[DIODE]^C^CINSERT;DIODE;\1.0;1.0;\                        16
[GROUND]^C^CINSERT;GRD;\1.5;1.5;0;;                       17
[ EXIT]^C                                                 18
```

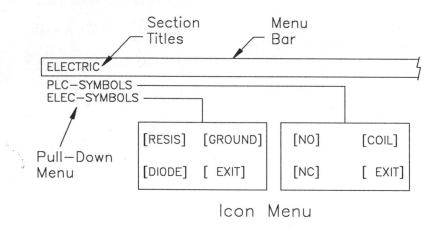

Figure 3 Design of pull-down and icon menu for Example 1

Line 1
***POP1
In this menu item ***POP1 is the section label and defines the first section of the pull-down menu.

Line 2
[ELECTRIC]
In this menu item [ELECTRIC] is the section title for the POP1 pull-down menu. It will be displayed in the menu bar.

Line 3
[PLC SYMBOLS]$I=ICON1 $I=*
In this menu item $I=ICON1 loads the submenu ICON1, and $I=* displays the current icon menu on the screen.

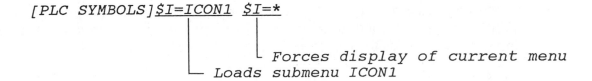

```
[PLC SYMBOLS]$I=ICON1 $I=*
```

                                    └ *Forces display of current menu*
                          └─ *Loads submenu ICON1*

Line 5
***ICON
In this menu item ***ICON is the section label of the icon menu. All the icon menus have to be defined within this section, otherwise AutoCAD can not locate the icon menus.

Line 6
**ICON1
In this menu item **ICON1 is the name of the icon submenu.

Line 7
[PLC-SYMBOLS]
When you select line 3 ([PLC SYMBOLS]$I=ICON1 $I=*), AutoCAD loads the submenu ICON1 and displays the title of the icon at the top of the dialogue box. This title is defined in line 7. If this line is missing, the next line will be displayed at the top of the dialogue box. The icon titles can be of any length as long as it fits the length of the dialogue box. The maximum number of icons is 16. Therefore, in addition to the first line, you can define a maximum of 16 icons in an icon menu.

Line 8
[NO]^C^CINSERT;NO;\1.0;1.0;0
In this menu item the first NO is the name of the slide and has to be enclosed within the brackets. The name should not have any trailing or leading blank spaces. Slide names can be up to 31 characters long. If the slides are not present AutoCAD will not display any graphical symbols in the icons. However, the menu items will be loaded and if you select this item, the command associated with icon will be executed.

The second NO is the name of the block that is to be inserted. The back slash (\) pauses for the user input, and in this case it is the block insertion point. The first 1.0 defines the X-Scale factor. The second 1.0 defines the Y-Scale factor, and the following 0 defines the rotation.

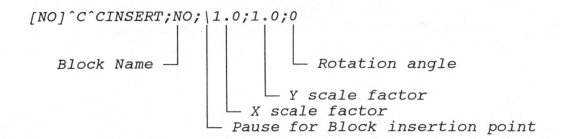

```
[NO]^C^CINSERT;NO;\1.0;1.0;0
```

          Block Name ─┘   └ *Rotation angle*
                           └ *Y scale factor*
                      └ *X scale factor*
                   └ *Pause for Block insertion point*

When you select this item, it will automatically answer all the prompts of the INSERT command and insert the NO block at the given location. The only input the user needs to enter is the insertion point of the block.

Line 10
[COIL]^C^CINSERT;COIL
In this menu item the block name is given, but the user needs to define other parameters when inserting this block.

Line 11
[EXIT]^C
Notice the blank space before EXIT. If there is such a space following the open bracket, AutoCAD does not look for a slide. AutoCAD instead displays the text, enclosed within the brackets, in the icon without any graphical symbol. When you select this icon, it will cancel the icon menu.

It is a good practice to provide a mechanism for cancelling an icon menu. Otherwise, you have to enter CTRL C or hit ESCAPE key on the key board to cancel the icon menu.

Line 12
Line 12 is a blank line that terminates the icon menu ICON1. When you swap the menus, the current items that are displayed on the screen must be cleared before loading the new items. This is made possible by providing a blank line at the end of every submenu. In this menu file line 12 clears the current menu items from the screen. If this line is missing, the submenus items will overlap, as a result of which some of the icons will not change when you load a new submenu that has fewer items.

Line 14
[RESIS]^C^CINSERT;RESIS;
This menu item inserts the block RESIS. The first back slash (\) is for block insertion point. The second, and third back slash are for X and Y scale factors. The fourth back slash is for the rotation angle. This menu item could also be written as:

[RESIS]^C^CINSERT;RESIS;
                   or
[RESIS]^C^CINSERT;RESIS

Line 15
[DIODE]^C^CINSERT;DIODE;\1.0;1.0;
If you select this menu item, AutoCAD will prompt you to enter the block insertion point and the rotation angle. The first back slash is for block insertion point and the second back slash is for rotation angle.

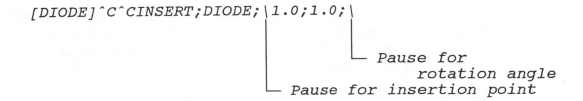

```
[DIODE]^C^CINSERT;DIODE;\1.0;1.0;\
```
                         └─ *Pause for*
                              rotation angle
          └─ *Pause for insertion point*

Line 16
[GROUND]^C^CINSERT;GRD;\1.5;1.5;0;;
This menu item has two semicolons (;) at the end. The first semicolon after 0 is for RETURN and completes the block insertion process. The second semicolon enters a RETURN and repeats the INSERT command. However, when the command is repeated you will have to respond to all the prompts. It does not accept the values defined in the menu item.

Note

1. The menu item repetition feature can not be used with the icon menus. For example, if the command definition starts with an asterisk ([GROUND]*^C^CINSERT;GRD;\1.5;1.5;0;;) the command is not automatically repeated, as is the case with a pull-down menu.

2. A blank line in an icon menu terminates the menu.

3. The menu command $I=* that displays the current menu can not be entered from the keyboard.

4. If you want to cancel or exit an icon menu, enter CTRL C or press ESCAPE key on the keyboard. AutoCAD ignores all other entries from the key board.

5. You can define any number of icon menus and submenus in the icon menu section of the menu file.

Slides for Icon Menus

The idea of creating slides for the icon menus is to display graphical symbols in the icons. This symbol makes it easier for the user to identify the operation that the icon will perform. Any slide can be used for the icon. However, the following guidelines should be kept in mind when creating slides for the icon menu.

1. When you make a slide for an icon menu, draw the object so that it fills the entire screen. The "MSLIDE" command makes a slide of the existing screen display, if the object is small the picture in the icon menu will be small. Use "ZOOM EXTENTS" or "ZOOM WINDOW" to display the object, before making a slide.

2. When you use the icon menu, it takes some time to load the slides for display in the icons. If the slides are complex, it will take more time to load them. Therefore, the slides should be kept as simple as possible and at the same time give the user enough information about the object.

3. Do not fill the object, because it takes a long time to load and display a solid object. If, there is a solid area in the slide, AutoCAD does not display the solid area in the icon.

4. If the objects are too long or too wide, it will be better to center the image with AutoCAD's PAN command before making a slide.

5. The space available on the screen for icon display is limited, especially if you have 16 icons on the screen. Make best use of this small area by giving only the relevant information in the form of a slide.

Loading Menus

AutoCAD software comes with a menu file ACAD.MNU that is automatically loaded when you get into drawing editor, provided the default settings have not been changed on your system. Otherwise, it will load the menu file that AutoCAD is configured to load, or the menu that is referenced by the prototype drawing. To load a new menu you can use AutoCAD's MENU command.

Command: MENU
Menu file name or . for none <current>: (file name)

To load the new menu, enter the file name of the icon menu (IM1) without the extension. AutoCAD will load the new menu, and then you can select the icon menus from the pull-down menu.

Note

1.   When you load the icon menu. some of the commands will be displayed on the screen menu area. This happens because the screen menu area is empty. If the menu file contained a screen menu also, the pull-down menu items will not be displayed in the screen menu area.

2.   When you load a new menu the original menu you had on the screen, prior to loading the new menu, is disabled. You can not select commands from the screen menu, pull-down menu, pointing device, or the digitizer, unless these sections are defined in the new menu file.

3.   To load the original menu, use the MENU command again and enter the name of the menu file.

Restrictions

The pull-down and icon menus are very easy to use and provide a quick access to some of the frequently used AutoCAD commands. However, the menu bar, the pull-down menus, and the icon menus are disabled during the following commands.

DTEXT Command
After you assign the text height and the rotation angle to a DTEXT command, the pull down-menu is automatically disabled.

SKETCH Command
The pull-down menus are disabled after you set the record increment in the SKETCH command.

VPOINT Command
The pull-down menus are disabled while the axis tripod and compass are displayed on the screen.

ZOOM Command
The pull-down menus are disabled when the dynamic zoom is in progress.

VIEWPORTS AND VPORTS
The pull-down menus are disabled when viewports and vports are active.

Exercise 1
Write an ICON menu for inserting the blocks as shown in Fig 4. Arrange the blocks in two groups so that you have two submenus in the icon menu.

<u>**PIPE FITTINGS**</u>	<u>**ELECTRIC SYMBOLS**</u>
GLOBE-P	BATTERY
GLOBE	CAPACITOR
REDUCER	COUPLER
CHECK	BREAKER

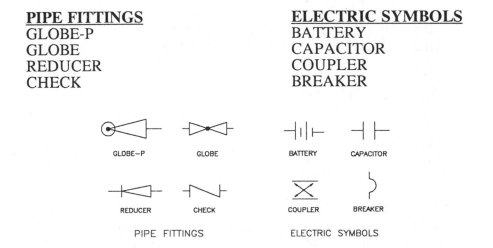

Figure 4 Block shapes for Exercise 1

Example 2

Write screen, tablet, pull down, and icon menu for inserting the following commands. B1 to B15 are the block names.

BLOCK
WBLOCK
ATTDEF
LIST
INSERT

BL1	BL6	BL11
BL2	BL7	BL12
BL3	BL8	BL13
BL4	BL9	BL14
BL5	BL10	BL15

The following file is a listing of the menu file for Example 2. The file contains the screen, tablet, pull-down and icon menu sections. The line numbers are not a part of the menu file. They are given for reference only.

```
***SCREEN                                              1
**INSERT1                                              2
[IM2-MENU]^C^C$S=INSERT1                               3
[* ---- *     ]                                        4
[-BLOCKS- ]                                            5
[         ]                                            6
[BLOCK:    ]^C^CBLOCK                                  7
[WBLOCK:   ]^C^CWBLOCK                                 8
[ATTDEF:   ]^C^CATTDEF                                 9
[LIST:     ]^C^CINSERT;?                              10
[INSERT-   ]                                          11
[         ]                                           12
[X,Y       ]                                          13
[   BL1:   ]^C^CINSERT;BL1;\1.0;1.0;\                 14
[   BL2:   ]*^C^CINSERT;BL2;\1.0;1.0;0               15
[   BL3:   ]*^C^CINSERT;BL3;\;;\                     16
[   BL4:   ]*^C^CINSERT;BL4;\;;;                     17
[   BL5:   ]^C^CINSERT;*BL5;\1.75                    18
[         ]                                           19
[         ]                                           20
[-CANCEL- ]^C                                         21
[- NEXT - ]^C^C$S=INSERT2                             22
[- ICON - ]$I=ICON1 $I=*                             23
                                                      24
**INSERT2 3                                            25
[INSERT-   ]                                          26
[         ]                                           27
[X,Y,Z]                                               28
[   BL6:   ]^C^CINSERT;BL6;\XYZ                       29
[   BL7:   ]*^C^CINSERT;BL7;\XYZ;;;\0                 30
                                                      31
[   BL8:   ]*^C^CINSERT;BL8;\XYZ;;;;;                 32
```

IM2–MENU
* –––– *
–BLOCKS–
BLOCK
WBLOCK
ATTDEF
LIST
INSERT
X,Y
BL1
BL2
BL3
BL4
BL5
– NEXT –
– ICON –
IM2–MENU
* –––– *
INSERT
X,Y,Z
BL6
BL7
BL8
BL9
BL10
BL11
BL12
CORNER
BL13
BL14
BL15
– PREV –
– ICON –
BLOCKS
BLOCK
WBLOCK
ATTDEF
LIST
INSERT
––––
ATTDIA–ON
ATTDIA–OFF
BL1 BL5 BL9 BL13
BL2 BL6 BL10 BL14
BL3 BL7 BL11 BL15
BL4 BL8 BL12 EXIT
SCREEN MENU
PULL–DOWN & ICON MENU

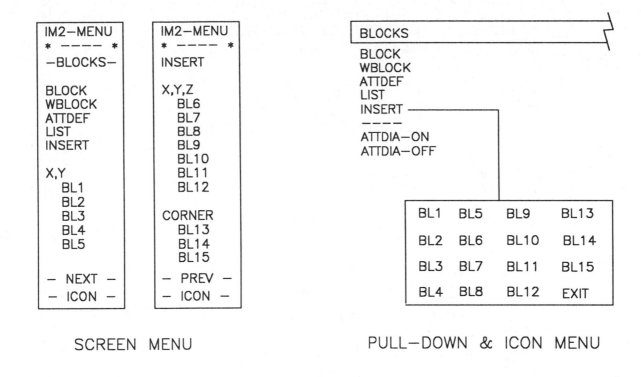

Figure 5A Design of screen and pull-down menu for Example 2

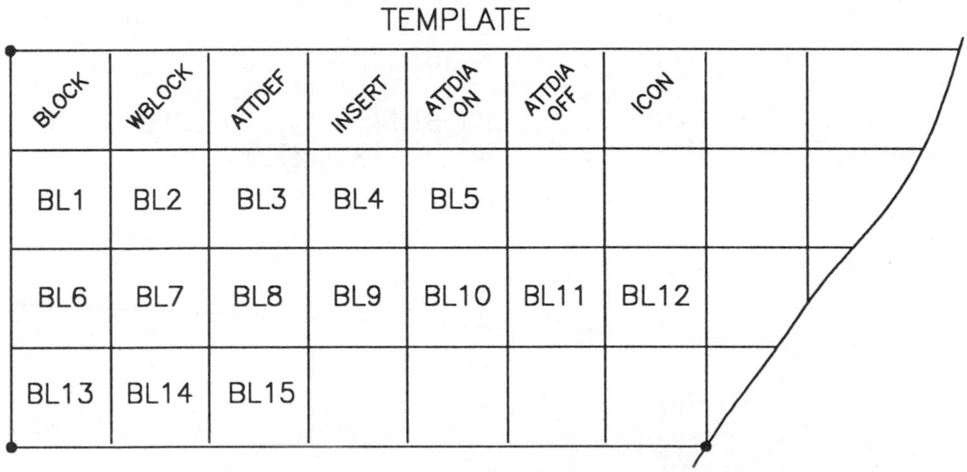

TEMPLATE
BLOCK
WBLOCK
ATTDEF
INSERT
ATTDIA ON
ATTDIA OFF
ICON
BL1 BL2 BL3 BL4 BL5
BL6 BL7 BL8 BL9 BL10 BL11 BL12
BL13 BL14 BL15

Figure 5B Design of tablet template for Example 2

```
[   BL9:      ]*^C^CINSERT;BL9;\XYZ;;;;\                          33
[   BL10:     ]*^C^CINSERT;*BL10;\XYZ;\                           34
[   BL11:     ]*^C^CINSERT;BL11;\XYZ;1.0;1.5;2.0;45              35
[   BL12:     ]^C^CINSERT;BL12;\XYZ;\\;;                          36
[            ]                                                    37
[CORNER      ]                                                    38
[   BL13:     ]*^C^CINSERT;*BL13;\\45                             39
[   BL14:     ]^C^CINSERT;BL14;\C;@1.0,1.0;0                      40
[   BL15:     ]^C^CINSERT;BL15;\C;@1.0,2.0;\                      41
[            ]                                                    42
[-CANCEL-   ]^C                                                  43
[- PREV -   ]^C^C$S=                                             44
[- ICON -   ]$I=ICON1 $I=*                                       45
                                                                 46
***TABLET1                                                       47
[1-1]^C^C$S=INSERT1 BLOCK                                        48
[1-2]^C^C$S=INSERT1 WBLOCK                                       49
[1-3]^C^C$S=INSERT1 ATTDEF                                       50
[1-4]^C^C$S=INSERT1 INSERT;?                                     51
[1-5]^C^CSETVAR ATTDIA 1                                         52
[1-6]^C^CSETVAR ATTDIA 0                                         53
[1-7]^C^C$I=ICON1 $I=*                                           54
[2-1]^C^C$S=INSERT1 INSERT;BL1;\1.0;1.0;\                        55
[2-2]*^C^C$S=INSERT1 INSERT;BL2;\1.0;1.0;0                       56
[2-3]*^C^C$S=INSERT1 INSERT;BL3;\;;\                             57
[2-4]*^C^C$S=INSERT1 INSERT;BL4;\;;;                             58
[2-5]^C^C$S=INSERT1 INSERT;*BL5;\1.75                            59
[2-6]                                                            60
[2-7]                                                            61
[3-1]^C^C$S=INSERT1 INSERT;BL6;\XYZ                              62
[3-2]*^C^C$S=INSERT1 INSERT;BL7;\XYZ;;;\0                        63
[3-3]*^C^C$S=INSERT1 INSERT;BL8;\XYZ;;;;;                        64
[3-4]*^C^C$S=INSERT1 INSERT;BL9;\XYZ;;;;\                        65
[3-5]*^C^C$S=INSERT1 INSERT;*BL10;\XYZ;\                         66
[3-6]*^C^C$S=INSERT1 INSERT;BL11;\XYZ;1;1.5;2;45                67
[3-7]^C^C$S=INSERT2 INSERT;BL12;\XYZ;\\;;                        68
[4-1]*^C^C$S=INSERT2 INSERT;*BL13;\\45                           69
[4-2]^C^C$S=INSERT2 INSERT;BL14;\C;@1.0,1.0;0                    70
[4-3]^C^C$S=INSERT2 INSERT;BL15;\C;@1.0,2.0;\                    71
[4-4]                                                            72
[4-5]                                                            73
[4-6]                                                            74
[4-7]                                                            75
                                                                 76
***POP1                                                          77
[INSERT]                                                         78
[BLOCK]^C^CBLOCK                                                 79
[WBLOCK]^C^CWBLOCK                                               80
[ATTRIBUTE DEFINITION]^C^CATTDEF                                 81
[LIST BLOCK NAMES]^C^CINSERT;?                                   82
[INSERT]^C^C$I=ICON1 $I=*                                        83
[--]                                                             84
[ATTDIA-ON]^C^CSETVAR ATTDIA 1                                   85
[ATTDIA-OFF]^C^CSETVAR ATTDIA 0                                  86
```

```
                                                                87
    ***ICON                                                     88
    **ICON1                                                     89
    [BLOCK INSERTION FOR EXAMPLE-2]                             90
    [BL1]^C^C$S=INSERT1 INSERT;BL1;\1.0;1.0;\                   91
    [BL2]^C^C$S=INSERT1 INSERT;BL2;\1.0;1.0;0                   92
    [BL3]^C^C$S=INSERT1 INSERT;BL3;\;;\                         93
    [BL4]^C^C$S=INSERT1 INSERT;BL4;\;;;                         94
    [BL5]^C^C$S=INSERT1 INSERT;*BL5;\1.75                       95
    [BL6]^C^C$S=INSERT1 INSERT;BL6;\XYZ                         96
    [BL7]^C^C$S=INSERT1 INSERT;BL7;\XYZ;;;\0                    97
    [BL8]^C^C$S=INSERT1 INSERT;BL8;\XYZ;;;;;                    98
    [BL9]^C^C$S=INSERT1 INSERT;BL9;\XYZ;;;;\                    99
    [BL10]^C^C$S=INSERT1 INSERT;*BL10;\XYZ;\                    100
    [BL11]^C^C$S=INSERT2 INSERT;BL11;\XYZ;1;1.5;2;45            101
    [BL12]^C^C$S=INSERT2 INSERT;BL12;\XYZ;\\;;                  102
    [BL13]^C^C$S=INSERT2 INSERT;*BL13;\\45                      103
    [BL14]^C^C$S=INSERT2 INSERT;BL14;\C;@1.0,1.0;0             104
    [BL15]^C^C$S=INSERT2 INSERT;BL15;\C;@1.0,2.0;\            105
    [ EXIT]^C                                                   106
```

Line 1
***SCREEN

In this menu item ***SCREEN is the section label for the screen menu. The menu items 2 through 46 are defined in this section.

Line 2
**INSERT1

In this menu item INSERT1 is the name of the submenu. The menu items 1 through 23 are a part of this submenu.

Line 14
^C^CINSERT;BL1;\1.0;1.0;\

This menu items inserts the block BL1. The input required for inserting the block is the block insertion point and the rotation angle. The X and Y scale factors are 1.0.

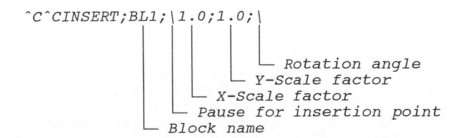

Line 17
*^C^CINSERT;BL4;\;;;

This menu item inserts the block BL4. The only input it requires is the block insertion point.

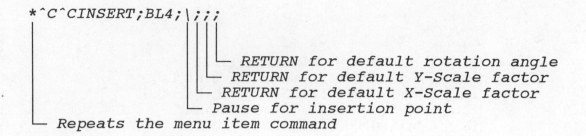

Line 18
^C^CINSERT;*BL5;\1.75
This menu item inserts the block BL5. The input required to insert the block is the insertion point and the scale factor. The asterisk in front of 5 (*5) is used to retain separate entities of the block. It is like inserting a block and then exploding it.

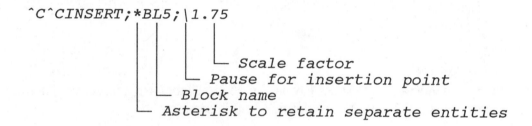

Note

*When you use asterisk in front of the block name (*BLK5) to retain separate entities of the block, AutoCAD prompts for the scale factor. The scale factor you enter is applied to both the X and Y axis. In the following example, AutoCAD will assume the scale factor as 1.75, insert the block, and then* **display an error message.**

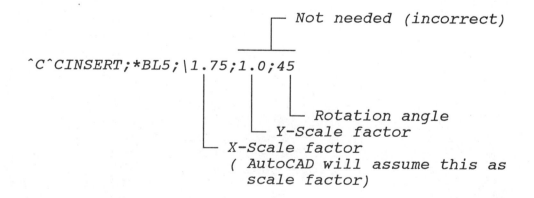

Line 22
^C^C$S=INSERT2

This menu item cancels the existing command twice and loads the submenu INSERT2

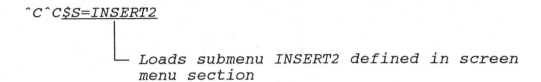

```
^C^C$S=INSERT2
                |
                |
                └─ Loads submenu INSERT2 defined in screen
                   menu section
```

Line 23
$I=ICON1 $I=*
In this menu item $I=ICON1 loads the icon submenu ICON1, and $I=* displays the dialogue box on the screen. This dialogue box contains the icons defined in the icon submenu ICON1.

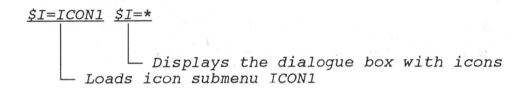

```
$I=ICON1 $I=*
    |        |
    |        |
    |        └─ Displays the dialogue box with icons
    └─ Loads icon submenu ICON1
```

Line 48
[1-1]^C^C$S=INSERT1 BLOCK
This menu item $S=INSERT1 loads the submenu INSERT1 on the screen. This submenu is defined in the screen menu section of the menu file. BLOCK is an AutoCAD command that allows the user to define a BLOCK. Therefore, when you select the BLOCK command from the tablet, you also load the corresponding menu on the screen.

[1-1] is for reference only and has no effect on the command. The first 1 indicates the first row, and the second 1 indicates that it is the first column. Giving reference numbers like this makes it easier for the user to identify the commands that will be assigned to a particular block on the template. For example, in the above line the BLOCK command will be assigned to the block that is in the first column of the first row.

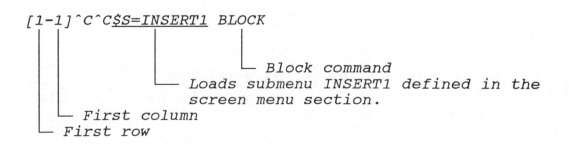

```
[1-1]^C^C$S=INSERT1 BLOCK
  | |         |       |
  | |         |       |
  | |         |       └─ Block command
  | |         └─ Loads submenu INSERT1 defined in the
  | |            screen menu section.
  | └─ First column
  └─ First row
```

Line 52
^C^CSETVAR ATTDIA 1
This menu item assigns a value of 1 to AutoCAD's ATTDIA system variable. When the value of this system variable is nonzero a dialogue box is displayed on the screen, when you select the INSERT command.

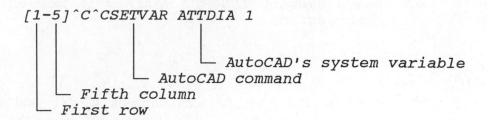

Line 54
^C^C$I=ICON1 $I=*
When you select this item from the template, it displays the dialogue box on the screen.   This dialogue box contains the icons that are defines in the icon submenu ICON1.

Line 60
[2-6]
This line does not contain any command definition and therefore creates an empty block on the template. If you select this block from the template, it will not enter any command. Line numbers 61, and 72 through 75 also create empty blocks on the template.

Line 77
***POP1
This is the section label of the first pull-down menu. The menu items defined on the lines 78 to 86 are defined in this section.

Line 88
***ICON
This is the section label of the icon menu.

Line 89
**ICON1
ICON1 is the name of the submenu, and the items on the lines 90 to 107 are defined in this submenu.

Line 91
[BL1]^C^C$S=INSERT1 INSERT;BL1;\1.0;1.0;
In this menu item BL1 is the name of the slide, and $S=INSERT1 loads the submenu INSERT1 on the screen.

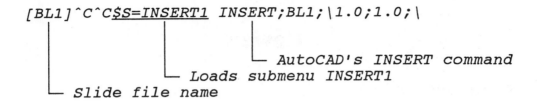

Exercise 2

Write a screen, tablet, and icon menu for inserting the following blocks. (The template of the tablet menu is shown in Figure 6)

B1	B4	B7
B2	B5	B8
B3	B6	B9

TEMPLATE

B1	B2	B3			
B4	B5	B6			
B7	B8	B9			

Figure 6 Tablet template for Exercise 2

Review

Fill in the blanks

1.   The icons are displayed in the .... box.

2.   An icon menu can be cancelled by entering .... or .... from the keyboard.

3.   The dialogue box can contain a maximum of .... icons.

4.   A blank line in an icon menu .... the icon menu.

5.   The menu item repetition feature .... be used with the icon menu.

6.   The drawing for slide should be .... on the entire screen before making a slide.

7.   It is .... recommended to fill a solid area in a slide for icon menu.

8.   The pull-down menus are disabled when the .... zoom is in progress.

9.   A menu item label like [3-5] is used in a tablet menu to reference .... and ....

10.   An icon menu .... be accessed from a tablet menu.

Exercises

Exercise 3

Write an icon menu for the following commands. Make the slides that will graphically illustrate the function of the command.

LINE	CIRCLE C,R
PLINE	CIRCLE C,D
	CIRCLE 2P

Exercise 4

Write a tablet and icon menu for inserting the following blocks. The B and C blocks should be in separate icons with CANCEL option. The layout of the template for the tablet menu is shown in Figure 7.

B1	B2	B3	C1	C2	C3
B4	B5	B6	C4	C5	C6
B7	B8	B9	C7	C8	C9

TEMPLATE

B1	B2	B3		C1	C2	C3
B4	B5	B6		C4	C5	C6
B7	B8	B9		C7	C8	C9

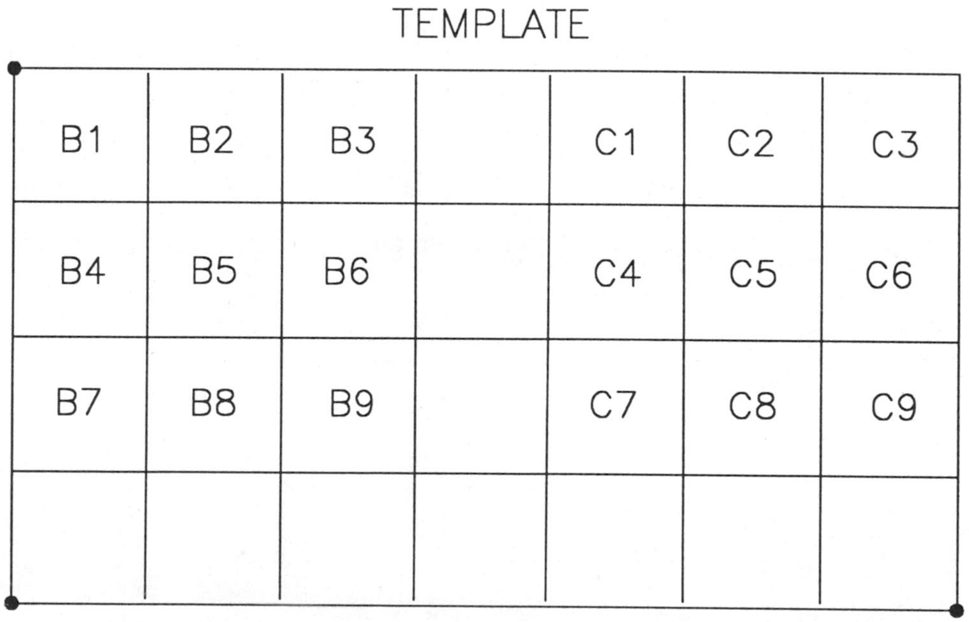

Figure 7 Tablet template for Exercise 4

Exercise 5

Write a screen, pull-down, and icon menu for the commands shown in Figure 8.   When the user selects a command from the pull down menu, it should automatically load the corresponding menu on the screen.

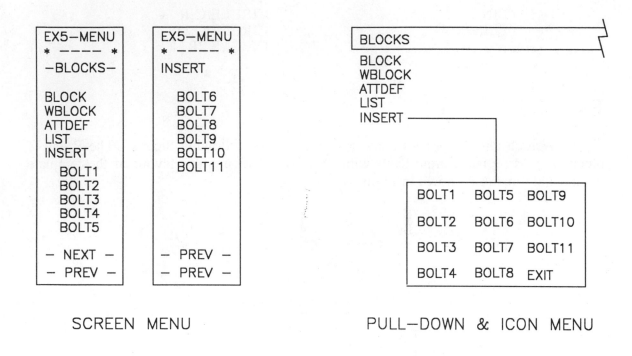

Figure 8   Design of screen, pull-down and icon menu for Exercise 5

Chapter **10**

Buttons and Aux1 Menus

You can use a multi-button pointing device to pick points, select objects or commands. These pointing devices come with different number of buttons, but 4 and 10 button pointing devices are very common. In addition to selecting points and objects, the multi-button pointing devices can be used to provide an easy and fast access to some of the frequently used AutoCAD commands. The commands can be selected by pressing the desired button, and AutoCAD automatically executes the command or the macro that is assigned to that button. Figure 1 shows one such pointing device with 12 buttons.

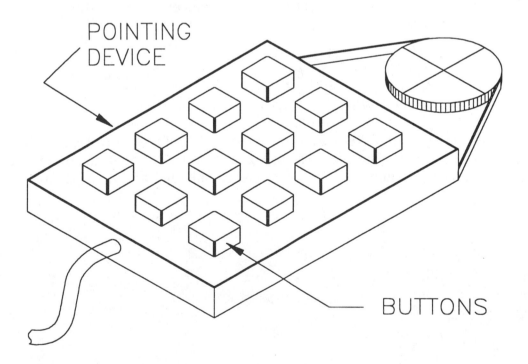

Figure 1   Pointing device with 12 buttons

The AutoCAD software package comes with a standard button menu that is a part of the ACAD.MNU file. The standard menu (ACAD.MNX) is automatically loaded when you start AutoCAD and get into the drawing editor. You can write your own button menu and assign the desired commands or macros to various buttons of the pointing device.

Writing a Button Menu

One of the buttons, generally the first button, is used as a pick button that picks the coordinates of the screen cross hairs and sends that information to AutoCAD. This button can also be used to select commands from various other menus like: tablet menu, screen menu, pull-down menu, and icon menu. This button can not be used for entering a command, but AutoCAD commands can be assigned to other buttons of the pointing device. Before writing a button menu, it is very important to decide the commands and options that you want to assign to various buttons, and know the prompts that are associated with those commands. Following example illustrates the working of the button-menu, and the procedure of assigning commands to different buttons.

Example 1

Write a Button-Menu for the following AutoCAD commands. The pointing device has 12 buttons (Figure 2) and the button number "1" is used as a pick button. (File name BM1.MNU)

2-RETURN	3-CANCEL	4-OSNAP
5-SNAP	6-ORTHO	7-AUTO
8-INT,END	9-LINE	10-CIRCLE
11-ZOOM Win	12-ZOOM Prev	

You can use AutoCAD's EDIT command, Edlin function of DOS, or any other text editor to write the menu file. The following file is a listing of the button menu for Example 1. The line numbers are for reference only and are not a part of the menu file.

***BUTTONS	1
;	2
^C^C	3
$S=OSNAP	4
^B	5
^O	6
AUTO	7
INT,ENDP	8
^C^CLINE	9
^C^CCIRCLE	10
'ZOOM;Win	11
'ZOOM;Prev	12

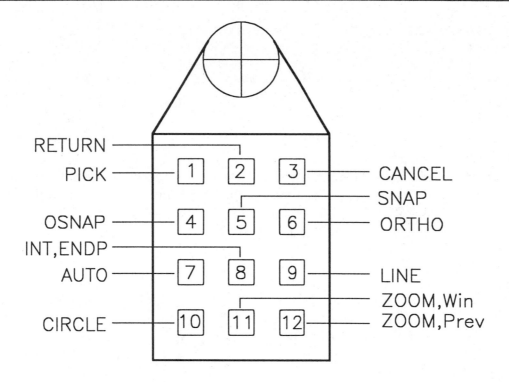

Figure 2   Pointing device

Line 1
***BUTTONS
***BUTTONS is the section label for the button menu. When the menu is loaded, AutoCAD compiles the menu file and assigns the commands to the buttons of the pointing device.

Line 2
;   This menu item assigns a semicolon (;) to button number 2. When you pick the second button on the pointing device, it enters a RETURN. It is like entering RETURN from the keyboard or the digitizer.

Line 3
^C^C
This menu item cancels the existing command twice (^C^C). This command is assigned to button number 3 of the pointing device. When you pick the third button on the pointing device, it cancels the existing command twice.

Line 4
$S=OSNAP
This menu item loads the submenu OSNAP that contains various object snap modes. The OSNAP submenu has been defined in the screen section of the menu file. This command is assigned to button number 4 of the pointing device. If you press this button, it will load the OSNAP submenu on the screen in the screen menu area.

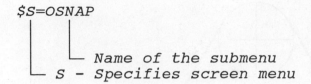

Line 5
^B
This menu item changes the snap mode. It is assigned to button number 5 of the pointing device. When you pick the 5th button on the pointing device, it turns the "SNAP" mode on, or off. It is like holding the CTRL key down on the key board and then pressing the key B.

Line 6
^O
This menu item changes the ORTHO mode, and it is assigned to the button number 6. When you pick the 6th button on the pointing device, it turns the ORTHO mode on, or off.

Line 7
AUTO
This menu item selects the AUTO option for creating a selection set. This command is assigned to button number 7 on the pointing device.

Line 8
INT,ENDP
In this menu item INT is for the intersection snap, and ENDP is for the end point snap. This command is assigned to button number 8 on the pointing device. When you pick this button, AutoCAD looks for the intersection point. If it can not find an intersection point then it starts looking for the end point of the object that is within the pick box.

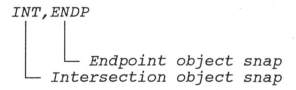

Line 9
^C^CLINE
This menu item defines the LINE command, and it is assigned to the button number 9. When you select this button, AutoCAD cancels the existing command, and then selects the LINE command.

Line 10
^C^CCIRCLE

This menu item defines the CIRCLE command. and it is assigned to button number 10. When you pick this button, AutoCAD automatically selects the CIRCLE command and prompts for the user input.

Line 11
'ZOOM;Win
This menu item defines a transparent ZOOM command with window option, and it is assigned to button number 11 of the pointing device.

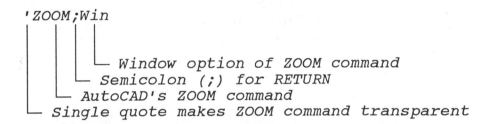

```
'ZOOM;Win
        Window option of ZOOM command
        Semicolon (;) for RETURN
        AutoCAD's ZOOM command
        Single quote makes ZOOM command transparent
```

Line 12
'ZOOM;Pre
This menu item defines a transparent ZOOM command with previous option, and it is assigned to button number 12 of the pointing device.

Note

1. *If the button menu has more menu items than the number of buttons on the pointing device, the menu items in excess of the number of buttons are ignored. This does not include the pick button. For example, if a pointing device has three buttons, in addition to the pick button, the first three menu items will be assigned to the three buttons. The remaining lines of the button menu are ignored.*

2. *The commands are assigned to the buttons in the same order in which they appear in the file. For example, the menu item that is defined on line 3 will be automatically assigned to the third button of the pointing device. Similarly, the menu item that is on line 4 will be assigned to the fourth button of the pointing device. Same is true with other menu items and buttons.*

Special Handling for Button Menu

When you press any button on the multi-button pointing device, AutoCAD receives the following information

1. **The button number.**
2. **The coordinates of the screen cross hairs.**

You can write a button menu that utilizes one, or both pieces of information. The following example uses only the button number and ignores the coordinates of the screen cross hairs.

Example
^C^CLINE

If this command was assigned to the second button of the pointing device and you select this button, AutoCAD will receive the button number, and the coordinates of the screen cross hair. AutoCAD will execute the command that is assigned to the second button, but it will ignore the coordinates of the cross hairs. The following example uses both, button number and the coordinates of the screen cross hairs.

Example
^C^CLINE;\

In this menu item the LINE command is followed by a semicolon (;) and a back slash (\). The semicolon enters a RETURN and the back slash normally causes a pause for the user input. However, in the buttons menu AutoCAD will not pause for the user input. The back slash (\) in this menu item will use the coordinates of the screen cross hair, supplied by the pointing device, as the starting point (From point) of the line. AutoCAD will then prompt for the second point of the line (To point).

Example 2

Write a button menu for the following AutoCAD commands. The menu items should utilize the information about the coordinate points of the screen cross hairs, where applicable. (File name BM2.MNU)

```
2. RETURN
3. AUTO;\
4. INT,END;\
5. LINE;\
6. PLINE;\
7. CIRCLE;\
```

The following file is a listing of the button menu for Example 2.

```
***BUTTON                                          1
;                                                  2
AUTO;\                                             3
INT,ENDP;\                                         4
LINE;\                                             5
PLINE;\                                            6
CIRCLE;\                                           7
```

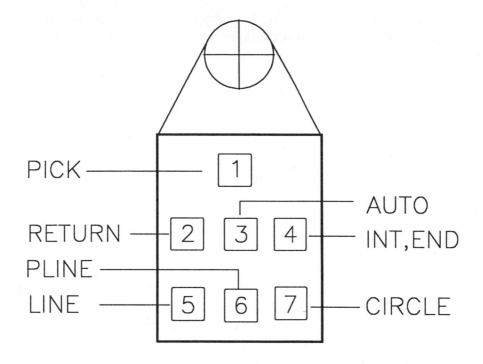

Figure 3   Pointing device with 7 buttons

Line 3
AUTO;
This menu item selects the AUTO option for creating a selection set, and the back slash is used to accept the coordinates supplied by the screen cross hairs. This command is assigned to button number 3 on the pointing device.

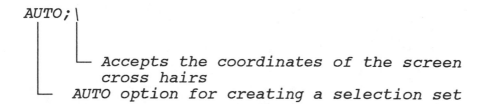

```
AUTO; \
      Accepts the coordinates of the screen
      cross hairs
   AUTO option for creating a selection set
```

Line 4
INT,ENDP;
In this menu item INT is for the intersection snap and ENDP is for the end point snap.   This command is assigned to button number 8 on the pointing device. When you pick this button, AutoCAD looks for the intersection point. If it can not find an intersection point then it starts looking for the end point of the object that is within the pick box. The back slash (\) is used here to accept the coordinates of the screen cross hairs. If the cross hairs are near an object,

within the pick box, AutoCAD will snap to the intersections point, or the end point of the object when you press button number 4 on the pointing device.

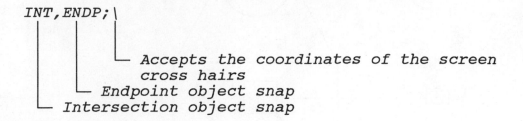

```
INT,ENDP;\
                    └─ Accepts the coordinates of the screen
                       cross hairs
              └─ Endpoint object snap
       └─ Intersection object snap
```

Line 7
CIRCLE;
This menu item generates a circle. The back slash (\) is used here to accept the coordinates of the screen cross hair as the center of the circle. If you press button number 7 of the pointing device to draw a circle, you do not need to enter the center of the circle. Because the current position of the screen cross hairs automatically become the center of the circle. You have to define the radius only, to generate the circle.

Note

1. *The coordinate information that is associated with the button can be utilized with the first back slash only.*

2. *If a menu item in a button menu has more than one back slash (\), the remaining back slashes are ignored. For example, in the following menu item the first back slash uses the coordinates of screen cross hairs as the insertion point and the remaining back slashes are ignored and do not cause a pause as in other menus.*

    Example
    INSERT;B1\\\0

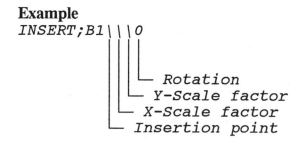

```
INSERT;B1\\\0
                └─ Rotation
             └─ Y-Scale factor
          └─ X-Scale factor
       └─ Insertion point
```

Submenus

The facility to define submenus is not limited to screen, pull-down and icon menus only. You can also define submenus in the button menu.

Submenu Definition

A submenu label consists of two asterisk signs (**) followed by the name of the submenu. The buttons menu can have any number of submenus, and every submenu should have a unique name. The items that follow a submenu, up to the next section label, or submenu label, belong to that submenu. The format of a submenu label is:

```
**Name
    |
    |  └─ Name of the submenu
    └─ Two asterisk signs (**) designate a submenu
```

Note

1. *The submenu name can be up to 31 characters long.*
2. *The submenu name can consist of letters, digits, and the special characters like: $ (dollar), - (hyphen), and _ (underscore).*
3. *The submenu name should not have any embedded blanks.*
4. *The submenu names should be unique in a menu file.*

Submenu Reference

The submenu reference is used to reference or load a submenu. It consists of a "$" sign followed by a letter that specifies the menu section. The letter that specifies a button menu section is B. The menu section is followed by "=" sign, and the name of the submenu that the user wants to activate. The submenu name should be without "**". Following is the format of a submenu reference:

```
$Section=Submenu
 |   |    |    |
 |   |    |    └─ Name of submenu
 |   |    └─ "=" sign
 |   └─ Menu section specifier
 └─ "$" sign
```

Example

```
$B=BUTTON1
 |    |
 |    └─ Name of submenu
 └─ B  Specifies buttons menu section
```

Loading Menus

From the buttons menu, you can load any menu that is defined in the screen, pull-down, or icon menu sections by using the appropriate load commands. It may not be needed in most of the applications, but if you want to, you can load the menus that are defined in other menu sections.

Loading Screen Menus

You can load any menu that is defined in the screen menu section, from the button menu, by using the following load commands.

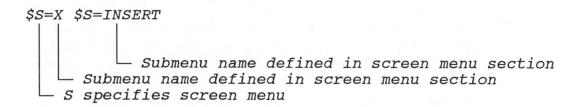

```
$S=X  $S=INSERT
 │     │     │
 │     │     └─ Submenu name defined in screen menu section
 │     └─ Submenu name defined in screen menu section
 └─ S specifies screen menu
```

The first load command ($S=X) loads the submenu X that has been defined in the screen menu section of the menu file. The X submenu can contain 21 blank lines, so that when it is loaded it clears the screen menu. The second load command ($S=INSERT) loads the submenu INSERT that has been defined in the screen menu section of the menu file.

Loading a Pull-down Menu

You can load a pull-down menu from the button menu by using the following command.

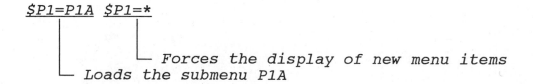

```
$P1=P1A  $P1=*
  │        │
  │        └─ Forces the display of new menu items
  └─ Loads the submenu P1A
```

The first load command $P1=P1A loads the submenu P1A that has been defined in the POP1 section of the menu file. The second load command $P1=* forces the new menu items to be displayed on the screen.

Loading an Icon Menu

You can also load an icon menu from the button menu by using the following load command.

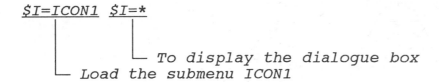

This menu item consists of two load commands. The first load command $I=ICON1 loads the icon submenu ICON1 that has been defined in the icon menu section of the file. The second load command $I=* displays the new dialogue box on the screen.

Example 3

Write a button menu for a pointing device that has 6 buttons. The functions assigned to different buttons is shown in the following table. (File name BM3.MNU)

SUBMENU B1	**SUBMENU B2**
1. PICK	1. PICK
2. RETURN	2. RETURN
3. LOAD OSNAPS SUBMENU	3. LOAD ICON1 SUBMENU
4. LOAD ZOOM1 SUBMENU	4. EXPLODE
5. LOAD BUTTON SUBMENU B1	5. LOAD BUTTON SUBMENU B1
6. LOAD BUTTON SUBMENU B2	6. LOAD BUTTON SUBMENU B2

Note

1.   OSNAPS submenu is defined in the POP1 section of the pull-down menu.

2.   ZOOM1 submenu is defined in the screen section of the menu file.

3.   ICON1 submenu is defined in the ICON section of the menu file. The ICON1 submenu contains 4 icons for inserting the blocks.

In this example there are two submenus. The submenus are loaded by picking button 5 for submenu B1, and button 6 for submenu B2. When the submenu B1 is loaded, AutoCAD assigns the commands that are defined under the submenu B1 to the buttons of the pointing device. Similarly, when the submenu B2 is loaded, AutoCAD assigns the commands that are defined under the submenu B2 to the buttons of the pointing device. Figure 3 shows the commands that are assigned to the buttons after loading submenu B1, and submenu B2

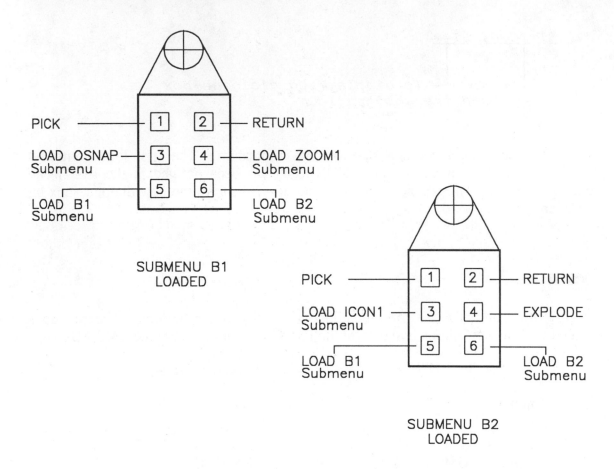

Figure 4 Commands assigned to different buttons of pointing device

You can use AutoCAD's EDIT command to write the file. The following file is the listing of the buttons menu for Example 3. The line numbers are not a part of the file. They are shown here for reference only.

```
***BUTTON                        1
**B1                             2
;                                3
$P1=*                            4
$S=X $S=ZOOM1 'ZOOM;Win          5
$B=B1                            6
$B=B2                            7
**B2                             8
```

```
;                                                    9
^C^C$I=ICON1 $I=*                                    10
EXPLODE;\                                             11
$B=B1                                                12
$B=B2                                                13
```

Line 2
**B1
This menu item defines a submenu. The name of the submenu is B1.

Line 4
$P1=*
This menu item loads and displays the pull-down menu that has been defined in the POP1 section of the pull-down menu.

Line 5
$S=X $S=ZOOM1 'ZOOM;Win
This menu item will load and display the ZOOM1 submenu on the screen, and enter a transparent ZOOM Window command. $S=X loads the submenu X that has been defined in the screen menu section of the menu file. $S=ZOOM1 loads the submenu ZOOM1 that has been also defined in the screen menu section. 'ZOOM;Win is a transparent zoom command with the window option.

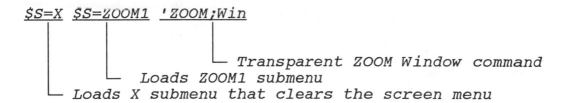

Line 8
**B2
This menu item defines the submenu B2

Line 10
^C^C$I=ICON1 $I=*
This menu item cancels the existing command twice and then loads the submenu ICON1 that has been defined in the ICON menu. $I=* displays the current dialogue box on the screen.

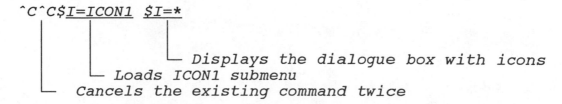

Line 11

EXPLODE;

This menu item will explode an entity. It utilizes the special feature of the pointing device buttons that supply the co-ordinates of the screen cross hair. When you select this button, it will explode the entity where the screen cross hair is located.

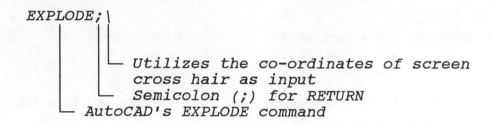

```
EXPLODE; \
  |       | |_ Utilizes the co-ordinates of screen
  |       |    cross hair as input
  |       |_ Semicolon (;) for RETURN
  |_ AutoCAD's EXPLODE command
```

Line 12

$B=B1

This menu item loads the submenu B1, and assigns the functions defined under this submenu to different buttons of the pointing device.

Line 13

$B=B2

This menu item loads the submenu B2, and assigns the functions defined under this submenu to different buttons of the pointing device.

Aux1 Menu

The auxiliary menu section (***Aux1) is similar to the buttons menu section. The difference is in the hardware. In the buttons menu the commands are assigned to the buttons of the pointing device, whereas in the auxiliary menu the commands are assigned to the buttons of a function-box. The function-box is a device that has several buttons like a pointing device, but does not need a digitizer to activate the functions. By pressing a button of the function-box, the command that is assigned to that particular button in the auxiliary menu is automatically activated.

Review

Fill in the blanks

1. A multi-button pointing device can be used to pick ...., or select ...., or enter AutoCAD ....

2. AutoCAD receives the button ...., and .... of screen cross hair, when a button is activated on the pointing device.

3. If the number of menu items in the buttons menu are more then the number of buttons on the pointing device, the excess lines are ....

4. The command are assigned to the buttons of the pointing device in the .... order in which they appear in the buttons menu.

5. The format of the load command for loading a submenu that has been defined in the screen menu is ....

6. The format of the load command for loading a submenu that has been defined in the pull-down menu is ....

7. The format of the load command for loading a submenu that has been defined in the icon menu is ....

Exercises

Exercise 1

Write a button menu for the following AutoCAD commands. The pointing device has 10 buttons and button number 1 is used for picking the points. The blocks are to be inserted with a scale factor of 1.00 and a rotation of 0 degrees.   (File name BME1.MNU)

1. PICK BUTTON   2. RETURN   3. CANCEL
4. OSNAPS   5. INSERT B1   6. INSERT B2
7. INSERT B3   8. ZOOM Window   9. ZOOM All
10.ZOOM Previous

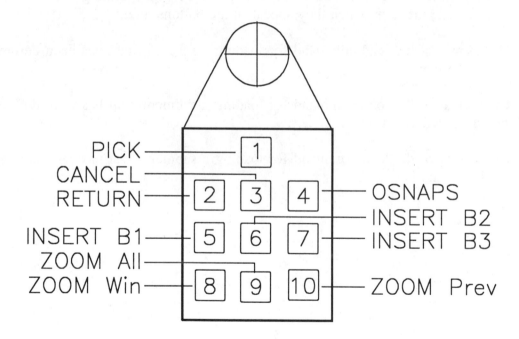

Figure 5   Pointing device with 10 buttons

Note

1.   B1, B2, B3 are the names of the Blocks or WBlocks that have already been created.

2.   It is assumed that the OSNAP submenu has already been defined in the screen menu section of the menu file.

3.   Use transparent ZOOM command for ZOOM Previous, and ZOOM Window.

Exercise 2

Write a button menu for a pointing device that has 10 buttons. The functions assigned to different buttons is shown in the following table. (File name BME2.MNU)

SUBMENU B1

1. PICK
2. RETURN
3. LINE
4. CIRCLE
5. LOAD OSNAPS
6. ZOOM Win
7. ZOOM Prev
8. ERASE
9. LOAD BUTTON MENU B1
10. LOAD BUTTON MENU B2

SUBMENU B2

1. PICK
2. RETURN
3. LOAD ICON1
4. LOAD ICON2
5. LOAD P2 (Pull-down)
6. LOAD P3 (Pull-down)
7. INSERT
8. EXPLODE
9. LOAD BUTTON MENU B1
10. LOAD BUTTON MENU B2

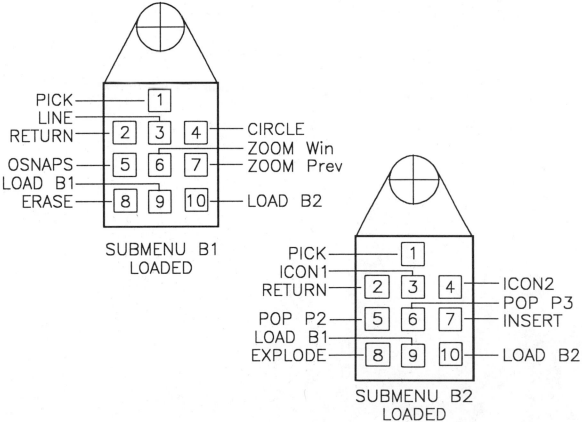

Figure 5 Commands assigned to different buttons of pointing device

Note

It is assumed that

1.   OSNAPS submenu is defined in the POP1 section of the pull-down menu.

2.   Pull-down menus P2 and P3 are defined in the POP2 and POP3 sections of the pull-down menu.

3.   ICON1 and ICON2 submenus are defined in the ICON section of the menu file. The ICON1 and ICON2 submenus contain 4 icons each for inserting the blocks.

Chapter 11

Customizing Standard AutoCAD Menu

Standard AutoCAD Menu

The AutoCAD software package comes with a standard menu file ACAD.MNU and a compiled menu file ACAD.MNX. The compiled file ACAD.MNX is loaded on the system when you install the AutoCAD software. The ACAD.MNU file is not loaded during the normal installation process. If you do a directory of the files, you will not find ACAD.MNU file in the directory listing. The ACAD.MNU file is contained on the "Support/Source" diskette under the "Source" subdirectory. You can use the following copy command to copy the file from the diskette in A drive to the ACAD11 subdirectory on C drive.

C > COPY A:\SOURCE\ACAD.MNU C:\ACAD11

When you load AutoCAD and get into the drawing editor, the menu file ACAD.MNX is automatically loaded. If the compiled file ACAD.MNX is missing then AutoCAD looks for ACAD.MNU file, compiles the file and then loads the compiled version of the menu. This menu file contains all commands that you see on the screen, digitizer, or the pull-down menus. If you make any changes in the menu file, AutoCAD senses the change and will automatically recompile the menu file and then load the updated ACAD.MNX file. The AutoCAD menu file contains the following section labels.

```
***BUTTONS
***AUX1
***POP1      ——— to ——— POP9
***ICON
***SCREEN
***TABLET1 ——— to ——— TABLET4
***TABLET1ALT —— to ——— TABLET4ALT
```

***COMMENT

The following file is a partial listing of ACAD.MNU file that shows some of the section labels.

***BUTTONS
;
$p1=*
^C^C
^B
^O
^G
^D
^E
^T
***AUX1
;
$p1=*
^C^C
^B
^O
^G
^D
^E
^T

***POP1
[Assist]
[Help!   ]'?
[~--]
[Cancel   ]^C^C
[~--]
[Osnap: <mode>]^C^C$p1= $p1=* OSNAP \
CENter
[ENDpoint   ]ENDP
INSert
[INTersection]INT

```
|
|
|
|
```

***POP2
**p2draw
[Draw]
[Line   ]^C^C$S=X $S=line line
[Point   ]*^C^C$S=X $S=point point

```
|
|
|
```

***SCREEN
**S

```
[AutoCAD]^C^C^P$S=X $S=S (setq T_MENU 0)(princ) ^P$P1=POP1
$P2=P2DRAW $P4=P4DISP $P6=P6OPT $P8=POP8
[* * * *]$S=OSNAPB
[BLOCKS]$S=X $S=BL
[DIM:]$S=X $S=DIM ^C^CDIM
[DISPLAY]$S=X $S=DS
[DRAW]$S=X $S=DR
[EDIT]$S=X $S=ED
[INQUIRY]$S=X $S=INQ
[LAYER:]$S=X $S=LAYER ^C^CLAYER
[MVIEW]$S=X $S=MV
[PLOT]$S=X $S=PLOT
[SETTINGS]$S=X $S=SET
```

```
***TABLET1
[A-1]
[A-2]
[A-3]
[A-4]
[A-5]
[A-6]
[A-7]
[A-8]
[A-9]
[A-10]
[A-11]
[A-12]
[A-13]
[A-14]
[A-15]
[A-16]
[A-17]
[A-18]
[A-19]
[A-20]
[A-21]
[A-22]
[A-23]
[A-24]
[A-25]
[B-1]^C^C^P(progn(setq m:err *error*)(princ))+
(defun *error* (msg)(princ msg)(setq *error* m:err m:err nil f nil)(princ))+
(if (null c:SOLMOVE)(defun c:SOLMOVE () (menucmd "S=X")(menucmd
"S=SOLLOAD");+
(terpri)(princ "ERROR:  Command not found. ")+
(princ "  Load AME or AMElite from the screen menu. ")+
(setq c:SOLMOVE nil)(princ))+
(progn (menucmd "S=X")(menucmd "S=SMOVE")))(princ);^PSOLMOVE
```

```
***TABLET2
^C^C^P(menucmd "S=X")(menucmd "S=HIDE1")(progn (initget "Yes
No")+
(setq ans (getkword "Do you want to HIDE? <Y> ")))(if (= ans "Yes")+
(command "HIDE")(progn (menucmd "S= ")(menucmd "S= ")))(princ);^P
$S=X $S=VPOINT VPOINT;;
$S=X $S=SHADE
$S=X $S=UCS1 ^C^CUCS
^C^CUCS;PREV
^C^CUCS;ORIGIN
;
$S=X $S=MV ^C^CMVIEW
$S=X $S=ZOOM 'ZOOM VMAX
$S=X $S=LINE ^C^CLINE
^C^CREGEN
```

```
***TABLET3
;
;
;
<<135
<<135
<<90
<<90
<<45
<<45
;
;
;
<<180
<<180
<\
<\
<<0
<<0
;
;
;
<<225
<<225
<<270
```

```
***TABLET4
```

```
;
;
;
;
;
;
;
;
;
;
;
;
;
;
;
;
;
;
;
;
[Tablet 1]^C^C^P(if (null T_MENU) (setq T_MENU 0))+
(if (= (logand 1 T_MENU) 1)(progn (setq T_MENU (- T_MENU 1))+
(if (< (getvar "EXPERT") 4)(princ "Alternate tablet area 1 unloaded.
"));+
```

```
***TABLET1ALT
[A-1]
[A-2]
[A-3]
[A-4]
[A-5]
[A-6]
[A-7]
[A-8]
[A-9]
[A-10]
[A-11]
[A-12]
[A-13]
[A-14]
[A-15]
[A-16]
[A-17]
[A-18]
[A-19]
[A-20]
```

```
***TABLET2ALT
```

```
^C^C^P(menucmd "S=X")(menucmd "S=HIDE1")(progn (initget "Yes
No")+
(setq ans (getkword "Do you want to HIDE? <Y>")))(if (= ans "Yes")+
(command "HIDE")(progn (menucmd "S= ")(menucmd "S= ")))(princ);^P
$S=X $S=VPOINT VPOINT;;
$S=X $S=SHADE
$S=X $S=UCS1 ^C^CUCS
^C^CUCS;PREV
^C^CUCS;ORIGIN
.
$S=X $S=MV ^C^CMVIEW
$S=X $S=ZOOM ^C^CZOOM VMAX
$S=X $S=LINE ^C^CLINE
^C^CREGEN
[VPOINT  ]^C^CVPOINT R;<<135;$S=X $S=VPOINT3D
[VPT rear]^C^CVPOINT R;<<90;$S=X $S=VPOINT3D
[VPOINT  ]^C^CVPOINT R;<<45;$S=X $S=VPOINT3D
$S=X $S=UCS1 ^C^CUCS
^C^CUCS;;
```

```
***TABLET3ALT
;
;
;
<<135
<<135
<<90
<<90
<<45
<<45
;
;
;
<<180
<<180
```

```
***TABLET4ALT
;
;
;
```

```
;
```

```
;
;
[Tablet 1]^C^C^P(if (null T_MENU) (setq T_MENU 0))+
(if (= (logand 1 T_MENU) 1)(progn (setq T_MENU (- T_MENU 1))+
```

Submenus

The number of items in a submenu section can be very large that can not be accommodated on one screen. For example, the maximum number of items that can be displayed on some of the menu devices is 21. If the pull-down menu or the screen menu has more than 21 items, the menu items in access of 21 are not displayed on the screen and can not therefore be accessed. Similarly, the maximum number of assignable blocks in tablet area-1 is 225. If the number of items in the TABLET1 or TABLET1ALT section are more than 225, the menu items in access of 225 are not assigned to any block on the template and are therefore inaccessible. The user can overcome this problem by using submenus that let the user define smaller groups of items within a menu section. When a submenu is selected, it loads the submenu items and displays them on the screen. In the case of a tablet menu the commands are assigned to various blocks on the template.

Submenu Definition

A submenu definition consists of two asterisk signs (**) followed by the name of the submenu. A menu can have any number of submenus, and every submenu should have a unique name. The items that follow a submenu, up to the next section label, or submenu label, belong to that submenu. Following is the format of a submenu label:

```
**Name
  |   |
  |   |
  |    └─ Name of the submenu
  └─ Two asterisk signs (**) designate a submenu
```

Note

1. *The submenu name can be up to 31 characters long.*

2. *The submenu name can consist of letters, digits, and the special characters like: $ (dollar), - (hyphen), and _ (underscore).*

3. *The submenu name should not have any embedded blanks.*

4. *The submenu names should be unique in a menu file.*

Submenu Reference

The submenu reference is used to reference or load a submenu. It consists of a "$" sign followed by a letter that specifies the menu section. For example, the letter S specifies screen menu, B specifies button menu, I specifies icon menu, and Pn species pull-down menu where n designates the number of the pull-down menu. Similarly, the letter that specifies a tablet menu section is Tn, where n designates the number of the tablet menu section. The menu section is followed by "=" sign, and the name of the submenu that the user wants to activate. The submenu name should be without "**". Following is the format of a submenu reference:

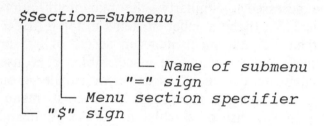

```
$Section=Submenu
```

```
              Name of submenu
        "=" sign
    Menu section specifier
  "$" sign
```

Example

```
$S=BLOCKS
```

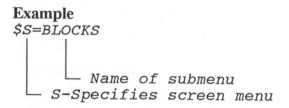

```
        Name of submenu
  S-Specifies screen menu
```

Loading Screen Menus

You can load a menu that is defined in the screen menu section, from any menu, by using the following load command.

$S = (name1) $S = (name2)
　　　　Where "name1" and "name2" are the names of the submenus

Example

```
$S=X $S=INSERT
```

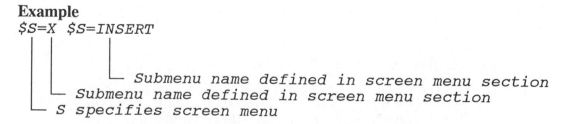

```
            Submenu name defined in screen menu section
      Submenu name defined in screen menu section
  S specifies screen menu
```

The first load command ($S=X) loads the submenu X that has been defined in the screen menu section of the menu file. The X submenu, defined in the screen menu section, contains 21 blank lines. When it is loaded, it clears the screen menu. The second load command ($S=INSERT) loads the submenu INSERT that has also been defined in the screen menu section of the menu file.

Loading Pull-down Menus

You can load a pull-down menu, from any menu, by using the following command.

$P(n)=(name) $P(n)=*
> Where "n" ranges from 1 to 10 (POP1 -- POP10) and "name" is the name of the submenu defined in the pull-down menu.

Example

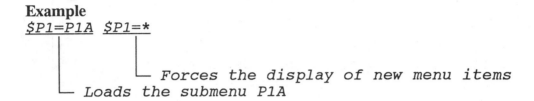

```
$P1=P1A  $P1=*
```
— Forces the display of new menu items
— Loads the submenu P1A

The first load command $P1=P1A loads the submenu P1A that has been defined in the POP1 section of the menu file. The second load command $P1=* is a special AutoCAD command that forces the new menu items to be displayed on the screen.

Loading Icon Menus

You can also load an icon menu, from any menu, by using the following load command.

$I=(name) $I=*
> Where "name" is the name of the submenu defined in the icon submenu

Example

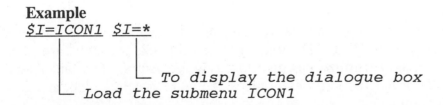

```
$I=ICON1  $I=*
```
— To display the dialogue box
— Load the submenu ICON1

This menu item consists of two load commands. The first load command $I=ICON1 loads the icon submenu ICON1 that has been defined in the icon menu section of the file. The second load command $I=* displays the new dialogue box on the screen.

Customizing Tablet Area-1

The tablet menu has four sections TABLET1, TABLET2, TABLET3 and TABLET4. AutoCAD provides an option that lets the user select the alternate tablet menu that also has four sections TABLET1ALT, TABLET2ALT, TABLET3ALT, and TABLET4ALT. Figure 1 shows the location of different tablet areas on the template.

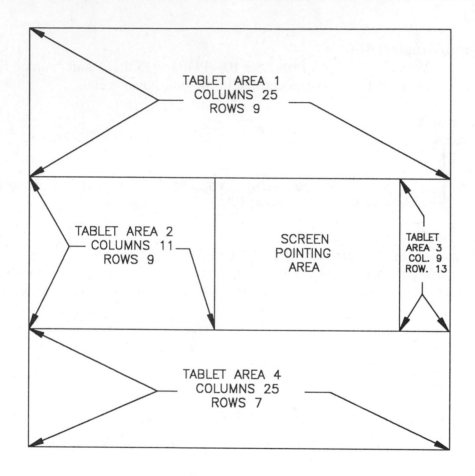

Figure 1   Four tablet areas of AutoCAD template

Tablet area 1 of the template has 25 columns numbered 1 to 25, and 9 rows designated by letters A through I. The total number of blocks for tablet area 1 is 225 (9 X 25 = 225). You can utilize this area to customize AutoCAD's tablet menu by assigning commands or macros to different blocks. Figure 2 shows tablet area-1 of the standard AutoCAD template.

The TABLET1 menu section uses the first 10 columns and 9 rows of tablet area 1 for AME functions. Therefore, the number of empty blocks that are not assigned any command are 120 (15 x 9 = 135). You can assign any command or macro to these blocks. Before making any changes or additions to the tablet menu it is very important to figure out the commands that you want to add to the tablet menu and determine their location on the template. A well thought out tablet design will save a lot of revision time in the long run. Figure 3 shows a drawing that has 25 columns and 9 rows. You can draw a similar drawing and make several copies of it for arranging the commands and designing the template.

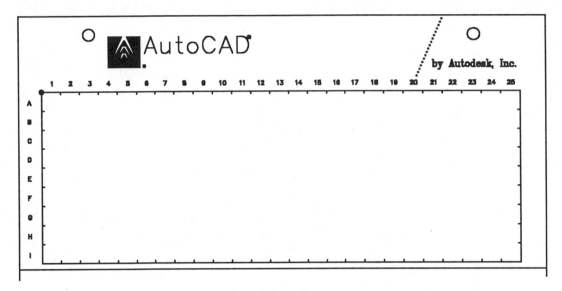

Fig. 2

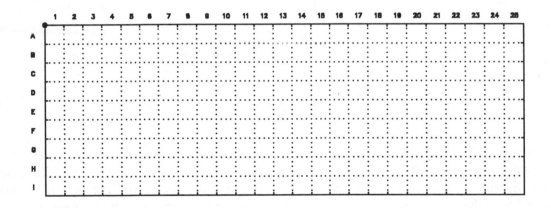

Figure 3   Tablet area-1 with 25 columns and 9 rows

Note

Before making any changes to the menu file make sure that the original file has been properly saved. You can also make a copy of the ACAD.MNU file and then make the changes in the new file. Use the following command to make a copy of the ACAD.MNU file. The name of the new menu file is CUSTOM.MNU. After you make the necessary changes you can load the new menu for testing by using AutoCAD's MENU command.

COPY ACAD.MNU CUSTOM.MNU

Example 1

Add the commands shown in Figure 4 to the TABLET1 section of CUSTOM.MNU file. B10 through B25 are the names of the blocks. The user should be able to insert the blocks with X and Y scale factors of 1.0, and a rotation angle of 0.

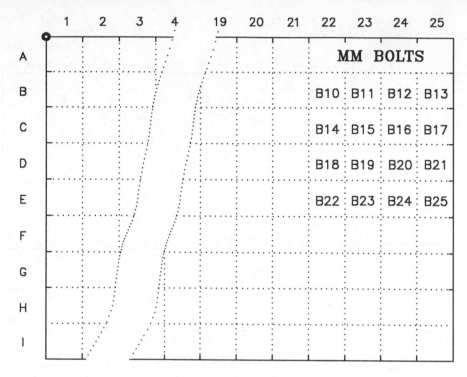

Figure 4   Commands assigned to tablet area-1

Before making any changes in the file, you need to determine the location of each block on the template. For example, the WBlock B10 is to be assigned to a block that is in row B and column number 22. Similarly, WBlock B17 is in row C and column 25. The following table shows the location of WBlocks in tablet area-1 of the template.

WBLOCK NAME	ROW	COLUMN	LOCATION IN TABLET1
B10	B	22	B-22
B11	B	23	B-23
B12	B	24	B-24
B13	B	25	B-25
B14	C	22	C-22
B15	C	23	C-23
B16	C	24	C-24
B17	C	25	C-25
B18	D	22	D-22

B19	D	23	D-23
B20	D	24	D-24
B21	D	25	D-25
B22	E	22	E-22
B23	E	23	E-23
B24	E	24	E-24
B25	E	25	E-25

You can use any word processor or text editor to load and edit the file. After CUSTOM.MNU file is loaded, search for ***TABLET1 section label. The letters and the numbers inside the brackets indicate the row and column. For example, in [A-1], A is for row number, and 1 is for column number in the template area-1.

```
[A-1]
 |  |
 |  |___ Column number
 |_____ Row
```

The location of the first WBlock B10 in the menu file is B-22. Locate the menu item B-22 in the menu file and add the INSERT command to the menu item command definition. The following file is a partial listing of the TABLET1 section of the menu file after editing.

```
***TABLET1
[A-1]
[A-2]
[A-3]
[A-4]
[A-5]
[A-6]
[A-7]
[A-8]
[A-9]
[A-10]
[A-11]
[A-12]
[A-13]
[A-14]
[A-15]
[A-16]
[A-17]
[A-18]
[A-19]
[A-20]
[A-21]
[A-22]
[A-23]
[A-24]
[A-25]
[B-1]^C^C^P(progn(setq m:err *error*)(princ))+
```

```
(defun *error* (msg)(princ msg)(setq *error* m:err m:err nil f nil)(princ))+
(if (null c:SOLMOVE)(defun c:SOLMOVE () (menucmd "S=X")(menucmd
"S=SOLLOAD");+
(terpri)(princ "ERROR:  Command not found. ")+
(princ "  Load AME or AMElite from the screen menu. ")+
(setq c:SOLMOVE nil)(princ))+
(progn (menucmd "S=X")(menucmd "S=SMOVE")))(princ);^PSOLMOVE
[B-2]^C^C^P(progn(setq m:err *error*)(princ))+
```



```
[B-22]^C^CINSERT;B10;\1.0;1.0;0
[B-23]^C^CINSERT;B11;\1.0;1.0;0
[B-24]^C^CINSERT;B12;\1.0;1.0;0
[B-25]^C^CINSERT;B13;\1.0;1.0;0
[C-1]
```



```
[C-21]
[C-22]^C^CINSERT;B14;\1.0;1.0;0
[C-23]^C^CINSERT;B15;\1.0;1.0;0
[C-24]^C^CINSERT;B16;\1.0;1.0;0
[C-25]^C^CINSERT;B17;\1.0;1.0;0
[D-1]
```



```
[D-20]
[D-21]
[D-22]^C^CINSERT;B18;\1.0;1.0;0
[D-23]^C^CINSERT;B19;\1.0;1.0;0
[D-24]^C^CINSERT;B20;\1.0;1.0;0
[D-25]^C^CINSERT;B21;\1.0;1.0;0
[E-1]
```



```
[E-21]
[E-22]^C^CINSERT;B22;\1.0;1.0;0
[E-23]^C^CINSERT;B23;\1.0;1.0;0
[E-24]^C^CINSERT;B24;\1.0;1.0;0
[E-25]^C^CINSERT;B25;\1.0;1.0;0
[F-1]
```

[I-10]^C^C^P(progn(setq m:err *error*)(defun *error*(msg)(princ"Error loading: ")+
(princ msg)(setq *error* m:err m:err nil #GTSPO nil)(princ))(princ));+
(cond((null #GTSPO)(vmon)(if(findfile"rman.lsp")(progn(load"rman")+
(menucmd"S=X")(menucmd"S=RMAN"))(progn(terpri);+
(prompt"The file 'Rman.lsp' was not found in your current search directories.")+
(terpri)(prompt"Check your AutoShade v2.0 Manual for installation instructions.");+
(princ)))(setq *error* m:err m:err nil)(princ))(T(menucmd"S=X")+
(menucmd"S=RMAN")(setq *error* m:err m:err nil)(princ))) ^P

Note

1.   To load the new menu CUSTOM.MNU, use AutoCAD's MENU command.

Command: MENU
Menu file name <ACAD>: <u>CUSTOM</u>

2.   When you select the block insert command from the template, AutoCAD will prompt you to enter insertion point. The X, Y scale factors and the rotation angle is already defined in the command definition.

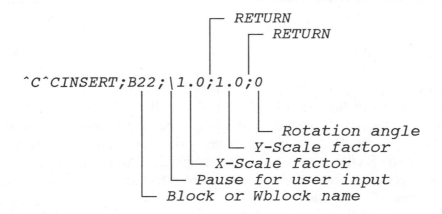

Submenus

The number of items in the TABLET1 or TABLET1ALT section of the menu file can be very large that may not accommodate on one template. For example, the maximum number of assignable blocks in tablet area-1 is 225. If the number of items in the TABLET1 or TABLET1ALT section are more than 225, the menu items in excess of 225 are not assigned to any block on the template and are therefore inaccessible. The user can overcome this problem by using submenus that let the user define any number of menu items in the tablet area-1 of the template. When the user selects the submenu, AutoCAD automatically loads the new submenu and assigns the commands to different blocks in template area-1. The format of the submenu reference is:

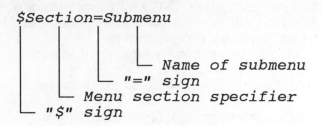

```
$Section=Submenu
              └─ Name of submenu
         └─ "=" sign
      └─ Menu section specifier
   └─ "$" sign
```

Example

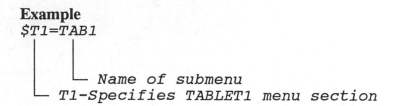

```
$T1=TAB1
        └─ Name of submenu
   └─ T1-Specifies TABLET1 menu section
```

Example 2

Edit the CUSTOM.MNU file to add the commands shown in Figure 5. Use the submenus and make a provision for swapping the submenus. When the user selects a block insert command from the tablet menu, AutoCAD should automatically load the corresponding screen menu.

In this example it is assumed that there is no room for adding more commands to tablet area-1, therefore submenus have to be created to make room for the commands in excess of 225. Two submenus TABA and TABB have been defined in the TABLET1 section of the menu file CUSTOM.MNU. When you load the menu file CUSTOM.MNU, the first submenu TABA is automatically loaded and you can select the block insert commands from the template. You can load the submenu TABB by selecting the **Load TABB** block from the template. AutoCAD loads the submenu TABB and now you can select the commands from the new submenu. If you want to load the submenu TABA back, select the **Load TABA** from the template. The following file is a partial listing of TABLET1 section of the menu file after inserting the new command definitions.

```
***TABLET1
**TABA
[A-1]
[A-2]
[A-3]
[A-4]
[A-5]
[A-6]
[A-7]
```

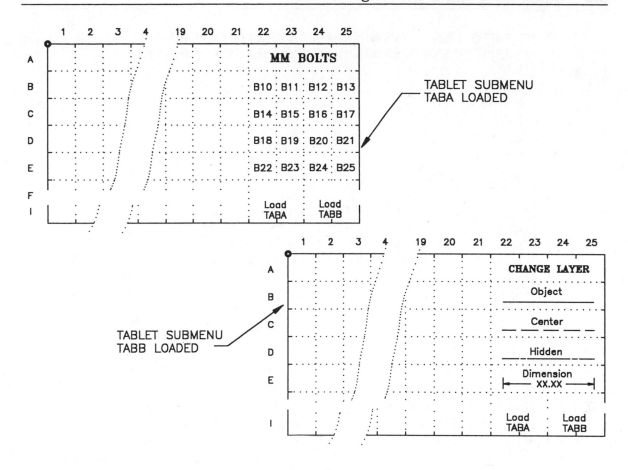

Figure 5   Commands assigned to tablet area-1

[A-8]

|

[B-18]
[B-19]
[B-20]
[B-21]
[B-22]^C^C$S=X $S=INSBLK INSERT;B10;\1.0;1.0;0
[B-23]^C^C$S=X $S=INSBLK INSERT;B11;\1.0;1.0;0
[B-24]^C^C$S=X $S=INSBLK INSERT;B12;\1.0;1.0;0
[B-25]^C^C$S=X $S=INSBLK INSERT;B13;\1.0;1.0;0
[C-1]

|

[C-21]
[C-22]^C^C$S=X $S=INSBLK INSERT;B14;\1.0;1.0;0
[C-23]^C^C$S=X $S=INSBLK INSERT;B15;\1.0;1.0;0

```
[C-24]^C^C$S=X $S=INSBLK INSERT;B16;\1.0;1.0;0
[C-25]^C^C$S=X $S=INSBLK INSERT;B17;\1.0;1.0;0
[D-1]


            |
            |
            |
            |


[D-20]
[D-21]
[D-22]^C^C$S=X $S=INSBLK INSERT;B18;\1.0;1.0;0
[D-23]^C^C$S=X $S=INSBLK INSERT;B19;\1.0;1.0;0
[D-24]^C^C$S=X $S=INSBLK INSERT;B20;\1.0;1.0;0
[D-25]^C^C$S=X $S=INSBLK INSERT;B21;\1.0;1.0;0
[E-1]


            |
            |
            |
            |


[E-21]
[E-22]^C^C$S=X $S=INSBLK INSERT;B22;\1.0;1.0;0
[E-23]^C^C$S=X $S=INSBLK INSERT;B23;\1.0;1.0;0
[E-24]^C^C$S=X $S=INSBLK INSERT;B24;\1.0;1.0;0
[E-25]^C^C$S=X $S=INSBLK INSERT;B25;\1.0;1.0;0
[F-1]


            |
            |
            |
            |


[H-19]
[H-20]
[H-21]
[H-22]^C^C$T1=TABA
[H-23]^C^C$T1=TABA
[H-24]^C^C$T1=TABB
[H-25]^C^C$T1=TABB
**TABB
[A-1]
[A-2]
[A-3]
[A-4]
[A-5]
[A-6]
[A-7]
[A-8]


            |
            |
            |
            |


[B-18]
```

[B-19]
[B-20]
[B-21]
[B-22]^C^CLAYER;SET;OBJECT;;
[B-23]^C^CLAYER;SET;OBJECT;;
[B-24]^C^CLAYER;SET;OBJECT;;
[B-25]^C^CLAYER;SET;OBJECT;;
[C-1]

[C-21]
[C-22]^C^CLAYER;SET;CENTER;;
[C-23]^C^CLAYER;SET;CENTER;;
[C-24]^C^CLAYER;SET;CENTER;;
[C-25]^C^CLAYER;SET;CENTER;;
[D-1]

[D-20]
[D-21]
[D-22]^C^CLAYER;SET;HIDDEN;;
[D-23]^C^CLAYER;SET;IIIDDEN;;
[D-24]^C^CLAYER;SET;HIDDEN;;
[D-25]^C^CLAYER;SET;HIDDEN;;
[E-1]

[E-21]
[E-22]^C^CLAYER;SET;DIM;;
[E-23]^C^CLAYER;SET;DIM;;
[E-24]^C^CLAYER;SET;DIM;;
[E-25]^C^CLAYER;SET;DIM;;
[F-1]

[H-19]
[H-20]
[H-21]
[H-22]^C^C$T1=TABA
[H-23]^C^C$T1=TABA
[H-24]^C^C$T1=TABB
[H-25]^C^C$T1=TABB

Note

1. *When you load the submenu TABB, the template overlay for tablet area-1 must be changed.*

2. *The menu items defined in H-22, H23 and H-24, H-25 load the submenus TABA and TABB respectively.*

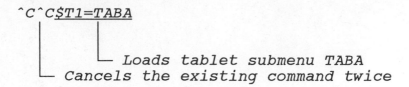

```
^C^C$T1=TABA
```
— Loads tablet submenu TABA
— Cancels the existing command twice

Customizing Tablet Area-2

If you take a look at the CUSTOM.MNU file you will find that there are two section labels for tablet area-2, TABLET2 and TABLET2ALT.   The first one, TABLET2, is automatically loaded when you get into drawing editor.   If you want to select the alternate tablet menu TABLET2ALT, you must swap the tablet menu by selecting the second tablet swap block from the template.

Tablet area-2 has 11 columns and 9 rows.   The columns are numbered from 1 to 11, and the rows are designated by the letters J through R.   The total number of blocks in tablet area-2 is 99 (9 x 11 = 99).   There are no empty blocks in this area like tablet area-1, and the commands that have been assigned to the blocks are defined in the TABLET2 and TABLET2ALT menu sections of the standard menu file.   You can change or delete the command definition assigned to these blocks.   You can even delete the entire TABLET2 or TABLET2ALT menu sections and write your own menu that best fits your needs.   However, you must be careful in developing a new menu and needs quite some time to come up with a reliable menu.   The following example illustrates the process of editing TABLET2ALT menu section of CUSTOM.MNU file.

Example 3

Assign the following commands to the blocks in the tenth column of alternate tablet area-2.   (The "Screen Menu" command assigned to the last block of 10th column does not change.)

```
LINE
PLINE
ARC,CSE
ARC,SCE
ARC,CSA
CIRCLE-C,R
CIRCLE-C,D
CIRCLE-2P
```

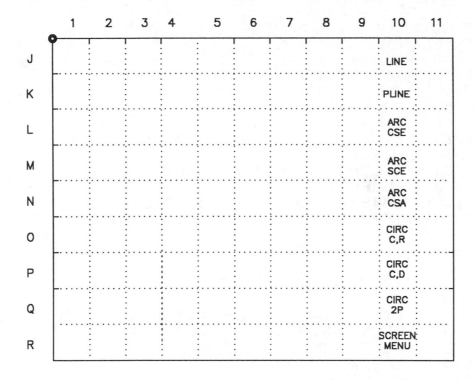

Figure 6   Commands assigned to tablet area-2

Use your word processor to load CUSTOM.MNU file and search for
***TABLET2ALT tablet menu section. Locate the lines that need to be changed and
assign the new menu definitions. The part of the menu item that is enclosed in the
brackets has no effect on the command definition. It can be used for reference to make
it easy to locate the revised commands in the menu file. The following file is the
listing of TABLET2ALT after making the necessary changes.

***TABLET2ALT
^C^C^P(menucmd "S=X")(menucmd "S=HIDE1")(progn (initget "Yes
No")+
(setq ans (getkword "Do you want to HIDE? <Y>")))(if (= ans "Yes")+
(command "HIDE")(progn (menucmd "S= ")(menucmd "S= ")))(princ);^P
$S=X $S=VPOINT VPOINT;;
$S=X $S=SHADE
$S=X $S=UCS1 ^C^CUCS
^C^CUCS;PREV
^C^CUCS;ORIGIN
;
$S=X $S=MV ^C^CMVIEW
$S=X $S=ZOOM ^C^CZOOM VMAX
[LINE]$S=X $S=LINE ^C^CLINE
^C^CREGEN
[VPOINT]^C^CVPOINT R;< <135;$S=X $S=VPOINT3D
[VPT rear]^C^CVPOINT R;< <90;$S=X $S=VPOINT3D
[VPOINT]^C^CVPOINT R;< <45;$S=X $S=VPOINT3D
$S=X $S=UCS1 ^C^CUCS

```
^C^CUCS;;
^C^CPLAN;W

;
$S=X $S=MV ^C^CMVIEW
$S=X $S=ZOOM ^C^CZOOM W
[PLINE]$S=X $S=PLINE ^C^CPLINE
^C^CREGENALL
[VPT left]^C^CVPOINT R;<<180;$S=X $S=VPOINT3D
[VPT plan]^C^CPLAN;;
[VPT rigt]^C^CVPOINT R;<<0;$S=X $S=VPOINT3D
$S=X $S=DVIEW ^C^CDVIEW
$S=X $S=DVIEW ^C^CSELECT;\DVIEW;P;;CA;\\;
$S=X $S=DVIEW ^C^C$S=X $S=DVIEW1 DVIEW;;

;
$S=X $S=MV ^C^CMVIEW ON
$S=X $S=ZOOM ^C^CZOOM D
[ARC,CSA]$S=X $S=ARC ^C^CARC C \\DRAG
'REDRAW
[VPOINT ]^C^CVPOINT R;<<225;$S=X $S=VPOINT3D
[VPT frnt]^C^CVPOINT R;<<270;$S=X $S=VPOINT3D
[VPOINT ]^C^CVPOINT R;<<315;$S=X $S=VPOINT3D
$S=X $S=DVIEW ^C^CDVIEW
$S=X $S=DVIEW ^C^CSELECT;\DVIEW;P;;Z;\;
$S=X $S=DVIEW ^C^CSELECT;\DVIEW;P;;PA;\\;

;
$S=X $S=MV ^C^CMVIEW OFF
$S=X $S=ZOOM ^C^CZOOM A
[ARC,SCA]$S=X $S=ARC ^C^CARC \C \DRAG
'REDRAW
$S=X $S=3D ^C^CRULESURF
$S=X $S=3D ^C^CREVSURF
$S=X $S=3DFACE ^C^C3DFACE
$S=X $S=VPLA ^C^CVPLAYER
$S=X $S=VPLA ^C^CVPLAYER THAW
$S=X $S=VPLA ^C^CVPLAYER FREEZE

;
$S=X $S=MV ^C^CMVIEW 2
$S=X $S=ZOOM ^C^CZOOM P
[ARC,CSA]$S=X $S=ARC ^C^CARC C \\A DRAG
'REDRAW
$S=X $S=3D ^C^CEDGESURF
$S=X $S=3D ^C^CTABSURF
$S=X $S=3DPOLY ^C^C3DPOLY
$S=X $S=VPLA ^C^CVPLAYER
$S=X $S=VPLA ^C^CVPLAYER NEW
$S=X $S=VPLA ^C^CVPLAYER RESET

;
$S=X $S=MV ^C^CMVIEW 3
$S=X $S=ZOOM ^C^CZOOM E
[CIRCLE-C,R]$S=X $S=CIRCLE ^C^CCIRCLE
'REDRAW
$S=X $S=XREF ^C^CXREF
$S=X $S=XREF ^C^CXREF;;
$S=X $S=XBIND ^C^CXBIND
```

```
$S=X $S=LAYER ^C^CDDLMODES
$S=X $S=LAYER ^C^CLAYER ON
$S=X $S=LAYER ^C^CLAYER OFF
;
$S=X $S=MV ^C^CMVIEW 4
$S=X $S=ZOOM ^C^CZOOM
[CIRCLE-C,D]$S=X $S=CIRCLE ^C^CCIRCLE \D
'REDRAW
$S=X $S=ATTDEF ^C^CATTDEF
$S=X $S=BLOCK ^C^CBLOCK
$S=X $S=INSERT ^C^CINSERT
$S=X $S=LAYER ^C^CLAYER
$S=X $S=LAYER ^C^CLAYER THAW
$S=X $S=LAYER ^C^CLAYER FREEZE
;
$S=X $S=MV ^C^CMSPACE
'PAN
[CIRCLE-2P]$S=X $S=CIRCLE ^C^CCIRCLE 2P
'REDRAWALL
$S=X $S=ATTEDIT ^C^CATTEDIT
$S=X $S=WBLOCK ^C^CWBLOCK
```

Note

[LINE]$S=X $S=LINE ^C^CLINE   *In this menu item $S=X loads the submenu X that has been defined in the screen menu section of the menu file. $S=LINE loads the submenu that has also been defined in the screen menu section.*

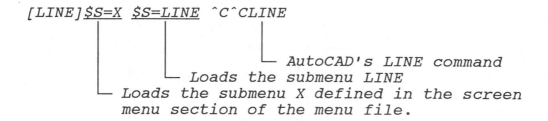

Customizing Tablet Area-3

Like tablet area-2, CUSTOM.MNU file has two section labels for tablet area-3, TBLET3 and TABLET3ALT. The first one TABLET3 is automatically loaded when you get into drawing editor. If you want to select the alternate tablet menu TABLET3ALT, you need to swap the tablet menu by selecting the third tablet swap block from the template.

Tablet area-3 has 9 columns and 13 rows. In Figure 7 the columns are numbered from 1 to 9, and the rows are numbered from 1 to 13. The total number of blocks in tablet area-3 are 117 (9 x 13 = 117). The size of the blocks in this area is smaller than the blocks in other sections of the tablet template. Also, the blocks are rectangular in shape, whereas in other tablet areas the blocks are square. You can modify or delete the command definitions assigned to these blocks. You can even delete the entire TABLET3 or TABLET3ALT menu sections and write your own menu that best fits your needs. However, you have to be careful in developing a new menu. The following example illustrates the editing process for adding commands to TABLET3ALT section of CUSTOM.MNU file.

Example 4

Add the following angles to TABLET3ALT section of CUSTOM.MNU file. The layout of the alternate tablet area-3 is shown Figure 7.

ANGLES
30
120
210
330

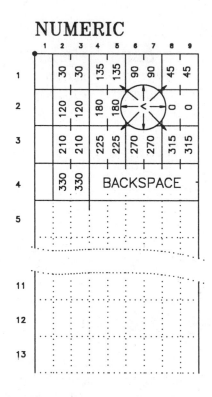

Figure 7   Angles assigned to alternate tablet area-3

Use your word processor or text editor to load CUSTOM.MNU file and search for **TABLET3ALT section of the menu file. Locate the lines that you want to edit and then assign the required command definitions to these lines. The following file is a partial listing of TABLET3ALT section of CUSTOM.MNU file after editing.

```
***TABLET3ALT
;
< <30
< <30
< <135
< <135
< <90
< <90
< <45
< <45
;
< <120
< <120
< <180
< <180
<\
<\
< <0
< <0
;
< <210
< <210
< <225
< <225
< <270
< <270
< <315
< <315
;
< <330
< <330
^H
^H
^H
^H
^H
^H
;
;
;
m\
m\
cm\
cm\
mm\
mm\
;
;
```

```
;
.\
.\
+\
+\
%%d\
%%d\
;
;
;
,\
,\
%%p\
%%p\
%%c\
%%c\
;
;
;
```

Customizing Tablet Area-4

Like other tablet areas, CUSTOM.MNU file has two section labels for tablet area-4, TBLET4 and TABLET4ALT. The first one TABLET4 is automatically loaded when you get into drawing editor. If you want to select the alternate tablet menu TABLET4ALT, you need to swap the menus by selecting the fourth tablet swap block on the template.

Tablet area-4 has 25 columns and 7 rows. As shown in Figure 8 the columns are numbered from 1 to 25, and the rows are designated by the letters S through Y. The total number of blocks in tablet area-4 are 175 (7 x 25 = 175).   You can modify or delete the command definition assigned to these blocks. You can even delete the entire TABLET4 or TABLET4ALT menu sections and write your own menu that best fits your needs. However, you have to be careful in developing a new menu. The following example illustrates the editing process for adding commands to TABLET4ALT section of CUSTOM.MNU file.   (CUSTOM.MNU is a copy of ACAD.MNU)

Example 5

Add the following commands to TABLET4 section of CUSTOM.MNU file. The partial layout of the tablet area-4 is shown Figure 8.

1. Load and run the AutoLISP routines TRANA.LSP and TRANB.LSP (It is assumed that the files TRANA.LSP and TRANB.LSP are pre-defined)

2. Run the script files SCR1 and SCR2

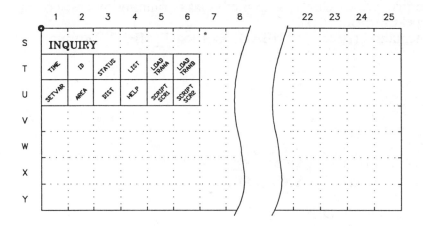

Figure 8   Commands assigned to tablet area-4

Use your word processor to load CUSTOM.MNU file and search for TABLET4 section. Before making any changes, make sure you know the commands that are needed to perform a given function. Locate the lines that need to be edited and then assign the new command definitions. The following file is a partial listing of TABLET4 section of CUSTOM.MNU file after editing.

***TABLET4
```
;
;
;
;
;
;
;
;
;
;
;
;
```

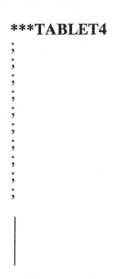

```
[Tablet 4]^C^C^P(if (null T_MENU) (setq T_MENU 0))+
(if (= (logand 8 T_MENU) 8)(progn(setq T_MENU (- T_MENU 8))+
(if (< (getvar "EXPERT") 4)(princ "Alternate tablet area 4 unloaded.
"));+
(menucmd "T4=TABLET4")(if (< (getvar "EXPERT") 1)(progn +
(terpri)(princ "Object snap modes issue overrides: commands do NOT
repeat.")(princ))))+
(progn(setq T_MENU (+ T_MENU 8))+
(if (< (getvar "EXPERT") 4)(princ "Alternate tablet area 4 loaded.  "));+
(menucmd "T4=TABLET4ALT")(if (< (getvar "EXPERT") 1)(progn +
```

```
(terpri)(princ "Object snap modes issue running modes: commands
repeat.")(princ)))))+
(menucmd (strcat "s=HEADER" (itoa T_MENU)))(princ);^P
;
;
;
^C^CTIME
^C^C$S=X $S=ID ID
^C^CSTATUS
^C^C$S=X $S=LIST LIST
^C^C(LOAD "TRANA");TRANA
^C^C(LOAD "TRANB");TRANB
;
^C^CDDEMODES
^C^CDDEMODES
^C^C$S=X $S=OSNAPC OSNAP
;
NONE
CENTER
ENDPOINT
INSERT
INTERSEC
MIDPOINT
NEAREST
NODE
PERPEND
QUADRANT
TANGENT
;
^C^CSAVE
^C^CSAVE
^C^CSETVAR ? *
^C^C$S=X $S=AREA AREA
^C^CDIST
'HELP
^C^CSCRIPT;SCR1
^C^CSCRIPT;SCR2
;
^C^CDDRMODES
^C^CDDRMODES
^C^C$S=X $S=OSNAPC OSNAP
;
UNDO B
^C^CU
^C^CREDO
AUTO
MULTIPLE
WINDOW
LAST
PREVIOUS
CROSSING
REMOVE
ADD
```

```
^C^CPLOT
^C^CPRPLOT
^C^C$S=X $S=DIMORD DIM ORDINATE
^C^C$S=X $S=DIM DIM LEADER
^C^C$S=X $S=DIMLINEAR DIM BASELINE
^C^C$S=X $S=DIMLINEAR DIM CONTIN
^C^C$S=X $S=DIMLINEAR DIM VERT
^C^C$S=X $S=DIMLINEAR DIM HORIZ
```

Note

1. **^C^C(LOAD "TRANA");TRANA**   *In this menu item (LOAD "TRANA") loads the AutoLISP file TRANA.   The TRANA that is outside the parenthesis, after the semicolon, executes the function TRANA.*

```
^C^C(LOAD "TRANA");TRANA
        |                |
        |                |__ Name of AutoLISP function
        |__ Loads AutoLISP program TRANA
```

2. **^C^CSCRIPT;SCR1**   *In this menu item SCR1 is the name of the script file and SCRIPT is an AutoCAD command for running a script file.*

```
^C^CSCRIPT;SCR1
      |      |
      |      |__ Name of the script file
      |__ AutoCAD's SCRIPT command
```

Customizing Buttons and Auxiliary Menus

The standard AutoCAD menu file ACAD.MNU contains a BUTTONS and an AUX1 menu section. The Buttons and Aux1 sections are identical and each section has 9 menu items. The following file is a listing of the Buttons and Aux1 sections of the standard AutoCAD menu file ACAD.MNU.

```
***BUTTONS
;
$p1=*
^C^C
^B
^O
^G
^D
^E
^T
***AUX1
;
$p1=*
^C^C
^B
^O
^G
^D
^E
^T
```

Note

The following table shows the function of the menu items that are defined in the BUTTONS section of CUSTOM.MNU file.

MENU ITEM	FUNCTION
***BUTTONS	Section label
;	RETURN
$p1=*	Loads POP1 pull-down menu
^C^C	Cancels the existing command twice
^B	SNAP ON/OFF (CTRL B)
^O	ORTHO ON/OFF (CTRL O)
^G	GRID ON/OFF (CTRL G)
^D	COORDINATE DIAL ON/OFF (CTRL D)
^E	ISOPLANE (CTRL E)
^T	TABLET ON/OFF (CTRL T)

Like any other menu you can make changes in the buttons menu to assign different commands to the buttons of the pointing device. The pointing devices generally come in 4 button or 10 button configuration. The first button is always the pick button and can not be used for any other purpose. AutoCAD commands can be assigned to the remaining buttons. The following example describes the editing procedure for the BUTTONS section of CUSTOM.MNU file. (CUSTOM.MNU file is a copy of ACAD.MNU file)

Example 6

Change the buttons sections of CUSTOM.MNU to assign the following commands to the four buttons of the pointing device (Figure 9).

> 1. PICK
> 2. RETURN
> 3. ZOOM Win
> 4. ZOOM Prev

The ZOOM Window command assigned to button number 3 should automatically zoom in an area that is 2 units from the selected point.

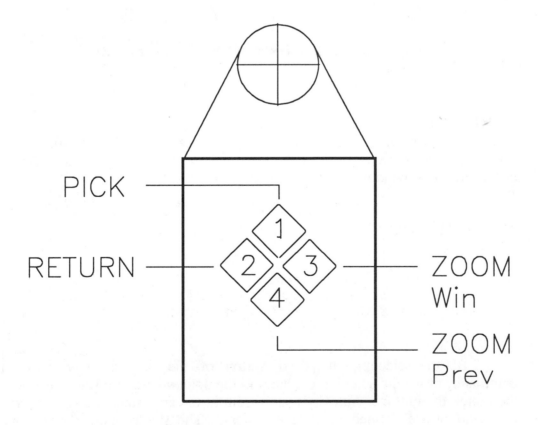

Figure 9 Commands assigned to 4 buttons of a pointing device

Before making any changes it is very important to know the commands and the prompt entries that are associated with the commands. Use your word processor to load the CUSTOM.MNU file and search for the ***BUTTONS section.   The lines that follow the ***BUTTONS section are the lines that need to be edited to assign new commands to the buttons of the pointing device. The following file is a listing of the button menu section of the CUSTOM.MNU file after making the required changes.

```
***BUTTONS                                          1
;                                                   2
'ZOOM;WIN;\@2,2                                     3
'ZOOM;PRE                                           4
^B                                                  5
^O                                                  6
^G                                                  7
^D                                                  8
^E                                                  9
^T                                                  10
```

Line 1
***BUTTONS
This is the section label for the BUTTONS menu section.

Line 2
;
The semicolon (;) causes a RETURN. It is like entering RETURN from the keyboard or template.

Line 3
'ZOOM;WIN;\\@2,2
When you select this menu item, it will zoom as shown in Figure 10. The first point you select becomes the first corner of the zoom window and the other corner of zoom window is 2.0,2.0 units from the selected point.

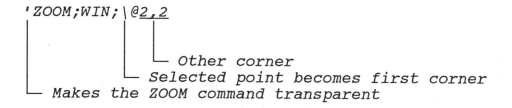

Before selecting the third button of the pointing device for this command, move the screen cross hairs to the point where you want to zoom and then click the button. AutoCAD will zoom in the area since the two corners of the window are defined in the menu item. The single quote (') in front of ZOOM makes the ZOOM Window command transparent.

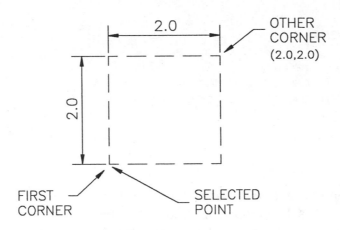

Figure 10   Zoom area

Line 4
'ZOOM;PRE
This menu item defines the ZOOM command with Previous option. The single quote (') in front of the ZOOM command makes the ZOOM Previous command transparent.

Note

The commands on the first three lines (2 - 4), excluding ***BUTTONS line, will be assigned to second, third, and fourth button of the 4-button pointing device. The remaining items will be ignored and do not effect the commands that are assigned to other buttons. Therefore you can leave them in the file.

Submenus

Like other menus, you can define submenus in buttons or auxiliary menus. For example, if you have 10 buttons on the pointing device, these buttons are assigned certain commands when you start AutoCAD or load a menu. You can define submenus within the buttons menu section that will assign different functions to the buttons of the pointing device. These submenus can be loaded by pressing the button that has been assigned the load command. The format of submenu reference is:

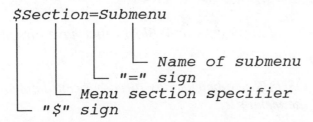

Example
```
$B=BUTTON1
```
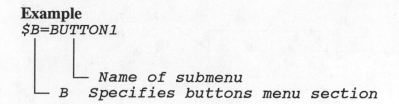

Name of submenu
B   Specifies buttons menu section

Example 7

Write a buttons and Auxiliary menu for the following AutoCAD commands. The pointing device has 10 buttons and button number 1 is used as a pick button. The blocks are to be inserted with a scale factor of 1.00 and a rotation angle of 0 degrees.

1. PICK BUTTON   2. RETURN   3. CANCEL
4. OSNAPS1   5. INSERT B1   6. INSERT B2
7. INSERT B3   8. ZOOM Window 9. ZOOM All
10.ZOOM Previous

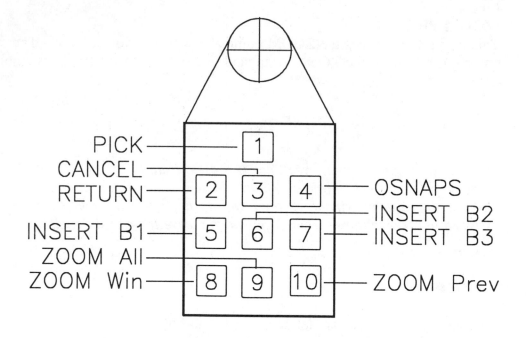

Figure 11   Commands assigned to different buttons of a 10 button pointing device

Note

1. *B1, B2, B3 are the names of the Blocks or WBlocks that have already been created.*

2. *It is assumed that the OSNAPS1 submenu has already been defined in the screen menu section of the menu file.*

3.   Use transparent ZOOM command for ZOOM Previous, and ZOOM Window.

The following file is a listing of the button menu section of the CUSTOM.MNU file after making the required changes.

```
***BUTTONS                          1
;                                   2
^C^C                                3
$S=X $S=OSNAPS1                     4
^C^CINSERT;B1;\1.0;1.0;0            5
^C^CINSERT;B2;\1.0;1.0;0            6
^C^CINSERT;B3;\1.0;1.0;0            7
'ZOOM;Win                          8
^C^CZOOM;All                       9
'ZOOM;Prev                        10
***AUX1                           11
;                                 12
^C^C                              13
$S=X $S=OSNAPS1                   14
^C^CINSERT;B1;\1.0;1.0;0          15
^C^CINSERT;B2;\1.0;1.0;01         16
^C^CINSERT;B3;\1.0;1.0;0          17
'ZOOM;Win                         18
^C^CZOOM;All                      19
'ZOOM;Prev                        20
```

Line 3
^C^C
This command definition is assigned to button number 3. It cancels the existing command twice.

Line 4
$S=X $S=OSNAPS1
In this menu item $S=X loads the submenu X that has been defined in the screen menu section of the menu file, and $S=OSNAPS1 loads the submenu OSNAPS1 that has also been defined in the screen menu section of the file and contains various object snap modes. This command definition is assigned to button number 4.

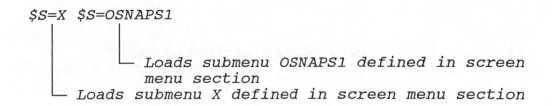

Line 5
^C^CINSERT;B1;\1.0;1.0;0

In this menu item ^C^C cancels the existing command twice and INSERT is an AutoCAD command that can be used to insert a Block or Wblock. B1 is the name of the block, and the back slash (\) pauses for the user input. In this menu item, it is the insertion point of the block. The first 1.0 is the X-Scale factor, and the second 1.0 is the Y-Scale factor of the block. The 0 at the end is for the rotation angle of the block.

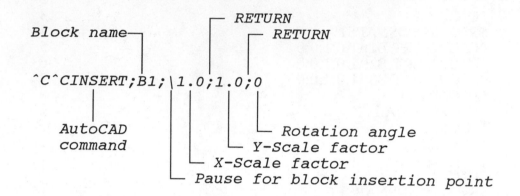

```
          RETURN
Block name    RETURN

^C^CINSERT;B1;\1.0;1.0;0

    AutoCAD
    command            Rotation angle
                     Y-Scale factor
                   X-Scale factor
                 Pause for block insertion point
```

Line 9
^C^CZOOM;All
The command definition of this menu item is assigned to button number 9 of the pointing device. If you select this key, it will enter a ZOOM All command.

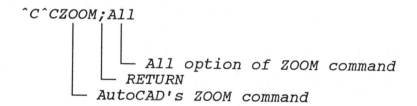

```
^C^CZOOM;All

           All option of ZOOM command
         RETURN
       AutoCAD's ZOOM command
```

Line 10
'ZOOM;Prev
This menu item defines the transparent ZOOM Previous command. It is assigned to the button number 10 of the pointing device.

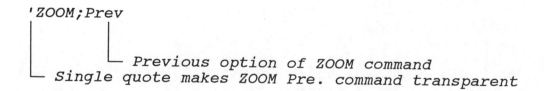

```
'ZOOM;Prev

           Previous option of ZOOM command
     Single quote makes ZOOM Pre. command transparent
```

Line 11
***AUX1
In this line AUX1 is the section label for auxiliary menu section, and the lines 12 through 20 are defined in this section.

Customizing Pull-down Menus

The pull-down menus are a part of standard AutoCAD menu file (ACAD.MNU) that comes with AutoCAD software package. The ACAD.MNU file is automatically loaded when you get into drawing editor, provided the standard configuration of AutoCAD has not been changed. The pull down menu can have a maximum of 10 sections defined as POP1, POP2, POP3 -- --- --- --- POP10. The standard AutoCAD menu uses only first nine sections POP1 through POP9.

Submenus

The number of items in a pull-down menu file can be very large that may not accommodate on one screen. For example, the maximum number of items that can be displayed on some of the menu devices is 21. If the pull-down menu has more than 21 items, the menu items in access of 21 are not displayed on the screen and can not therefore be accessed. The user can overcome this problem by using submenus that let the user define smaller groups of items within a menu section. When a submenu is selected, it loads the submenu items and displays them on the screen. The format of submenu reference is:

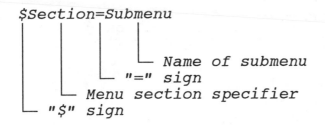

```
$Section=Submenu
```
            └── Name of submenu
         └── "=" sign
      └── Menu section specifier
   └── "$" sign

Example

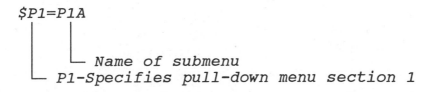

```
$P1=P1A
```
      └── Name of submenu
   └── P1-Specifies pull-down menu section 1

Example 8

Redefine the menu item that contains the **"insert"** command in the pull-down menu section POP2, so that when you select **insert** from the pull-down menu, it replaces POP2 with the following pull-down menu. Also, when you select **insert** from the pull-down menu, it should display the corresponding menu BL in the screen menu area.

INSERTDW
DOOR1
DOOR2

WINDOW1
WINDOW2

PREVIOUS
CANCEL

Note

1. *The doors and windows are saved as WBLOCKS in the SYMBOLS subdirectory on D drive.*

2. *User should be able to insert the block at the selected point with X and Y scale factors of 1.25, and rotation angle of 0.*

3. *Do not edit ACAD.MNU file. Make a copy of ACAD.MNU file and then edit the new file (CUSTOM.MNU).*

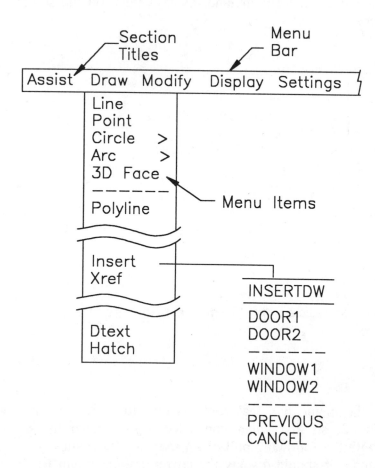

Figure 12 POP2 section of pull-down menu

Use your word processor to load the menu file CUSTOM.MNU and search for the **insert** command in the pull-down menu section ***POP2. Redefine the line that contains the **insert** function so that it loads the INSERT submenu as shown in Figure 12. The following file is a partial listing of CUSTOM.MNU file after editing the POP2 section of the pull-down menu and adding a new submenu.

```
***POP1
[Assist]
[Help!        ]'?
[~--]
[Cancel       ]^C^C
[~--]
[Osnap: <mode>]^C^C$p1= $p1=* OSNAP \
CENter
[ENDpoint    ]ENDP
INSert
[INTersection]INT
MIDpoint
NEArest
NODe
[PERpendicular]PER
QUAdrant
[Quick, <mode> ]QUICK,^Z$p1=*
TANgent
NONE
[~--]
[FILTERS     >]$p1=filters $p1=*

**filters
[Filters]
.X
.Y
.Z
.XY
.XZ
.YZ
[~--]
[ASSIST >]$p1= $p1=*

***POP2
**p2draw
[Draw]
[Line      ]^C^C$S=X $S=line line
[Point     ]*^C^C$S=X $S=point point
[Circle    >]^C^C^P$p2=p2cir $p2=* (if (not c:ct)(defun c:ct




[3D Face   ]^C^C$S=X $S=3dface 3dface
[~--]
[Polyline  ]^C^C^P$S=X $S=pline pline
```

```
[3D Poly   ]^C^C$S=X $S=3dpoly 3dpoly
[Donut     ]^C^Cdonut ;;
[Ellipse   ]^C^C$S=X $S=ellipse ellipse
[Polygon   ]^C^C^P$S=X $S=polygon (if (not c:mpg)+
```

```
[~--]
[Insert    ]^C^C$S=X $S=BL $P2=INSERTDW $P2=*
[Xref      ]$S=X $S=XREF ^C^CXREF
[~--]
[Surfaces...]$I=surf1 $I=*
[Objects... ]$I=3dobjects $I=*
[~--]
[Dtext     ]^C^C^P(if (not c:dt)(defun c:dt (/ m:err m:ta0 setq *error*
m:err)(prin1)))(princ);dt;^P
```

```
[Hatch]^C^C^P$S=X $S=hatch (if (not c:hatchm)(defun c:hatchm (/ m:err
m:hp1)+
(setq m:err *error*)(defun *error* (msg)(setq *error* m:err)(princ))+
(if(/ =(type m:hp)'STR)(setq m:hp pause))(if(/ =(type m:hs)'STR)(setq m:hs
""));+
(if(/ =(type m:hsc)'REAL)(setq m:hsc pause))(if(/ =(type m:hr)'REAL)(setq
m:hr +
pause))(setq m:hp1 (strcat m:hp m:hs))(if (= m:hp "U")(command
"HATCH" m:hp1)+
(if (= m:hp pause)(command "HATCH" pause m:hsc m:hr pause);+
(command "HATCH" m:hp1 m:hsc m:hr pause)))(setq *error*
m:err)(princ)))+
(princ);hatchm;^P
[Dim...    ]^C^C$S=X $S=dim DIM $I=drdim $I=*
```

```
**INSERTDW
[INSERTDW]
[DOOR1]^C^CINSERT;D:/SYMBOLS/DOOR1;\1.25;1.25;0
[DOOR2]^C^CINSERT;D:/SYMBOLS/DOOR2;\1.25;1.25;0
[~--]
[WINDOW1]^C^CINSERT;D:/SYMBOLS/WINDOW1;\1.25;1.25;0
[WINDOW2]^C^CINSERT;D:/SYMBOLS/WINDOW2;\1.25;1.25;0
[~--]
[PREVIOUS]$P2=P2DRAW $P2=*
[CANCEL]$P2=P2DRAW ^C^C
```

```
**p2arc
[Arc]
[3-point          ]$p2=p2draw ^C^C^P(defun c:at () +
(setq m:err *error*)(defun *error* (msg)(menucmd "p2=p2draw")+
```

(setq *error* m:err m:err nil)(princ))(command "ARC" pause pause
pause)+
(setq *error* m:err m:err nil)(princ))(princ);at;^P
[~--]$p2=p2draw

***POP3
[Modify]
[Erase   ]*^C^C$S=X $S=erase erase si auto
[Oops!]^C^Coops
[Move   ]^C^C$S=X $S=move move

Note

1. **[Insert   ]^C^C$S=X $S=BL $P2=INSERTDW $P2=***
    *In this menu item $S=X loads the submenu X, defined in the screen menu
    section of the menu file, and $S=BL loads the submenu BL that is also
    defined in the screen menu section. $P2=INSERTDW load the submenu
    INSERTDW that has been defined in the POP2 section of the pull-down
    menu. $P2=* forces the display of the current pull-down menu on the
    screen.*

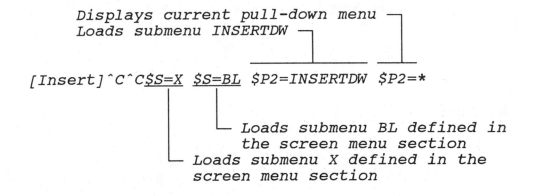

2. **[DOOR1]^C^CINSERT;D:/SYMBOLS/DOOR1;\1.25;1.25;**   *When you
    define the search path in the menu file, replace the back slashes (\) by
    forward slashes (/).   To load the file DOOR1 from the SYMBOLS
    subdirectory in D drive the search path normally will be defined as
    D:\SYMBOLS\DOOR1.   But the same statement in a menu file will be
    defined as D:/SYMBOLS/DOOR1.   In the menu file back slash is used for
    user input.*

Customizing Icon Menus

The icon menus are extremely useful when the user is inserting blocks, selecting a hatch pattern or a text font. You can also use the icon menus to load an AutoLISP routine or a pre-defined macro. Therefore the icon menu is a powerful tool for customizing AutoCAD.

The icon menus can be accessed from the pull-down, tablet, button, or the screen menu. When the user selects an icon, a dialogue box is displayed on the screen that contains different icons. The title of the icon menu is displayed at the top of the dialogue box. Also, an arrow appears on the screen that can be moved to select any icon. You can cancel an icon menu by entering CTRL C, pressing ESCAPE key on the keyboard, or selecting the EXIT icon from the icon menu display.

The dialogue box can display 4,9, or 16 icons depending on the number of items in the icon menu section. For example, if there are 5 items in a submenu, AutoCAD will display 9 icons in the dialogue box. Out of these nine icons, the first five icons will display the slides as referenced in the corresponding menu item, and the remaining icons will be empty.

An icon menu will work only if the device driver that you are using supports AutoCAD's Advanced User Interface (AUI). AutoCAD ignores the icon menu section (***ICON) if the display driver does not support AUI. Also, the system should be configured so that the status line is not disabled. Otherwise, the icon menus, or the pull down menus can not be used. The icon menu consists of a section label ***ICON. There is only one icon menu section in a file and all the icon menus are defined in this section.

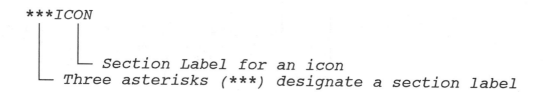

```
***ICON
  |   |
  |   └─ Section Label for an icon
  └─ Three asterisks (***) designate a section label
```

Submenus

The number of items in an icon menu file can be very large that may not accommodate on one screen. For example, the maximum number of items in an icon menu is 16. If the icon menu has more than 16 items, the menu items in access of 16 are not displayed on the screen, and can not therefore be accessed. The user can overcome this problem by using submenus that let the user define smaller groups of items within an icon menu section. When a submenu is selected, it loads the submenu items and displays them on the screen. The format of submenu reference is:

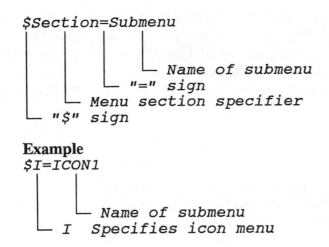

Example
```
$I=ICON1
```

Example 9

Write an icon menu that can be accessed from POP10 for inserting the following blocks

BL1	BL4
BL2	BL5
BL3	BL6

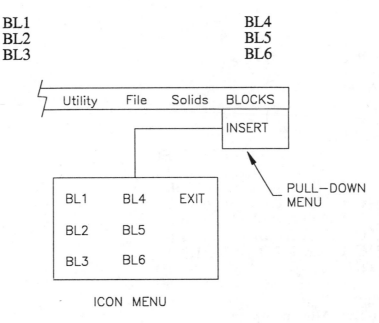

Figure 13   Commands defined in the icon menu

Note

1. *It is assumed that the slides have already been created and the names of the slides are the same as blocks.*

2. *Do not edit ACAD.MNU file. Make a copy of ACAD.MNU file and then edit the new file (CUSTOM.MNU).*

Use your word processor to load the CUSTOM.MNU file and search for the
***ICON section label. The standard ACAD.MNU file does not have the POP10
section in the pull-down menu. Therefore you can define POP10 just before ***ICON
section label. Similarly, you can define the INSTBLK icon menu just before the icon
section label ***ICON. The following file is a partial listing of the CUSTOM.MNU
file after the necessary editing.

```
***POP9
[Solids]
[~--        ]
[   Load AME   ]^C^C^P(progn(setq m:err *error*)(princ))+
(defun *error* (msg)(princ msg)(setq *error* m:err m:err nil f nil)(princ))+
(cond ((null c:solbox)(princ "Loading AME...")+
(cond ((setq f (findfile "ame")) (xload f))+
((setq f (findfile "ame.exp")) (xload f));+
(T (terpri)(princ "ERROR:  File not found. ")))+
(if f (progn(terpri)(princ "AutoCAD AME executable loaded. ")+
(menucmd "p9=p9prim")(menucmd "p9=*")(princ))+**P9Prim
```

```
***POP10
[BLOCKS]
[INSERT]^C^C$I=INSTBLK $I=*
```

```
***icon
**INSTBLK
[INSERT CUSTOMIZED BLOCKS]
[BL1]^C^CINSERT;BL1;\1.0;1.0;0
[BL2]^C^CINSERT;BL2;\1.0;1.0;0
[BL3]^C^CINSERT;BL3;\1.0;1.0;0
[BL4]^C^CINSERT;BL4;\1.0;1.0;0
[BL5]^C^CINSERT;BL5;\1.0;1.0;0
[BL6]^C^CINSERT;BL6;\1.0;1.0;0
[ EXIT]^C^C
```

```
**txtalign
[Select Text Alignment]
[acad(j-tleft)]^P(setq m:ta "TLeft") ^P
[acad(j-mleft)]^P(setq m:ta "MLeft") ^P
[acad(j-start)]^P(setq m:ta "BLeft") ^P
[acad(j-bleft)]^P(setq m:ta "BLeft") ^P
[acad(j-tcen)]^P(setq m:ta "TCenter") ^P
[acad(j-mcen)]^P(setq m:ta "MCenter") ^P
[acad(j-center)]^P(setq m:ta "C") ^P
[acad(j-bcen)]^P(setq m:ta "BCenter") ^P
[acad(j-tright)]^P(setq m:ta "TRight") ^P
```

Note

1. **[INSERT]^C^C$I=INSTBLK $I=***

    In this menu item $I=INSTBLK loads the icon submenu INSTBLK that has been defined in the icon menu section. $I= forces the display of the dialogue box with the icons.*

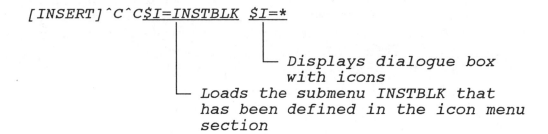

2. *****ICON**

    This is the section label of the ICON menu.   All icon menus have to be defined in this section (***ICON) of the menu file.

3. ****INSTBLK**

    This is the submenu label. The name of the submenu is INSTBLK

4. **[INSERT CUSTOMIZED BLOCKS]**

    This menu item describes the contents of the icon menu and it is displayed at the top of the dialogue box.

5. **[BL1]^C^CINSERT;BL1;\1.0;1.0;0**

    The BL1 that is inside the brackets is the name of the slide that is displayed in one of the icons of the dialogue box.   ^C^C cancels the existing command twice and INSERT command inserts the block BL1 with the X,Y scale factor of 1.0 and the rotation angle of 0 degrees.

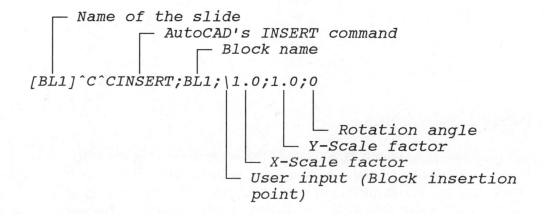

Customizing Screen Menu

Like other menu sections, screen menu section can be edited to modify or delete the existing commands or add new command and submenus. Before writing a menu, it is very important to design a menu, know the exact sequence of AutoCAD commands, and the prompts associated with the commands. You can edit the standard AutoCAD menu and arrange the commands in a way that provides the user an easy and quick access to most frequently used commands. A careful design will save quite some time in the long run. Therefore, it is strongly recommended to consider several possible alternatives and then select the one that is best suited for the job.

Submenus

The number of items in the screen menu file can be very large that may not accommodate on one screen. For example, the maximum number of items that can be displayed on some of the menu devices is 21. If the screen menu has more than 21 items, the menu items in access of 21 are not displayed on the screen and can not therefore be accessed. The user can overcome this problem by using submenus that let the user define smaller groups of items within a menu section. When a submenu is selected, it loads the submenu items and displays them on the screen.

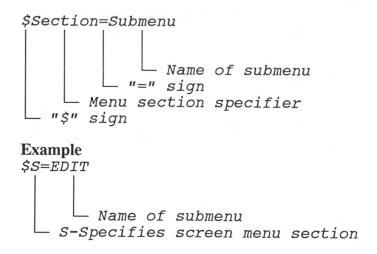

Example
```
$S=EDIT
```

Nested Submenus

When a submenu is activated, the current menu is copied to a stack. If you select another submenu, the submenu that was current will be copied or pushed to the top of the stack. The maximum number of menus that can be stacked is 8. If the stack size increases more than 8, the menu that is at the bottom of the stack is removed and forgotten. You can call the previous submenu by using the nested submenu call. The format of the call is:

```
$S=
 | | |
 | |  └─ "=" sign
 |  └─ Screen menu specifier
  └─ "$" sign
```

The maximum number of nested submenu calls that the user can have is 8. Each time you call a submenu, this pops the last item off the stack, and reactivates them.

Example 10

Edit the standard AutoCAD menu to add the commands as shown in Figure 14.

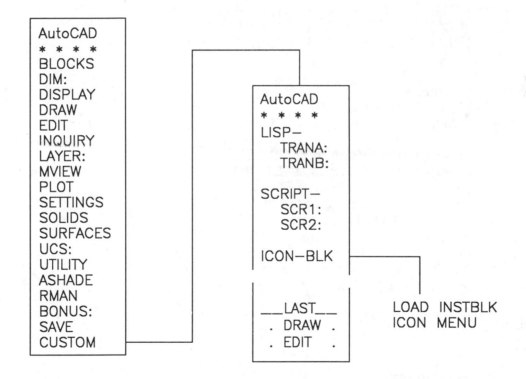

Figure 14   Modified screen menu

Note

1.   *It is assumed that the icon submenu* **INSTBLK** *has already been defined in the icon menu section of the menu file.*

2.   *Do not edit ACAD.MNU file.   Make a copy of ACAD.MNU file and then edit the new file (CUSTOM.MNU).*

You can use your word processor to load the menu file CUSTOM.MNU and search for ***SCREEN** section label. Add the new menu item at the end of the submenu **S**, and then define the submenu **CUSTOM** and the menu items as shown in Figure 14. The following file is a partial listing of the **CUSTOM.MNU** file after editing.

```
[PRIMITIVES  >]^C^C$P9=P9Prim;$P9=*;
[MODIFY     >]^C^C$P9=p9Modify;$P9=*;
[INQUIRY    >]^C^C$P9=p9Inquiry;$P9=*;
[DISPLAY    >]^C^C$P9=P9Display;$P9=*;
[~]^C^C$P9=P9Utility;$P9=*;


***ICON
**INSTBLK
[INSERT CUSTOMIZED BLOCKS]
[BL1]^C^CINSERT;BL1;\1.0;1.0;0
[BL2]^C^CINSERT;BL2;\1.0;1.0;0
[BL3]^C^CINSERT;BL3;\1.0;1.0;0
[BL4]^C^CINSERT;BL4;\1.0;1.0;0
[BL5]^C^CINSERT;BL5;\1.0;1.0;0
[BL6]^C^CINSERT;BL6;\1.0;1.0;0
[ EXIT]^C^C

**txtalign
[Select Text Alignment]
[acad(j-tleft)]^P(setq m:ta "TLeft") ^P
[acad(j-mleft)]^P(setq m:ta "MLeft") ^P
[acad(j-start)]^P(setq m:ta "BLeft") ^P
[acad(j-bleft)]^P(setq m:ta "BLeft") ^P
[acad(j-tcen)]^P(setq m:ta "TCenter") ^P
[acad(j-mcen)]^P(setq m:ta "MCenter") ^P
[acad(j-center)]^P(setq m:ta "C") ^P
[acad(j-bcen)]^P(setq m:ta "BCenter") ^P
[acad(j-tright)]^P(setq m:ta "TRight") ^P
[acad(j-mright)]^P(setq m:ta "MRight") ^P
[acad(j-right)]^P(setq m:ta "R") ^P



***SCREEN
**S
[AutoCAD]^C^C^P$S=X $S=S (setq T_MENU 0)(princ) ^P$P1=POP1
$P2=P2DRAW $P4=P4DISP $P6=P6OPT $P8=POP8
[* * * *]$S=OSNAPB
[BLOCKS]$S=X $S=BL
[DIM:]$S=X $S=DIM ^C^CDIM
[DISPLAY]$S=X $S=DS
[DRAW]$S=X $S=DR
[EDIT]$S=X $S=ED
[INQUIRY]$S=X $S=INQ
[LAYER:]$S=X $S=LAYER ^C^CLAYER
```

```
[MVIEW]$S=X $S=MV
[PLOT]$S=X $S=PLOT
[SETTINGS]$S=X $S=SET
```

```
[RMAN]^C^C^P(progn(setq m:err *error*)(defun *error*(msg)(princ"Error
loading: ")+
(princ msg)(setq *error* m:err m:err nil #GTSPO nil)(princ))(princ));+
(cond((null #GTSPO)(vmon)(if(findfile"rman.lsp")(progn(load"rman")+
(menucmd"S=X")(menucmd"S=RMAN"))(progn(terpri);+
(prompt"The file 'Rman.lsp' was not found in your current search
directories.")+
(terpri)(prompt"Check your AutoShade v2.0 Manual for installation
instructions.");+
(princ)))(setq *error* m:err m:err nil)(princ))(T(menucmd"S=X")+
(menucmd"S=RMAN")(setq *error* m:err m:err nil)(princ))) ^P
[BONUS]$S=X $S=SAMP1
[SAVE:]^C^CSAVE
[CUSTOM]^C^C$S=X $S=CUSTOM
```

```
**CUSTOM 3
[LISP-]
[  TRANA:]^C^C(LOAD "TRANA");TRANA
[  TRANB:]^C^C(LOAD "TRANB");TRANB
[  ]
[SCRIPT-]
[  SCR1:]^C^CSCRIPT;SCR1
[  SCR2:]^C^CSCRIPT;SCR2
```

```
[ICON-BLK]^C^C$I=INSTBLK $I=*
```

```
**HEADER
[AutoCAD]^C^C^P$S=X $S=S (setq T_MENU 0)(princ) ^P$P1=POP1
```

Note

1. **[CUSTOM]^C^C$S=X $S=CUSTOM** *In this menu item $S=X loads the submenu X that has been defined in the screen menu section. $S=CUSTOM loads the submenu CUSTOM that has also been defined in the screen menu section of the menu file CUSTOM.MNU.*

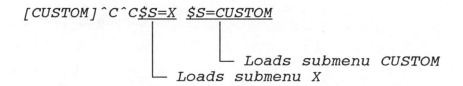

2. ****CUSTOM 3**   *In this menu item CUSTOM is the name of the submenu. The 3 that follows the submenu name, prints the menu items defined in the submenu CUSTOM from the line number 3. Nothing is printed on the first two lines, therefore the first two lines AutoCAD and * * * * stay on the screen.*

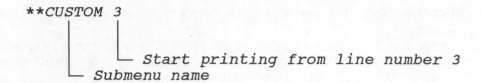

3. **[ICON-BLK]^C^C\$I=INSTBLK \$I=***   *In this menu item \$I=INSTBLK loads the icon submenu INSTBLK that has been defined in the icon section of the menu file. \$I=* forces the display of the new icon menu on the screen.*

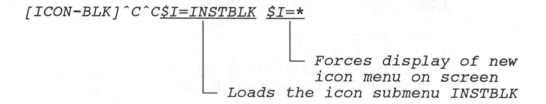

Customizing Comment Section

You can use the comment section for providing the information about the menu file. It can be any information of any length that is relevant and helps to understand different sections of the menu file. It is a good practice to give the comments in the file when you make any changes in the menu item. It will help you and other users to keep a track of the changes made from time to time. The comments are ignored when the file is compiled.

Like other menu sections, the comments section is designated by three asterisks followed by COMMENT (***Comment or ***COMMENT). The lines that follow the ***Comment section, until the next menu section label or submenu label, are a part of this section.

Review

Fill in the blanks

1.   The AutoCAD menu file can have up to .... sections.

2.   Tablet menu can have up to .... sections.

3.   The section label is designated by ....

4.   The submenu label is designated by ....

5.   In a menu file you can use .... to cancel the existing command.

6.   Submenu names can be .... characters long.

7.   You .... assign same command to more than one block on the template.

8.   AutoCAD's .... command is used to configure the tablet menu template.

9.   AutoCAD's .... command is used to load a new menu.

10.   You need to enter .... points that are at .... degrees to configure different tablet areas.

11.   The commands are assigned to the buttons of the pointing device in the .... order in which they appear in the buttons menu.

12.   The format of the command used for loading a submenu that has been defined in the screen menu section is ....

13.   The format of the command used for loading a submenu that has been defined in the pull-down menu section is ....

14.   The format of the command used for loading a submenu that has been defined in the icon menu section is ....

15.   The command that is used to force the display of the current pull-down menu is ....

Exercises

Exercise 1

Add the following commands to the TABLET1ALT section of the standard AutoCAD menu file ACAD.MNU. Figure 16 shows the layout of the tablet area-1 of the template.

VIEW-POINTS

0,0,1	1,0,0	0,1,0
1,-1,1	1,1,1	-1,1,1

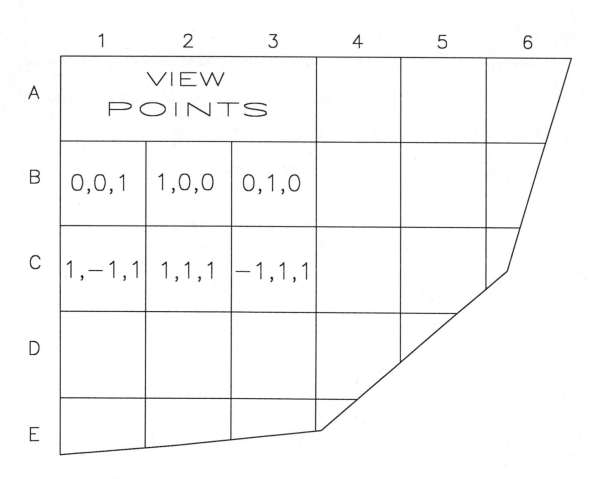

Figure 15   Commands assigned to alternate tablet area-1

Exercise 2

Add the following commands to the TABLET1 section of the standard AutoCAD menu file ACAD.MNU. The layout of the tablet area-1 is shown in Figure 15.

INSERT NO	PLOT 12x18	SETLAYER OBJ
INSERT NC	PLOT 18x24	SETLAYER HID
INSERT COIL	PLOT 24x36	SETLAYER CEN
INSERT RESIS	PRPLOT	SETLAYER DIM

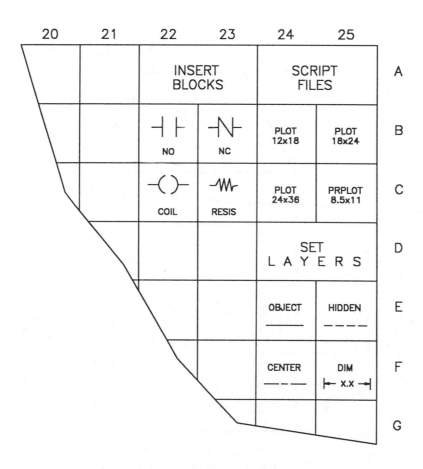

Figure 16   Commands assigned to tablet area-1

Exercise 3

Write a button menu for the following AutoCAD commands. The pointing device has 10 buttons; button number 1 is used for picking the points. The blocks are to be inserted with a scale factor of 1.00 and a rotation of 0 degrees. (File name BME1.MNU)

1. PICK BUTTON	2. RETURN	3. CANCEL
4. OSNAPS	5. END PT	6. CENTER
7. NEAR	8. ZOOM Window	9. ZOOM Prev
10. PAN		

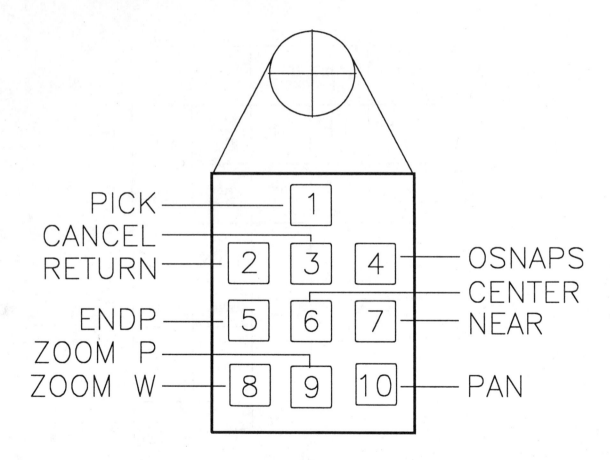

Figure 17   Commands assigned to different buttons of a pointing device

Exercise 4

Add the commands shown in Figure 18 to POP10 section of the standard AutoCAD menu ACAD.MNU

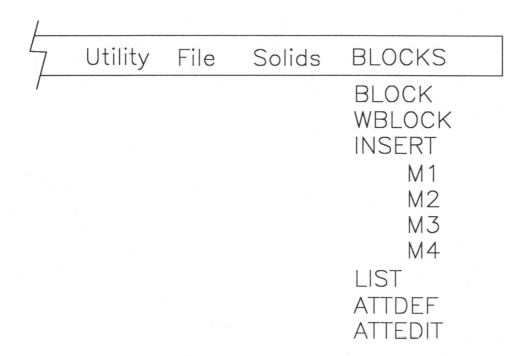

Figure 18   POP10 section of pull-down menu

Exercise 5

Write an icon menu that can be accessed through POP10 section of Example 4, for inserting the following blocks.

SYMBOL-X	SYMBOL-Y	SYMBOL-Z
LOGO-1	LOGO-2	LOGO-3
TBLOCK-1	TBLOCK-2	TBLOCK-3

Note

It is assumed that the blocks have already been created.

Chapter 12

Shapes and Text Fonts

AutoCAD provides a facility to define the shapes and text fonts. These files are ASCII files with an extension .SHP. You can write these files by using Edlin function of DOS, AutoCAD's EDIT command (provided the ACAD.PGP file is present and EDIT command is defined in the file), or any other text editor.

Shape Files

Shape files contain information about various entities that constitute the shape of an object. The basic entities that are used in these files are lines and arcs. User can define any shape by using these basic entities, and then insert them anywhere in a drawing. The shape files are easy to insert and take less disk space compared to blocks. However, there are some disadvantages in using shapes. For example, you can not edit a shape or make changes to it. The blocks, on the other hand, can be edited after exploding them with AutoCAD's EXPLODE command.

Shape Description

Shape description consists of the following two parts

1. Header
2. Shape Specification

1. Header

The Header line has the following format

*SHAPE NUMBER, DEFBYTES, SHAPENAME

Example
```
*201,21,HEXBOLT
```

Shape name
Number of data bytes in
shape specification
Shape number

Every header line starts with a asterisk (*) followed by the **SHAPE NUMBER**. The shape number could be any number between 1 and 255 in a particular file, but these numbers can not be repeated within the same file. However, these numbers could be repeated in another shape file with a different name.

DEFBYTES is the number of data bytes used in the shape specification that includes the terminating zero.

SHAPE NAME is the name of a shape in upper case characters. The name is ignored if the letters are in lower case characters. The file must not contain two shapes with the same name.

2. Shape Specification:

The shape specification line contains the complete definition of the shape of an object. The shape is described by using special codes, hexadecimal numbers and decimal numbers. A hexadecimal number is designated by leading zero (012) and a decimal number is a regular number without any leading zero (12). The data bytes are separated by a comma (,). The maximum number of data bytes is 2000 bytes per shape. In a particular shape file there can be more than one shape and the number of bytes in the shape specification line should not exceed 2000 bytes. The shape specification can have multiple lines. It is a recommended practice to define the shape in some logical blocks and enter each block on a separate line. It makes it much easier to edit and debug the files. The number of characters on any line must not exceed 80 characters. The Shape Specification is terminated by a zero at the end of the shape specification.

Vector Length and Direction Encoding

For direction encoding, 360 degrees angle has been divided into 16 equal parts. Each angle is equal to 22.5 degrees. A direction vector is defined after every 22.5 degrees as shown in Figure 1.

All these vectors have the same magnitude or length specification. To define a vector you need its magnitude and direction. That means each shape specification byte contains vector length and direction code. The maximum length of the vector is 15 units. Let us consider the following example to illustrate the use of vectors.

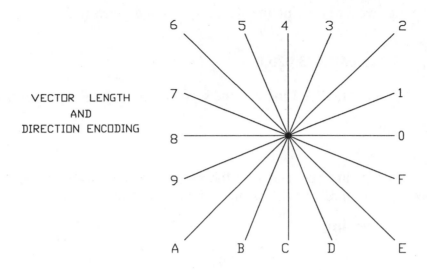

Figure 1   Vector length and direction encoding

Example 1

Write a Shape File for the resistor as shown in Figure 2. The name of the file is SH1.SHP and the shape name is RESIS.

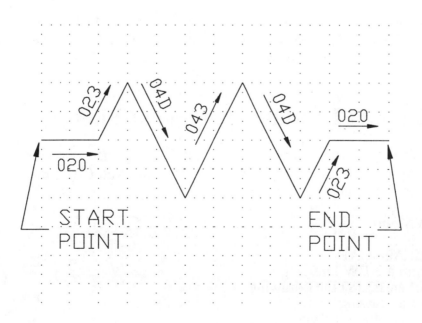

Figure 2   Resistor

The following two lines define the shape file for the given resistor.

*201,8,RESIS
020,023,04D,043,04D,023,020,0

The fist line is the **Header Line** and the second line is the **Shape Specification**.

Header Line

*201,8,RESIS
*201 is the shape number, and 8 is the number of data bytes contained in the shape specification line. RESIS is the name of the shape.

Shape Specification

020,023,04D,043,04D,023,020,0

```
L Direction Code
L Vector length
L Hexadecimal notation
```

Each data byte in this line, except the terminating zero, has three elements. The first element (0) is the hexadecimal designation. The second element is the length of the vector, and the third element is the direction code. For the first data byte 020, the length of the vector is 2, and the direction is along the direction vector 0.

Similarly, for the second data byte 023, the first element 0 is for hexadecimal, the second element 2 is the length of the vector, and the third element 3 is the direction code for the vector.

Compiling and Loading Shape/Font Files

The shape or font files can be compiled by using option number 7 of AutoCAD's main menu. To compile a shape file, start AutoCAD, the main menu will be displayed on the screen.

Main Menu

0. Exit AutoCAD
1. Begin a NEW Drawing
2. Edit an EXISTING drawing
3. Plot a drawing
4. Printer plot a drawing

5. Configure AutoCAD
6. File utilities
7. **Compile shape/font description file**

8. Convert old drawing file
9. Recover damaged drawing

After you have selected the option number 7, AutoCAD will display the following prompt:

Enter NAME of shape file: (Name of Shape file) <u>SH1</u>

In response to this prompt enter the name of the file you want to compile. For Example 1, the name of the file is SH1. Type SH1 and hit the ENTER key. AutoCAD assumes the extension .SHP, therefore do not include the extension with the file name. AutoCAD will compile the file and if the compilation process is successful, the following prompt will be displayed on the screen.

Compilation successful
Output file name.shx contains nn bytes

For Example 1, the name of the compiled output file is SH1.SHX and the number of bytes is 49. This is the file that is loaded when you use AutoCAD's LOAD command to load a shape.

If AutoCAD encounters any error in compiling a shape file, an error message will be displayed on the screen indicating the type of error and the line number where the error occurred.

To insert a shape in the drawing, you have to be in the drawing editor, and then use the LOAD command to load the shape file.

Command: <u>Load</u>
Name of shape file to load (or ?): (Name of file) <u>SH1</u>

SH1 is the name of the shape file for Example 1. Do not include the extension .SHX with the name, because AutoCAD automatically assumes .SHX extension. If the shape file is present, AutoCAD will display the shape names that are loaded. To insert the loaded shapes, use AutoCAD's SHAPE command.

Command: SHAPE
Shape name (or ?) <default>: (Shape name)
Start point: (Shape Origin)
Height <1.0>: (number or point)
Rotation angle <0.0>: (number or point)

For Example 1, the shape name is RESIS. After you enter the information about the start point, height and rotation, the shape will be displayed on the screen.

Special Codes

Generating the shapes with the direction vectors has some limitations. For example, you can not draw an arc or draw a line that is not along the standard direction vectors. These limitations can be overcome by using the special codes that add much flexibility and give the user a better control over the shapes he wants to create.

Following is a list of the Standard Codes:

000	End of shape definition
001	Activate draw mode (pen down)
002	Deactivate draw mode (pen up)
003	Divide vector lengths by next byte
004	Multiply vector lengths by next byte
005	Push current location from stack
006	Pop current location from stack
007	Draw sub-shape numbers given by next byte
008	X-Y displacement given by the next two bytes
009	Multiply X-Y displacement, terminated by (0,0)
00A	Octant arc defined by next two bytes
00B	Fractional arc defined by next five bytes
00C	Arc defined by X-Y displacement and bulge
00D	Multiply bulge-specified arcs
00E	Process next command only if vertical text style

Code 0: End of shape definition.

This code marks the end of a shape definition.

Code 1: Activate draw mode.

This code turns the draw mode on. When you start a shape, the draw mode is on and you do not need to use this code. However, if the draw mode has been turned off, then you can use Code 001 to turn it on.

Code 2: Deactivate draw mode.

This code turns the draw mode off. It is used when you want to move the pen without drawing a line.

Example

```
_____              _____
1              2             3              4
```

Let us say the distance from point 1 to 2, from point 3 to 4, and from point 2 to 3 is 2 units. The shape specification for this line is:

020,002,020,001,020,0

The first data byte 020 generates a line of 2 units long along the direction vector 0. The second data byte 002 deactivates the draw mode, and the third byte 020 generates a blank line of 2 units long. The fourth data byte 001 activates the draw mode, and the next byte 020 generates a line that is 2 units long along the direction vector 0. The last byte 0 terminates the shape description.

Example 2

Write a shape file for generating the character "G" as shown in Figure 3.

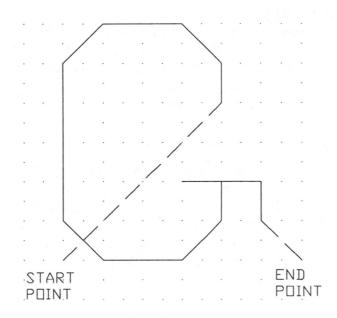

Figure 3   Shape of the character "G"

You can use the Edlin function of DOS or any other text editor to write a shape file. The name of the file is CHRGEE and the shape name is GEE. In the following file the line numbers are not a part of the file. They are for reference only.

*215,20,GEE	**1**
002,042,	**2**
001,014,016,028,01A,	**3**
04C,01E,020,012,014,	**4**
002,018,	**5**
001,020,01C,	**6**
002,01E,0	**7**

Explanation

Line1
*215,28,GEE

The first data byte contains asterisk (*) and shape number 215. The second data byte is the number of data bytes that are contained in the shape specification, including the terminating zero. GEE is the name of shape.

Line2
002,042,
The data byte 002 deactivates the draw mode (pen up), and the next databyte defines a vector that is 4 units long along the direction vector 2.

Line 3
001,014,016,028,01A,
The data byte 001 activates the draw mode (pen down), and 014 defines a vector that is 1 unit long at 90 degrees (direction vector 4). The data byte 016 defines a vector that is 1 unit long along the direction vector 6. The data byte 028 defines a vector that is 2 units long along the direction vector 8 (180 degrees). The data byte 01A defines a unit vector along the direction vector A.

Line4
04C,01E,020,012,014,
The data byte 04C defines a vector that is 4 units long along the direction vector C. The data byte 01E defines a direction vector that is 1 unit along the direction vector E. The data byte 020 defines a direction vector that is 2 units long along the direction vector 0 (0 degrees). The data byte 012 defines a direction vector that is 1 unit long along the direction vector 2. Similarly, 014 defines a vector that is 1 unit long along the direction vector 4.

Line 5
002,018,
The data byte 002 deactivates the pen (pen up), and 018 defines a vector that is 1 unit long along the direction vector 8.

Line 6
001,020,01C,
The data byte 001 activates the pen (pen down), and 020 defines a vector that is 2 unit long along the direction vector 0. The data byte 01C defines a vector that is 1 unit long along the direction vector C.

Line 7
002,01E,0
The data byte 002 deactivates the pen and the next data byte 01E defines a vector that is 1 unit long along the direction vector E. The data byte 0 terminates the shape specification.

Code 3: Divide Vector Lengths.

This code is used if you want to Divide a vector by a certain number. In Example 2, if you want to divide the vectors by 2. The shape description can be written as:

003,2,020,002,020,001,020,0

The first byte 003 is the division code, and the next byte 2 is the number by which all the remaining vectors are divided. The length of the lines, and the gap between the lines will be equal to 1 unit now.

Also the scale factors are cumulative within a shape. For example, if we insert another Code 003 in the above mentioned shape description, the length of the last vector 020 will be divided by 4 (2*2).

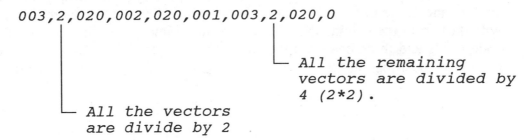

```
003,2,020,002,020,001,003,2,020,0
```

└─ All the remaining vectors are divided by 4 (2*2).

└─ All the vectors are divide by 2

Following is the output of this shape file:

Code 4: Multiply Vector Lengths.

This code is used if you want to multiply the vectors by a certain number. It could also be used to reverse the effect of Code 003.

Example
```
003,2,020,002,020,001,004,2,020,0
```

└─ Multiplies all the vectors on the right by 2

└── Divides all the vectors on the right by 2

In this example, the Code 003 divides all the vectors to the right by 2. Therefore, a vector that was one unit long will be 0.5 units long now. The second Code 004 multiplies the vectors to the right by 2. We know the scale factors are cumulative, and therefore the vectors that were divided by 2 earlier will be multiplied by 2 now. Because of this cumulative effect, the length of the last vector will remain unchanged. This file will produce the following shape

Codes 5 & 6 Location Save/Restore.

Code 5, lets the user save the current location of the pen, and Code 6 restores the saved location. Let us consider the following example to illustrate the use of Code 5 & 6.

Example

Figure 4(a) shows three lines that are unit vectors, and intersect at one point. After drawing the first line the pen has to return to origin to start second vector. This is done by using Code 005 that saves the starting point (origin) of the first vector, and Code 006 restores the origin. Now, if you draw another vector, it will start from the origin. Since there are three lines, therefore you need three code 005's and three code 006's. The following file shows the header line and the shape specification for generating three lines as shown in Figure 4 (a).

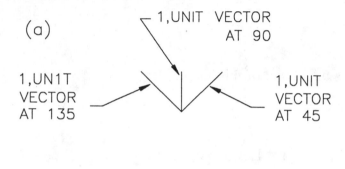

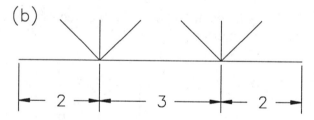

Figure 4   (a) Three unit vectors intersecting at a point (b) Repeating predefined subshapes

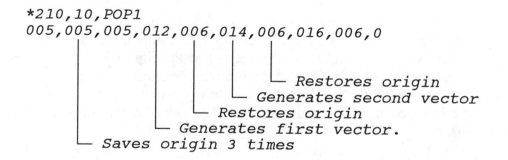

The number of saves (Code 005) has to be equal to the number of restores (Code 006). If the number of saves (Code 005) are more than the number of

restores (Code 006), AutoCAD will display the following message when the shape is drawn.

Position stack overflow in shape (Shape Number)

Similarly, if the number of restores (Code 006) are more than the number of saves (Code 005), following message will be displayed:

Position stack underflow in shape (Shape Number)

Also, the maximum number of saves and restores you can use in a particular shape definition is 4.

Code 7: Subshape.

You can define a subshape like a subroutine in a program. To reference a subshape, the subshape Code 007 has to be followed by the shape number of the subshape. The subshape has to be defined in the same shape file, and the shape number has to be from 1 to 255.

Example

```
         ┌─ Shape Number
      ┌
      │ ·
*210,10,POP1
005,005,005,012,006,014,006,016,006,0
*211,8,SUB1
020,007,210,030,007,210,020,0
      │     │
      │     └─ Shape number
      └─ Subshape reference
```

The shape that this example will generate is shown in Figure 4(b).

Code 8: X-Y Displacement.

In the previous examples, you might have noticed that there are some limitations with the vectors. As mentioned earlier, you can draw vectors only in the 16 predefined directions, and the length of the vector can not exceed 15 units. These restrictions make the shape files easier and efficient, but at the same time are limiting. Therefore, codes 8 and 9 allow the user to generate nonstandard vectors by entering the displacements along X and Y direction. The general format is:

8, X-DISPLACEMENT, Y-DISPLACEMENT
or
8, (X-DISPLACEMENT, Y-DISPLACEMENT)

X and Y displacements can range from +127 to -128. Also, a positive displacement is designated by a positive (+) number, and a negative displacement is designated by a negative (-) number. The leading positive sign (+) is optional in a positive number. The parentheses are used to improve readability and these have no effect on the shape specification.

Example:

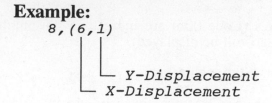

```
8,(6,1)
        └── Y-Displacement
     └── X-Displacement
```

The shape that this vector definition will produce is shown in Figure 5.

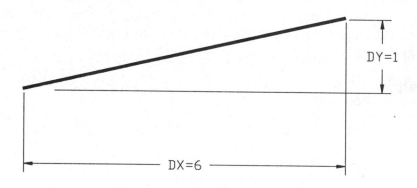

Figure 5   Generate nonstandard vectors by defining X-Y displacement

Code 9: Multiple X-Y Displacements

Whereas code 8 allows the user to generate a nonstandard vectors by entering a single X and Y displacement, code 9 allows the user to enter multiple X and Y displacements. It is terminated by a pair of 0 displacement (0,0). The general format is:

9,(X-Displ, Y-Displ), (X-Disp, Y-Displ),.......(0,0)

Example

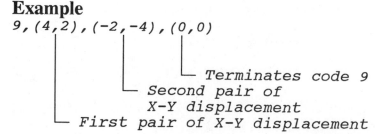

```
9,(4,2),(-2,-4),(0,0)
                  └── Terminates code 9
          └── Second pair of
             X-Y displacement
    └── First pair of X-Y displacement
```

The shape that this vector definition will generate is shown in Figure 6.

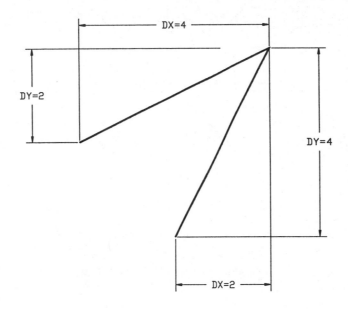

Figure 6   Using multiple X-Y displacements

Code 00A or 10: Octant Arc

If you divide 360 degrees into 8 equal parts, each angle will be 45 degrees. Each 45 degree angle segment is called an Octant, and the two lines that contain an octant are called octant boundary. The octant boundaries are numbered from 0 to 7 as shown in Figure 7. The general format is:

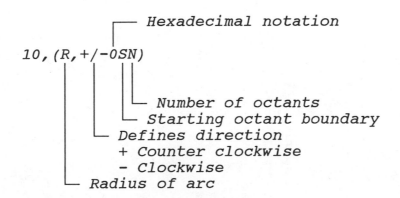

Example
10,(3,-043)

The first number 10 is the Code 00A for the Octant Arc. The second number 3 is the radius of the octant arc

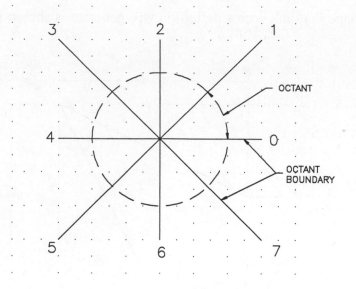

Figure 7   Octant boundaries

The negative sign indicates that the arc is to be generated in clockwise direction. If it was positive (+), or if there was no sign, then the arc will be generated in counter clockwise direction. 0 is the hexadecimal notation, and the following number 4 is the number of the octant boundary where the octant arc will start. Next element, 3 is the number of octants that this arc will extend. This example will generate an arc as shown in Figure 8A.

The following shape file will generate a shape as shown in Figure 8A.

```
*214,5,FOCT1
001,10,(3,-043),0
```

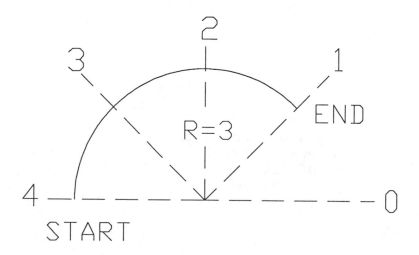

Figure 8A   Octant arc

Code 00B or 11: Fractional Arc

You can generate a nonstandard fractional arc by using Code 00B or 11. This code will allow the user to start and end an arc at any angle. The definition uses five bytes, and the general format is

11,(START OFFSET, END OFFSET, HIGH-RADIUS, LOW-RADIUS, +/-0SN)

The START OFFSET represents how far from an octant boundary the arc starts, and the END OFFSET represents how far from an octant boundary the arc ends. The HIGH-RADIUS is 0 if the radius is equal to or less than 255 units, and the LOW-RADIUS is the radius of the arc. The positive (+) or negative (-) sign indicates if the arc is drawn counter clockwise or clockwise. The next element "S" is the number of octant where the arc starts, and the element "N" is the number of octants the arc goes through. Let us consider the following example to illustrate the fractional arc concept.

Example
Draw a fractional arc of radius 3 units that starts at 20 degree angle and ends at 140 degree angle (counter clockwise).

The solution involves the following steps:

1   Find the nearest octant boundary whose angle is less than 140 degrees. The nearest octant boundary is the number 4 octant boundary whose angle is 135 (3*45 = 135).

2   Calculate end offset to the nearest whole number (Integer).

      Start offset   = (140-135) * 256/45
                              = 28.44
                              = 28

3   Find the nearest octant boundary whose angle is less than 20 degree. The nearest octant boundary is 0 whose angle is 0.

4   Calculate start offset to the nearest whole number.

      End offset   = (20-0) * 256/45
                              = 113.7
                              = 114

5   Find the number of octants the arc passes through. In this example, the arc starts in the first octant and it ends in the fourth octant. Therefore, the number of octants the arc passes through is 4 (counter clockwise).

6   Find the octant where the arc starts. In this example it starts in the 0th octant.

7   Substitute the values in the general format of the fractional arc.

11,(114,28,0,3,004)

The following shape file will generate a fractional arc as shown in Figure 8B

```
*221,8,FOCT2
001,11,(114,28,0,3,004),0
```

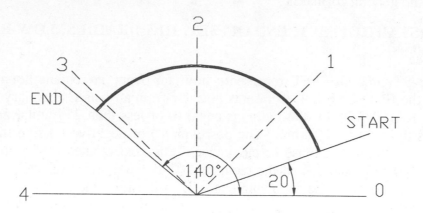

Figure 8B   Fractinal arc

Code 00C or 12: Arc Definition by Displacement & Bulge.

Code C can be used to define an arc by specifying the displacement of the end point of an arc, and the bulge factor. X and Y displacements may range from -127 to +127, and the bulge factor can also range from -127 to +127. A semicircle will have a bulge factor of 127, and a straight line will have a bulge factor of 0. If the bulge factor has a negative sign, the arc is drawn clockwise.

```
Bulge Factor = ((2 * H)/D) * 127
                       |   |
                       |   └─ Displacement
                       └─ Height of arc
```

For a semicircle 2H	**= D**
Therefore Bulge	**= (D/D) * 127**
	= 127
For a straight line H	**= 0**
Therefore bulge	**= (0/D) * 127**
	= 0

Example
In Figure 9, the distance between the start and end point of an arc is 4 units and the height is 1 unit. Therefore, bulge can be calculated by substituting the values in the above mentioned relation.

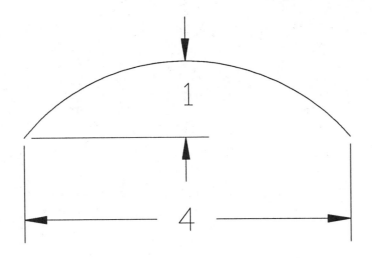

Figure 9   Calcualting bulge

Bulge   = (2 * 1/4) * 127
                   = 63.5
                   = 63 (Integer)

The following shape description will generate an arc as shown in Figure 9.

```
*213,5,BULGE1
12,(4,0,-63),0
```

             ┌── Bulge factor
          ┌── Negative (-), generates
                         clockwise arc
       ┌── Y-Displacement
     ┌── X-Displacement

Code 00D or 13: Multiple Bulge Specified ARC.

Code 00D or 13 can be used to generate multiple arcs with different bulge factors. It is terminated by a (0,0).

Example:
The following shape description defines the arc configuration of Figure 10.

```
*214,16,BULGE2
13,(4,0,-111),
(0,4,63),
(-4,0,-111),
(0,-4,63),(0,0),0
```

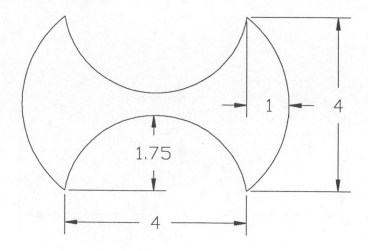

Figure 10 Different arc configuration

Code 00E or 14: Flag Vertical Text.

Code 00E or 14 is used when the same text font description is to be used in both horizontal and vertical orientation. If the text drawn is in a horizontal direction, then the vector that is next to Code 14 is ignored. If the text is drawn in a vertical position, then the vector that is next to Code 14 is not ignored. This lets the user generate text in vertical or horizontal direction with the same shape file.

For the horizontal text the start point is the lower left point, and the end point is on the lower right as shown in Fig 10-3. In the vertical text the start point is at the top center, and the end point is at the bottom center of the text as shown in Fig 10-11. At first, it appears that you need two separate shape files to define the shape of a horizontal and a vertical text. However, with Code 14 you can avoid the dual shape definition as shown in the following example.

Example
Figure 11 shows the pen movements for generating text character "G". If the text is horizontal the line that is next to Code 14 is automatically ignored. However, if the text is vertical then the line is not ignored.

```
1*15,28,FLAG
002,14,
008,(-2,-6),
042,001,
014,016,028,01A,
04C,01E,020,012,014,
002,018,
001,020,01C,
002,01E,
14,
008,(-4,-1),
0
```

If text is horizontal, Code 14 automatically ignores next line.
008, (-2,-6),

If text is horizontal, Code 14 automatically ignores next line.
008,(-4,-1),

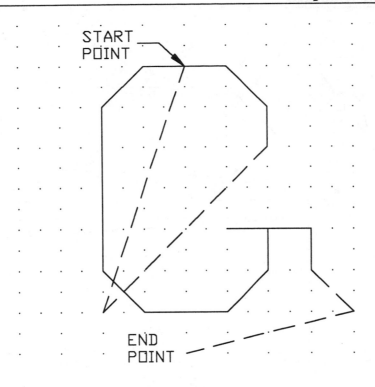

Figure 11   Pen movement for generating the character "G"

Example 3

Write a shape file for a hammer as shown in Figure 12. (The name of the shape file is HMR.SHP and the shape name is HAMMER). The following file defines the shape of a hammer. The line numbers are not a part of the file. They are for reference only.

```
*204,34,HAMMER             1
003,22                     2
002,8,(2,-1),              3
001,024                    4
8,(-1,4),                  5
00A,(1,004),               6
8,(-1,-4),06C,             7
00C,(4,0,63),              8
044,8,(17,-1),             9
00C,(0,4,63),             10
8,(-17,-1),0              11
```

Explanation

Line1
*204,34,HAMMER
This is the header line that consists of shape number (204), number of data bytes in the shape specification (34), and name of the shape (HAMMER)

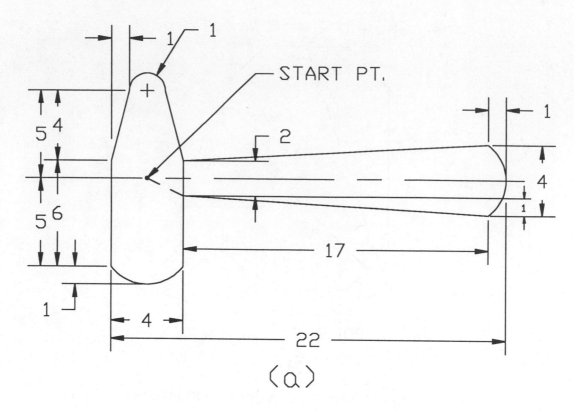

Figure 12A   Dimensions of hammer in units

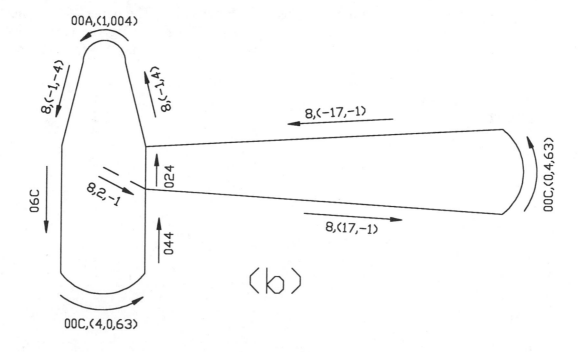

Figure 12B   Pen movements for generating the shape of a hammer

Line 2
003,22
The data byte 003 has been used to divide the vectors by the next data byte 22. This reduces the hammer shape to a unit size that facilitates the scaling operation when the user inserts the shape in a drawing.

Line 3
002,8,(2,-1),
The data byte 002 deactivates the pen (pen up), and the next data byte (code 8) defines a vector that has X-displacement of 2 units and Y-displacement of 1 unit. No line is drawn because the pen is deactivated.

Line 4
001,024
The data byte 001 activates the pen (pen down), and the next data byte defines a vector that is 2 units long along the direction vector 2.

Line 5
8,(-1,-4)
The first data byte 8 (code 8) defines a vector whose X and Y displacement is given by the next two data bytes. The X-displacement of this vector is -1 and the Y-displacement is -4 units.

Line 6
00A,(1,004)
The data byte 00A defines an octant arc that has a radius of 1 unit as defined by the next data byte. The first element (0) of the data byte 004 is a hexadecimal notation. The second element (0) defines the starting octant of the arc, and the third element (4) defines the ending octant of the arc.

Line 7
8,(-1,-4),06C
The data byte 8 (code 8) defines a vector that has X-displacement of -1 unit, and Y-displacement of -4 units. The next data byte defines a vector that is 6 units long along the direction vector C.

Line 8
00C,(4,0,63)
The first data byte 00C defines an arc that has X-displacement of 4 units, Y-displacement of 0 units and a bulge factor of 63.

$$
\begin{aligned}
\textbf{Bulge Factor} \quad &= (2 * H)/D * 127 \\
&= (2 * 1)/4 * 127 \\
&= 63.5 \\
&= 63 \text{ (integer)}
\end{aligned}
$$

Line 9
044,8,(17,-1)
The first data byte defines a vector that is 4 units long along the direction vector 4. The second data byte (8) defines a vector that has X-displacement of 17 units, and Y-displacement of -1 unit.

Line 10
00C,(0,4,63)

The first data byte (00C) defines an arc that has X-displacement of 0 units, Y-displacement of 4 units and a bulge factor of 63.

$$\textbf{Bulge Factor} \qquad = \textbf{(2 * H)/D * 127}$$
$$= \textbf{(2 * 1)/2 * 127}$$
$$= \textbf{63.5}$$
$$= \textbf{63 (integer)}$$

Line 11
8,(-17,-1),0
The first data byte (8) defines a vector that has X-displacement of -17 units and Y-displacement of -1 units. The data byte 0 terminates the shape definition.

Text Font Files

In addition to shape files, AutoCAD provides a facility to create new text fonts. After you have created and compiled a text font file, text can be inserted in a drawing like regular text using the new font. These text files are regular shape files with some additional information about the text font description and the line feed. The following is the general layout of the text font file.

Text Font Description
Line feed
Shape Definition

Text Font Description

The text font description consists of the following two lines

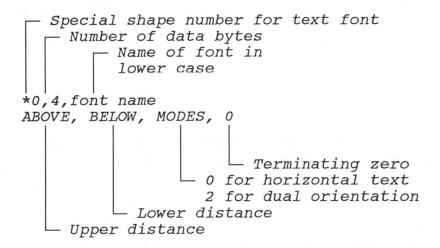

```
*0,4,font name
ABOVE, BELOW, MODES, 0
```

Special shape number for text font
Number of data bytes
Name of font in lower case
Terminating zero
0 for horizontal text
2 for dual orientation
Lower distance
Upper distance

Example
    *0,4,ucm
    10,4,2,0

The first data byte 0 is a special shape number for the text font, and every text font file will have this shape number. The next data byte 4 is the number of data bytes in the next line, and ucm is the shape name (name of font). The shape names in all text font files should be in lower case letters so that the computer does not have to save the names in memory. You can still reference the shape names for editing.

The first data byte 10 in the second line specifies the height of upper case letter above the base line. For example, in Figure 13 the height of the letter "M" is 10 units above the base line. The next data byte 4 specifies the distance of lower case letters below the base line. This information is used by AutoCAD to automatically scale the text. For example, if you enter the height of text as 1 unit then the text will be 1 unit although it was drawn 10 units high text in the text font definition.

The third data byte 2 defines the mode. It can have only two values 0 or 2.   If the text is horizontal then the mode is 0, and if the text has dual orientation (horizontal or vertical) then the mode is 2.

The fourth data byte 0 is the terminating zero that terminates the definition.

Line Feed

The Line Feed is used to space the lines so that the characters do not overlap, and maintain a desired distance between the lines.   AutoCAD has reserved shape number 10 to define the line feed.

Example

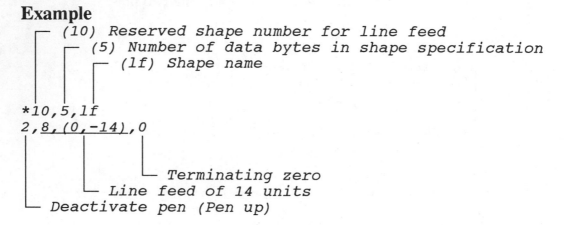

```
       ┌─ (10) Reserved shape number for line feed
       │  ┌─ (5) Number of data bytes in shape specification
       │  │   ┌─ (lf) Shape name
       │  │   │
       │  │   │
  *10,5,lf
  2,8,(0,-14),0
  │   │        │
  │   │        └─ Terminating zero
  │   └─ Line feed of 14 units
  └─ Deactivate pen (Pen up)
```

The first data byte 10 is reserved shape number for line feed, and the next data byte (5) is the number of characters in the shape specification.   The data byte "lf" is the name of the shape.

The first data byte 2 in the second line deactivates the pen.   The next data byte 8 is a special code 008 that defines a vector by X and Y displacement.   Third and fourth data bytes (0,-14) are X-Displacement and Y-Displacement of the displacement vector, and produces a line feed that is 14 units below the base line.   The fifth data byte 0 is the terminating zero that terminates the shape definition.

Shape Definition

The shape number in the shape definition of the text font are corresponding to the ASCII code for that character.   For example, if you are writing a shape definition for the upper case character "M" then the shape number is 77

Example
```
*77,50,ucm
```
```
      Shape name
    Number of data bytes
  Shape number - ASCII code of upper case
  Character "M"
```

The ASCII codes can be obtained from the following ASCII character table that gives the ASCII codes for all characters, numbers and punctuation marks.

32	space	56	8	80	P	104	h
33	!	57	9	81	Q	105	i
34	"	58	:	82	R	106	j
35	#	59	;	83	S	107	k
36	$	60	<	84	T	108	l
37	%	61	=	85	U	109	m
38	&	62	>	86	V	110	n
39	,	63	?	87	W	111	o
40	(	64	@	88	X	112	p
41	)	65	A	89	Y	113	q
42	*	66	B	90	Z	114	r
43	+	67	C	91	[	115	s
44	,	68	D	92	\	116	t
45	-	69	E	93	]	117	u
46	.	70	F	94	^	118	v
47	/	71	G	95		119	w
48	0	72	H	96	`	120	x
49	1	73	I	97	a	121	y
50	2	74	J	98	b	122	z
51	3	75	K	99	c	123	{
52	4	76	L	100	d	124		
53	5	77	M	101	e	125	}
54	6	78	N	102	f	126	~
55	7	79	O	103	g		

Example 4

Write a text font shape file for the upper case character "M" as shown in Figure 13. The font file should be able to generate horizontal and vertical text. Each grid is one unit, and the directions of vectors is designated with leader lines. In the following file the line numbers are not a part of the file. They are for reference only.

```
*0,4,upper case m                                          1
10,2,2,0                                                   2
*10,13,lf                                                  3
002,8,(0,-14),14,9,(0,14),(14,0),(0,0),0                   4
*77,51,ucm                                                 5
2,14,8,(-5,-10),                                           6
```

```
001,009,(0,10),(1,0),(4,-6),(4,6),(1,0),            7
(0,-10),(-1,0),(0,0),                               8
003,2,                                              9
009,(0,17),(-7,-11),(-2,0),(-7,11),                 10
(0,-17),(-2,0),(0,0),                               11
002,8,(28,0),                                       12
004,2,                                              13
14,8,(-9,-4),0                                      14
```

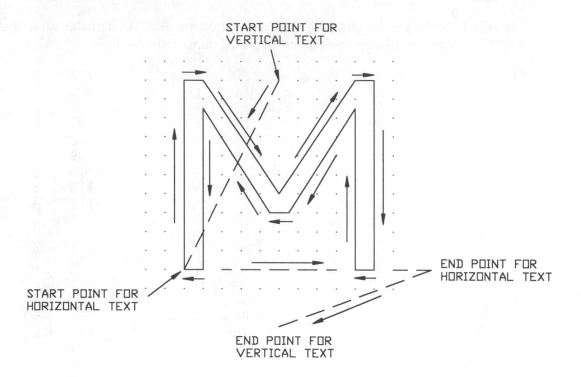

Figure 13   Shape and pen movement of the upper case character "M"

Explanation

Line 1
*0,4,upper case m
The first data byte *0 is the special shape number for the text font file. The next data byte 4 is the number of data bytes, and the third data byte is the name of the shape.

Line 2
10,0,2,0
The fist data byte 10 represents total height of the character "M", and the second data byte 0 represents the length of the lower case letters that extend below the base line. The data byte 2 is the text mode for dual orientation (horizontal and vertical) of the text. If the text was required in the horizontal direction only then the mode is 0. The fourth data byte 0 is the terminating zero that terminates the definition of this particular shape.

Line 3
*10,13,lf
The first data byte 10 is the reserved code for line feed, and the second data byte 13 is the number of data bytes in the shape specification. The third data byte (lf) is the name of the shape.

Line 4
002,8,(0,-14),14,9,(0,14),(14,0),(0,0),0
The first data byte 002 or 2 is the code for deactivating the pen (pen up). The next three data bytes 8,(0,-14) define a displacement vector whose X and Y displacement is 0 and -14 units respectively. This will cause a carriage return that is 14 units below the text insertion point of the first text line. This will work fine if the text is drawn in horizontal direction only. However, if the text is vertical then the carriage return should produce a displacement to the right of the existing line. This is accomplished by the next 7 data bytes. The data byte 14 ignores the next code if the text is horizontal. If the text is vertical then the next code is processed. The next set of data bytes (0,14) defines a displacement vector that is 14 units up from the previous point, D1 in Figure 14.

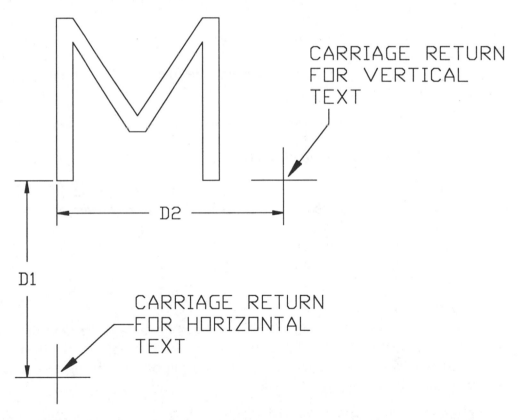

Figure 14   Carriage return for vertical and horizontal text

The data bytes (14,0) define a displacement vector that is 14 units to the right, D2 in Fig 10-14. These four data bytes combined together will result in a carriage return that is 4 units to the right of the existing line. The next set of data bytes (0,0) terminate the code 9, and the last data byte 0 terminates the shape specification.

Line 5
*77,51,ucm
The first data byte 77 is the ASCII code of the upper case character "M". The second data byte 51 is the number of data bytes in the shape specification. The next data byte (ucm) is the name of the shape file in lower case letters.

Line 6
2,14,8,(-5,-10),
The first data byte code 2 deactivates the pen (pen up), and the next data byte code 14 will cause the next code to be ignored if the text is horizontal. In the horizontal text the insertion point of the text is the starting point of that text line, Figure 13. However, if the text is vertical then the starting point of the text is upper middle point of the character "M". This is accomplished by the next three data bytes 8,(-5,-10) that displace the starting point of the text 5 units (width of character M is 10) to left and 10 (height of character M is 10) units down.

Line 7,8
001,009,(0,10),(1,0),(4,-6),(4,6),(1,0),
(0,-10),(-1,0),(0,0),
The first byte 001 activates the draw mode (pen down), and the remaining bytes define the next 7 vectors.

Line 9,10,11
003,2,
009,(0,17),(-7,-11),(-2,0),(-7,11),
(0,-17),(-2,0),(0,0),
The inner vertical line of the right leg of character "M" is 8.5 units long, and you can not define a vector that is not an integer. However, you could define a vector that is 17 units (2 * 8.5) long and then divide that vector by 2 to get a vector that is 8.5 units long. This is accomplished by the code 003 and the next data byte 2. All the vectors defined in the next two lines will be divided by 2.

Line 12
002,8,(28,0),
The fist data byte 002 deactivates the draw mode, and the next three data byte define a vector that is 14 units (28/2=14) to right. This means the next character will start 4 units (14-10) to the right of the existing character that will produce a horizontal text.

Line 13
004,2,
The code 004 multiplies the vectors that follow it by 2, and therefore it nullifies the effect of code 003,2.

Line 14
14,8,(-9,-4),0

If the text is vertical then the next letter should start below the previous letter. This is accomplished by the data bytes 8,(-9,-4) that define a vector which is -9 units along X-Axis, and -4 units along Y-Axis. The data byte 0 terminates the definition of the shape.

Example 5

Write a text font shape file for the lower case character "m" as shown in the Figure 15. The font file should be able to generate horizontal and vertical text. Each grid is one unit and the directions of the vectors is designated with the leader lines.

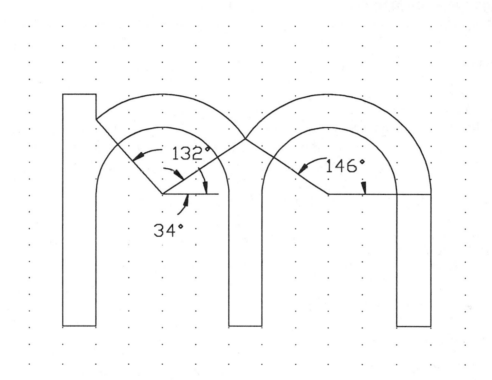

Figure 15   Shape of lower case character "m"

The following file is a listing of the text font shape file for Example 5. The line numbers are not a part of the file. They are shown here for reference only.

```
*0,4,lower-case m                           1
14,3,2,0                                    2
*10,13,1f                                   3
002,8,(0,-18),14,9,(0,18),(27,0),(0,0),0    4
*109,57,lcm                                 5
2,14,8,(-11,-14),                           6
005,005,001,020,084,                        7
00A,(4,-044),                               8
08C,020,084,                                9
```

```
00A,(4,-044),                         10
08C,020,084,                          11
00B,(0,62,0,6,004),                   12
00B,(193,239,0,6,003),                13
006,9,(0,14),(2,0),(0,0)              14
003,5,07C,004,5                       15
006,2,8,(27,0),                       16
14,8,(-16,-5),0                       17
```

The format of most of the lines is same as the previous example, except the following lines that use save/restore origin, octant, and fractional arcs

Line 7
005,005,001,020,084,
The first and second data bytes 005 have been used to save the location of the point twice. The remaining data bytes activate the draw mode and define the vectors.

Line 8
00A,(4,-044),
The first data byte code 00A is the code for octant arc, and the second data byte 4 defines the radius of the arc. The negative sign (-) in the third data byte generates an arc in clockwise direction. The first element 0 is a hexadecimal notation. The second element defines the starting octant, and the third element 4 defines the number of octants that the arc passes through.

Line 12
00B,(0,62,0,6,004),
The first data byte 00B is the code for fractional arc that is defined by the next five data bytes. The second data byte 0 is the starting offset of the first arc as shown in the following calculations.

1st Arc

Starting Angle	**= 0**	**Ending Angle = 146**
Starting Octant	**= 0**	**Ending Octant= 4**
Starting Offset	**= (0-0)*256/45**	
	= 0	
Ending Offset	**= (146-135)*256/45**	
	= 62.57	
	= 62 (integer)	

The third data byte 62 is the ending offset of the arc, and the fourth data byte 0 is the high radius. The fifth data byte 6 defines the radius of the arc. The second element 0 of the next data byte is the starting octant, and the third element 4 is the number of octants that the arc goes through.

Line 13
00B,(193,239,0,6,003),

The first data byte 00B is the code for the fractional arc. The remaining data bytes define various parameters of the fractional arc as explained earlier. The offset angles have been obtained from the following calculations.

2nd Arc

Starting Angle	= 34	**Ending Angle** = 132
Starting Octant	= 0	**Ending Octant** = 3

Starting Offset = (34-0)*256/45
= 193.4
= 193 (integer)

Ending Offset = (132-90)*256/45
= 238.9
= 239 (integer)

Note

Since the offset values have been rounded, it is not possible to describe an arc that is very accurate. Therefore, in this example the origin has been restored after two arcs were drawn. This origin was then used to draw the remaining lines.

Line 14
006,9,(0,14),(2,0),(0,0)
The first data byte 006 restores the previously saved point, and the remaining data bytes define the vectors using code 9.

Review

Fill in the blanks

1. The basic entities that are used in the shape files are .... and ....

2. The shape files are easy to insert and take less disk space compared to .... However, there are some disadvantages in using Shapes. For example, you can not .... a shape.

3. The Shape Number could be any number between 1 and .... in a particular file and these numbers can not be repeated within the same file.

4. The shape file may not contain two .... with the same name.

5. A hexadecimal number is designated by leading ....

6. The maximum number of data bytes is .... bytes per shape.

7. To define a vector you need its magnitude and ....

8. Do not include the extension with the ....

9. To load the shape file use AutoCAD's .... command.

10. Generating the shapes with the direction vectors has some limitations. For example, you can not draw an arc or draw a line that is not along the .... vectors. These limitations can be overcome by using the .... that add a lot of flexibility and give the user a better control over the shapes he wants to create.

11. Code 001 activates the .... mode, and Code .... deactivate the draw mode.

12. The byte that follows the division code divides the .... vectors.

13. Code 4 is used if you want to multiply the vectors by a certain number. It could also be used to .... the effect of Code 003.

14. Scale factors are ....

15. The number of saves (Code 005) has to be equal to the number of .... code ....

16.   The maximum number of saves and restores you can use in a particular shape definition is ....

17.   You can define a subshape like a subroutine in a program. To reference the subshape use Code ....

18.   Vector can be drawn in the 16 predefined directions only, and the length of the vector can not exceed .... units.

19.   A nonstandard fractional arc can be generated by using Code 00B or ....

20.   Code .... can be used to define an arc by specifying the displacement of the end point of an arc and the bulge factor.

21.   Bulge factor can range from -127 to ....

22.   Code 00E or .... is used when the same text font description is to be used in both horizontal and vertical orientation.

23.   The text files are regular .... files with some additional information about the text font description and the line feed.

24.   The shape names in all text font files should be in lower case letters so that the computer does not have to save the names in its ....

25.   The Line Feed is used to space the lines so that the characters do not ....

26.   The shape number in the shape definition of the text font are corresponding to the .... code for that character.

Exercises

Exercise 1

Write a Shape File for letter "M" as shown in Figure 16.

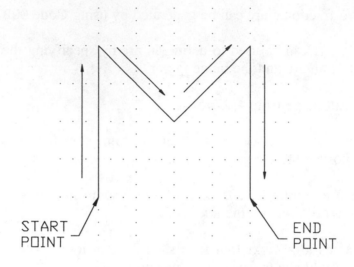

Figure 16   Upper case letter "M"

Exercise 2

Write a shape file for generating the Taper Gib-Head key as shown in Figure 17.

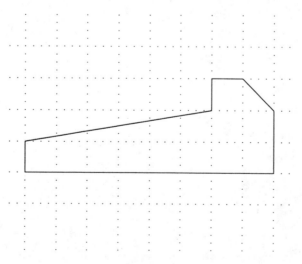

Figure 17   Tapered gib-head key

Exercise 3

Write a text font shape file for upper case character "G" as shown in Figure 18.

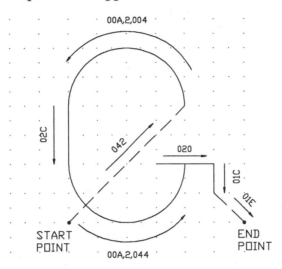

Figure 18   Upper case character "G"

Exercise 4

Write a text font shape file for upper case character "W" as shown in Figure 19. The font file should be able to generate horizontal and vertical text.

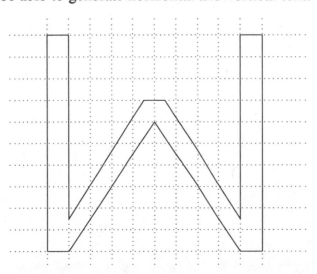

Figure 19   Upper case character "W"

Chapter 13

AutoLISP

AutoLISP developed by Autodesk Inc. is an implementation of the **LISP** programming language. The first reference of LISP was by John McCarthy in the April 1960 issue of "The Communications of the ACM". The LISP is an acronym of **LISt Processor**.

Except for **FORTRAN**, most of the languages developed in early 1960's have become obsolete, but LISP continued to survive and has become a leading programming language for artificial intelligence (AI). Some of the dialects of the LISP programming language are: Common LISP, BYSCO LISP, ExperLISP, GCLISP, IQLISP, LISP/80, LISP/88, MuLISP, TLCLISP, UO-LISP, Waltz LISP, and XLISP. XLISP is a public domain LISP interpreter. The LISP dialect that resembles AutoLISP is Common LISP. The AutoLISP interpreter is embedded within AutoCAD software package. However, AutoCAD version 2.17 and lower do not have the AutoLISP interpreter, therefore you can use the AutoLISP programing language only with AutoCAD release 2.18 and up. The name of the AutoLISP program file for 640k DOS systems is acadl.ovl and for AutoCAD 386, it is acadl.exp

AutoCAD software package contains most of the commands that are used in generating and editing a drawing. However, there are some commands that are not provided in AutoCAD. For example, AutoCAD does not have a command for drawing a rectangle or making global changes in the drawing text entities. With AutoLIPS user can write a program in AutoLISP programming language that will draw a rectangle, or make global or selective changes in the drawing text entities. As a matter of fact, you can use AutoLISP to write any program or imbed it into the menu and thus customize your system to make it more efficient.

AutoLISP programming language has been used by several third-party software developers to write software packages for various applications. For example, the author of this text has developed a software package **"SMLayout"** that generates flat layout of various geometrical shapes like: transitions, intersection of pipes and cylinders, elbows, cones, and tank heads. There is a good demand for AutoLISP programmers as consultants for developing application software and custom menus.

This chapter assumes that the reader is familiar with AutoCAD commands, and AutoCAD system variables. However, you need not be an AutoCAD or programming expert to begin learning AutoLISP. The chapter also assumes that the reader has no prior programming knowledge. If you are familiar with any other programming language, learning AutoLISP might be easier. A thorough discussion of various functions and a step by step explanation of the examples should make it a fun to learn AutoLISP. This chapter discusses the most frequently used AutoLISP functions and their application in writing a program. For those functions that are not discussed in this chapter, please refer to the AutoLISP Programmers Reference manual from Autodesk.

AutoLISP does not require any special hardware. If your system runs AutoCAD, it will also run AutoLISP. However, before using AutoLISP make sure that AutoLISP is enabled and enough memory has been set aside for running the programs. In some of the systems you can also utilize extended AutoLISP. To write AutoLISP programs you can use **EDLIN** command of DOS, **EDIT** function of DOS 5.0, or any other ASCII text editor. You can also use AutoCAD's **EDIT** command, provided ACAD.PGP file is present and EDIT command is defined in the file.

Mathematical Operations

A mathematical function constitute an important feature of any programming language. Most of the mathematical functions that are commonly used in programming and mathematical calculations are available in AutoLISP. You can use AutoLISP to add, subtract, multiply and divide the numbers. You can also use it to find sine, cosine and arctangent of angles expressed in radians. There is a host of other calculations you can do with AutoLISP. This section discusses the most frequently used mathematical functions that are supported by the AutoLISP programming language.

Addition

Format **(+ num1 num2 num3 - - -)**

This function (+) calculates the sum of all the numbers that are to the right of the plus (+) sign (num1 + num2 + num3 +.......). The numbers can be integers or real. If the numbers are integers then the sum is an integer number. If the numbers are real then the sum is real. However, if some numbers are real and some integers then the sum is real.

Examples
(+ 2 5)	returns 7
(+ 2 30 4 50)	returns 86
(+ 2 30 4 50.0)	returns 86.0

(+ 5.5 11.25)   returns 16.75

In the first example, all numbers are integers therefore the result is an integer. In the third example, one number is a real number (50.0), therefore the sum is a real number.

Subtraction

Format (- num1 num2 num3 - - -)

This function (-) subtracts the second number from the first number (num1-num2). If there are more than two numbers then the second and the subsequent numbers are added and the sum is subtracted from the first number [num1 - (num2 + num3 +.......)]. In the first example, 14 is subtracted from 28 and returns 14. Since both the numbers are integers, the result is an integer number. In the second example, 20 and 10.0 are added, and the sum of these two numbers (30.0) is subtracted from 50, returning a real number 20.0

Examples
(- 28 14)   returns 14
(- 25 7 11)   returns 7
(- 50 20 10.0)   returns 20.0
(- 50.0 20.0 10.0)   returns 20.0
(- 20)   returns -20
(- 20.0)   returns -20.0
(- 20 30)   returns -10
(- 20.0 30.0)   returns -10.0

Multiplication

Format (* num1 num2 num3 - - -)

This function (*) calculates the product of the numbers that are to the right of asterisk (num1 x num2 x num3 x...........). If the numbers are integers, then the product of these numbers is an integer. If one of the numbers is a real number, then the product is a real number.

Examples
(* 2 5)   returns 10
(* 2 5 3)   returns 30
(* 2 5 3 2.0)   returns 60.0
(* 2 -5.5)   returns -11.0
(* 2.0 -5.5 -2)   returns 22.0

Division

Format   (/ num1 num2 num3 - - -)

This function (/) divides the first number by the second number (num1/num2). If there are more then two numbers then the first number is divided by the product of the second and subsequent numbers [num1 / (num2 x num3 x ....)]. In example 4, 200 is divided by the product of 5 and 4.0 [200 / (5 * 4.0)].

Examples
(/ 30)	returns 30
(/ 3 2)	returns 1
(/ 3.0 2)	returns 1.5
(/ 200 5 4)	returns 10
(/ 200 5 4.0)	returns 10.0
(/ 200.0 5.5)	returns 36.363636
(/ 200 -5)	returns -40
(/ -200 -5.0)	returns 40.0

Incremented, Decremented and Absolute Numbers

Incremented number

Format **(1+ number)**

This function **(1+)** adds 1 (integer) to **number** and returns a number that is incremented by 1. In the second example below, 1 is added to -10.5 and returns -9.5

Examples
(1+ 20)	returns 21
(1+ -10.5)	returns -9.5

Decremented number

Format   **(1- <number>)**

This function **(1-)** subtracts 1 (integer) from the **number** and returns a number that is decremented by 1. In the second example below, 1 is subtracted from -10.5 and returns -11.5

Examples
(1- 10)	returns 9
(1- -10.5)	returns -11.5

Absolute number

Format **(abs <num>)**

The **abs** function returns the absolute value of a number. The number may be an integer number or a real number. In the second example below, the function returns 20 because the absolute value of -20 is 20.

Examples

(abs 20)	returns 20
(abs -20)	returns 20
(abs -20.5)	returns 20.5

Trigonometrical Functions

sin

Format   **(sin angle)**

The **sin** function calculates the sine of an angle, where the angle is expressed in radians. In the second example below, the **sin** function calculates the sine of pi (180 degrees) and return 0.

Examples

(sin 0)	returns 0.0
(sin 1.0472)	returns 0.866027

cos

Format   **(cos angle)**

The **cos** function calculates the cosine of an angle, where the angle is expressed in radians. In the second example below, the **cos** function calculates the cosine of pi (180 degrees) and return -1.0.

Examples

(cos 0)	returns 1.0
(cos 0.0)	returns 1.0
(cos pi)	returns -1.0
(cos 1.0)	returns 0.540302

atan

Format   **(atan num1)**

The **atan** function calculates the arctangent of **num1**, and the calculated angle is expressed in radians. In the second example below, the **atan** function calculates the arctangent of 1.0 and returns 0.785398 (radians).

Examples

(atan 0.5)	returns 0.463648
(atan 1.0)	returns 0.785398
(atan -1.0)	returns -0.785398

You can also specify a second number in atan function. The format of atan function is:

Format   **(atan num1 num2)**

If the second number is specified then the function returns the arctangent of (num1/num2) in radians. In the first example above, the first number (0.5) is divided by the second number (1.0), and then **atan** function calculates the arctangent of the product (0.5/1.0 = 0.5).

Examples

(atan 0.5 1.0)	returns 0.453648 radians
(atan 2.0 3.0)	returns 0.588003 radians
(atan 2.0 -3.0)	returns 2.55359 radians
(atan -2.0 3.00	returns -0.588003 radians
(atan -2.0 -3.0)	returns -2.55359 radians
(atan 1.0 0.0)	returns 1.5708 radians
(atan -0.5 0.0)	returns -1.5708 radians

angtos

Format   **(angtos angle [mode [precision]])**

The **Angtos** function returns the angle expressed in radians in a string format. The format of the string is controlled by the settings of **mode** and **precision**.

Examples

(angtos 0.588003 0 4)	returns "33.6901"
(angtos 2.55359 0 4)	returns "146.3099"
(angtos 1.5708 0 4)	returns "90.0000"
(angtos -1.5708 0 2)	returns "270.00"

Note

In (angtos angle [mode [precision]])

angle	*is angle in radians*
mode	*is the angtos mode that corresponds to the AotoCAD system variable AUNITS.*

Following modes are available in AutoCAD

ANGTOS MODE	*EDITING FORMAT*
0	*Degrees*
1	*Degrees/minutes/seconds*

2	*Grads*
3	*Radians*
4	*Surveyor's Units*

*precision is an integer number that controls the number of decimal places. Precision corresponds to AutoCAD system variable **AUPREC**. The minimum value of **precision** is 0 and the maximum is 4*

*In the first example above, **angle** is 0.588003 radians, **mode** is 0 (angle in degrees), and **precision** is 4 (4 places after decimal) and the function will return "33.6901"*

Relational Statements

Programs generally involve features that test a particular condition. If the condition is true then the program performs a certain functions, and if the condition is not true then the program performs other functions. For example, the relational statement (if (< x 5)) tests if the value of variable x is less then 5. This is a type of test condition that is very frequently used in programming. The following section discusses various relational statements as used in AutoLISP programming.

Equal to

Format   (= atom1 atom2 - - - -)

This function (=) checks if the two atoms are equal. If they are equal then the conditions is true and the function will return **T**. Similarly, if the specified atoms are not equal then the condition is false and the function will return **nil**

Examples
(= 5 5)	returns T
(= 5 5.0)	returns T
(= 5 4.9)	returns nil
(= 5.5 5.5 5.5)	returns T
(= 5.5 5.5 4.0)	returns nil
(= "yes" "yes")	returns T
(= "yes" "no")	returns nil
(= "yes" "yes" "no")	returns nil
(= 5 -5)	returns nil

Not equal to

Format   (/= atom1 atom2 - - - -)

This function (/=) checks if the two atoms are not equal. If they are not equal then the conditions is true and the function will return **T**. Similarly, if the specified atoms are equal then the condition is false and the function will return **nil**

Examples

(/= 50 4)	returns T
(/= 50 50)	returns nil
(/= 50 50 50)	returns T
(/= 2 2 2 2)	returns nil
(/= 50 -50)	returns T
(/= "yes" "yes")	returns nil
(/= "yes" "no")	returns T

Less than

Format   (< atom1 atom2 - - - -)

This function (<) checks if the first atom (**atom1**) is less than the second atom (**atom2**). If it is true then the function will return **T**. If it is not true then the function will return **nil**.

Examples

(< 3 5)	returns T
(< 5 3)	returns nil
(< 3.0 5)	returns nil
(< 5 3 4 2)	returns nil
(< 2 3 4 5)	returns T
(< "x" "y")	returns T
(< "b" "a")	returns nil

Less than or equal to

Format   (<= atom1 atom2 - - - -)

This function (<=) checks if the first atom (**atom1**) is less than or equal to the second atom (**atom2**). If it is true then the function will return **T**. If it is not true then the function will return **nil**.

Examples

(<= 10 15)	returns T
(<= 19 10)	returns nil
(<= 5 15 15)	returns T
(<= 5 15 13 20)	returns nil
(<= "a" "a")	returns T
(<= "a" "b")	returns T
(<= "c" "b")	returns nil
(<= -2.0 0)	returns T

Greater than

Format   **(> atom1 atom2 - - - -)**

This function (>) checks if the first atom **(atom1)** is greater than the second atom **(atom2)**. If it is true then the function will return **T**. If it is not true then the function will return **nil**. In the fourth example below, 15.0 is greater than 10.5, and 10.5 is greater than 2.5. Therefore this relational function is true and the function will return **T**. In the fifth example, 10 is greater than 9, but this number is not greater than the second 9, therefore this function will return **nil**.

Examples

(> 15 10)	returns T
(> 20 30)	returns nil
(> 15.0 10.5)	returns T
(> 15.0 10.5 2.5)	returns T
(> 10 9 9)	returns nil
(> "c" "b")	returns T

Greater than or Equal to

Format   **(> = atom1 atom2 - - - -)**

This function (> =) checks if the first atom **(atom1)** is greater than or equal to the second atom **(atom2)**. If it is true then the function returns **T**, otherwise it will return **nil**. In the fourth example below, 80 is greater than 78 but, 78 is not greater than 79, therefore it will return **nil**.

Examples

(> = 78 50)	returns T
(> = 78 88)	returns nil
(> = 80 78 78)	returns T
(> = 80 78 79)	returns nil
(> = "x" "x")	returns T
(> = "x" "y")	returns T
(> = "y" "x")	returns nil

defun, setq, getpoint, and command functions

defun

The **defun** function is used to define a function in an AutoLISP program. The format of **defun** function is:

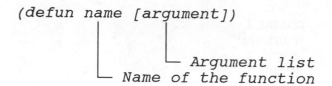

```
(defun name [argument])
```
— Argument list
— Name of the function

Examples

(defun ADNUM ()

Defines a function ADNUM with no arguments or local symbols. This means that all variables used in the program are global variables. A global variable does not loose its value after the programs ends.

(defun ADNUM (a b c)

Defines a function ADNUM that has three arguments a b and c. The variables a, b and c receive the value from outside the program.

(defun ADNUM (/ a b)

Defines a function ADNUM that has two local variables a and b. A local variable is one that retains the value during the program execution and can be used within that program only.

(defun C:ADNUM ()

By using **C:** in front of the function name the function can be executed by entering the name of the function at AutoCAD's Command prompt. If **C:** is not used, the function name has to be enclosed in parenthesis.

Note

AutoLISP contains some built-in function. Do not use these names for function or variable names. The following is a list of some of the names reserved for AutoLISP's built-in functions. (Refer to AutoLISP Programmer's Reference manual for a complete list of AutoLISP's built-in functions.)

abs	ads	alloc
and	angle	angtos
append	apply	atom
ascii	assoc	atan

atof	atoi	distance
equal	fix	float
if	length	list
load	member	nil
not	nth	null
open	or	pi
read	repeat	reverse
set	T	type
while		

setq

The **setq** function is used to assign a value to variable. The format of **setq** function is:

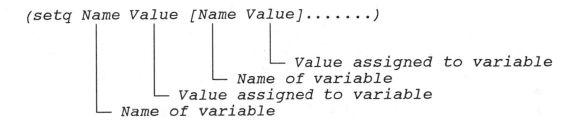

```
(setq Name Value [Name Value].......)
```

The value assigned to a variable can be a numeric value or a string. If the value is a string, the string length can not be more than 100 characters long.

Command: (setq X 12)

Command: (setq X 6.5)

Command: (setq X 8.5 Y 12)
> In this expression, the number 8.5 is assigned to variable X and the number 12 is assigned to variable Y

Command: (setq answer "YES")
> In this expression the string value "YES" is assigned to variable answer

The **setq** function can also be used in an AutoLISP program to assign a value to a variable. In the following examples the **setq** function has been used to assign values to a different variable.

```
(setq pt1 (getpoint "Enter start point: "))
(setq ang1 (getangle "Enter included angle: "))
(setq answer (getstring "Enter YES or NO: "))
```

Note

AutoLISP uses some built-in function names and symbols. Do not assign values to these functions. The following function are valid functions, but pi and angle functions that are reserved functions will be redefined.

(setq pi 3.0)
(setq angle (......))

getpoint

The getpoint function pauses for user to enter the X, Y coordinates or X, Y, Z coordinates of a point. The coordinates of the point can be entered from the key board or by using the screen cursor. The format of **getpoint** function is:

```
(getpoint [point] [prompt])
                        └─ Prompt to be displayed on the
                           screen
          └─ Enter a point, or select a point
```

Example
(setq pt1 (getpoint))
(setq pt1 (getpoint "Enter starting point"))

Note

1. You can not enter the name of another AutoLISP routine in response to getpoint function.

2. A 2D or a 3D point is always defined with respect to the current User Coordinate System (UCS).

command

The **command** function is used to execute standard AutoCAD commands from within an AutoLISP program. The AutoCAD command name and the command options have to be enclosed in double quotation marks. The format of **command** function is:

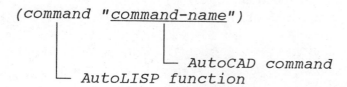

```
(command "command-name")
          │                │
          │                └─ AutoCAD command
          └─ AutoLISP function
```

Examples

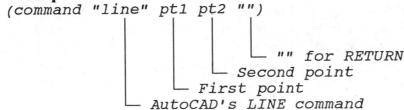

```
(command "line" pt1 pt2 "")
```
— "" for RETURN
— Second point
— First point
— AutoCAD's LINE command

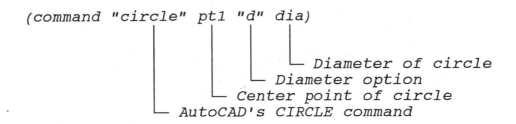

```
(command "circle" pt1 "d" dia)
```
— Diameter of circle
— Diameter option
— Center point of circle
— AutoCAD's CIRCLE command

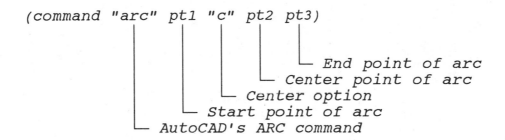

```
(command "arc" pt1 "c" pt2 pt3)
```
— End point of arc
— Center point of arc
— Center option
— Start point of arc
— AutoCAD's ARC command

Note

*1. The **command** function can not be used for executing AutoCAD's PRPLOT or PLOT command. For example: (command "prplot".........) or (command "plot".........) are not valid functions.*

*2. The **command** function can not be used for entering data with AutoCAD's DTEXT or TEXT command. (You can use the DTEXT and TEXT command with the command function. You can also enter text height and text rotation, but you can not enter the text when AutoCAD prompts for text entry.)*

3. You can not use the input functions of AutoLISP with the command function. The input functions are getpoint, getangle, getstring, and getint. For example, (command "getpoint".....) or (command getangle........) are not valid functions. If the program contains such a function, it will display an error message when the program is loaded.

Example 1

Write a program that will prompt the user to select three points of a triangle and then draw lines through those points to generate a triangle as shown in Fig. 2

Most of the programs essentially consist of three parts. The first part is **input**, the second part is **output**, and the third part is the **process** involved is generating the desired output from the given input (Figure 1). Before writing a program it is very important to identify them. In Example 1 above, the input to the program is the coordinates of the three points. The desired output is a triangle. The process or the operations needed to generate a triangle is to draw three lines from P1 to P2, P2 to P3, and P3 to P1. By clearly identifying these three sections the programming process becomes easier and less confusing.

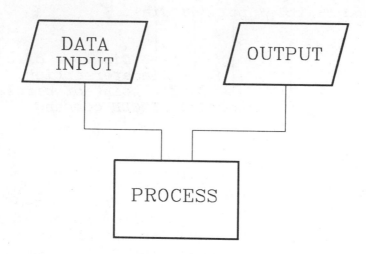

Figure 1   Three elements of a program

The process section of the program is vital to the success of the program. Sometime, it is simple, but sometimes it involves complicated calculations. If the program involves lot of calculations, divide it into sections and may be subsections that are laid out in a logical and systematic order. Also, remember the programs need to be edited from time to time, may be by other programmers. Therefore, document the programs as clearly as possible in an unambiguous manner so that other programmers can understand what the program is doing at different stages of its execution. Give sketches and identify points where possible.

INPUT

Location of point P1
Location of point P2
Location of point P3

OUTPUT

Triangle P1, P2, P3

PROCESS

Line from P1 to P2
Line from P2 to P3
Line from P3 to P1

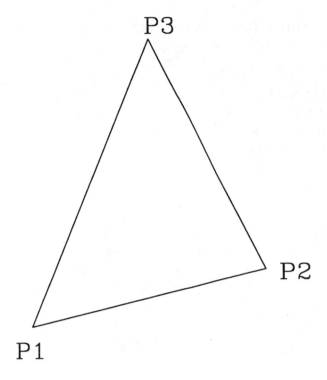

Figure 2   Triangle P1 P2 P3

The following file is a listing of the AutoLISP program for Example 1. The line numbers are not a part of the program, they are shown here for reference only.

```
;This program will prompt the user to enter three points        1
;of a triangle from the key board, or select three points       2
;by using screen cursor.  P1, P2, P3 are triangle corners.      3
                                                                 4
(defun c:TRIANG1()                                               5
(setq P1 (getpoint "\n Enter first point of Triangle: "))        6
(setq P2 (getpoint "\n Enter second point of Triangle: "))       7
(setq P3 (getpoint "\n Enter third point of Triangle: "))        8
(command "LINE" P1 P2 P3 "C")                                    9
)                                                               10
```

Line 1-3
The first three lines are comment lines describing the function of the program. These lines are important for the reason that it makes it easier for the programmer to edit a program. Comments should be used where needed. All comment lines must start with a semicolon (;). The lines that start with a semicolon are ignored when the program is executed.

Line 4
This is a blank line that separates the comment section from the program. Blank lines can be used to separate different modules of a program. This makes

it easier to identify different sections that constitute a program. The blank lines do not have any effect on the program.

Line 5
(defun c:TRIANG1()
In this line **defun** is an AutoLISP function that defines the function **TRIANG1**. **TRIANG1** is the name of the function. By using **c:** in front of the function name, **TRIANG1** can be executed like an AutoCAD command. If **c:** is missing then the **TRIANG1** command can be executed only by enclosing it in parenthesis (TRIANG1).

Line 6

(setq P1 (getpoint "\n Enter first point of Triangle: "))
In this line the **getpoint** function pauses for the user to enter the first point of the triangle. The prompt, **Enter first point of Triangle**, is displayed in the prompt area of the screen. User can enter the coordinates of this point from the keyboard or select a point by using the screen cursor. The **setq** function then assigns these coordinates to the variable **P1**. \n is used for the carriage return so that the statement that follows \n is printed on the next line.

Line 7,8
(setq P2 (getpoint "\n Enter second point of Triangle: "))
(setq P3 (getpoint "\n Enter third point of Triangle: "))
These two lines prompt the user to enter the second, and third corner of the triangle. These coordinates are then assigned to the variables P2 and P3. \n causes a carriage return so that the input prompts are displayed on the next line.

Line 9

command "LINE" P1 P2 P3 "C")
In this line the **command** function is used to enter AutoCAD's LINE command and then draw a line from P1 to P2, and P2 to P3. "C" (for close option) joins the last point P3 with the first point P1. All AutoCAD command and options, when used in an AutoLISP program, have to be enclosed in double quotation marks. The variables P1, P2, P3 are separated by a blank space.

Line 10
This line consist of a close parenthesis that completes the definition of the function, TRIANG1. This parenthesis could have been combined with the previous line. It is a good practice to keep it on a separate line so that a programmer can easily identify the end of a definition. In this program there is only one function defined, therefore it is not a problem to locate the end of a definition. But in some programs there could be a number of definitions, or modules within the same program that need to be clearly identified. The parenthesis and blank lines help to identify the start and end of a definition or a section in the program.

Loading an AutoLISP Program

There are generally two names associated with a AutoLISP program. One is the program file name and the second is the function name. For example, TRIANG.LSP is the name of the file, not a function name. All AutoLISP file names have the extension .LSP. An AutoLISP file can have one or several functions defined within the same file. For example, TRIANG1 in Example 1 is the name of a function. To execute a function, the AutoLISP program file that defines that function must be loaded. Use the following command to load an AutoLISP file when you are in the drawing editor.

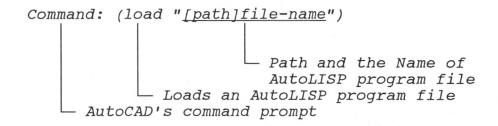

The AutoLISP file name and the optional path name must be enclosed in double quotes. The **load** and the **file-name** must be enclosed in parenthesis. If the parenthesis are missing, AutoCAD will try to load a shape or a text file, not an AutoLISP file. The space between load and file name is not required. If AutoCAD is successful in loading the file, it will display the name of the function in the command prompt area of the screen.

C:TRIANG1

To run the program type the name of the function at AutoCAD's command prompt and press the ENTER key. If the function name did not contain **C:** in the program then you can run the program by enclosing the function name in parenthesis.

Command: TRIANG1
or
Command: (TRIANG1)

Note

Use forward slash when defining the path for loading an AutoLISP program. For example, if the AutoLISP file TRIANG is in LISP subdirectory on C drive use the following command to load the file. You can also use a double backslash (\\) in place of the forward slash.

Command (load "c:/lisp/triang")

Command (load "c:\\lisp\\triang")

getcorner, setvar, car, cdr, and cadr functions

getcorner

The **getcorner** function pauses for user to enter the coordinates of a point. The coordinates of the point can be entered from the key board or by using the screen crosshairs. This function requires a base point, and it displays a rectangle with respect to the base point as the user moves the screen crosshairs on the screen. The format of **getcorner** function is:

```
(getcorner point [prompt])
                │         │
                │         └─ Prompt displayed on screen
                └─ Base point
```

Examples
(getcorner pt1)
(setq pt2 (getcorner pt1))
(setq pt2 (getcorner pt1 "Enter second point: "))

Note

1. *The base point, and the point that the user selects in response to the getcorner function, are located with respect to the current UCS.*

2. *If the point selected by the user is a 3D point, having X, Y, and Z coordinates, the Z coordinate is ignored. The point assumes current elevation as its Z coordinate.*

setvar

The **setvar** function assigns a value to an AutoCAD system variable. The name of the system variable must be enclosed in double quotes. The format of **setvar** function is:

```
(setvar "variable name" value)
                │             │
                │             └─ Value to be assigned to
                │                the system variable
                └─ AutoCAD system variable
```

Examples
(setvar "cmdecho" 0)
(setvar "dimscale" 1.5)
(setvar "ltscale" 0.5)
(setvar "dimcen" -0.25)

car

The **car** function returns the first element of a list. If the list does not contain any elements, the function will return **nil**. The format of **car** function is:

```
(car list)
       └── list of elements
    └── Returns the first element
```

Examples

(car '(2.5 3 56)	returns 2.5
(car '(x y z))	returns X
(car '((15 20) 56))	returns (15 20)
(car '())	returns nil

cdr

The **cdr** function returns a list with the first element removed from the list. The format of **cdr** function is:

```
(cdr list)
       └── list of elements
    └── Returns a list with the first element removed
```

Examples

(cdr '(2.5 3 56)	returns 3 56
(cdr '(x y z))	returns (Y Z)
(cdr '((15 20) 56))	returns 56
(cdr '())	returns nil

cadr

The **cadr** function performs two operations, **cdr** and **car**. The **cdr** function removes the first element, and the **car** function then returns the first element of the new list. The format of **cadr** function is:

```
(cadr list)
       |      |
       |      |___ list of elements
       |___ Performs two operations   (car (cdr '(x y z))
```

Examples

(cadr '(2 3)	returns 3
(cadr '(2 3 56)	returns 3
(cadr '(x y z))	returns Y
(cadr '((15 20) 56 24))	returns 56

In these examples cadr performs two functions

(cadr '(x y z))   = (car (cdr '(x y z)
                               = (car (y z)
                                  returns y

Note

*In addition to the above mentioned functions (**car, cdr, cadr**) there are several other functions that can be used to extract different elements of a list. Following is a list of these functions, where the function f consists of a list '((x y) z w))*

(setq f '((x y) z w))

(caar f) = (car (car f))	*returns x*
(cdar f) = (cdr (car f))	*returns y*
(cadar) = (car (cdr (car f)))	*returns y*
(cddr f) = (cdr (cdr f))	*returns w*
(caddr f) = (car (cdr (cdr f)))	*returns w*

graphscr, textscr, princ, and terpri functions

graphscr

The **graphscr** function switches from the text screen to graphics screen, provided the system has only one screen. If the system has two screens then this function is ignored.

textscr

The **textscr** function switches from the graphics screen to text screen, provided the system has only one screen. If the system has two screens then this function is ignored.

princ

The **princ** function prints the value of the variable. If the variable is enclosed in double quotes, it prints the expression that is enclosed in the quotes. The format of **princ** function is:

(princ [variable or expression)]

Examples

(princ)	prints a blank on the screen
(princ a)	prints the value of variable a on the screen
(princ "Welcome")	prints Welcome on the screen

terpri

The **terpri** function prints a new line on the screen. This function is used to print the line, that follows the **terpri** function, on a separate line.

Example

(setq p1 (getpoint "Enter first point: "))(terpri)
(setq p2 (getpoint "Enter second point: "))

The first line (Enter first point:) will be displayed on the screen's command prompt area. The **terpri** function causes a carriage return, therefore the second line (Enter second point) will be displayed on a new line, just below the first line. If terpri function was missing, the two lines will be displayed on the same line (Enter first point: Enter second point:).

Example 2

Write a program that will prompt the user to enter two opposite corners of a rectangle and then draw the rectangle on the screen as shown in Figure 3.

INPUT	OUTPUT
Coordinates of point P1	Rectangle
Coordinates of point P3	

PROCESS

1. Calculate the coordinates
   of the points P2, P4
2. Draw the following lines.
   Line from P1 to P2
   Line from P2 to P3
   Line from P3 to P4
   Line from P4 to P1

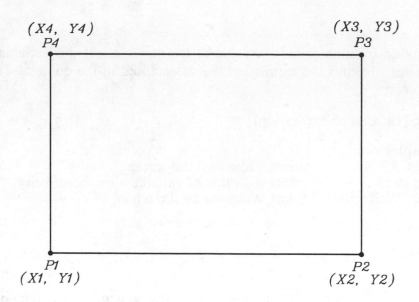

Figure 3   Rectangle P1 P2 P3 P4

The X and Y coordinates of the points P2 and P4 can be calculated by using the **car** and **cadr** functions. The **car** function extracts the X coordinate and **cadr** function extracts the Y coordinate of a given list.

> **X coordinate of point p2**
> x2 = x3
> x2 = car (x3 y3)
> x2 = car p3
>
> **Y coordinate of point p2**
> y2 = y1
> y2 = CADR (x1 y1)
> y2 = CADR p1
>
> **X coordinate of point p4**
> x4 = x1
> x4 = car(x1 y1)
> x4 = car p1
>
> **Y coordinate of point p4**
> y4 = y3
> y4 = cadr (x3 y3)
> y4 = cadr p3
>
> **Therefore points p2 and p4 are**
> p2 = (list (car p3) (cadr p1))
> p4 = (list (car p1) (cadr p3))

The following file is a listing of the program for Example 2. The line numbers are for reference only and are not a part of the program.

```
;This program will draw a rectangle.  User will            1
;be prompted to enter the two opposite corners             2
;                                                          3
(defun c:RECT1()                                          4
  (graphscr)                                              5
  (setvar "cmdecho" 0)                                    6
  (prompt "RECT1  command  draws  a rectangle")(terpri)   7
  (setq p1 (getpoint "Enter first corner"))(terpri)       8
  (setq p3 (getpoint "Enter opposite corner"))(terpri)    9
  (setq p2 (list (car p3) (cadr p1)))                     10
  (setq p4 (list (car p1) (cadr p3)))                     11
(command "line" p1 p2 p3 p4 "c")                          12
(setvar "cmdecho" 1)                                      13
(princ)                                                   14
)                                                         15
```

Lines 1-3
The first three lines are comment lines that describe the function of the program. All comment lines that start with a semicolon are ignored when the program is compiled.

Line 4
(defun c:RECT1()
The **defun** function defines the function **RECT1**.

Line 5
(graphscr)
This function switches the text screen to graphics screen, if the current screen happens to be text screen. Otherwise this function has no effect on the display screen.

Line 6
(setvar "cmdecho" 0)
The **setvar** function assigns a value 0 to AutoCAD system variable **cmdecho** that turns the echo off. When **cmdecho** is off, the AutoCAD command prompts are not displayed in the command prompt area of the screen.

Line 7
(prompt "RECT1 command draws a rectangle")(terpri)
The **prompt** function will display the information that is in double quotes ("RECT1 command draws a rectangle") on the screen. The function **terpri** causes a carriage return so that the next line is printed on a separate line.

Line 8
(setq p1 (getpoint "Enter first corner"))(terpri)
The **getpoint** function pauses for the user to enter a point (first corner of rectangle), and the **setq** function assigns that value to variable p1.

Line 9
(setq p3 (getpoint "Enter opposite corner"))(terpri)

The **getpoint** function pauses for the user to enter a point (opposite corner of rectangle), and the **setq** function assigns that value to variable p3.

Line 10

(setq p2 (list (car p3) (cadr p1)))
The **cadr** function extracts the y coordinate of the point p1, and the **car** function extracts the x coordinate of the point p3. These two values form a list and the function **setq** assigns that value to variable p2.

Line 11

(setq p4 (list (car p1) (cadr p3)))
The **cadr** function extracts the y coordinate of point p3, and the **car** function extracts the x coordinate of point p1. These two values form a list and the function **setq** assigns that value to variable p4.

Line 12

(command "line" p1 p2 p3 p4 "c")
The command function uses AutoCAD's **LINE** command to draw lines between the points p1, p2, p3, p4, and c (close) joins the last point p4 with the first point p1.

Line 13

(setvar "cmdecho" 1)
The **setvar** function assigns a value of 1 to the AutoCAD system variable **cmdecho**, that turns the echo on.

Line 14

(princ)
The **princ** function prints a blank on the screen. If this line is missing, AutoCAD will print the value of the last expression. This value does not effect the program in any way. However, it might get confusing at times. The **princ** function is merely used to prevent the display of the last expression in the command prompt area.

Line 15

The close parenthesis completes the definition of the function **RECT1** and ends the program.

Note

In this program the rectangle is generated after the user defines the two corners of the rectangle. The rectangle is not dragged as you move the screen crosshairs to enter the second corner. However, the rectangle can be dragged by using the getcorner function as shown in the following program listing.

```
;This program will draw a rectangle with the
;drag mode on and using getcorner function
;
```

```
(defun c:RECT2()
  (graphscr)
  (setvar "cmdecho" 0)
  (prompt "RECT2 command draws a rectangle")(terpri)
  (setq p1 (getpoint "enter first corner"))(terpri)
  (setq p3 (getcorner p1 "Enter opposite corner" ))(terpri)
  (setq p2 (list (car p3) (cadr p1)))
  (setq p4 (list (car p1) (cadr p3)))
(command "line" p1 p2 p3 p4 "c")
(setvar "cmdecho" 1)
(princ)
)
```

getangle, getorient, and getdist functions

getangle

The **getangle** function pauses for the user to enter the angle and then it returns the value of that angle in radians. The format of **getangle** function is:

```
(getangle [point] [prompt])
                     │
                     │
                     └── Any prompt that needs to be
                         displayed on the screen
           └── First point of the angle
```

Examples
(getangle)
(setq ang (getangle))
(setq ang (getangle pt1))   --------------- pt1 is a predefined point
(setq ang (getangle "Enter taper angle"))
(setq ang (getangle pt1 "Enter second point of angle"))

The angle that you enter is effected by the angle setting. The angle settings can be changed by using AutoCAD's **UNITS** command or by changing the value of AutoCAD's system variables **ANGBASE** and **ANGDIR**. Following are the default settings for measuring an angle:

1. The angle is measured with respect to positive X axis or 3-OClock position. The value of this setting is saved in AutoCAD system variable **ANGBASE**.

2. The angle is positive if it is measured in counterclockwise direction and the angle is negative if it is measured in clockwise direction. The value of this setting is saved in AutoCAD system variable **ANGDIR**.

If the angle has default setting (Figure 4a), the **getangle** function will return 2.35619 radians for an angle of 135 (Figue 5a).

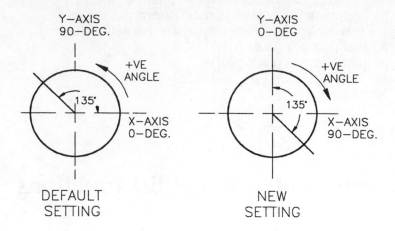

Figure 4a   **Figure 4b**

Example
(setq ang (getangle "Enter angle")) will return 2.35619 for the angle of 135 degrees.

Figure 4b shows the new settings of the angle, where Y axis is 0 degree and the angles measured clockwise are positive.   The **getangle** function will return 3.92699 for an angle of 135 degrees. The getangle function calculates the angle in counter-clockwise direction, **ignoring the direction set in the system variable ANGDIR**, with respect to the angle base as set in the system variable **ANGBASE** (Figure 5b).

Example
(setq ang (getangle "Enter angle")) will return 3.92699

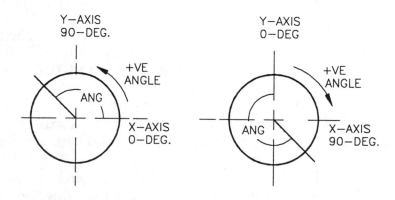

Figure 5a   **Figure 5b**

getorient

The **getorient** function pauses for the user to enter the angle and then it returns the value of that angle in radians. The format of **getorient** function is:

```
(getorient [point] [prompt])
```
— Any prompt that needs to be displayed on the screen
— First point of the angle

Examples
(getorient)
(setq ang (getorient))
(setq ang (getorient pt1))
(setq ang (getorient "Enter taper angle"))
(setq ang (getorient pt1 "Enter second point of angle"))

The getorient function is just like getangle function. Both return the value of the angle in radians. However, the getorient function always measures the angle with positive X axis (3-OClock position) and in counter-clockwise direction. **It ignores the settings of ANGBASE and ANGDIR.** If the settings have not been changed as shown in Figure 6a (default settings for ANGDIR and ANGBASE) then for an angle of 135 degrees the getorient function will rcturn 2.35619 radians. If the settings are changed as shown in Figure 6b then for an angle of 135 degrees the getorient function will return 5.49778 radians. Although the settings have been changed where the angle is measured with the positive Y axis and in clockwise direction, the getorient function ignores the new settings and measures the angle from positive X axis and in counter-clockwise direction.

Note

1. For **getangle** and **getorient** functions the angle can be entered by typing the angle from the keyboard or by selecting two points on the screen. For example, if the assignment is **(setq ang (getorient))** the angle can be entered by selecting two points on the screen or typing the angle. If the assignment is **(setq ang (getorient pt1))** where the first point pt1 is already defined, user will be prompted to enter the second point. This point can be entered by selecting a point on the screen or by entering the coordinates of the second point.

2. 180 degrees is equal to **pi** (3.14159) radians. To calculate an angle in radians use the following relation.
   Angle in radians = (pi x angle)/180

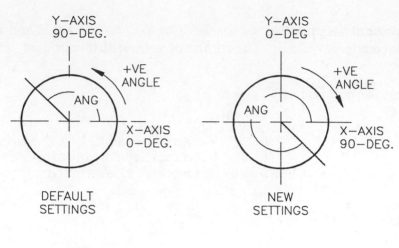

Figure 6a   Fig 6b

getdist

The **getdist** function pauses for the user to enter distance and it then returns the distance as a real number. The format of **getdist** function is:

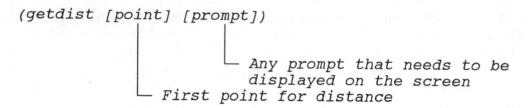

```
(getdist [point] [prompt])
```

Any prompt that needs to be displayed on the screen

First point for distance

Examples
(getdist)
(setq dist (getdist))
(setq dist (getdist pt1))
(setq dist (getdist "Enter distance"))
(setq dist (getdist pt1 "Enter second point for distance"))

The distance can be entered by selecting two points on the screen. For example, if the assignment is **(setq dist (getdist))** you can enter a number or select two points. If the assignment is **(setq dist (getdist pt1))** where the first point pt1 is already defined, you need to select the second point only.

The getdist function will always return the distance as a real number. For example, if the current setting is architectural and the distance is entered in architectural units, the getdist function will return the distance as a real number.

Example 3

Write an AutoLISP program that will generate a chamfer between two given lines by entering the chamfer angle and the chamfer distance.

To generate a chamfer AutoCAD uses the values assigned to system variables CHAMFERA and CHAMFERB. When you select AutoCAD's CHAMFER command, the first and second chamfer distances are automatically assigned to the system variables CHAMFERA and CHAMFERB. The chamfer command then uses these assigned values to generate a chamfer. However, in most of the engineering drawings, the preferred way of generating the chamfer is by entering the chamfer length and the chamfer angle as shown in Figure 7.

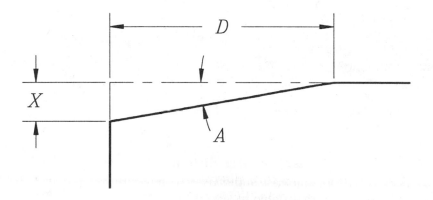

Figure 7 Chamfer with angle A and distance D

INPUT	**OUTPUT**
Chamfer distance (D)	Chamfer between any two
Chamfer angle (A)	selected lines.

PROCESS

1. Calculate second chamfer distance
2. Assign these values to the system variables CHAMFERA and CHAMFERB
3. Use AutoCAD's CHAMFER command to generate chamfer.

Calculations

X/D = TAN A
X   = D * (TAN A)
    = D * [(SIN A) / (COS A)]

The following file is a listing of the program for Example 3. The line numbers are not a part of the file, they are for reference only.

```
;This program generates a chamfer by entering              1
;the chamfer angle and the chamfer distance                2
;                                                           3
(defun c:chamf (/)                                         4
(setvar "cmdecho" 0)                                       5
(graphscr)                                                 6
(setq d (getdist "\n Enter chamfer distance: "))           7
(setq a (getangle "\n Enter chamfer angle: "))             8
(setvar "chamfera" d)                                      9
(setvar "chamferb" (* d (/ (sin a) (cos a))))            10
(command "chamfer")                                       11
(setvar "cmdecho" 1)                                      12
(princ)                                                   13
)                                                         14
```

Line 7
(setq d (getdist "\n Enter chamfer distance: "))
The **getdist** function pauses for the user to enter the chamfer distance and then **setq** function assigns that value to variable d.

Line 8
(setq a (getangle "\n Enter chamfer angle: "))
The **getangle** pauses for the user to enter the chamfer angle and then the **setq** function assigns that value to variable a.

Line 9
(setvar "chamfera" d)
The **setvar** function assigns the value of variable d to AutoCAD system variable **chamfera**.

Line 10
(setvar "chamferb" (* d (/ (sin a) (cos a))))
The **setvar** function assigns the value obtained from the expression **(* d (/ (sin a) (cos a))** and assigns that value to AutoCAD's system variable **chamferb**

Line 11
(command "chamfer")
The **command** function uses AutoCAD's **chamfer** command to generate a chamfer.

getint, getreal, getstring and getvar functions

getint

The **getint** function pauses for the user to enter an integer number and the function always returns an integer, even if the number that the user enters is a real number. The format of **getint** function is:

```
(getint [prompt])
```
              └── Optional prompt that the user wants to
                  display on the screen

Examples
(getint)
(setq numx (getint))
(setq numx (getint "Enter number of rows: "))
(setq numx (getint "\n Enter number of rows: "))

getreal

The **getreal** function pauses for the user to enter a real number and it always returns a real number, even if the number that the user enters is a integer number. The format of getreal function is:

```
(getreal [prompt])
```
              └── Optional prompt that is displayed on
                  the screen.

Examples
(getreal)
(setq realnumx (getreal))
(setq realnumx (getreal "Enter distance: "))
(setq realnumx (getreal "\n Enter distance: "))

getstring

The **getstring** function pauses for the user to enter a string value and it always returns a string, even if the string that the user enters contains numbers only. The format of **getstring** function is:

```
(getstring [prompt])
```

└─ *Optional prompt that is displayed on the screen*

Examples
(getstring)
(setq answer (getstring))
(setq answer (getstring "Enter Y for yes, N for no:))
(setq answer (getstring "\n Enter Y for yes, N for no:))

Note

The maximum length of the string is 132 characters. If the length of the string exceeds 132 characters, the characters in excess of 132 are ignored.

getvar

The **getvar** function lets the user retrieve the value of an AutoCAD system variable. The format of **getvar** function is:

```
(getvar "variable")
```

└─ *AutoCAD system variable name*

Examples
(gatvar)
(getvar "dimcen")   returns 0.09
(getvar "ltscale")   returns 1.0
(getvar "limmax")   returns 12.00,9.00
(getvar "limmin")   returns 0.00,0.00

Note

1. The system variable name should always be enclosed in double quotes.

2. You can retrieve only one variable value in one assignment. To retrieve the values of several system variables use a separate assignments for each variable.

polar, and sqrt functions

polar

The **polar** function defines a point at a given angle and distance from the given point. The angle is expressed in radians, measured positive in counter-clockwise direction (Assuming default settings for ANGBASE and ANGDIR). The format of this function is:

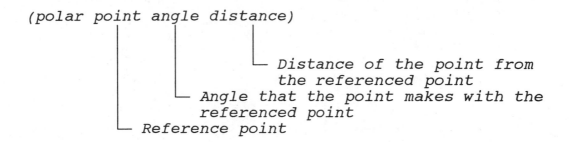

```
(polar point angle distance)
                         └─ Distance of the point from
                            the referenced point
                   └─ Angle that the point makes with the
                      referenced point
           └─ Reference point
```

Example
(polar pt1 ang dis)
(setq pt2 (polar pt1 ang dis))
(setq pt2 (polar '(2.0 3.25) ang dis))

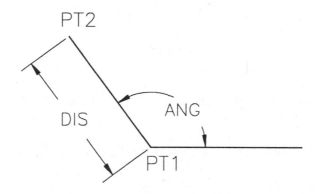

(setq pt2 (polar pt1 ang dis))

Figure 8   Using polar function to define a point

sqrt

The **sqrt** function calculates the square root of a number and the value that this function returns is always a real number. The format of **sqrt** function is:

(sqrt number)

└─── *Number that the user wants to find the square root of (real or integer)*

Examples

(sqrt 144)	returns 12.0
(sqrt 144.0)	returns 12.0
(setq x (sqrt 57.25))	returns 7.566373
(setq x (sqrt (* 25 36.5)))	returns 30.207615
(setq x (sqrt (/ 7.5 (cos 0.75))))	returns 3.2016035
(setq hyp (sqrt (+ (* base base) (* ht ht))))	

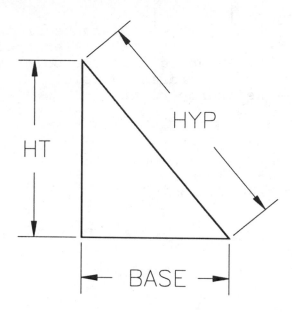

(setq hyp (sqrt (+ (* base base) (* ht ht))))

Figure 10   Application of **sqrt** function

Example 4

Write an AutoLISP program that will draw a congruent triangle outside the circle. The sides of the triangle are tangent to the circle. The program should prompt the user to enter the radius and the center point of the circle.

The following file is the listing of the AutoLISP program for Example 4.

```
;This program will draw a triangle outside
;the circle with the lines tangent to circle
:
(defun dtr (a)
```

```
     (* a (/ pi 180.0))
     )
(defun c:trgcir()
(setvar "cmdecho" 0)
(graphscr)
     (setq r(getdist "\n Enter circle radius: "))
     (setq c(getpoint "\n Enter center of circle: "))
     (setq d(/ r (sin(dtr 30))))
     (setq p1(polar c (dtr 210) d))
     (setq p2(polar c (dtr 330) d))
     (setq p3(polar c (dtr 90) d))
(command "circle" c r)
(command "line" p1 p2 p3 "c")
(setvar "cmdecho" 1)
(princ)
)
```

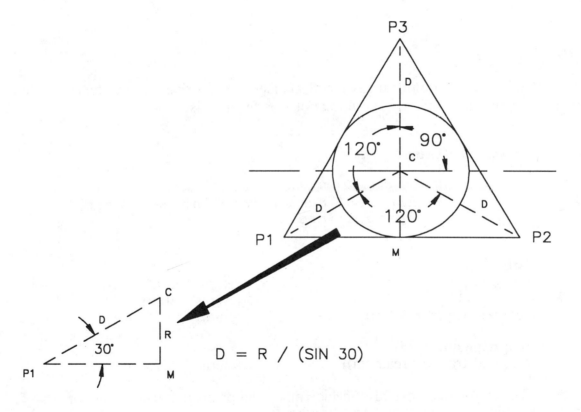

Figure 9 Congruent triangle outside the circle

itoa, rtos, strcase, and prompt functions

itoa

The **itoa** function changes an integer into a string and returns the integer as a string. The format of **itoa** function is:

```
(itoa number)
         └── The integer number that you want to convert
             into a string
```

Examples

(itoa 89)   returns "89"
(itoa -356)   returns "-356"

(setq intnum 7)
(itoa intnum)   returns "7"

(setq intnum 345)
(setq intstrg (itoa intnum))   returns "345"

rtos

The **rtos** function changes a real number into a string and the function returns the real number as a string. The format of **rtos** function is:

```
(rtos realnum)
         └── The real number that the user want to
             convert into a string
```

Examples

(rtos 50.6)   returns "50.6"
(rtos -30.0)   returns "-30.0)
(setq realstrg (rtos 5.25))   returns "5.25"

(setq realnum 75.25)
(setq realstrg (rtos realnum))   returns "75.25"

The rtos function can also include mode and precision. The format of **rtos** function with mode and precision is:

(rtos realnum [mode] [precision])

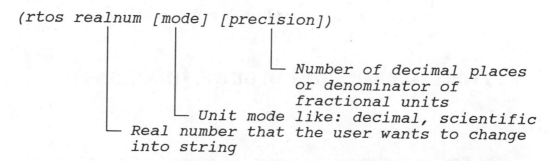

```
                                    └── Number of decimal places
                                        or denominator of
                                        fractional units
                      └── Unit mode like: decimal, scientific
         └── Real number that the user wants to change
             into string
```

strcase

The **strcase** function converts the characters of a string into upper-case or lower-case. The format of **strcase** function is:

```
(strcase string [true])
                    |
                    |__ If it is not nil, all characters
                        are converted to lower-case
              |__ String that needs to be converted to
                  upper-case or lower-case
```

true is optional. If it is missing or if the value of **true** is nil, then the string is converted to upper-case. If the value of true is not nil then the string is converted to lower case.

Examples
(strcase "Welcome Home")   returns "WELCOME HOME"

(setq t 0)
(strcase "Welcome Home" t)   rcturns "welcome home"

(setq answer (strcase (getstring "Enter Yes or No: ")))

prompt

The **prompt** function is used to display a message on the screen in the command prompt area. The contents of the message must be enclosed in double quotes. The format of **prompt** function is:

```
(prompt message)
             |
             |__ Message that the user wants to display
                 on the screen
```

Examples
(prompt "Enter circle diameter: ")
(setq d (getdist (prompt "Enter circle diameter: ")))

Note

On a two screen system the prompt function displays the message on both the screens.

Example 5

Write a program that will draw two circles of radii r1 and r2, representing two pulleys, that are separated by a distance d. The line joining the centers of the two circles makes an angle a with X axis as shown in Figure 11.

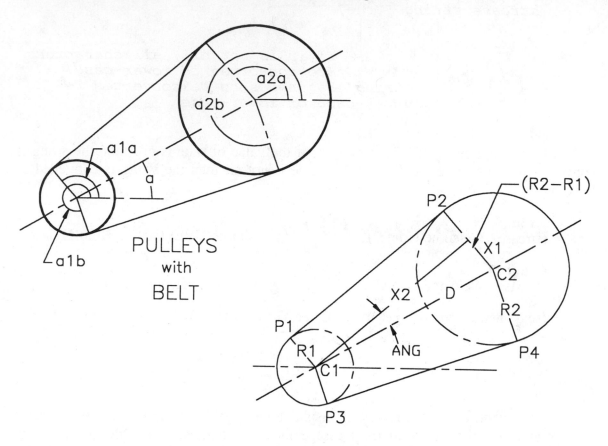

Figure 11   Two circles with tangent lines

INPUT

Radius of small circle r1
Radius of large circle r2
Distance between circles d
Angle of center line a
Center of small circle c1

OUTPUT

Small circle of radius r1
Large circle of radius r2
Lines tangent to circles

PROCESS

1. Calculate distance x1, x2
2. Calculate angle ang
3. Locate point c2 with respect to point c1
4. Locate point p1, p2, p3, p4

5. Draw small circle with radius
r1 and center c1
6. Draw large circle with radius
r2 and center c2
7. Draw lines p1 to p2 and p3 p4

Calculations
x1 = r2 - r1
x2 = SQRT [d**2 - (r2 - r1)**2]
tan ang = x1 / x2
ang = atan (x1 / x2)

a1a = 90 + a + ang
a1b = 270 + a - ang
a2a = 90 + a + ang
a2b = 270 + a - ang

The following file is a listing of the AutoLISP program for Example 4. The line numbers are not a part of the file. These numbers are for reference only.

```
;This program draws a tangent (belt) over two                  1
;pulleys that are separated by a given distance.               2
                                                               3
;This function changes degrees into radians                    4
(defun dtr (a)                                                 5
  (* a (/ pi 180.0))                                           6
  )                                                            8
                                                               9
(defun c:belt()                                               10
(setvar "cmdecho" 0)                                          11
(graphscr)                                                    12
(setq r1(getdist "\n Enter radius of small pulley: "))        13
(setq r2(getdist "\n Enter radius of larger pulley: "))       14
(setq d(getdist "\n Enter distance between pulleys: "))       15
(setq a(getangle "\n Enter angle of pulleys: "))              16
(setq c1(getpoint "\n Enter center of small pulley: "))       17
(setq x1 (- r2 r1))                                           18
(setq x2 (sqrt (- (* d d) (* (- r2 r1) (- r2 r1)))))          19
(setq ang (atan (/ x1 x2)))                                   20
(setq c2 (polar c1 a d))                                      21
(setq p1 (polar c1 (+ ang a (dtr 90)) r1))                    22
(setq p3 (polar c1 (- (+ a (dtr 270)) ang) r1))               23
(setq p2 (polar c2 (+ ang a (dtr 90)) r2))                    24
(setq p4 (polar c2 (- (+ a (dtr 270)) ang) r2))               25
                                                              26
(command "circle" c1 p3)                                      28
(command "circle" c2 p2)                                      29
(command "line" p1 p2 "")                                     30
(command "line" p3 p4 "")                                     31
(setvar "cmdecho" 1)                                          32
(princ)                                                       33
)                                                             34
```

Line 5
(defun dtr (a)
In this line the **defun** function defines a function **dtr (a)** that converts degrees into radians.

Line 6
(* a (/ pi 180.0))
(/ pi 180) divides the value of **pi** by 180 and the product is then multiplied by the angle a. (180 degrees is equal to **pi** radians)

Line 10
(defun c:belt()
In this line the function **defun** defines a function c:belt that generates two circles with tangent lines.

Line 18
(setq x1 (- r2 r1))
In this line the function **setq** assigns the value of r2 - r1 to variable x1.

Line 19
(setq x2 (sqrt (- (* d d) (* (- r2 r1) (- r2 r1)))))
In this line **(- r2 r1)** subtracts the value of r1 from r2 and **(* (- r2 r1) (- r2 r1))** calculates the square of (- r2 r1). **(sqrt (- (* d d) (* (- r2 r1) (- r2 r1))))** calculates the square root of the difference, and **setq x2** assigns the product of this expression to variable x2.

Line 20
(setq ang (atan (/ x1 x2)))
In this line **(atan (/ x1 x2))** calculates the arc tangent of the product of **(/ x1 x2)**. The function **setq ang** assigns the value of the angle in radians to variable **ang**.

Line 21
(setq c2 (polar c1 a d))
In this line **(polar c1 a d)** uses the **polar** function to locate the point c2 with respect to c1 at a distance of d and making an angle **a** with the positive X axis.

Line 22
(setq p1 (polar c1 (+ ang a (dtr 90)) r1))
In this line **(polar c1 (+ ang a (dtr 90)) r1))** locates the point p1 with respect to c1 at a distance r1 and making an angle of **(+ ang a (dtr 90))** with the positive X axis.

Line 28
(command "circle" c1 p3)
In this line the **command** function uses AutoCAD's **CIRCLE** command to draw a circle with the center c1 and radius defined by the point p3.

Line 30
(command "line" p1 p2 "")

In this line the **command** function uses AutoCAD's **LINE** command to draw a line from p1 to p2. The pair of double quotes ("") at the end introduce a return to terminate the LINE command.

Flowchart

A flowchart is a graphical representation of the algorithm and can be used to analyze a problem systematically. It gives a better understanding of the problem, especially if the problem involves some conditional statements. It consists of some standard symbols that represent a certain function in the program. For example, a rectangle is used to represent a process that takes place when the program is executed. The blocks are connected by lines indicating the sequence of operations. Figure 12 illustrates the standard symbols that can be used in a flowchart.

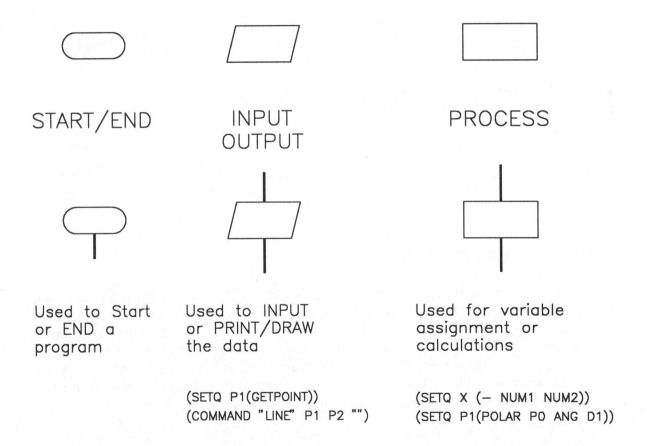

START/END

INPUT OUTPUT

PROCESS

Used to Start or END a program

Used to INPUT or PRINT/DRAW the data

Used for variable assignment or calculations

(SETQ P1(GETPOINT))
(COMMAND "LINE" P1 P2 "")

(SETQ X (− NUM1 NUM2))
(SETQ P1(POLAR P0 ANG D1))

Figure 12a   Flowchart symbols

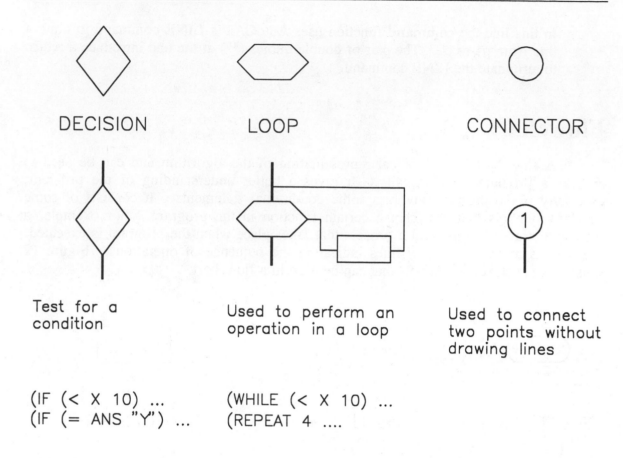

DECISION

LOOP

CONNECTOR

Test for a
condition

Used to perform an
operation in a loop

Used to connect
two points without
drawing lines

(IF (< X 10) ...
(IF (= ANS "Y") ...

(WHILE (< X 10) ...
(REPEAT 4 ....

Figure 12b   Flowchart symbols

Conditional Functions

The relational functions, discussed earlier in the chapter, establish a relationship between two atoms. For example, (< x y) describes a test condition for an operation. In order to use such functions in a meaningful way a conditional function is required. For example, (if (< x y) (setq z (- y x)) (setq z (- x y))) describes the action to be taken if the condition is true (T) or false (nil). If the condition is true then z = y - x. If the condition is not true then z = x - y. Therefore the conditional functions are very important for any programming language, including AutoLISP.

if

The **if** function evaluates the first expressions (then) if the specified condition returns T, and it evaluates the second expression (else) if the specified condition returns nil. The format of **if** function is:

```
(if condition then [else])
```

        └── *Expression evaluated if the*
            condition returns nil
        └── *Expression evaluated if*
            the condition returns T
    └── *Specified conditional statement*

Examples

(if (= 7 7) ("true"))   returns "true"
(if (= 5 7) ("true") ("false"))   returns "false"

(setq ans "yes")
(if (= ans "yes") ("Yes") ("No"))   returns "Yes"

(setq num1 8)
(setq num2 10)
(if (> num1 num2)
    (setq x (- num1 num2))
    (setq x (- num2 num1))
)   returns 2

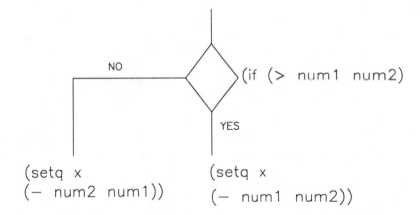

Figure 13   If function

Example 6

Write an AutoLISP program that will subtract a smaller number from a larger number. The program should also prompt the user to enter two numbers.

INPUT	OUTPUT
Number (num1)	x = num1 - num2
Number (num2)	or
	x = num2 - num1

PROCESS

If num1 > num2 then x = num1 - num2
if num1 < num2 then x = num2 - num1

The flow chart shown in the following figure , Figure 11 describes the process that is involved in writing the program by using standard flow chart symbols.

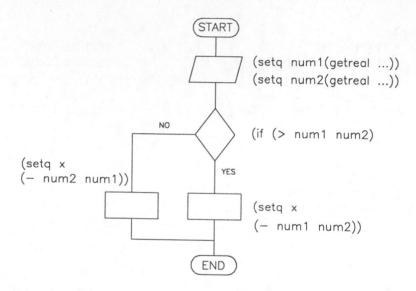

Figure 14   Flow diagram for Example 6

The following file is a listing of the program for Example 5. The line numbers are not a part of the file. These numbers are for reference only.

```
;This program subtracts smaller number          1
;from larger number                             2
;                                               3
(defun c:subnum()                               4
(setvar "cmdecho" 0)                            5
(setq num1 (getreal "\n Enter first number: ")) 6
(setq num2 (getreal "\n Enter second number: "))7
(if (> num1 num2)                               8
    (setq x (- num1 num2))                      9
    (setq x (- num2 num1))                      10
    )                                           11
(setvar "cmdecho" 1)                            12
(princ)                                         13
)                                               14
```

Line 8
(if (> num1 num2)

In this line the **if** function evaluates the test expression (**> num1 num2**). If the condition is true it returns T, and if the condition is not true it returns nil.

Line 9
(setq x (- num1 num2))
This expression is evaluated if the test expression **(if (> num1 num2)** returns T. The value of variable num2 is subtracted from num1 and the resulting value is assigned to variable x.

Line 10
(setq x (- num2 num1))
This expression is evaluated if the test expression **(if (> num1 num2)** returns nil. The value of variable num1 is subtracted from num2 and the resulting value is assigned to variable x.

Line 11
The close parenthesis completes the definition of the **if** function.

Example 7

Write an AutoLISP program that will enable the user to multiply or divide two numbers. The program should prompt the user to enter the choice of multiplication or division. The program should also display an appropriate message if the user does not enter the right choice.

The following file is a listing of the AutoLISP program for Example 6.

```
;This program multiplies or divides
;two given numbers
(defun c:mdnum()
(setvar "cmdecho" 0)
(setq num1 (getreal "\n Enter first number: "))
(setq num2 (getreal "\n Enter second number: "))
(prompt "Do you want to multiply or divide. Enter M or D: ")
(setq ans (strcase (getstring)))
(if (= ans "M")
   (setq x (* num1 num2))
   )
(if (= ans "D")
   (setq x (/ num1 num2))
   )
(if (and (/= ans "D")(/= ans "M"))
   (prompt "Sorry!  Wrong entry, Try again")
   )
(setvar "cmdecho" 1)
(princ)
)
```

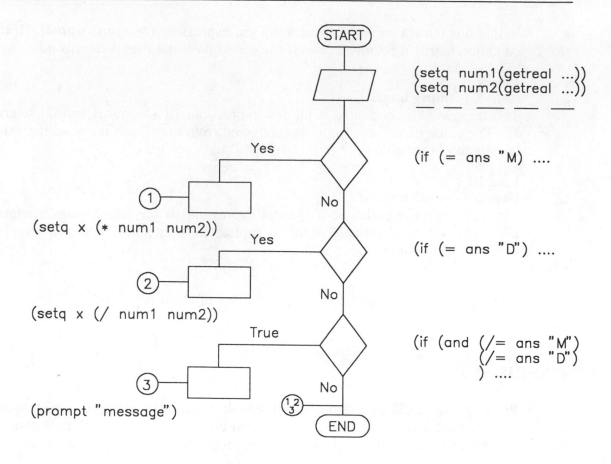

Figure 15 Flow diagram for Example 7

progn

The **progn** function can be used with **if** function to evaluate several expressions. The format of **progn** function is:

(progn expression expression ......)

The **if** function evaluates only one expression, if the test condition returns **T**. The **progn** function can be used in conjunction with **if** function to evaluate several expressions.

Example
```
(if (= ans "yes")
    (progn
    (setq x (sin ang))
    (setq y (cos ang))
    (setq tanang (/ x y))
    )
)
```

while

The **while** function evaluates the test condition, if the condition is true (expression does not return nil) the operations that follow the while statement are repeated till the test expression returns **nil**. The format of **while** function is:

```
(while test-expression operations)
                │                │
                │                └─ Operations to be
                │                   performed till the test
                │                   expression returns nil
                └─ Expression that tests a condition
```

Examples
```
(while (= ans "yes")
     (setq x (+ x 1))
     (setq ans (getstring "Enter yes or no: "))
     )

(while (< n 3)
     (setq x (+ x 10))
     (setq n (1+ n))
     )
```

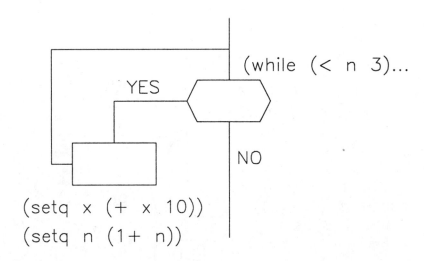

Figure 16   While function

Example 8

Write an AutoLISP program that will find the nth power of a given number. The power is an integer number. The program should prompt the user to enter the number, and the nth power.

INPUT   **OUTPUT**

Number x   product x^n
nth power n

PROCESS

1. set the value of t = 1
   and c = 1
2. multiply t * x and assign
   that value to the variable t
3. repeat the process till the
   counter c is less than or
   equal to n

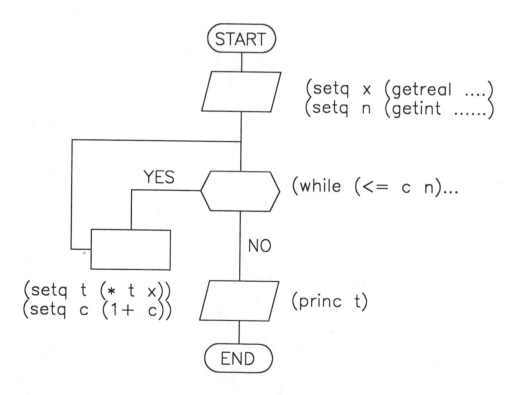

Figure 17   Flow chart for Example 8

The following file is a listing of the AutoLISP program for Example 7.

```
;This program calculates the nth
;power of a given number
(defun c:npower()
(setvar "cmdecho" 0)
(setq x(getreal "\n Enter a number: "))
(setq n(getint "\n Enter Nth power-integer number: "))
(setq t 1) (setq c 1)
(while (< = c n)
  (setq t (* t x))
  (setq c (1+ c))
  )
(setvar "cmdecho" 1)
(princ t)
)
```

Example 9

Write an AutoLISP program that will generate the holes of a bolt circle. The program should prompt the user to enter the center point of bolt circle, bolt circle diameter, bolt circle hole diameter, number of holes, and the start angle of the bolt circles.

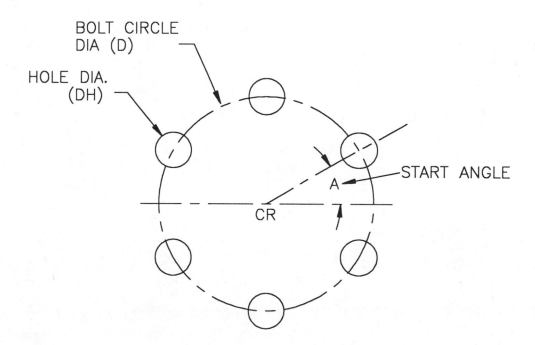

Figure 18   Bolt circle with 6 holes

```
;This program generates a bolt circle
;
(defun c:bc1()
(graphscr)
(setvar "cmdecho" 0)
   (setq cr(getpoint "\n Enter center of Bolt-Circle: "))
   (setq d(getdist "\n Dia of Bolt-Circle: "))
   (setq n(getint "\n Number of holes in Bolt-Circle: "))
   (setq a(getangle "\n Enter start angle: "))
   (setq dh(getdist "\n Enter diameter of hole: "))
   (setq inc(/ (* 2 pi) n))
   (setq ang 0)
   (setq r (/ dh 2))
(while (< ang (* 2 pi))
   (setq p1 (polar cr (+ a inc) (/ d 2)))
   (command "circle" p1 r)
   (setq a (+ a inc))
   (setq ang (+ ang inc))
   )
(setvar "cmdecho" 1)
(princ)
)
```

repeat

The **repeat** function evaluates the expressions n number of times as specified in the **repeat** function. The variable n must be an integer. The format of the **repeat** function is:

```
repeat n
      |
      |___ n is an integer that defines the number of
           times the expressions are to be evaluated.
```

Example
```
(repeat 5
 (setq x (+ x 10))
 )
```

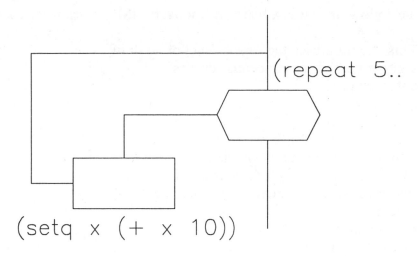

Figure 19   repeat function

Example 10

Write an AutoLISP program that will generate a given number of concentric circles. The program should prompt the user to enter the center point of circles, start radius, and the radius increment.

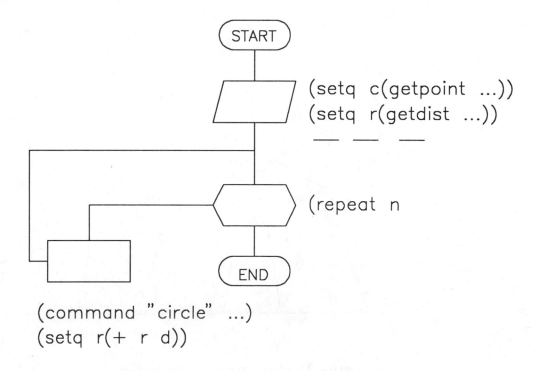

Figure 20   Flow chart for Example 10

The following file is a listing of the AutoLISP program for Example 9.

```
;This program uses the repeat function to draw
;a given number of concentric circles.
(defun c:concir()
(graphscr)
(setvar "cmdecho" 0)
(setq c (getpoint "\n Enter center point of circles: "))
(setq n (getint "\n Enter number of circles: "))
(setq r (getdist "\n Enter radius of first circle: "))
(setq d (getdist "\n Enter radius increment: "))
(repeat n
  (command "circle" c r)
  (setq r (+ r d))
  )
(setvar "cmdecho" 1)
(princ)
)
```

Example 11

Write an AutoLISP program that will generate flat layout drawing of a transition and then dimension the layout. The transition and the layout without dimensions is shown in Figure 21

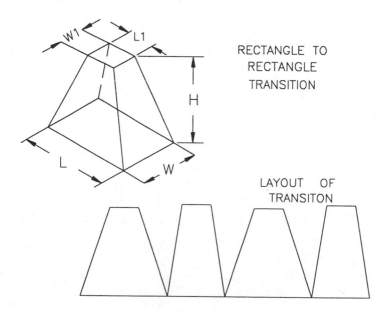

Figure 21   Flat layout of a transition

The following file is a listing of the AutoLISP program for Example 11. It is not necessary that the programs be in lowercase letters. It could uppercase or a combination of upper and lower case letters.

```
;This program generates flat layout of
;a rectangle to rectangle transition
;
(defun c:TRANA(/)
(graphscr)
(setvar "cmdecho" 0)

(setq L (getdist "\n Enter length of bottom rectangle: "))
(setq W (getdist "\n Enter width of bottom rectangle: "))
(setq H (getdist "\n Enter height of transition: "))
(setq L1 (getdist "\n Enter length of top rectangle: "))
(setq W1 (getdist "\n Enter width of top rectangle: "))

(setq X1 (/ (- W W1) 2))
(setq Y1 (/ (- L L1) 2))
(setq D1 (SQRT (+ (* H H) (* X1 X1))))
(setq D2 (SQRT (+ (* D1 D1) (* Y1 Y1))))
(setq S1 (/ (- L L1) 2))
(setq P1 (SQRT (- (* D2 D2) (* S1 S1))))
(setq S2 (/ (- W W1) 2))
(setq P2 (SQRT (- (* D2 D2) (* S2 S2))))

(setq T1 (+ L1 S1))
(setq T2 (+ L W))
(setq T3 (+ L S2 W1))
(setq T4 (+ L S2))
(setq PT1 (LIST 0 0))
(setq PT2 (LIST S1 P1))
(setq PT3 (LIST T1 P1))
(setq PT4 (LIST L 0))
(setq PT5 (LIST T4 P2))
(setq PT6 (LIST T3 P2))
(setq PT7 (LIST T2 0))
(command "LAYER" "MAKE" "CCTO" "C" "1" "CCTO" "")
(command "LINE" PT1 PT2 PT3 PT4 PT5 PT6 PT7 "C")

(setq SF (/ (+ L W) 12))
(setvar "DIMSCALE" SF)
(setq C1 (LIST 0 (- 0 (* 0.75 SF))))
(setq C7 (LIST (- 0 (* 0.75 SF)) 0))
(setq C8 (LIST (- L (* 0.75 SF)) 0))

(command "LAYER" "MAKE" "CCTD" "C" "2" "CCTD" "")
(command "DIM" "HOR" PT1 PT2 C1 "" "BASE" PT3 "" "BASE" PT4 ""
```

```
"EXIT")
(command "DIM" "HOR" PT4 PT5 C1 "" "BASE" PT6 "" "BASE" PT7 ""
"EXIT")
(command "DIM" "VERT" PT1 PT2 PT2 "" "EXIT")
(command "DIM" "VERT" PT4 PT5 PT5 "" "EXIT")
(command "DIM" "ALIGNED" PT1 PT2 C7 "" "EXIT")
(command "DIM" "ALIGNED" PT4 PT5 C8 "" "EXIT")
(setvar "CMDECHO" 1)
(princ)
)
```

Example 12

Write an AutoLISP program that can generate flat layout of a cone as shown in Figure 22. The program should also dimension the layout.

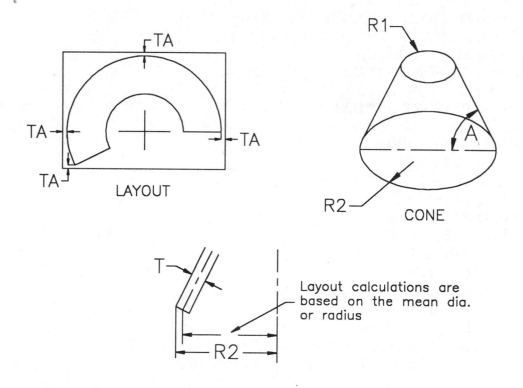

Figure 22   Flat layout of a cone

The following file is listing of the AutoLISP program for Example 12.

```
;This program generates layout of a cone
;
```

```
;DTR function changes degrees to radians
(defun DTR (a)
 (* PI (/ A 180.0))
 )

;RTD Function changes radians to degrees
(DEFUN RTD (A)
(* A (/ 180.0 PI))
)

(DEFUN TAN (A)
(/ (SIN A) (COS A))
)
(defun C:CONE-1P(/)
(GRAPHSCR)
(SETVAR "CMDECHO" 0)
(SETQ R2 (getdist "\n ENTER OUTER RADIUS AT LARGER END: "))
(SETQ R1 (GETDIST "\n ENTER INNER RADIUS AT SMALLER END: "))
(SETQ T (GETDIST "\n ENTER SHEET THICKNESS:-"))
(SETQ A (GETANGLE "\n ENTER CONE ANGLE:-"))

;THIS PART OF THE PROGRAM CALCULATES VARIOUS
PARAMETERS
;NEEDED IN CALCULATING THE STRIP LAYOUT.
(SETQ X0 0)
(SETQ Y0 0)
(SETQ SF (/ R2 3))
(SETVAR "DIMSCALE" SF)
(SETQ AR A)
(SETQ TX (/ (* T (SIN AR)) 2))
(SETQ RX2 (- R2 TX))
(SETQ RX1 (+ R1 TX))
(SETQ W (* (* 2 PI) (COS AR)))
(SETQ RL1 (/ RX1 (COS AR)))
(SETQ RL2 (/ RX2 (COS AR)))

;THIS PART OF THE PROGRAM CALCULATES THE X CO-ORDINATE
;OF THE POINTS.
  (SETQ X1 (+ X0 RL1)
      X3 (+ X0 RL2)
      X2 (- X0 (* RL1 (COS (- PI W))))
      X4 (- X0 (* RL2 (COS (- PI W))))
      )

;THIS PART OF THE PROGRAM CALCULATES THE Y CO-ORDINATE
;OF THE POINTS
  (SETQ Y1 Y0
      Y3 Y0
```

```
            Y2 (+  Y0 (* RL1 (SIN (- PI W))))
            Y4 (+  Y0 (* RL2 (SIN (- PI W))))
            )

    (SETQ P0 (LIST X0 Y0)
        P1 (LIST X1 Y1)
        P2 (LIST X2 Y2)
        P3 (LIST X3 Y3)
        P4 (LIST X4 Y4)
        )
    (COMMAND "LAYER" "MAKE" "CCTO" "C" "1" "CCTO" "")
    (COMMAND  "ARC" P1 "C" P0 P2)
    (COMMAND  "ARC" P3 "C" P0 P4)
    (COMMAND  "LINE" P1 P3 "")
    (COMMAND  "LINE" P2 P4 "")

    (SETQ F1 (/ R2 24))
    (SETQ F2 (/ R2 2))
    (SETQ D1 (LIST (+ X3 F2) Y3))
    (SETQ D2 (LIST X0 (- Y0 F2)))

(COMMAND "LAYER" "MAKE" "CCTD" "C" "2" "CCTD" "")
(SETVAR "DIMTIH" 0)
(COMMAND "DIM" "HOR" P0 P1 D2 "" "BASELINE" P3 "" "BASELINE"
P2 "" "BASELINE" P4 "" "EXIT")
(COMMAND "DIM" "VERT" P0 P2 D1 "" "BASELINE" P4 "" "EXIT")
(SETVAR "DIMSCALE" 1)
(SETVAR "CMDECHO" 1)
(PRINC)
)
```

Exercises

Exercise 1

Write an AutoLISP program that will draw a congruent triangle inside the circle (Figure 23). The program should prompt the user to enter the radius and the center point of the circle.

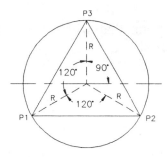

Figure 23   Congruent triangle inside a circle

Exercise 2

Write an AutoLISP program that will delete all the objects that are contained within upper (limmax) and lower (limmin) limits. Use AutoCAD's setvar and erase command to delete the entities.

Exercise 3

A. Write an AutoLISP program that will draw two lines tangent to two circles. The program should prompt the user to enter the circle diameter and the center distnace between the circles, Figure 24(A).

B. Re-write the program where the user is prompted to enter angle A, Figure 24(B)

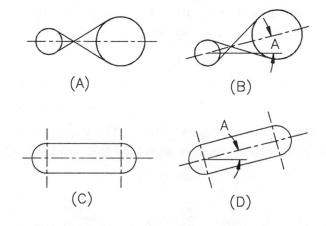

Figure 24   Circle with tangent lines, and slot.

Exercise 4

A.   Write a program that will draw a slot with center lines. The program should prompt the user to enter slot length, slot width, and the layer name for center lines, Figure 24(C).

B.   Re-write the program with slot angle as shown in Figure 24(D).

Exercise 5

Write an AutoLISP program that will draw a line and then generate a given number of lines, parallel to the first line.

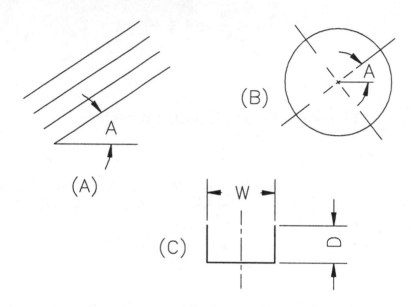

Figure 25   Line with offset, Circle with center lines, and key-way slot

Exercise 6

Write an Autolisp program to draw a circle with center lines. The program should prompt for the circle diameter and the angle of center lines as shown in Figure 25(B).

Exercise 7

Write a program to draw a key-way slot. The program should prompt the user to enter the width of slot, depth of slot, angle of slot, and the starting point, Figure 25(C).

Chapter 14

AutoLISP
Editing the Drawing Database

In addition to writing programs for creating new commands, you can use the AutoLISP programing language to edit the drawing database. This is a powerful tool to make changes in a drawing. For example, you can write a program that will delete all text entities in the drawing, or change the layer and color of all circles just by entering one command. Ones you know and understand how AutoCAD stores the information of the drawing entities, and how it can be retrieved and edited, you can manipulate the database in any way you want to, limited only by ones imagination.

This chapter discusses some of the commands that are frequently used in editing the drawing database. For other commands, not discussed in this section, please refer to the reference manual "AutoLISP Programmers Reference", published by Autodesk.

ssget

The **ssget** function enables the user to select any number of entities in a drawing. The object selection modes (window, crossing, previous, last) and the points that define the corners of the window can be included in the **ssget** assignment. The format of **ssget** function is:

```
(ssget [selection-mode] [point1 point2])
```

> └ Second point of
>   window (Optional)
> └ First point of window
>   (Optional)
> └ Object selection mode (w,c,l,p)

Examples

(ssget)	For general entity selection
(ssget "L")	For selecting last entity
(ssget "p")	For selecting previous selection set

(ssget "w" (list 0 0) (list 12.0 9.0))

Entity selection using window object selection mode, where the window is defined by points 0,0 and 12.0,9.0

(ssget "c" pt1 pt2)

Entity selection using crossing object selection mode, where the window is defined by the predefined points pt1 and pt2

Example 1

Write an AutoLISP program that will erase all entities within the drawing limits, limmax and limmin. Use ssget function to select the entities.

The following file is a listing of the AutoLISP program for Example 1. The line numbers are not a part of the program, they are shown here for reference only

```
;This program will delete all entities            1
;that are within the drawing limits               2
;                                                  3
(defun c:delall()                                  4
(setvar "cmdecho" 0)                               5
   (setq pt1 (getvar "limmin"))                    6
   (setq pt2 (getvar "limmax"))                    7
   (setq ss1 (ssget "c" pt1 pt2))                  8
(command "erase" ss1 "")                           9
(command "redraw")                                 10
(setvar "cmdecho" 1)                               11
(princ)                                            13
)                                                  14
```

Lin 1-3
The first three lines are comment lines that describe the function of the program. Notice that all comment lines start with a semicolon (;).

Line 4
(defun c:delall()
In this line **defun** function defines the function delall.

Line 6
(setq pt1 (getvar "limmin"))

The **getvar** function secures the value of the lower left corner of the drawing limits (limmin) and the setq function assigns that value to variable pt1.

Line 7
(setq pt2 (getvar "limmax"))
The **getvar** function secures the value of the upper right corner of the drawing limits (limmax) and the setq function assigns that value to variable pt2.

Line 8
(setq ss1 (ssget "c" pt1 pt2))
The **ssget** function uses the "crossing" objection selection mode to select the objects that are within or touching the window defined by the points pt1 and pt2. The setq function then assigns this object selection set to variable ss1.

Line 9
(command "erase" ss1 "")
The **command** function uses AutoCAD's **ERASE** command to erase the predefined object selection set ss1.

line 10
(command "redraw")
In this line the **command** function uses AutoCAD's **REDRAW** command to redraw the screen and get rid of the blip marks left after erasing the objects.

ssget "X"

The **ssget "X"** function enables the user to select specified type of entities in the entire drawing database, even if the layers are frozen or turned off. The format of **ssget "X"** function is:

```
(ssget "X" specified-criteria)
                  |
                  |
                  └─ List of the specified criteria
                     for selecting the entities
        └─ Filter mode of the ssget function
```

Examples
(ssget "X" (list (cons 0 "TEXT")))

returns a selection set that consists of all TEXT entities in the drawing

(ssget "X" (list (cons 7 "ROMANC")))

returns a selection set that consists of all TEXT entities in the drawing with the text style name ROMANC.

(ssget "X" (list (cons 0 "LINE")))

returns a selection set that consists of all LINE entities in the drawing

(ssget "X" (list (cons 8 "OBJECT")))

returns a selection set that consists of all entities in the layer OBJECT.

The **ssget "X"** function can contain more than one selection criteria. This option can be used to select a specific set of entities in a drawing. For example, if the user wants to select the LINE entities that are in the OBJECT layer, there are two selection criteria. First one is that the entity has to be a LINE, and the second one is that the LINE entity has to be in the layer OBJECT. As shown in the following example, these two selection criteria can be combined together to filter out the entities that satisfy these two conditions.

(ssget "X" (list (cons 0 "LINE")(cons 8 "OBJECT")))

Group Codes for ssget "X"

The following table is a list of AutoCAD group codes that can be used with the function **ssget "X"**.

Group Code	Code Function
0	Entity type
2	Block name for Block reference
3	Dimension entity DIMSTYLE name
6	Linetype name
7	Text style name
8	Layer name
38	Elevation
39	Thickness
62	Color number
66	Attributes
210	3D extrusion direction

Example 2

Write an AutoLISP program that will erase all text entities in a drawing on a specified layer. Use the filter option of ssget function (ssget "X") to select text entities in the specified layer.

The following file is a listing of the AutoLISP program for Example 2.

```
;This program will delete all text
;in the user specified layer
;
(defun c:deltext()
(setvar "cmdecho" 0)
(setq layer (getstring "\n Enter layer name: "))
(setq ss1 (ssget "x" (list (cons 8 layer) (cons 0 "text"))))
(command "erase" ss1 "")
(command "redraw")
(setvar "cmdecho" 1)
(princ)
)
```

sslength

The **sslength** function determines the number of entities in a selection set and returns an integer number corresponding to the number of entities found. The format of **sslength** function is:

```
(sslength selection-set)
                 |
                 └─ Name of the selection set
```

Examples
```
(setq ss1 (ssget))
(setq num (sslength ss1))
```
        returns the number of entities in the predefined selection set ss1.

```
(setq ss2 (ssget "l"))
(setq num (sslength ss2))
```
        returns the number of entities (1) in the selection set ss2, where the selection set ss2 has been defined as the last entity in the drawing.

ssname

The **ssname** function returns the name of the entity, from a predefined selection set, as referenced by the index that designates the entity number. The name of the entity returned by this function is in the hexadecimal format (60000014). The format of **ssname** function is:

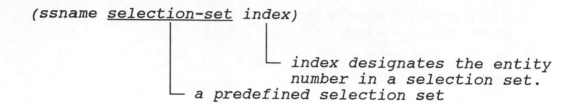

```
(ssname selection-set index)
```

index designates the entity
number in a selection set.

a predefined selection set

Examples
(setq ss1 (ssget))
(setq index 0)
(setq entname (ssname ss1 index))

returns the name of the first entity that is contained in the predefined selection set ss1.

Note

If the index is 0, the ssname function returns the name of the first entity in the selection set. Similarly if the index is 1, it returns the name of the second entity.

entget

The **entget** function retrieves the entity list from the entity name. The name of the entity can be obtained by using the function ssname. The format of **entget** function is:

```
(entget entity-name)
```

Name of the entity as obtained by
ssname

Example
(setq ss1 (ssget))
(setq index 0)
(setq entname (ssname ss1 index))

(setq entlist (entget entname))

> returns the list of the first entity from the variable, entname and assigns the list to variable entlist.

assoc

The **assoc** function searches for a specified code in the entity list and returns the element that contains that code. The format of **assoc** function is:

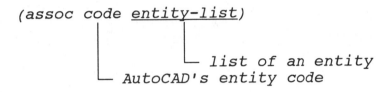

```
(assoc code entity-list)
                        list of an entity
            AutoCAD's entity code
```

Example
(setq ss1 (ssget))
(setq index 0)
(setq entname (ssname ss1 index))
(setq entlist (entget entname))
(setq entasso (assoc 0 entlist))

> returns the element that is associated with AutoCAD's entity code 0, from the list defined by variable entlist.

cons

The **cons** function constructs a new list from the given elements or lists. The format of the **cons** function is:

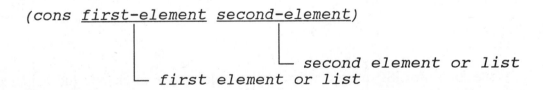

```
(cons first-element second-element)
                                second element or list
            first element or list
```

Examples
(cons 'x 'y)   returns (X . Y)
(cons '(x y) 'z)   returns ((X Y) . Z)
(cons '(x y z) '(0.5 5.0))   returns ((X Y Z) 0.5 5.0)

subst

The **subst** function substitutes the new item in place of old items. The old items can be a single item or multiple items, provided they are in the same list. The format of **subst** function is:

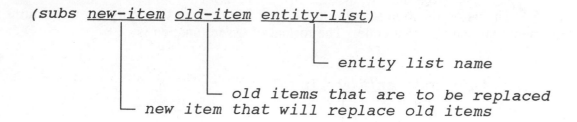

```
(subs new-item old-item entity-list)
```
— entity list name

— old items that are to be replaced

— new item that will replace old items

Example
(setq entlist '(x y x))
(setq newlist (subs '(z) '(x) entlist)

                  returns (z y z). The subst function replaces x in
                  the entity list (entlist) by z.

entmod

The **entmod** function updates the drawing by writing the modified list back to drawing database. The format of the **entmod** function is:

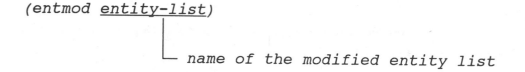

```
(entmod entity-list)
```
— name of the modified entity list

Example 3

Write an AutoLISP program that will enable a user to change the height of a text entity. The program should prompt the user to enter the new height of the text.

<u>INPUT</u>	<u>OUTPUT</u>
New text height	Text with new
Text entity	text height

<u>PROCESS</u>

1. After selecting the text entity, obtain the name of the entity using the function **ssname**.

2. Extract the list of the entity using the function **entget**

3. Separate the element associated with AutoCAD entity code 0, from the list, using the function **assoc**.

4. Construct a new element where the height of text is changed to new height, using the function **cons**.

5. Substitute the new element back into the original list, using **subst** function.

6. Update the drawing database using **entmod** function.

The following file is a listing of the AutoLISP program for Example 3. The line numbers are not a part of the program, they are shown here for reference only.

```
;This program changes the height of the                          1
;selected text, only one text at a time.                         2
;                                                                 3
(defun c:chgtext1()                                              4
(setvar "cmdecho" 0)                                             5
(setq newht (getreal "\n Enter new text height: "))              6
(setq ss1 (ssget))                                               7
(setq namc (ssnamc ss1 0))                                       8
(setq ent (entget name))                                         9
  (setq oldlist (assoc 40 ent))                                 10
  (setq conlist (cons (car oldlist) newht))                     11
  (setq newlist (subst conlist oldlist ent))                    12
  (entmod newlist)                                              13
(setvar "cmdecho" 1)                                            14
(princ)                                                         15
)                                                               16
```

How Database is Retrieved and Edited

To change the entities in a drawing it is very important to understand the structure of the drawing database and how it can be manipulated. Ones a programmer understands this concept, it is easy, and at times a fun to edit the drawing database, and therefore the drawing. The following step by step explanation describes the process involved in changing the height of a selected text entity in a drawing. It is assumed that the text that needs to be edited is "CHANGE TEXT" and this text is already drawn on the screen. The height of the text is 0.3 units. Before going through the following steps, load the AutoLISP program of Example 3 above, and run it so that the variables are assigned a value.

Step 1

Select the text by using the functions **ssget** or **ssget "X"** and assign it to a variable ss1.   AutoCAD creates a selection set that could have one, or more than one entity. In line number 7 **(setq ss1 (ssget))** of the program for Example 3, the selection set is assigned to variable ss1. Use the following command to check the variable ss1.

       Command: !ss1
       <Selection set: 2>

Step 2

There could be several entities in a selection set and the entities need to be separated, one at a time, before any change is made to an entity. This is made possible by using the function **ssname** that extracts the name of an entity. The index number used in the function **ssname** determines the entity whose name is being extracted. For example, if the index is 0 the ssname function will extract the name of the first entity, and if the index is 1 the ssname function will extract the name of second entity, and so on. In line number 8 **(setq name (ssname ss1 0))** of the program, the ssname extracts the name of the first entity and assigns it to variable, name. Use the following command to check the variable, name.

       Command: !name
       <Entity name: 60000018>

Step 3

Extract the entity list by using the function **entget**. In line number 9 **(setq ent (entget name))** of the program, the value of the list has been assigned to variable ent. Use the following command to check the value of the variable ent.

       Command: !ent
       ((-1.<Entity name: 600000018> (0 . "TEXT") (8 . "0") (10 4.91227
       5.36301 0.0) **(40 . 0.3)** (1 . "CHANGE TEXT") (50 .0.0) (41 . 1.0) (51
       .0.0) (7 . "standard") (71 .0)) (72 . 1) (11 6.51227 5.36302 0.0) (210
       0.0 0.0 1.0))

This list contains all the information about the selected text entity (CHANGE TEXT), but we are only interested in changing the height of the text. Therefore, we need to identify the element that contains the information about the text height (40 . 0.3) and separate that from the list.

Step 4

Use the function **assoc** to separate the element that is associated with code 40 (text height).   The statement in line 10 **(setq oldlist (assoc 40 ent))** of the program, uses assoc function to separate the value and assign it to variable oldlist. Use the following command to check the value of this variable.

       Command: !oldlist
       (40 . 0.3)

Step 5
The **(40 . 0.3)** element consist of the code for text height (40), and the text height (0.3). In order to change the height of the text, the text height value (0.3) needs to be replaces by the new value. This is accomplished by constructing a new list as described in line number 11 **(setq conlist (cons (car oldlist) newht))** of the program. This line also assigns the new element to variable, conlist. For example, if the value assigned to variable newht is 0.5, the new element will be (40 . 0.5). Use the following command to check the value of conlist.

        Command: !conlist
        (40 . 0.5)

Step 6
After constructing the new element, use the function **subst** to substitute the new element back into the original list, ent. This is accomplished by line number 12 **(setq newlist (subst conlist oldlist ent))** of the program. Use the following command to check the value of the variable newlist.

        Command: !newlist
        ((-1. <Entity name: 600000018> (0 . "TEXT") (8 . "0") (10 4.91227
        5.36301 0.0) **(40 . 0.5)** (1 . "CHANGE TEXT") (50 .0.0) (41 . 1.0) (51
        .0.0) (7 . "standard") (71 .0)) (72 . 1) (11 6.51227 5.36302 0.0) (210
        0.0 0.0 1.0))

Step 7
The last step is to update the drawing database. This is done by using the function **entmod** as shown in line number 13 **(entmod newlist)** of the program.

Example 4

Write an AutoLISP program that will enable a user to change the height of all text entity in a drawing. The program should prompt the user to enter the new height of the text.

The following file is a listing of the AutoLISP program for Example 16. The line numbers are not a part of the program, they are for reference only.

```
;This program changes the height of              1
;all text entities in a drawing.                 2
;                                                3
(defun c:chgtext2()                              4
(setvar "cmdecho" 0)                             5
(setq newht (getreal "\n Enter new text height: ")) 6
(setq ss1 (ssget "x" (list (cons 0 "text"))))    7
(setq index 0)                                   8
(setq num (sslength ss1))                        9
(repeat num                                      10
   (setq name (ssname ss1 index))                11
```

```
        (setq ent (entget name))                          12
        (setq oldlist (assoc 40 ent))                     13
        (setq conlist (cons (car oldlist) newht))         14
        (setq newlist (subst conlist oldlist ent))        15
        (entmod newlist)                                  16
        (setq index (1+ index))                           17
    )                                                     18
  (setvar "cmdecho" 1)                                    19
  (princ)                                                 20
)                                                         21
```

Flowchart

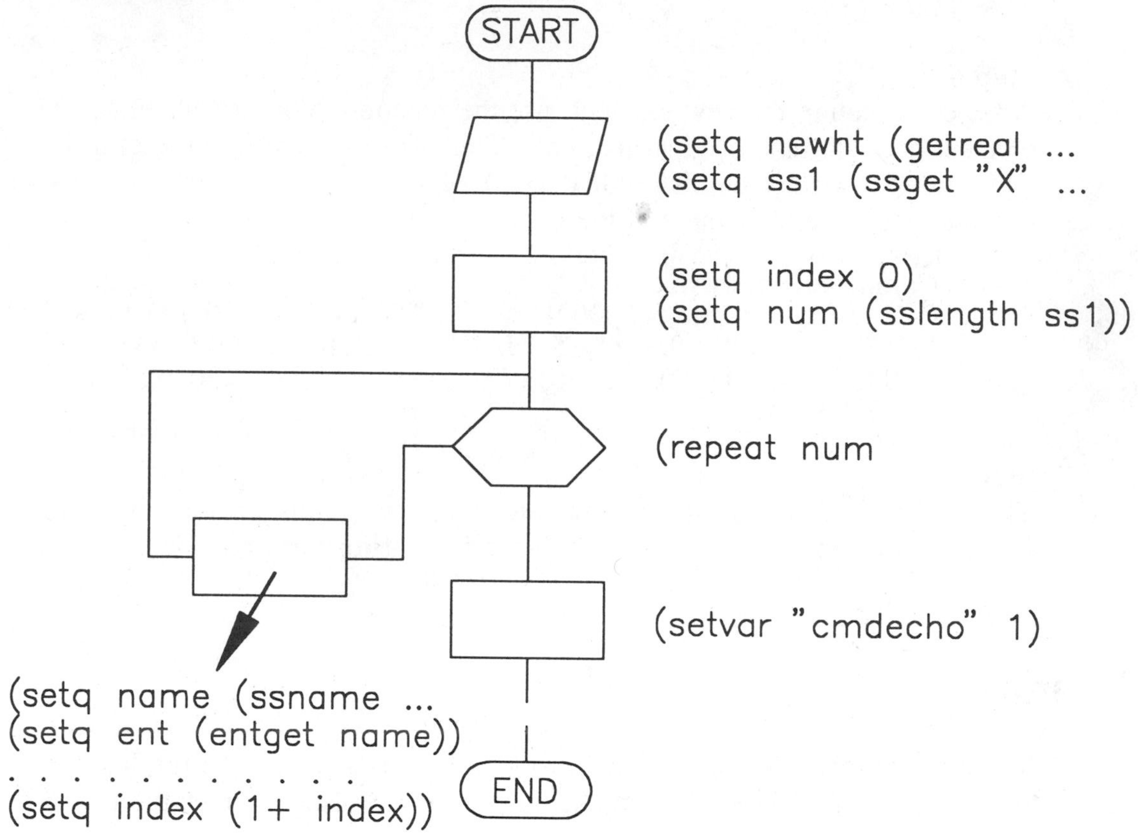

Figure 1   Flowchart for Example 4

Line 7
(setq ss1 (ssget "x" (list (cons 0 "text"))))
The **ssget "X"** function filters the text entities from the drawing database, and the **setq** function assigns that selected set of text entities to variable **ss1**.

Line 8
(setq index 0)
The **setq** function sets the value of the variable **Index** to 0. This variable is later on used by the program to select different entities.

Line 9
(setq num (sslength ss1))
The function **sslength** determines the number of entities in the selection set ss1
and the setq function assigns that number to variable **num**.

Line 10
(repeat num
The **repeat** function will repeat the processes defined within the repeat function
num number of times.

Example 5

Write an AutoLISP program that will enable a user to change the height of the
selected text entities in a drawing. The program should prompt the user to enter the
new height of the text.

Flowchart

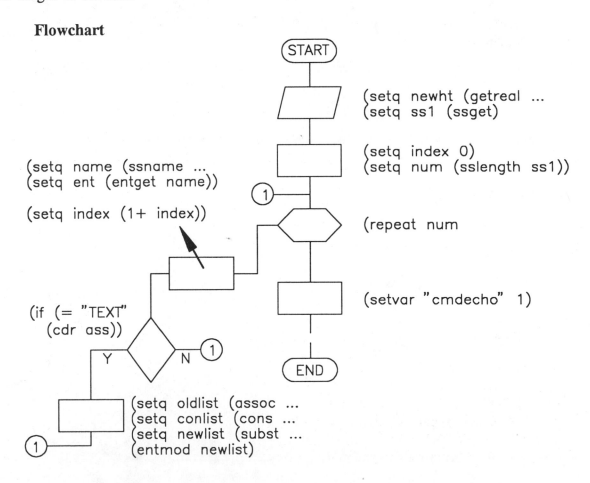

Figure 2 Flowchart of Example 5
;This program changes the height of the
;selected text entities.

```
;
(defun c:chgtext3()
(setvar "cmdecho" 0)
(setq newht (getreal "\n Enter new text height: "))
(setq ss1 (ssget))
(setq index 0)
(setq num (sslength ss1))
(repeat num
   (setq name (ssname ss1 index))
   (setq ent (entget name))
   (setq ass (assoc 0 ent))
   (setq index (1+ index))
   (If (= "TEXT" (cdr ass))
        (progn
        (setq oldlist (assoc 40 ent))
        (setq conlist (cons (car oldlist) newht))
        (setq newlist (subst conlist oldlist ent))
        (entmod newlist)
        )
     )
   )
(setvar "cmdecho" 1)
(princ)
)
```

Exercises

Exercise 1

Write an AutoLISP program that will enable a user to change the layer of the selected entities in a drawing. The program should prompt the user to enter the new layer name.

Exercise 2

Write an AutoLISP program that will change the text style name of the selected text entities in a drawing. The program should prompt the user to enter the new text style.

Exercise 3

Write an AutoLISP program that will change the layer of the selected entities in a drawing to a new layer. The user should be able to enter the new layer by selecting an object in that layer.

Appendix A

DOS Commands

This chapter contains a brief description of some of the DOS commands that are frequently used in a CAD environment. The examples that follow the DOS commands are some possible applications of these commands. For a detailed explanation of the DOS commands and the command options, check your disk operating system reference manual.

ASSIGN Command
(Assign Drive)

This command will route the disk input and output (I/O) from one drive to another. The format of the command is:

```
ASSIGN [X[=]Y]
           |    |
           |    |__ Drive, where you want to send I/O
           |_____ Drive, where current I/O is sent
```

Example
ASSIGN A=B
This command will assign drive B to drive A. For example, if you do a directory of A drive (DIR A:), the files in B drive will be listed. If you want to restore the default drive specification, use the ASSIGN command without any parameters (ASSIGN).

CHDIR Command
(Change Directory)

This command changes the directory. The format of the command is:

```
CHDIR [d:][path]
or
CD [d:][path]
             │          │
             │          └─ path specification
             └─ Drive whose directory you want to change
```

Example
CHDIR ACAD
or
CD ACAD
```
This command will change the directory to ACAD
subdirectory.
```

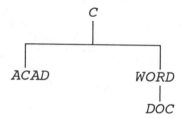

Example
CD\WORD\DOC
This command will change the directory to DOC subdirectory of WORD.

Example
CHDIR
or
CD

These commands will change the current directory to the root directory.

CHKDSK Command
(Check Disk)

You can use the DOS command CHKDSK, to check the status of your diskette and the system. It provides information about disk space, how much memory the system has, and how much is available for program use. The format of the command is:

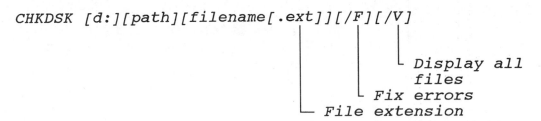

```
CHKDSK [d:][path][filename[.ext]][/F][/V]
```
└─ File extension
  └─ Fix errors
    └─ Display all
       files

Example
```
CHKDSK A:
```

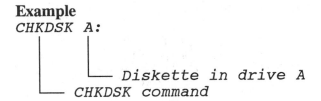

└── Diskette in drive A
└── CHKDSK command

This command will check the diskette in A drive and then display the information on the screen.

Example
CHKDSK C:/F
This command will check C drive and fix any errors that are found in the disk directory or the file allocation table.

CLS Command
(Clear Screen)

This command clears the display screen. The format of the command is:

CLS

COPY Command
(Copying Files)

The COPY command is used to copy files from one disk to another. COPY is an internal command that is loaded in the computer memory when you boot the computer. The format of the command is:

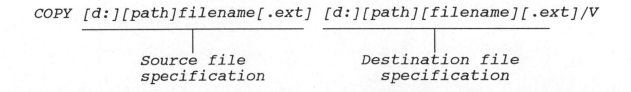

```
COPY [d:][path]filename[.ext] [d:][path][filename][.ext]/V
```

Source file   Destination file
specification   specification

Source file specification:

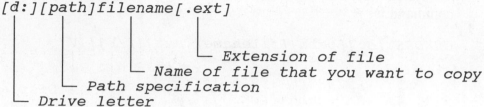

```
[d:][path]filename[.ext]
                            └─ Extension of file
                  └─ Name of file that you want to copy
          └─ Path specification
    └─ Drive letter
```

Destination file specification:

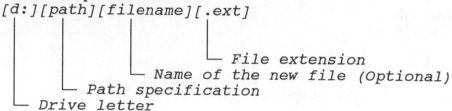

```
[d:][path][filename][.ext]
                          └─ File extension
                └─ Name of the new file (Optional)
          └─ Path specification
    └─ Drive letter
```

If you use /V at the end of the copy command line, it causes DOS to verify the sectors written on the target diskette. Because of the verification process, the copy command with /V option is relatively slow.

When you copy the files, it is very important to know the structure of the files on your drive. In the following examples, it is assumed that there are two drives C and D. Each drive has subdirectories as shown in the following figure. Also, **it is assumed that DWG1 subdirectory is the current directory.**

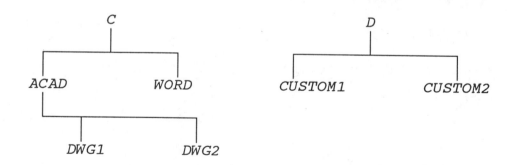

Example

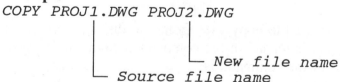

```
COPY PROJ1.DWG PROJ2.DWG
                     └─ New file name
         └─ Source file name
```

This COPY command will copy a file PROJ1.DWG to PROJ2.DWG.

Example
COPY C:\ACAD\SPLINE.LSP D:\CUSTOM1

```
                                    └─ CUSTOM1 subdirectory
                                       on D drive

            SPLINE.LSP file in
            ACAD subdirectory
            on C drive
```

This command will copy the file SPLINE.LSP in ACAD subdirectory to CUSTOM1 subdirectory on D drive. The name of the file that is copied to CUSTOM1 subdirectory does not change.

Example
COPY C:\ACAD\PROJ1.DWG D:\CUSTOM1\PROJ2.DWG
This command will copy a file PROJ1.DWG in ACAD subdirectory to a file PROJ2.DWG in CUSTOM1 subdirectory on D drive.

Example
COPY *.DWG D:\CUSTOM2
This command will copy all the drawing files with the extension DWG, from the current sub-directory to CUSTOM2 sub-directory on D Drive

Example
COPY *.* D:\CUSTOM1
This command will copy all files from the current subdirectory to CUSTOM1 subdirectory on D drive.

Example
COPY SHOW.SCR+DEMO.SCR SHOWDEMO.SCR

```
                        └─ Plus sign combines the two files
                           (SHOW.SCR and DEMO.SCR)
```

This command will combine the two files SHOW.SCR and DEMO.SCR, and copy them to a new file SHOWDEMO.SCR.

Example
COPY SHOW.SCR+C:\WORD\DEMO.SCR
D:\CUSTOM1\SHOWDEMO.SCR
This command will combine the SHOW.SCR file in the current subdirectory, with the DEMO.SCR file in the WORD subdirectory and copy the file to SHOWDEMO.SCR in the CUSTOM1 subdirectory of D drive.

DATE Command
(Change Date)

This command allows you to change the date that is saved on the system. The format of the command is:

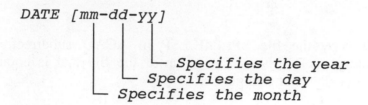

```
DATE [mm-dd-yy]
              └── Specifies the year
           └── Specifies the day
        └── Specifies the month
```

Example
DATE 12-31-91
This command will change the date to December 31, 1991 and save the information on the system.

Example
DATE
If you type DATE without specifying any parameters, the following prompt will be displayed on the screen.

Current date is mm-dd-yy
Enter new date (mm-dd-yy) :

If you want to change the date, type the new date in the same format as displayed on the screen and press the RETURN key. If you do not want to change anything, just press the RETURN key to accept the default date.

DIR Command
(File Directory)

You can use the DOS command, DIR, to display a list of files on a diskette. It is an internal command that is loaded in the computer memory when you boot the computer. The format of the command is:

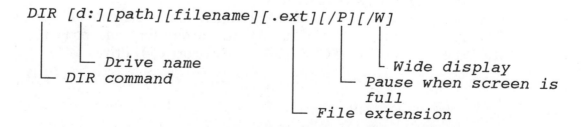

```
DIR [d:][path][filename][.ext][/P][/W]
        └── Drive name              └── Wide display
     └── DIR command              └── Pause when screen is
                                      full
                           └── File extension
```

Example
DIR D:
This command will display a list of files on D drive, together with their size in bytes, the time and date when they were last opened.

Example
DIR B:/P
This command of DOS will display the files on B drive one page at a time. When you press a key, another page of files is displayed.

Example
DIR B:/W
This command will display files on B drive in wide format. The file listing on the screen has five columns across the screen. Only file names, file types, and total number of files are displayed.

Example
DIR B:SCRMENU.MNU
This command will display the specified file only. It will display the file SCRMENU.MNU, with its size and date.

Example
DIR B:*.DWG
This command will display files that have an extension DWG. "*" is a wild card.

Example
DIR C:\ACAD\CUST1*.DWG
This command will display all files that have the extension DWG in CUST1 subdirectory of ACAD directory.

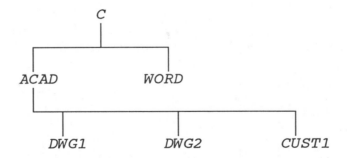

DISKCOPY Command
(Copying Disks)

If you have a computer system that has two floppy disk drives, you can use the DOS command, DISKCOPY, to make a backup copy of the entire disk. DISKCOPY copies all the contents on the source disk to the target disk. Before copying the files it automatically formats the target disk, if the diskette has not been formatted before. Therefore, make sure that you do not have any files on the target diskette that you do not want to be erased. This command can be used for making copies of diskettes only. If you specify a fixed drive, an error message will be displayed. The format of the DISKCOPY command is:

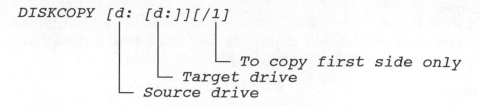

```
DISKCOPY [d: [d:]][/1]
```
To copy first side only
Target drive
Source drive

Example
```
DISKCOPY A: B:
```
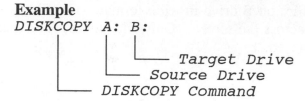

Target Drive
Source Drive
DISKCOPY Command

This command will prompt you to insert the source diskette in A drive and the destination diskette in B drive.

Example
DISKCOPY A: A:
If the source and the target drives are same, you will be prompted to insert the source diskette in A drive. After reading the source diskette you will be prompted to enter the target diskette in A drive.

Example
DISKCOPY
If both, the source and the target drive specifications are missing, the user is prompted to insert the source diskette in the default drive. After reading the source diskette, you will be prompted to insert the target diskette.

ERASE Command
(Erase Files)

This command is used to erase the specified files from a disk. The format of the command is:

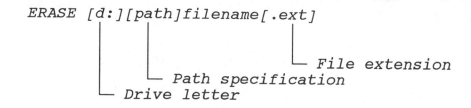

```
ERASE [d:][path]filename[.ext]
```
File extension
Path specification
Drive letter

Example
ERASE B:PROJ101.DWG
This command will erase the file PROJ101.DWG from the diskette in B drive.

Example
ERASE *.BAK
This command will erase all the files with the extension BAK from the current directory. If the drive specification is missing, the current drive is assumed.

Example
ERASE A:*.*
If you want to delete all files from the specified drive by specifying *.*, the following prompt is displayed to make sure that you really want to erase all files.

Are you sure (Y/N)?

If you want to erase all files on the specified drive, type Y and press the ENTER key. If you do not want to erase all files, type N and press the ENTER key.

FORMAT Command
(Disk Formatting)

A new diskette is like a blank sheet of paper. Before DOS can write any data on disk, the disk must be formatted. Formatting divides the disk in tracks and sectors so that DOS can keep track of where the file are located on disk. When DOS formats a disk, it erases all the files on the disk, unless it is write protected. Before formatting, make sure that you do not need the files that are on this disk, and the disk is not write protected. (The FORMAT command described below does not list all the available options. Refer to a DOS manual for details). The format of the FORMAT command is:

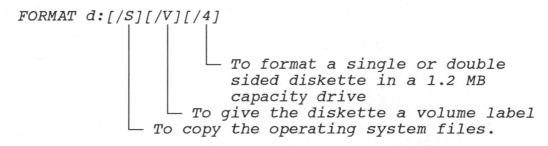

```
FORMAT d:[/S][/V][/4]
```

To format a single or double sided diskette in a 1.2 MB capacity drive
To give the diskette a volume label
To copy the operating system files.

Example

```
FORMAT A:
```

Diskette in A drive
FORMAT Command

This command will FORMAT a diskette that is in drive A.

Example
Format B:
This command will FORMAT a diskette that is in drive B.

Example
FORMAT A:/S/V
This command will format the diskette in A drive. The /V option will prompt for a volume label and that information will be saved on the diskette. The /S option will copy the system files on the diskette in A drive.

Example
C:\DOS\FORMAT A:
This command will format the diskette that is in A drive. If the path has not been set in the Autoexec.BAT file, use C:\DOS to define the path where the DOS files are located. In this example, it is assumed that the DOS files are in the DOS subdirectory on C drive.

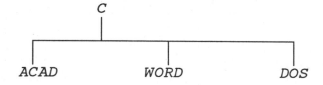

Note

Do not format the hard drives (FORMAT C:, FORMAT D:) unless you are familiar with hard disk formatting procedure. If you format the hard drives, it will destroy the DOS partition, including all subdirectories and their contents. Consult you DOS reference manual for detailed information.

MKDIR Command
(Make Directory)

This command creates a subdirectory on the disk. The format of the command is:

```
MKDIR [d:]path
or
MD [d:]path
```

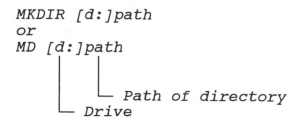

Example
C > MKDIR ACAD
C > MKDIR WORD
These commands will create subdirectories ACAD and WORD on C drive. You can create any number of subdirectories, provided the maximum length of the path from the root directory to the specified directory is not more than 63 characters long.

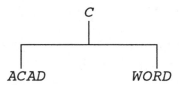

Example
MD C:\ACAD\DWG1\HOUSE
This command will make a subdirectory HOUSE in the DWG1 directory.

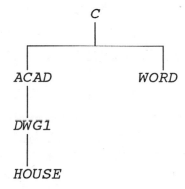

PATH Command
(Set Search Directory)

The PATH command sets the path for searching commands and batch files in the directories specified in the path command. The format of the command is:

```
PATH [[d:]path[[;d:]path]]]
```

Path name
Drive

Example
```
PATH C:\ACAD;D:\SYMBOLS\ARCH;
```

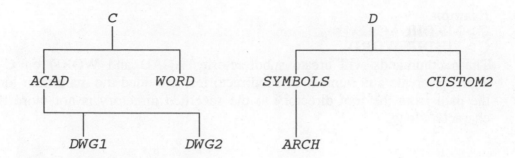

If the command or the batch file is not found in the current directory, DOS searches the subdirectories named in the path. In above example, DOS will search all the directories in the same sequence as specified in the path.

Example
PATH
If no parameters are specified in the PATH command, it displays the current path.

Example
PATH;
If the PATH command is followed by a semicolon (;), it resets the search path to null. DOS will search for the commands and the batch files in the current directory only.

RENAME Command
(Rename a file)

The RENAME command lets you change the name of a file. The format of the command is:

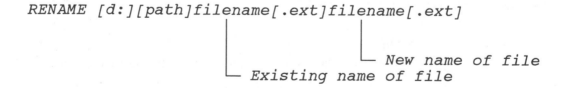

```
RENAME [d:][path]filename[.ext]filename[.ext]
```

└ New name of file
└ Existing name of file

Example
RENAME C:\ACAD\PROJ1.DWG NEWPROJ.DWG
or
REN C:\ACAD\PROJ1.DWG NEWPROJ.DWG
This command will change the name of the PROJ1.DWG file in ACAD subdirectory to NEWPROJ.DWG. The path name can be specified with the first file name only.

RMDIR Command
(Remove Directory)

The RMDIR command removes the subdirectory from a disk. The format of the command is:

```
RMDIR [d:]path
or
RD [d:]path
```

        Path specification
    Drive

Example
RMDIR OLDDWG
This command will remove the OLDDWG subdirectory from the current directory. The subdirectory has to be empty to remove it.

Example
RMDIR C:\ACAD\OLDDWG
This command will remove the OLDDWG subdirectory from the ACAD directory.

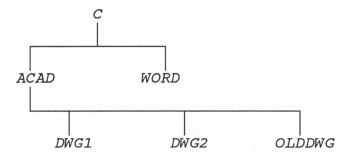

TIME Command
(Display, Change Time)

The TIME command lets you display or change the time of the system. The format of the command is:

```
TIME [hh:mm:ss]
```

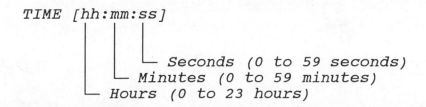

            Seconds (0 to 59 seconds)
        Minutes (0 to 59 minutes)
    Hours (0 to 23 hours)

Example
TIME

If you enter the command, TIME, without any parameters, the following prompt will be displayed.

Current time is hh:mm:ss
Enter new time:

If you want to change the system time, enter the time in the same format as displayed on the screen and press the ENTER key. The time you entered will be saved on the system. If you do not want to change time, just press the ENTER key.

Example
TIME 14:54:32

This command will change the time to 14:54:32 and save that information on the system.

TYPE Command
(Display, Print Files)

The TYPE command displays the listing of the specified file on the screen or on the output device. The format of the command is:

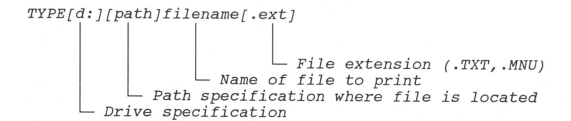

```
TYPE[d:][path]filename[.ext]
```
File extension (.TXT, .MNU)
Name of file to print
Path specification where file is located
Drive specification

Example
TYPE C:\ACAD\PLOT1.SCR

This command will display the contents of the file PLOT1.SCR that is located in the ACAD subdirectory.

Example
TYPE CUTMENU.MNU > PRN

This command will print the contents of the file on the printer.

XCOPY Command
(Copy files)

The XCOPY command is used to copy a group of files. This command can also copy the files that are in a subdirectory. The format of the command is:

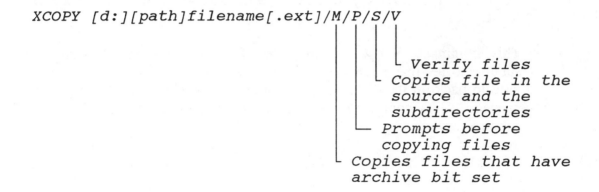

```
XCOPY [d:][path]filename[.ext]/M/P/S/V
```

        Verify files
        Copies file in the source and the subdirectories
        Prompts before copying files
        Copies files that have archive bit set

Example
```
XCOPY C:\ACAD\DWG1\*.DWG A: /S
```

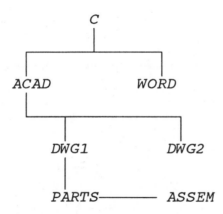

This command will copy all the files in the DWG1 subdirectory and the subdirectories within the DWG1 subdirectory (PARTS, ASSEM), to A drive. On A drive it will automatically create the subdirectories, if needed, and copy the files.

Example
XCOPY *.DWG A:/M
This command will copy the files from the current directory that have the archive bit set. This command can therefore be used to back up the disk.

Example
XCOPY *.DWG A:/M/S

```
                          └─ Copies all files in the source and
                             subdirectories
                        └ Copies files that have archive bit set
                     └─ A drive (files are copied to A drive)
                └.DWG extension (all files with DWG extension)
```

This command will copy the files from the current directory and the subdirectories that have the archive bit set.   This command can therefore be used to back up the disk.   Use the following command to set the archive bit, if needed.   This command will set the archive bit of all the files in DWG1 subdirectory.

ATTRIB +a C:\ACAD\DWG1*.*

Appendix B

Edlin
(The Line Editor)

What is EDLIN

You can use the DOS line editor, EDLIN, to create text files and save them on your diskette. With EDLIN you can update the existing files, and delete, edit, insert, or display any number of lines. You can also search for a text, and replace or delete text within the file. With a line editor you can edit only one line at a time.

How EDLIN Works

When you enter different lines in the file, EDLIN automatically numbers the lines consecutively. The line numbers that you see on the screen are not a part of the file. When you insert or delete a line in the file, the lines are automatically renumbered. The lines can be of any length, up to 253 characters per line.

How to Start EDLIN

To start EDLIN from the AutoCAD drawing editor, type SH or SHELL at AutoCAD command prompt. Type the word EDLIN, followed by file name with extension and then press the RETURN key.

```
Command: SHELL
OS Commands: (File name.ext)
```

Example
```
OS Commands: EDLIN SCRMENU.MNU
                │      │      │
                │      │      └─ File extension
                │      └─ File name
                └─ EDLIN command
```

You can also use AutoCAD's EDIT command to edit a file. If you want to use the EDIT command, type EDIT at AutoCAD command prompt and press the ENTER key. Next, type the name of the file that you want to edit, with the file extension. The SHELL, SH or EDIT command will work if the ACAD.PGP file is present.

```
Command: EDIT
File name: (File name with extension)
```

Example
```
Command: EDIT
File name: SCRMENU.MNU
```

Sometimes, you may have to define the path, if the path has not been defined in the AUTOEXEC.BAT file. For example, if the DOS files are in the DOS subdirectory on C drive, you can invoke the EDLIN command by defining the search path before the EDLIN command.

```
Command: SHELL
OS Commands: C:\DOS\EDLIN SCRMENU.MNU
                │
                └─ Search path
```

You can also start EDLIN from outside the drawing editor by using the following command at system prompt.

```
C>EDLIN (File name with extension)
```

Example
```
C>EDLIN SCRMENU.MNU
```

If the EDLIN command does not find the file in the existing directory or the directory that is defined in the EDLIN command statement, it creates a new file, and the following prompt is displayed on the screen.

New file
*

To begin entering text, type I for insert, and line number 1 is displayed on the screen followed by *. Now, you can type lines or use any EDLIN commands.

If the EDLIN command finds the file that is specified in the command line, it will load it and display the following message.

End of input file
*

At this point you're ready to start editing.

EDLIN Commands

The EDLIN commands are easy to use, especially when you are editing a small text files. The following is a description of some of the EDLIN commands that are frequently used to edit a file.

C   (Copy Lines Command)

This command copies a specified number of lines and places them ahead of the line that is specified as the third parameter in the command line. Notice, the third parameter in the copy command line is not optional. The format of the command is:

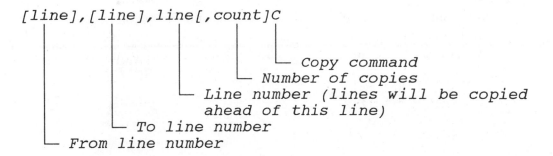

```
[line],[line],line[,count]C
```

Example
1,3,8,2C
This command copies lines 1 through 3 ahead of line 8, twice. The following files are a listing of the script file before and after copying the line.

```
 1:   VSLIDE SLIDE1
 2:   VSLIDE *SLIDE2
 3:   DELAY 15000
 4:   VSLIDE
 5:   VSLIDE *SLIDE3
 6:   DELAY 15000
 7:   VSLIDE
 8:   VSLIDE *SLIDE4
 9:   DELAY 15000
10:   VSLIDE
11:   DELAY 15000
12:   RSCRIPT
```

1,3,8,2C

1: VSLIDE SLIDE1
2: VSLIDE *SLIDE2
3: DELAY 15000
4: VSLIDE
5: VSLIDE *SLIDE3
6: DELAY 15000
7: VSLIDE
8: VSLIDE SLIDE1
9: VSLIDE *SLIDE2
10: DELAY 15000
11: VSLIDE SLIDE1
12: VSLIDE *SLIDE2
13: DELAY 15000
14: VSLIDE *SLIDE4
15: DELAY 15000
16: VSLIDE
17: DELAY 15000
18: RSCRIPT

Example
2,2,4C

If you want to copy one line only, the first and the second parameter specified in the command line should be same. In the following file, line number 2 is copied ahead of line number 4. The file is then automatically renumbered.

1:    VSLIDE SLIDE1
2:    VSLIDE *SLIDE2
3:    DELAY 15000
4:    VSLIDE

2,2,4C

1:    VSLIDE SLIDE1
2:    VSLIDE *SLIDE2
3:    DELAY 15000
4:    VSLIDE *SLIDE2
5:    VSLIDE

D   (Delete Lines Command)

This command deletes a specified number of lines from the file. The lines that follow the deleted lines are automatically renumbered. The line that follows the deleted lines becomes the current line. The format of the command is:

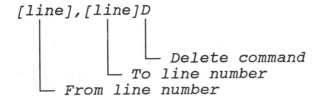

```
[line],[line]D
```
— Delete command
— To line number
— From line number

Example
1,5D
This command deletes the lines 1 through 5. The following file uses this delete command to delete the lines 1 through 5 from the file.

```
 1:   VSLIDE SLIDE1
 2:   VSLIDE *SLIDE2
 3:   DELAY 15000
 4:   VSLIDE
 5:   VSLIDE *SLIDE3
 6:   DELAY 15000
 7:   VSLIDE
 8:   VSLIDE *SLIDE4
 9:   DELAY 15000
10:   VSLIDE
```

1,5D

```
1:   DELAY 15000
2:   VSLIDE
3:   VSLIDE *SLIDE4
4:   DELAY 15000
5:   VSLIDE
```

Example
,5D
If the first parameter is omitted (,5D), the lines from the current line to the line number specified in the command line will be deleted. In the following file, lines 2 through 5 will get deleted.

```
1:   DELAY 15000
2*   VSLIDE                ——————————— Current line
3:   VSLIDE *SLIDE4
4:   DELAY 15000
5:   VSLIDE
6:   DELAY 15000
7:   RSCRIPT
```

,5D

```
1:   DELAY 15000
2:   DELAY 15000
3:   RSCRIPT
```

Example
2D
or
2,D
If the second parameter is omitted, only the specified line will be deleted. In the following file line number 2 gets deleted.

   1:   DELAY 15000
   2:   DELAY 15000
   3:   RSCRIPT

2D
or
2,D

   1:   DELAY 15000
   2:   RSCRIPT

Line (Edit Line Command)

This command allows you to revise a line of text. To edit the line, type the line number and press the ENTER key. **If you want to edit an existing line, type period (.) and press the ENTER key. If you press ENTER without a line number, the line that follows the current line will be edited.** After making the changes in the line, if you decide not to save the changes, press the CTRL-BREAK or ESCAPE key instead of ENTER key. The format of the command is:

[line]

Example
3
In the following file if you want to edit line number 3. Type 3 and press the ENTER key. Line number 3 will be displayed on the screen.

   1:   VSLIDE SLIDE1
   2:   VSLIDE *SLIDE2
   3:   DELAY 15000
   4:   VSLIDE
   5:   VSLIDE *SLIDE3

3

   3:* DELAY 15000
   3:*

E   (End Edit Command)

This command ends EDLIN and also saves the edited file on the disk. The file is saved under the same name and on the same drive that you entered when you started EDLIN. If there is not enough space on the disk, the portion of the file that was not saved on the disk will be lost. Therefore make sure that there is enough space on the disk before editing a file.

Example
EDLIN SHOW.SCR
In this example the file has been loaded from the current drive. When you end EDLIN the file SHOW.SCR will be automatically saved on the current drive.

Example
EDLIN C:\ACAD\SHOW.SCR
In this example the file has been loaded from the ACAD subdirectory. When you end EDLIN, the file will be automatically saved in ACAD subdirectory with the same name.

Example
EDLIN A:SHOW.SCR
In this example the file has been loaded from A drive. When you end EDLIN, the file will be saved on A drive.

I   (Inset Line Command)

This command inserts the lines just before the line number that you specify in the command line. If you do not specify the line number in the insert command, the line is inserted before the current line. The format of the command is:

```
[line]I
     |     |
     |     |__ Insert command
     |__ Line number
```

Example
3I
This command will display 3* on the screen and the lines you enter will be inserted before line 3. Once you are done entering the lines enter CTRL-BREAK form the key board. The lines will be automatically renumbered. In the following file the insert command (I) has been used to insert one line before line number 3.

```
1:    VSLIDE SLIDE1
2:    VSLIDE *SLIDE2
3:    DELAY 15000
4:    VSLIDE
5:    VSLIDE *SLIDE3
6:    DELAY 15000
```

3I
3:*DELAY 1000
4:

1:    VSLIDE SLIDE1
2:    VSLIDE *SLIDE2
3*   DELAY 1000
4:    DELAY 15000
5:    VSLIDE
6:    VSLIDE *SLIDE3
7:    DELAY 15000

Example
8I
If you want to insert a line at the end of the file, the line number that you define in the insert command should be higher than the last line in the file.   For example, if the last line in the file is 6 and you want to add more lines at the end of the file, type 7I or 8I and press ENTER.   The lines you enter will be added to the file at the end.

1:    VSLIDE SLIDE1
2:    VSLIDE *SLIDE2
3:    DELAY 15000
4:    VSLIDE
5:    VSLIDE *SLIDE3
6:    DELAY 15000

7I

7* RSCRIPT
8*

1:    VSLIDE SLIDE1
2:    VSLIDE *SLIDE2
3:    DELAY 15000
4:    VSLIDE
5:    VSLIDE *SLIDE3
6:    DELAY 15000
7:   RSCRIPT

Example
I
If you do not specify the line number in front of the insert command I, the lines will be inserted ahead of the current line.

1:    VSLIDE SLIDE1
2:    VSLIDE *SLIDE2
3*   DELAY 15000   ——————— Current line
4:    VSLIDE

I

3:*VSLIDE SLIDE3

4:*

```
1:    VSLIDE SLIDE1
2:    VSLIDE *SLIDE2
3:    VSLIDE SLIDE3
4:    DELAY 15000
5:    VSLIDE
```

L   (List Lines Command)

This command displays the lines as specified in the command line. The format of the command is:

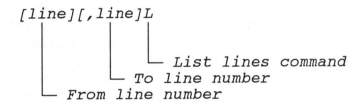

```
[line][,line]L
```

List lines command
To line number
From line number

Example
2,5L
This command will list the lines 2 through 5, including line number 2 and 5. The following files show the lines that will be displayed by this command.

```
1:    VSLIDE SLIDE1
2:    VSLIDE *SLIDE2
3:    DELAY 15000
4:    VSLIDE
5:    VSLIDE *SLIDE3
6:    DELAY 15000
```

2,5L

```
2:    VSLIDE *SLIDE2
3:    DELAY 15000
4:    VSLIDE
5:    VSLIDE *SLIDE3
```

If the first and second parameters are missing (L), a total of 23 lines will be displayed. The first 11 of these lines are before the current line, then the current line, and the remaining 11 lines are after the current line. This will happen if there are enough lines before the current line, at least 11. For example, if there are only five lines before the current line, the first five lines will be displayed, followed by the current line, and then the remaining lines so that the total is 23 lines. If the first line is the current line, in that case the first 23 lines will be displayed.

Example
,46L

If the first parameter is missing(,23L), 11 lines before the current line will be displayed followed by the current line and the lines from the current line to the line number specified in the command line..

Example
24,L

Similarly, if the second parameter is missing (24,L), a total of 23 lines are displayed. The line that is specified in the command line becomes the first line of the display.

M   (Move Lines Command)

This command moves a group of lines that are specified by the first two parameters in the command line, ahead of the line number specified in the third parameter of the command line. The format of the command is:

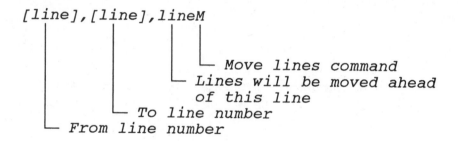

```
[line],[line],lineM
```
- Move lines command
- Lines will be moved ahead of this line
- To line number
- From line number

Example
1,3,6M

This command line will move lines 1 through 3 ahead of line 6. If the first or second parameter is missing (LineM, Example: 6M), only the current line will be moved. Notice, the third parameter in the move command line is not optional. After moving the lines the lines are automatically renumbered. The following files show the lines that are moved by using the move command.

```
1:    VSLIDE SLIDE1
2:    VSLIDE *SLIDE2
3:    DELAY 15000
4:    VSLIDE
5:    VSLIDE *SLIDE3
6:    DELAY 15000
```

1,3,6M

```
1:    VSLIDE SLIDE1
2:    VSLIDE *SLIDE2
3:    DELAY 15000
4:    VSLIDE
```

```
5:    VSLIDE *SLIDE3
6:    VSLIDE SLIDE1
7:    VSLIDE *SLIDE2
8:    DELAY 15000
9:    DELAY 15000
```

Example
1,1,4M

If you want to move one line only, the first and the second parameter in the command line has to be same. In the following file line number 1 has been moved before line number 4.

```
1:    VSLIDE SLIDE1
2:    VSLIDE *SLIDE2
3:    DELAY 15000
4:    VSLIDE
```

1,1,4M

```
1:    VSLIDE *SLIDE2
2:    DELAY 15000
3:    VSLIDE SLIDE1
4:    VSLIDE
```

P   (Page Command)

This command displays a specified number of lines on the screen. The format of the command is:

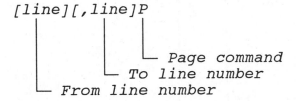

```
[line][,line]P
```
— Page command
— To line number
— From line number

Example
2,4P

This command will list the lines 2 through 4, including the line number 2 and 4. If the first line parameter is omitted, the current line plus the next line will be displayed. If the second line parameter is omitted, the command will display 23 lines. **You can use this command to page through 23 lines at a time.** The following file uses 2,4P command to list lines 2 through 4.

```
1:    VSLIDE SLIDE1
2:    VSLIDE *SLIDE2
3:    DELAY 15000
4:    VSLIDE
5:    VSLIDE *SLIDE3
```

```
6:    DELAY 15000
```

2,4P

```
2:    VSLIDE *SLIDE2
3:    DELAY 15000
4:    VSLIDE
```

Q   (Quit Edit Command)

This command quits the editing process without saving the changes that are made in the file. When you quit, the following message is displayed on the screen to make sure that you really want to discard the changes made to the file.

Abort edit (Y/N)?

If you do not want to save the changes, type Y and then press the ENTER key. If you do not want to abort, type N, or any other key to continue editing the file.

R   (Replace Text Command)

This command replaces all strings specified by the first string parameter of the command line in the specified group of lines with a new string that is defined as the second string parameter.

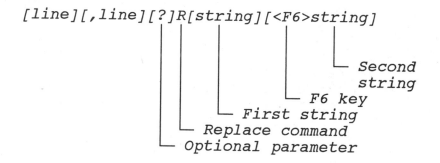

```
[line][,line][?]R[string][<F6>string]
```
                                            └─ Second
                                               string
                                    └─ F6 key
                          └─ First string
              └─ Replace command
          └─ Optional parameter

Example
3,5RSLIDE2 < F6 > SLIDE5
This command will search for the string SLIDE2 from line number 3 through 5 and replace all SLIDE2 strings by SLIDE5. If you use the optional question mark (?) in the command line, an **O.K.?** prompt will be displayed. If you want to retain the changes that have been made in the line, type Y or press the ENTER key. If you do not want to retain the changes, press any other key. In the following file SLIDE2 has been replaced by SLIDE5.

```
1:    VSLIDE SLIDE1
```

```
2:    VSLIDE *SLIDE2
3:    DELAY 15000
4:    VSLIDE
5:    VSLIDE *SLIDE3
6:    DELAY 15000
```

3,5RSLDE2 < F6 > SLDE5

```
1:    VSLIDE SLIDE1
2:    VSLIDE *SLIDE5
3:    DELAY 15000
4:    VSLIDE
5:    VSLIDE *SLIDE3
6:    DELAY 15000
```

.i.S   (Search Text Command);

This command searches a specified number of lines to locate a string specified in the command line.

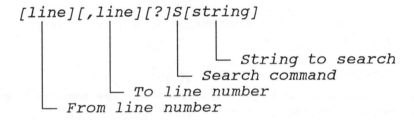

```
[line][,line][?]S[string]
```
- String to search
- Search command
- To line number
- From line number

Example
1,6SVSLIDE
This command will locates the first occurrence of the word "VSLIDE" in lines 1 through 6. The search command searches for the same characters as defined in the command line. If the string defined in the command line is uppercase, it will search for uppercase. Same is true for the lowercase strings. If you use the optional parameter ?, a prompt **O.K.?** will be displayed after displaying the line containing the specified string. If the string that is defined in the command line is not found, the search is terminated and a message **Not found** is displayed on the screen.

T   (Transfer Lines Command)

This command transfers the lines from the file specified in the command line into the file that is currently being edited.

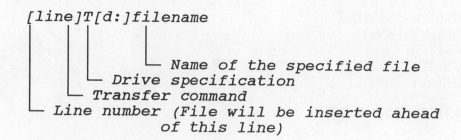

```
[line]T[d:]filename
```
- Name of the specified file
- Drive specification
- Transfer command
- Line number (File will be inserted ahead of this line)

Example
3TA:SCRIPT2.SCR
In this command line the file SCRIPT2.SCR, located on A drive will be merged with the file that is currently being edited. The lines of the specified file will be transferred ahead of line 3. If line number is omitted from the command line, the lines will be transferred ahead of the current line. If the drive name is not specified with the file, the file is read from the default drive. The path that was specified when using the EDLIN command will become the default drive.

Note

1. *You can enter the EDLIN commands in uppercase, lowercase, or a combination of both.*

2. *After entering a command press the ENTER key.*

3. *You can stop a command by pressing CTRL-BREAK key. To stop the display of the lines on the screen press the CTRL-NUM LOCK key.*

4. *You can use the control keys and DOS editing keys to edit a line.*

5. *You can enter multiple commands in one command line. The commands should be separated by a semicolon (;).*

Appendix C

Screen Menus

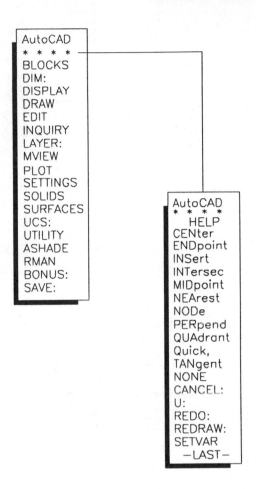

Object Snap Menu

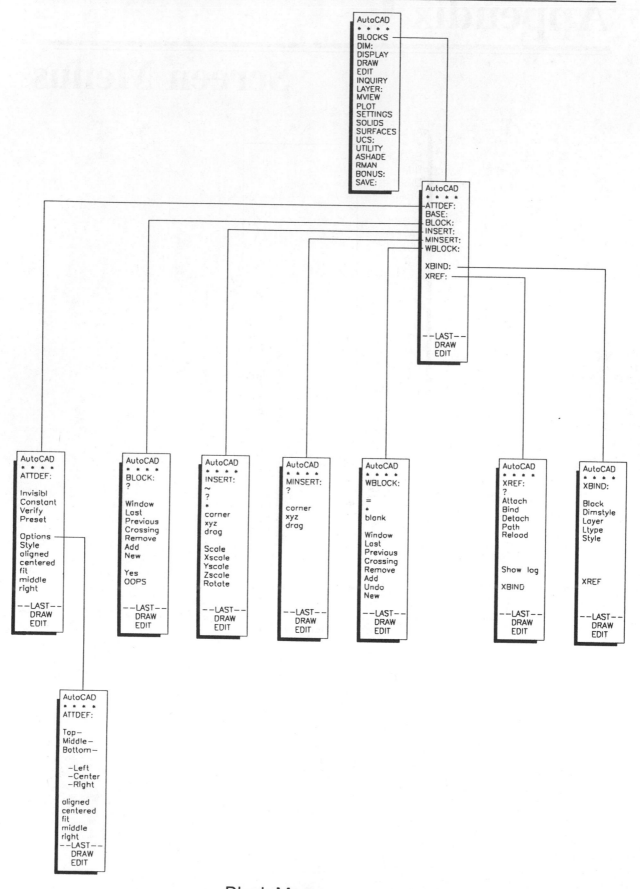

Block Menus

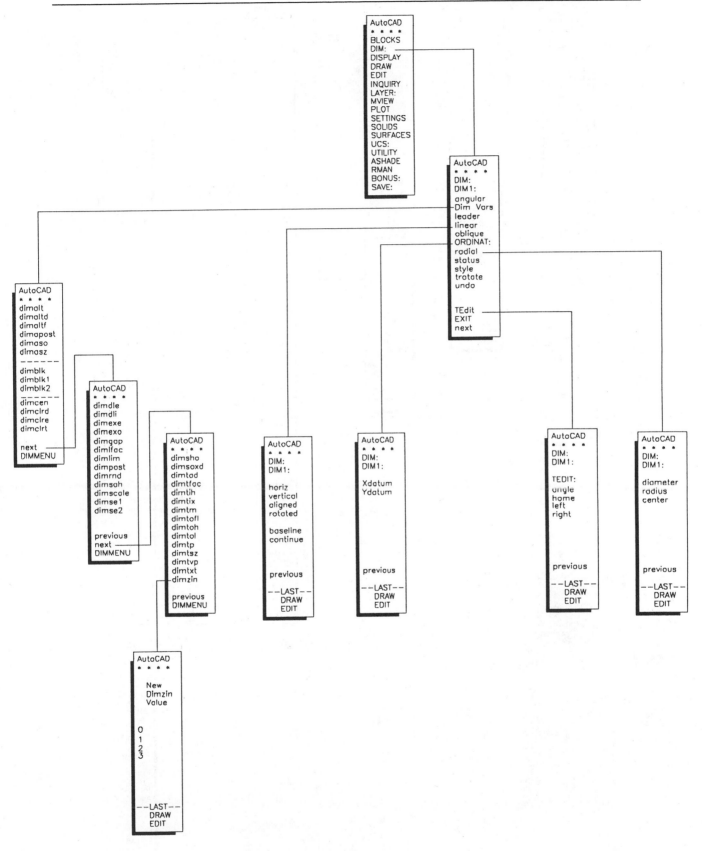

Dimension Menus

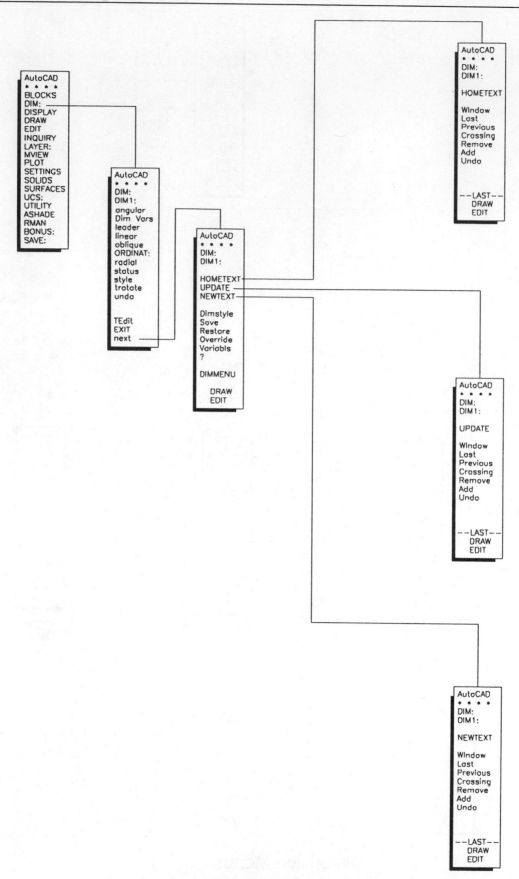

Dimension Menus (Next)

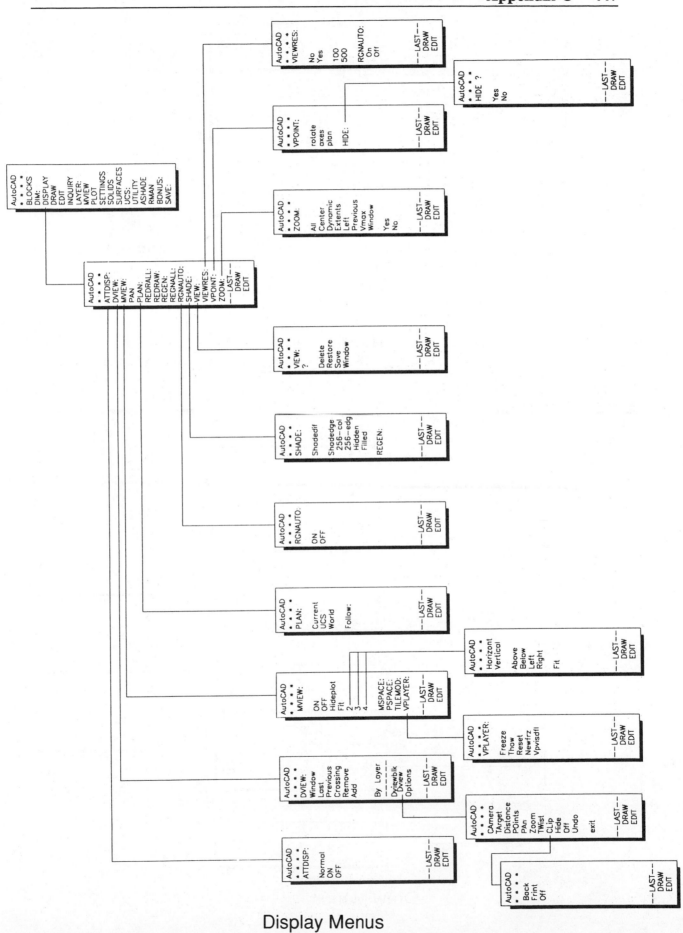

Display Menus

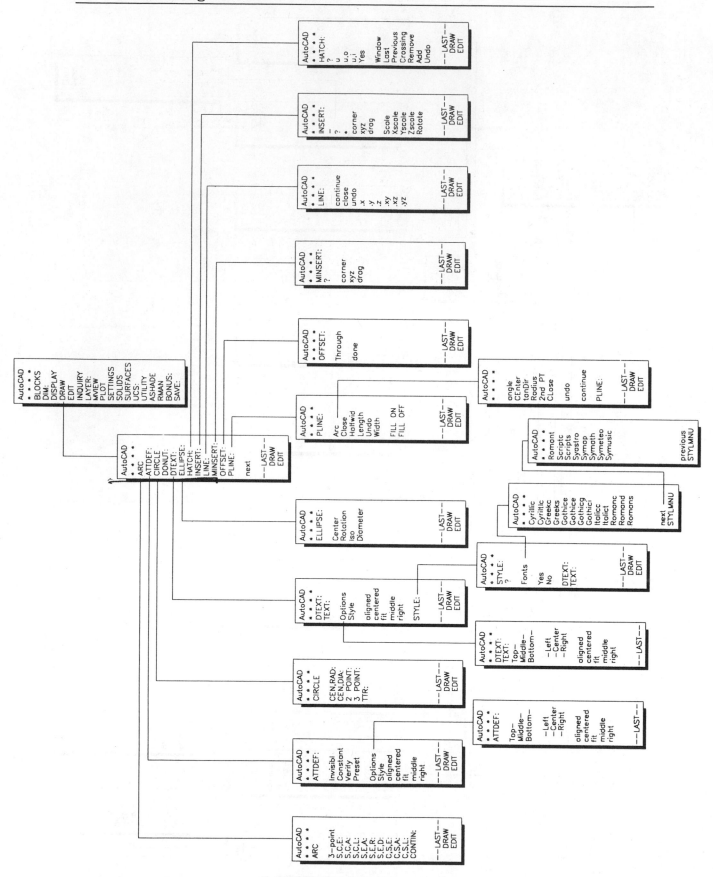

Draw Menus

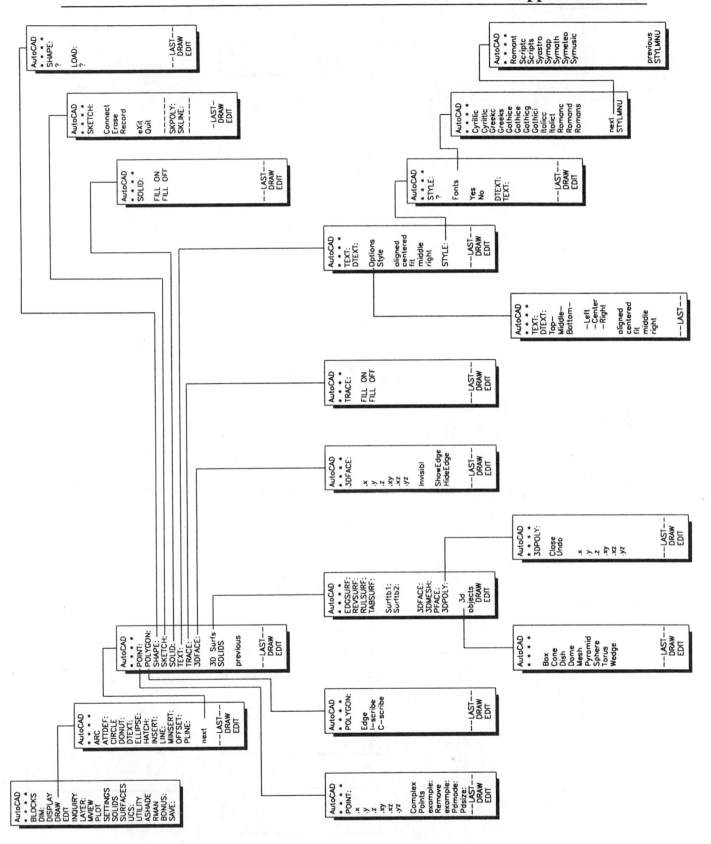

Draw Menus (Next)

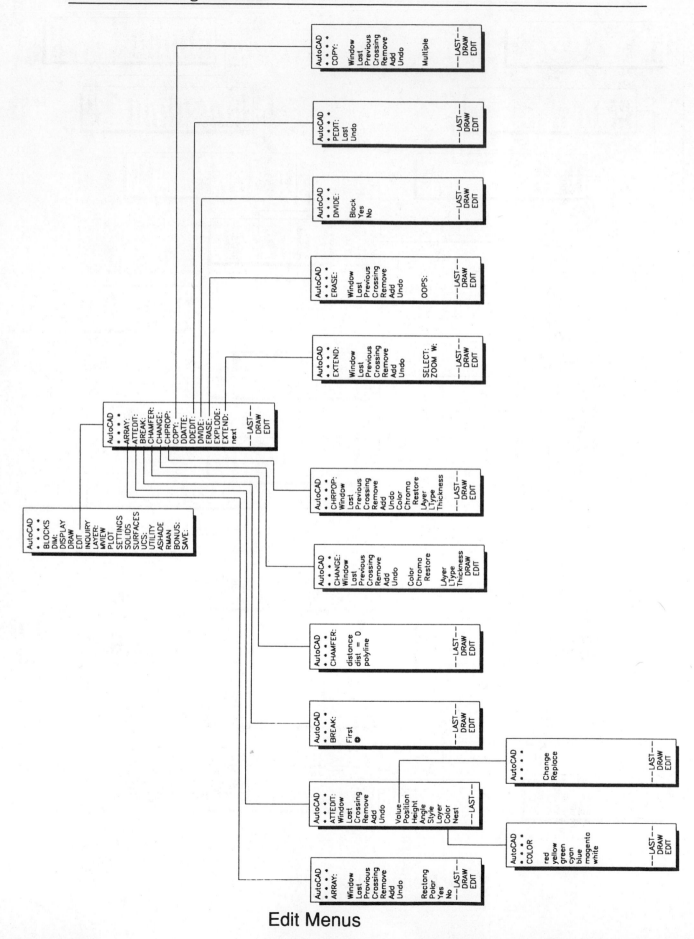

Edit Menus

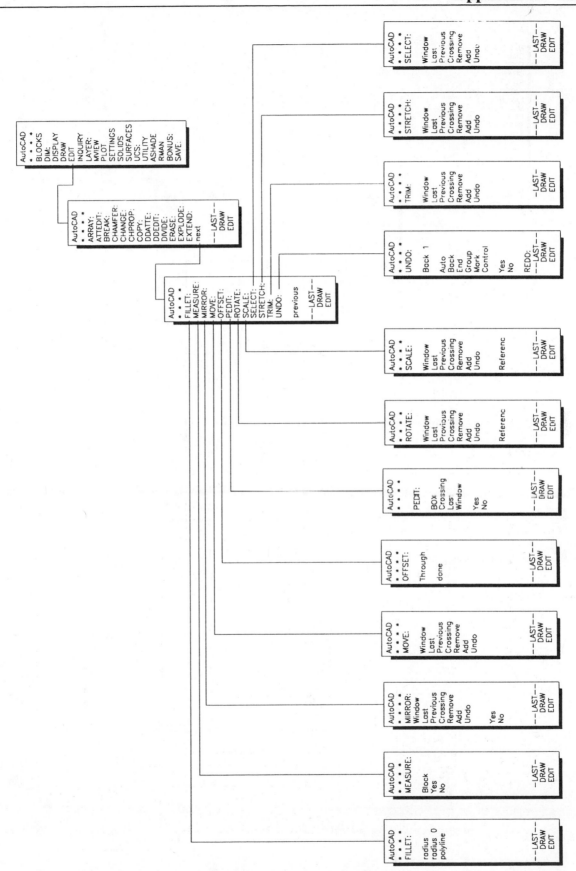

Edit Menus (Next)

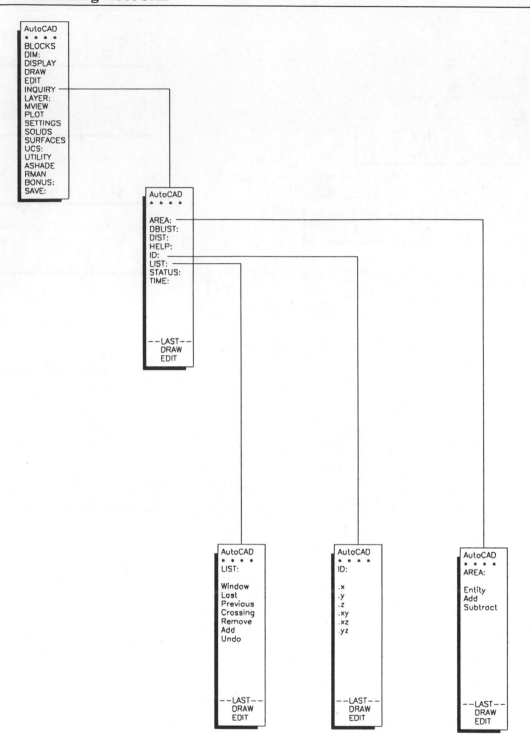

Inquiry Menus

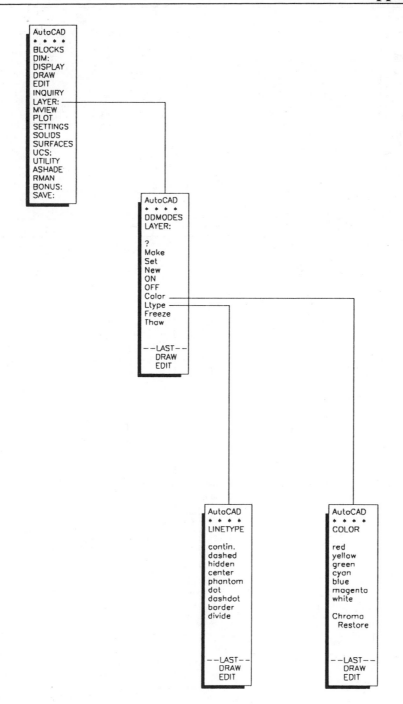

Layer Menus

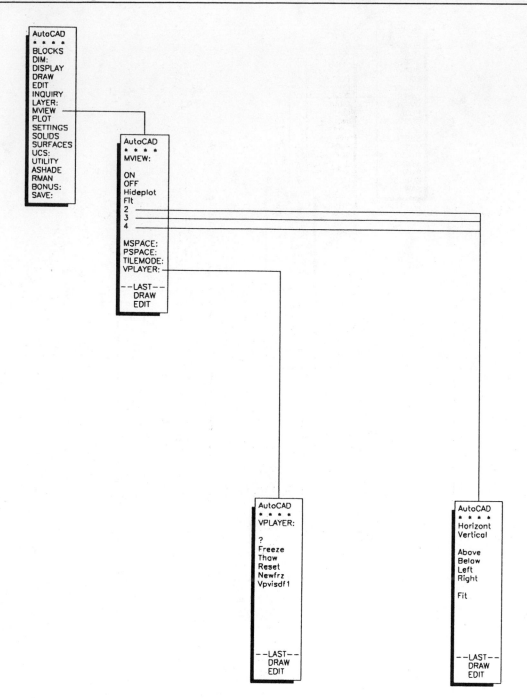

MView Menus

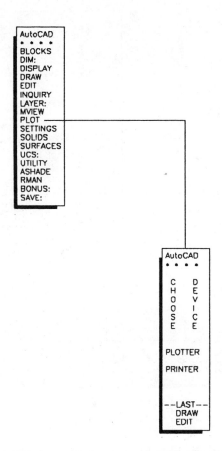

Plot Menus

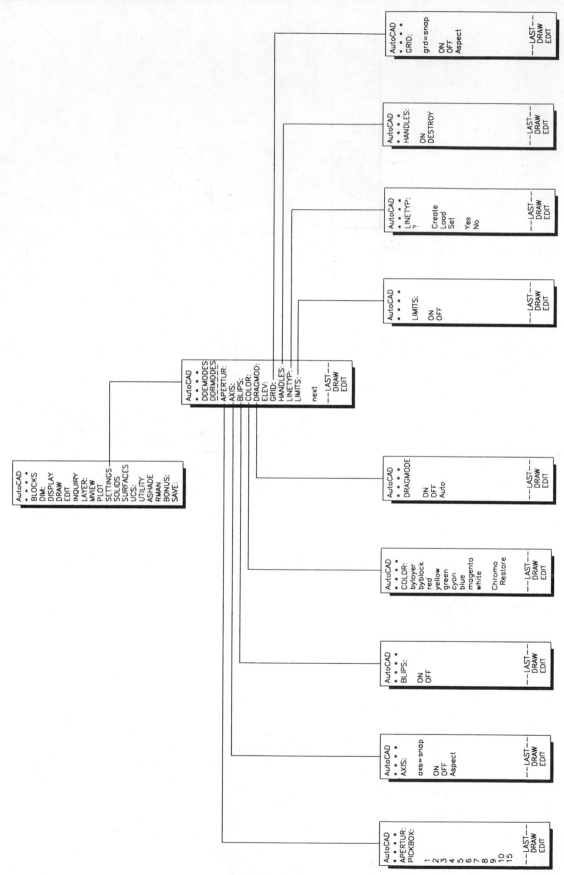

Settings Menus

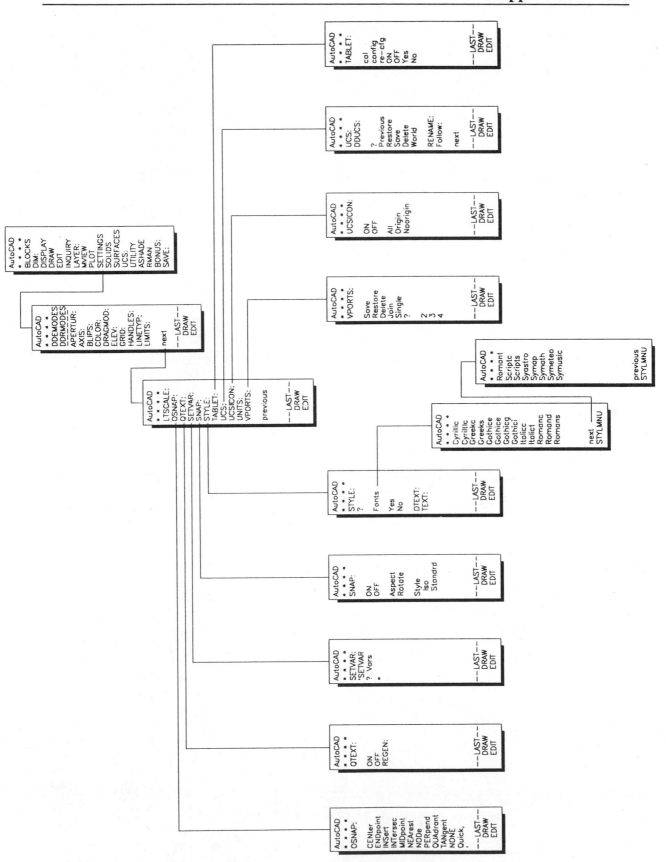

Settings Menus (Next)

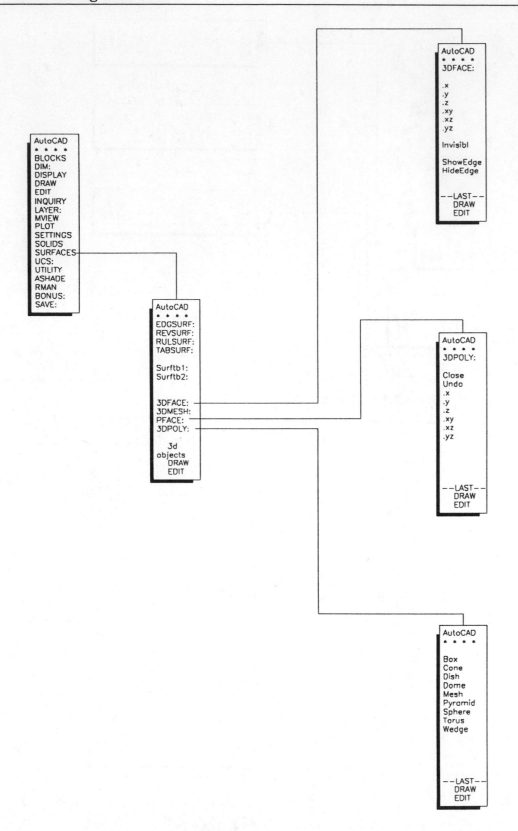

Surfaces Menus

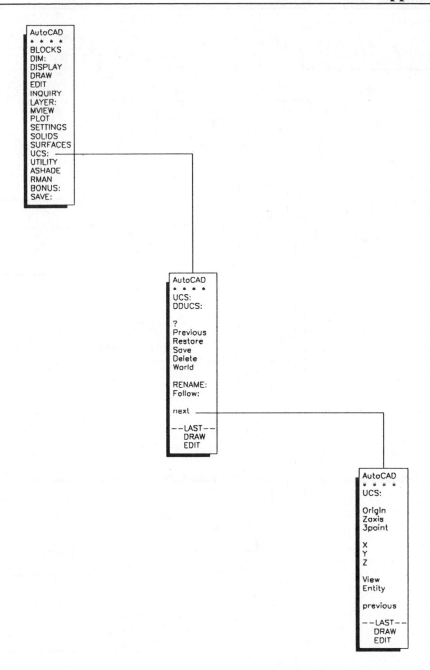

UCS Menus

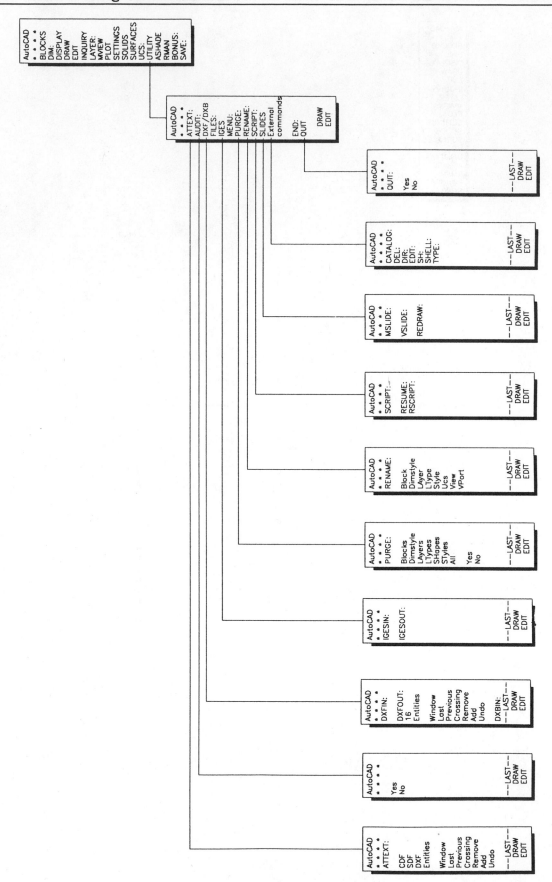

Utility Menus

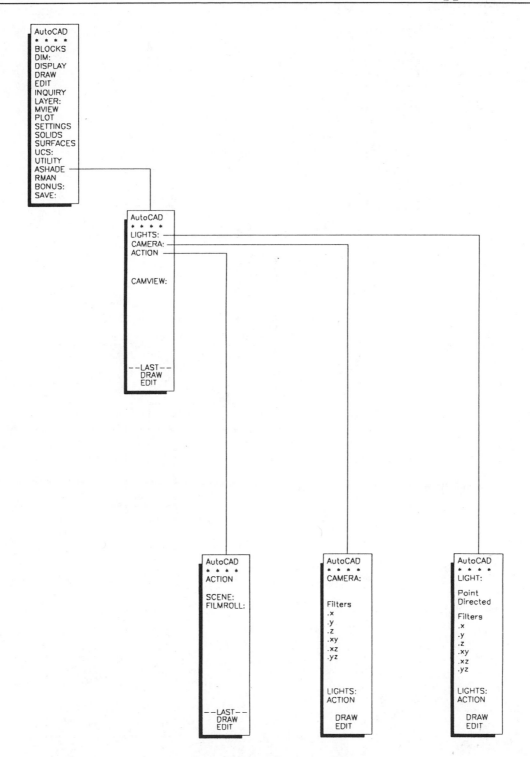

ASHADE Menus

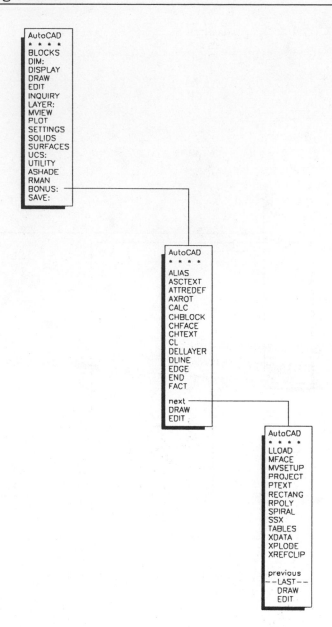

Bonus Menus

Appendix D

Pull-down Menus

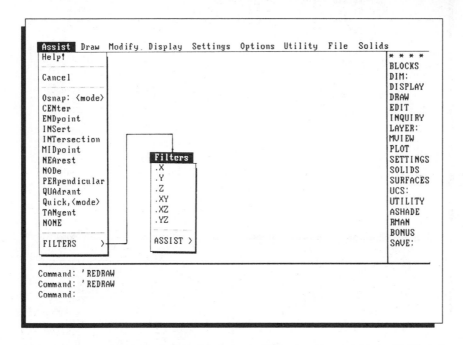

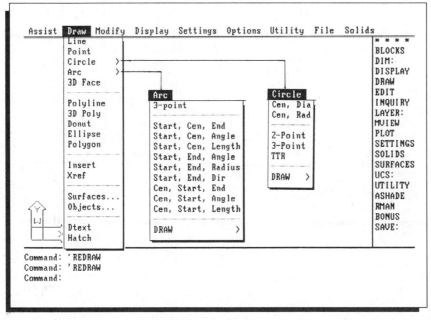

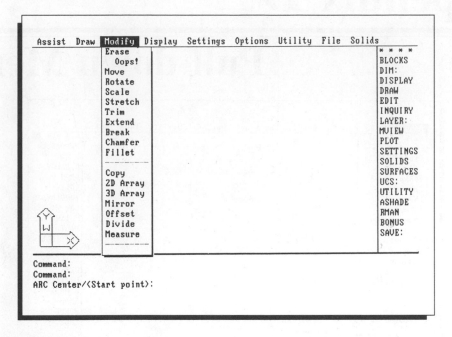

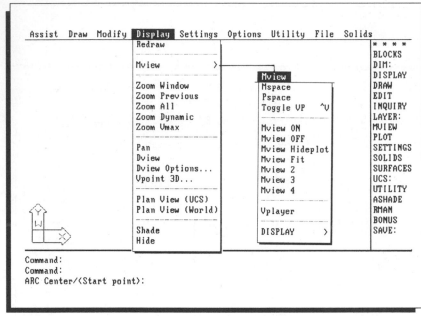

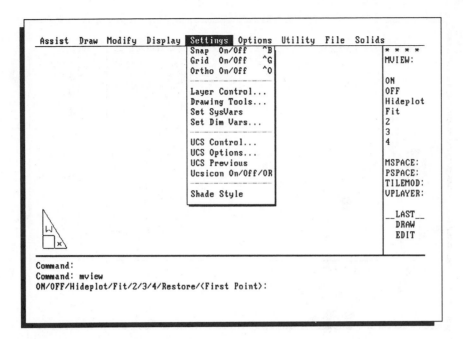

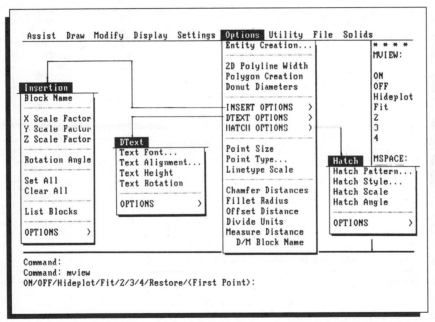

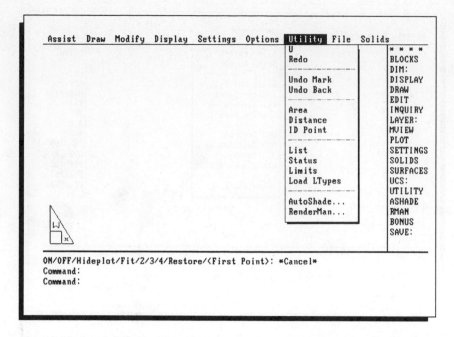

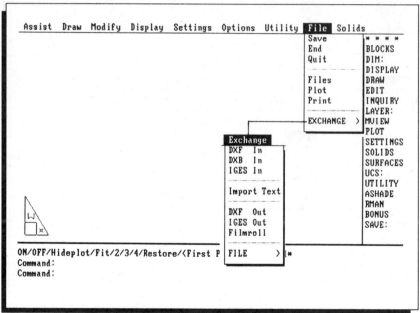

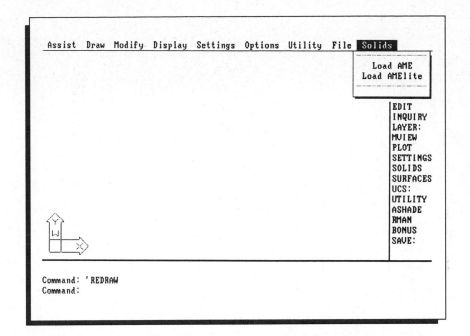

Assist Draw Modify Display Settings Options Utility File Solids

    Load AME
    Load AMElite

    EDIT
    INQUIRY
    LAYER:
    MVIEW
    PLOT
    SETTINGS
    SOLIDS
    SURFACES
    UCS:
    UTILITY
    ASHADE
    RMAN
    BONUS
    SAVE:

Command: 'REDRAW
Command:

Appendix E

Icon Menus

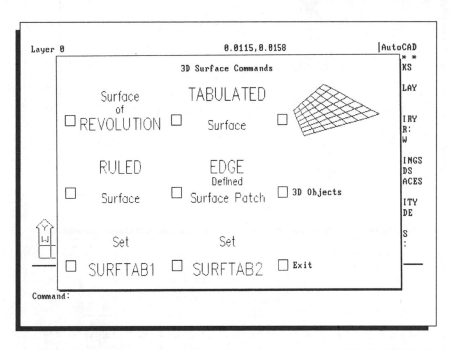

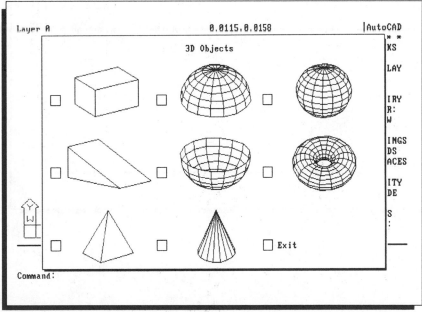

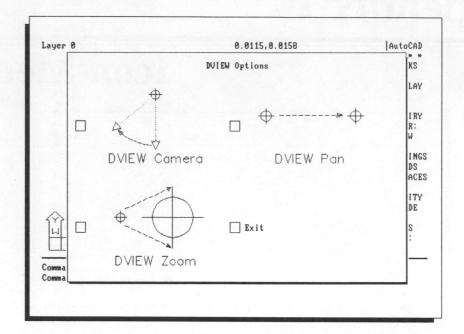

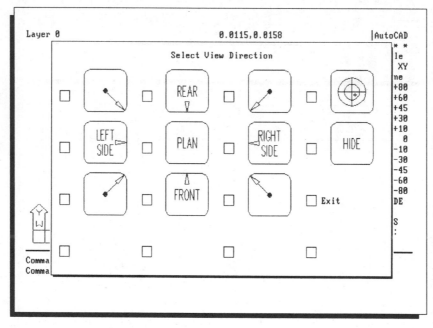

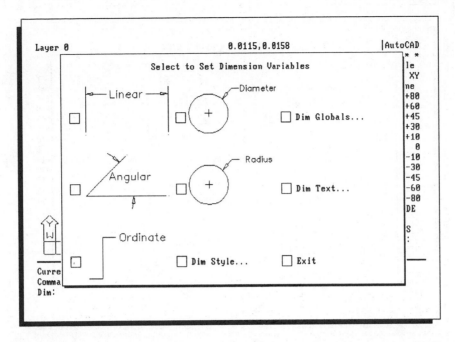

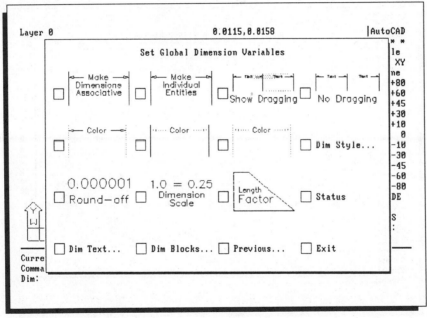

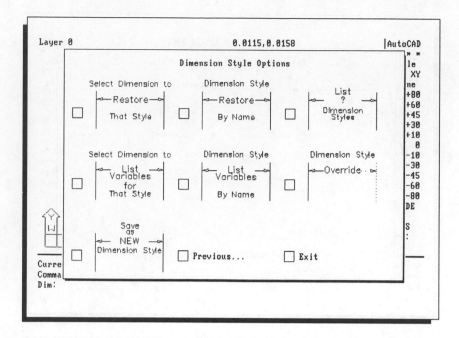

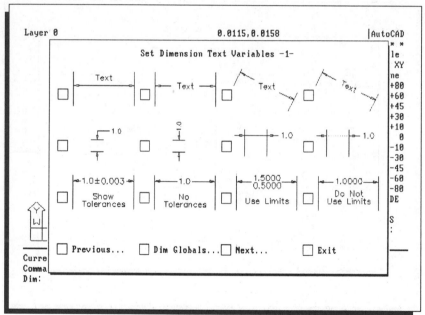

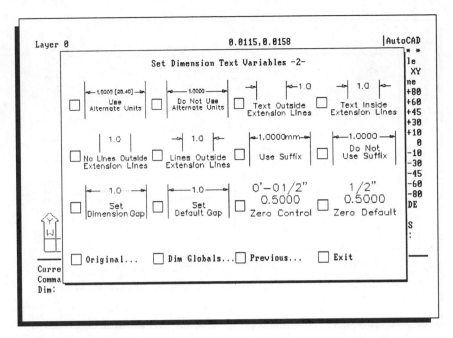

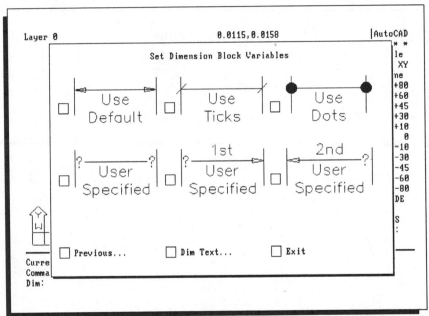

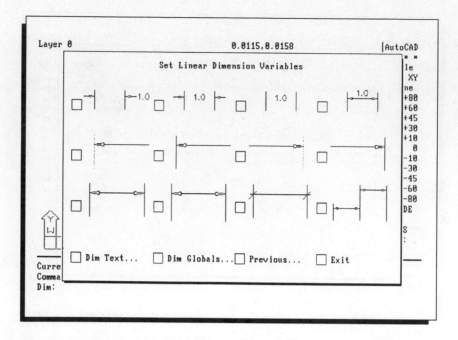

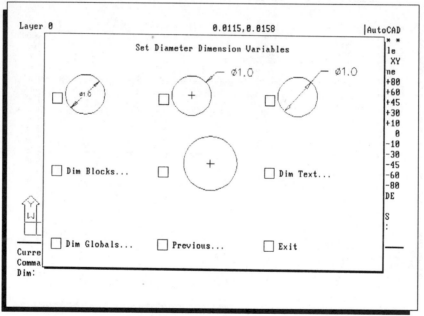

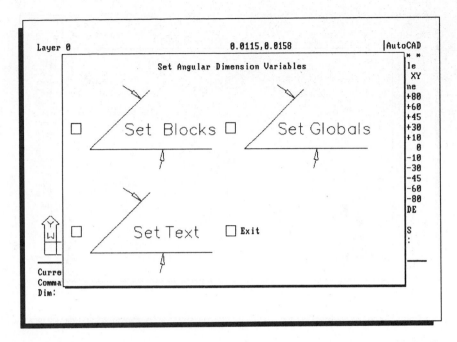

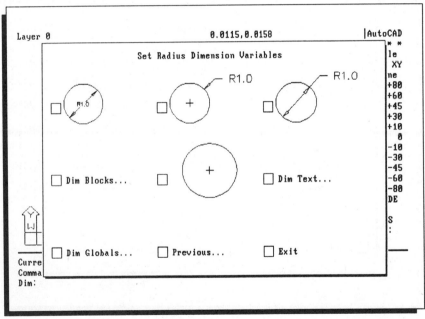

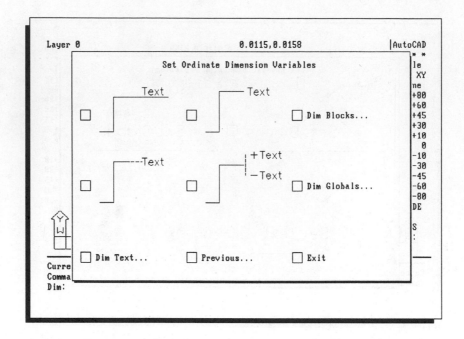

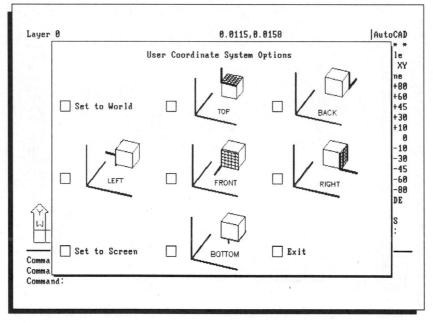

Layer 0   0.0115,0.0158 |AutoCAD

Select Text Font

ROMAN SIMPLEX   ROMAN DUPLEX   MONOTXT

☐   ABC123   ☐   ABC123   ☐   ABC123

ROMAN COMPLEX   ROMAN TRIPLEX

☐   ABC123   ☐   ABC123   ☐ Next

ITALIC COMPLEX   ITALIC TRIPLEX

☐   ABC123   ☐   ABC123   ☐ Exit

New
Comma
Command:

Layer 0   0.0115,0.0158 |AutoCAD

Select Text Font

GOTHIC ENGLISH   GOTHIC GERMAN   GOTHIC ITALIAN

☐   ABC123   ☐   ABC123   ☐   ABC123

GREEK SIMPLEX   GREEK COMPLEX

☐   ΣΩ   ☐   ΣΩ   ☐ Next

SCRIPT SIMPLEX   SCRIPT COMPLEX

☐   ABC123   ☐   ABC123   ☐ Exit

New
Comma
Command:

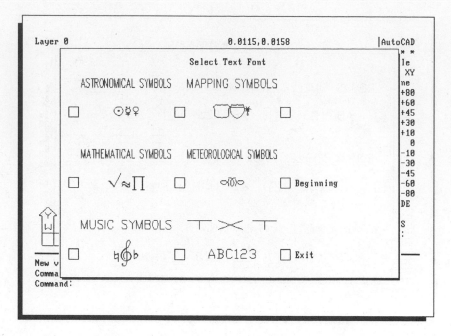

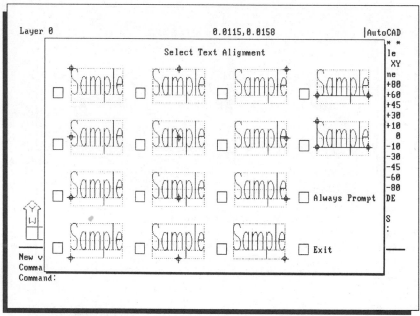

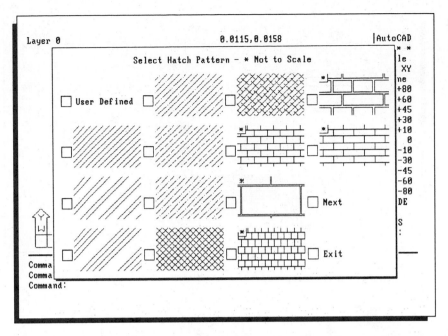

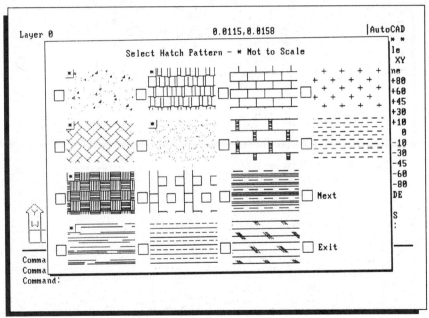

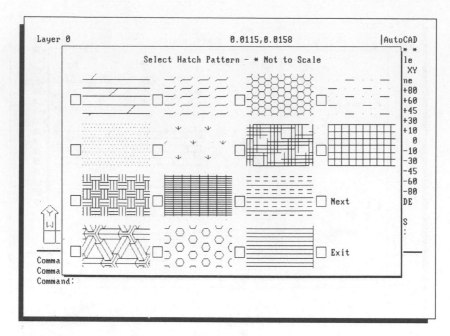

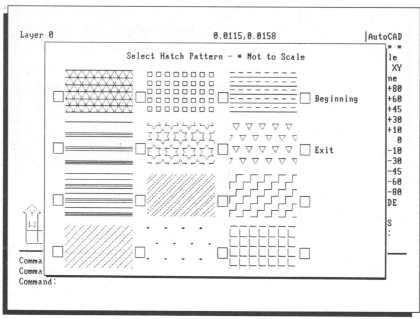

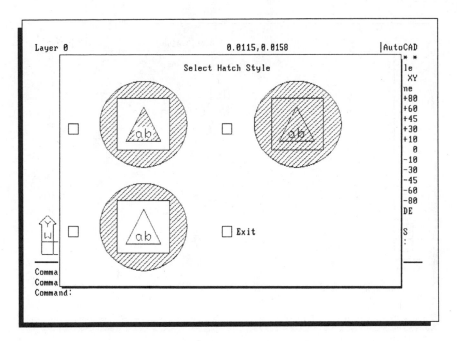

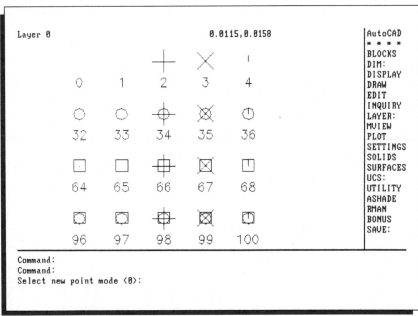

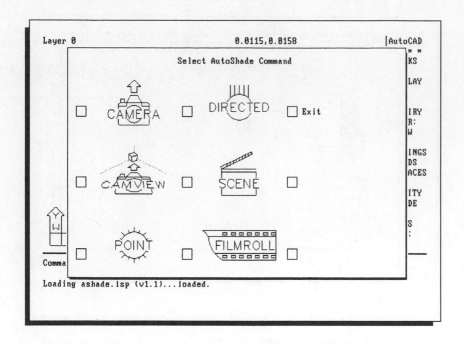

Layer 0   0.0115,0.0158 |AutoCAD

Select AutoShade Command

☐ CAMERA   ☐ DIRECTED   ☐ Exit

☐ CAMVIEW   ☐ SCENE   ☐

☐ POINT   ☐ FILMROLL   ☐

Comma

Loading ashade.lsp (v1.1)...loaded.

Appendix F

Dialogue Boxes

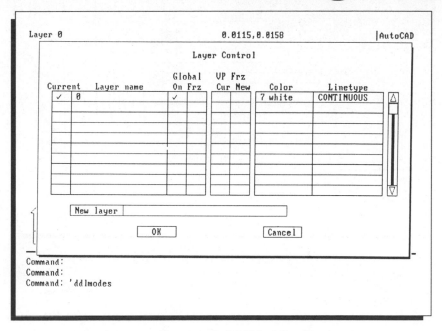

Layer Control (DDL Modes)

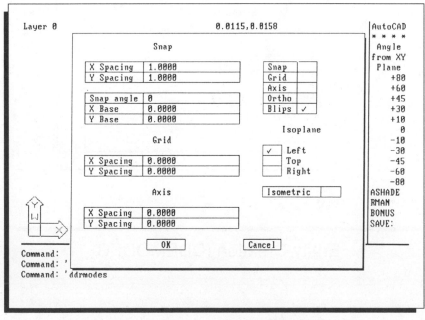

Drawing Tools (DDR Modes)

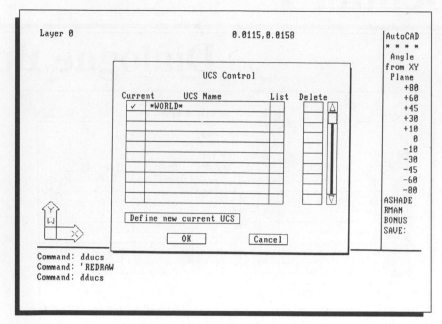

UCS Options (DDUCS)

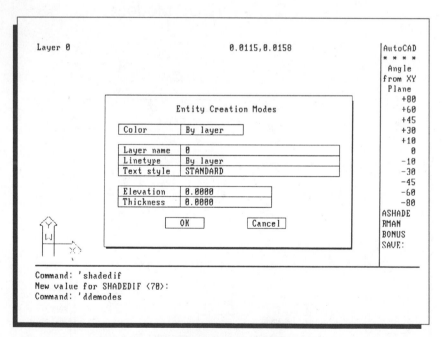

Entity Creation (DDEMODES)

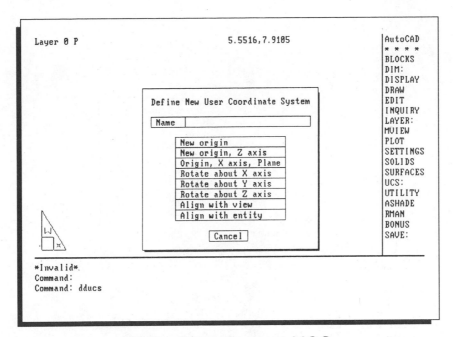

Define New Current UCS
(Branches from UCS options dialogue box)

Index